A Time

Trevor Royle is a broadcaster and author specialising in the history of war and empire. His most recent books include *Montgomery: Lessons in Leadership from the Soldier's General* and *The Wars of the Roses: England's First Civil War*. His acclaimed history of Scotland and the First World War, *The Flowers of the Forest*, was published by Birlinn in 2006. He is a Fellow of the Royal Society of Edinburgh and is also a member of the Scottish Government's Advisory Panel for Commemorating the First World War.

A Time of Tyrants

Scotland and the Second World War

Trevor Royle

BIRLINN

This edition published in 2013 by
Birlinn Limited
West Newington House
10 Newington Road
Edinburgh
EH9 1QS

www.birlinn.co.uk

ISBN: 978 1 84341 064 5

British Library Cataloguing-in-Publication Data
A catalogue record for this book is available from the British Library

Typeset by Iolaire Typesetting, Newtonmore
Printed and bound by Grafica Veneta
www.graficaveneta.com

Always in the darkest loam
A birthday is begun;
And from its catacomb
A candle lights the sun.

William Soutar,
'In the Time of Tyrants',
1937

Contents

List of Illustrations

12. Fairfield drillers at work on a gun-shield for the battleship HMS *Howe* prior to commissioning in August 1942.

13. Hugh MacDiarmid working at Mechan's Engineering Company, 1942.

14. A group of women workers preparing ration packs of tea, milk and sugar at the Scottish Co-operative and Wholesale Society (SCWS) factory at Shieldhall in Glasgow in 1942.

15. Commandos cross a toggle bridge at the Commando Training Depot at Achnacarry in Inverness-shire.

16. Men of the 2nd Argyll and Sutherland Highlanders engaged in jungle training in Malaya in 1941.

17. Blindfolded survivors from the *Scharnhorst* are led ashore at Scapa Flow after the German battle-cruiser was sunk by a naval force led by HMS *Duke of York* on 26 December 1943.

18. The two of the four-man crew of the X-class midget submarine HMS *Extant* (*X-25*) prepare to dock in the Holy Loch.

19. A line of allied merchant ships makes its way around the north cape of Norway to the Russian ports of Murmansk and Archangel.

20. The pipes and drums of the 51st Highland Division play in the main square of Tripoli on 28 January 1943.

21. Led by a piper soldiers of the 2nd Argyll and Sutherland Highlanders move up to the attack during Operation Epsom on 26 June 1944 to outflank Caen.

22. Major-General T.G. Rennie, commander of the 51st Highland Division in Rouen in September 1944.

23. A De Havilland Mosquito VI fighter-bomber of 143 Squadron fires rockets at German merchant ship during an attack by the Banff Strike Wing on the harbour at Sandefjord in Norway.

24. Soldiers of 10th Highland Light Infantry come ashore after crossing the Rhine at the end of March 1945 as part of the final push into Germany.

25. Victory parade in Bremerhaven on 12 May 1945 led by the pipes and drums of the 51st Highland Division.

26. Crowds celebrate VE Day in Princes Street Gardens in Edinburgh.

Preface and Acknowledgements

This book was conceived as a sequel to *The Flowers of the Forest*, an account of the part played by Scotland in the First World War, which was published in 2006. It is similar in structure and sets out to bring together the military history of the Second World War with an narrative about Scotland's political, social and economic role during the conflict. Like its predecessor the intention is not simply to write a history of the war as seen through Scottish eyes or to wrap its main events in a kilt. Rather, it is the story of the role played by Scotland and Scots in the British (and wider Allied) management of a war which was very different from the preceding global conflict. Inevitably, many of the concerns of *The Flowers of the Forest* are revisited in this book: the role of women; the contribution of the heavy industries; the ever-changing kaleidoscope of Scottish domestic politics; and Scotland's contribution to the war effort through the armed forces, especially the roles played by the three Scottish infantry divisions and other Scottish forces on all the main battle fronts. Some personalities reappear from the earlier conflict – politicians such as Tom Johnston and James Maxton, and poets Hugh MacDiarmid and William Soutar, for example – and some issues resurface, such as the question of home rule which was one of the casualties of August 1914 and which remained unresolved until the passing of the Scotland Act in 1998.

Otherwise the war of 1939–45 was a completely different experience, and it threw up problems and issues which were quite dissimilar from the events of the earlier conflict. For a start, between the fall of France in May 1940 and the decision of the USA to enter the war following the Japanese attack on its Pacific naval base of Hawaii in December 1941, Britain prosecuted the war against Germany alone, with the support of Dominion forces and the free forces of those

European powers which had managed to escape from Nazi occupation. That gave Scotland a distinctive role as many of the émigré forces, notably the Poles, were stationed in the country and added to the sense that – in the closing stages, at least – the Allies were indeed a 'united nations'. Many of the Poles stayed on in Scotland after the war, either because they had married Scottish girls or were persuaded not to return to their homeland following the carve-up at Yalta in February 1945 which laid the basis for the creation of a Communist government in post-war Poland. Norwegians, French, British Hondurans, Italians and Americans added to the racial mix, and for the first time in many years Scotland became a more variegated place socially and culturally, even if it was only a temporary innovation.

There were other factors. The Scottish land mass provided ideal territory for training, especially in the remote Highlands and Western Islands, most of which was a Protected Area throughout the conflict. Industry, mainly in the central belt, also played a part, and it is true to say that the war came as a lifeline to shipbuilding, steel and munitions. Whether that was for good or for ill in the longer term is still a moot point. As happened in the earlier conflict, women played a full role with thousands being conscripted under the terms of the National Service Acts of 1941. It is also fair to claim that the arts in Scotland flourished during the war, especially in literature where a new generation of younger writers such as J.K. Annand, Hamish Henderson, Maurice Lindsay, Alexander Scott and Douglas Young built on the example of Hugh MacDiarmid's renaissance movement of the 1920s. But it was in the world of politics that the war had the deepest impact on Scotland. Although the country remained part of the union, and political nationalism was never a determining factor in national life until the 1970s, Scotland was offered a tantalising glimpse of what devolution might be like under the guardianship of Secretary of State Tom Johnston.

Most of the research for this volume was conducted in the National Archives of Scotland in Edinburgh and the National Archives at Kew. In both places I received nothing but courteous assistance from the ever-helpful staff. Thanks are also due to the staff of the National Library of Scotland, where I have been a reader for over four decades, and the University of Edinburgh Library, where extended loans of key texts greatly aided my research. I am also grateful to Professor Tom

Devine for making it possible for me to hold an Honorary Fellowship in the School of History, Classics and Archaeology at the University of Edinburgh, where I enjoyed the ready support of my friend Dr Jeremy Crang during his tenure as director of the Centre for the Study of the Two World Wars. After many years writing as an independent historian this was a singular privilege. It has also been of some significance to me that most of the book was written at my home in Portobello which stands less than a hundred yards from targets machine-gunned during the Luftwaffe's first major attack on the UK mainland in October 1939.

For permission to quote copyright material I would like to thank the following: Carcanet Press for 'The New Divan 99' by Edwin Morgan from Edwin Morgan, *The New Divan*, Carcanet Press, 1977; Eric Glass Ltd for 'Consanguinity' by Ronald Duncan from Ronald Duncan, *The Perfect Mistress*, Rupert Hart Davis, 1969; Robert Hale Ltd for excerpts from Maurice Lindsay, *Thank You for Having Me*, Robert Hale Ltd, 1983; Cath Scott for 'Coronach for the Dead of the 5/7th Battalion The Gordon Highlanders' by Alexander Scott MC, from Alexander Scott, *Selected Poems 1943–1974*, Akros Publications, Preston 1975. Extracts from regimental histories are produced by kind permission of the trustees of regiments concerned. Every effort has been made to contact copyright holders and any omissions will be made good in future editions.

No writer could hope to have a more agreeable or supportive publisher than Birlinn. Hugh Andrew welcomed the proposal with enthusiasm, and I received nothing but professional help and support from him and his colleagues. They all have my thanks.

Trevor Royle
Edinburgh/Angus
Spring 2011

Prologue
The Last Hurrah; Bellahouston 1938

To the casual observer with only a passing knowledge of Glasgow's history, a visit to Bellahouston Park is not very different from a stroll in the park in any other municipal recreational area in Scotland or the United Kingdom The grassland is well manicured, the pathways are meandering and discreet, trees punctuate the rolling terrain, locals and visitors mingle or take their ease in the sun. Hanging over the acres there is an air of gentle if poignant contemplation. It is still used for civic and national events – the park has been the scene of two recent papal visits and masses, for Pope John Paul II in the summer of 1982 and again in September 2010 for Pope Benedict XVI – and it is well used by those who live on the south side of the city. Once part of the lands of Govan and surrounding Ibroxhill and Drumbreck, Bella-houston came into civic ownership at the end of the nineteenth century, and at one time its 175 acres made it the largest public park in Britain. There are the usual sports facilities such as a bowling green, a golfing pitch-and-putt course and modern all-weather pitches, but Bellahouston Park is not just a civic amenity in which the locals take considerable pride. It is all that remains of a short-lived monument to a year, 1938, when everything seemed to be for the best in the best of all possible worlds. As such, the park was a last hurrah for a way of life that might have turned out very differently had Scotland and the rest of the world not gone to war in the following summer.

Look again at the park and its contours, especially the central whaleback ridge which dominates the area, and let your imagination roam. That neat white building near the centre with the bold proclamation 'Palace of Art' gives a clue. Squat but angular, and book-ended by two small pavilions, its colonnaded front still catches the eye and it is as neat and robust as it was when it was first created all

those years ago by Launcelot Ross, a well-known Glasgow architect
with strong links to the Territorial Army. Today it acts as a centre of
sporting excellence but it is also a reminder of one of the most
extraordinary events in Glasgow's history, a beacon of hope in a year
when Scotland had put behind it the misery of the Great Depression,
and national self-confidence was once again in the ascendant. Apart
from the mirage of memory and a plinth marking the spot where over
140 buildings were thrown up between Mosspark Boulevard and
Paisley Road West, it is all that remains of the Empire Exhibition of
1938, an event which has been described as 'the last durbar', a
gathering place for an empire which would soon be swept away
by the great storm of war. It is just possible to visualise other points of
reference in the park, and a modern three-dimensional computerised
project launched in 2008 has resurrected something of the original
grandeur, but to all intents and purposes the Empire Exhibition is now
part of the irretrievable past.[1]

In common with many other similar events associated with the city
of Glasgow, the planning for the 1938 Empire Exhibition was replete
with civic confidence and was certainly not lacking in ambition. The
original motivation was to promote Scotland as an important commercial and industrial centre, but the overarching aspiration was to
create a bold and brash event which would provide a lasting impression of what Scotland had to offer the rest of the world. Quite
simply, its organisers were determined that the exhibition should be
the best of its kind, not a parochial event in a post-industrial city, but a
prestigious exposition that would place Scotland at the heart of the
British Empire. That much became clear at the first meeting of the
steering committee which was held in the Merchant's House in
Glasgow on 5 October 1936. The gathering was organised under
the auspices of the Scottish National Development Council (SNDC),
which itself had been founded on 8 May 1931 by the Convention of
Royal Burghs, to promote the cause of Scotland's industries at a time
when they had been battered by the effects of the economic depression of the 1930s and to attempt to find solutions to the prevailing
malaise. Amongst those involved in the creation of the SNDC were
Sir Henry Keith, former Provost of Hamilton and a prominent
Unionist MP, William Watson of Glasgow, organiser of the Scottish
Trades Development Association and Edward James Bruce, 10th Earl

of Elgin, a director of the Royal Bank of Scotland, who outlined what the exhibition should attempt to produce: 'The effort must embrace Scotland as a whole, it must aim at expanding Scottish industry and employment and must not overlook the great asset Scotland has in its charms of scenery and opportunities for holiday, sport and pleasure.'[2]

It was a stirring call to arms but almost immediately the committee had a problem. Under the rules for regulating and staging international exhibitions agreed by the Bureau International des Expositions (International Exhibitions Bureau) there was no vacancy until 1947. This was clearly too far ahead for the organising committee and as a result it was decided to hold an exhibition which would be centred on the British Empire, similar to one which had been held at Wembley in London in 1924. Not only would such an event fall outside the international regulations but it would also commemorate an entity – the British Empire – which covered 25 per cent of the globe and was home to some 450 million inhabitants.

For Glasgow that had added resonance. Somewhat self-consciously it was styled the 'Second City of Empire' (Liverpool also laid claim to the title, as did Calcutta), Clyde-built ships helped to hold the empire together and the heavy industries of the Clyde valley looked to the empire for their main markets. The city was also home to the manufacture of a huge variety of goods, from marine engines and locomotives to carpets and foodstuffs, which were sold all over the world. There was also the experience of the recent past. Glasgow was no stranger to mounting this type of international exhibition: the first, held in Kelvingrove Park in 1888, was the largest to its kind since London's 'Great Exhibition of the Works of Industry of all Nations' of 1851 with its magnificent centrepiece of the Crystal Palace, a great cathedral of iron and glass which dominated the open ground on the south side of Hyde Park between Queen's Gate and Rotten Row. Glasgow's effort was equally successful in promoting 'the wealth, the productive enterprise and the versatility of the great people who flourish under Her Majesty's reign' and it was followed by two further events in 1901 and 1911, the latter of which had the laudable aim of raising funds for the creation of a chair in Scottish history and literature at Glasgow University. (In this it was successful.)

More than any other factor, though, the driving force behind the 1938 Empire Exhibition was the need to galvanise the industries of the west of Scotland in the aftermath of the recent economic downturn. By then twenty years had passed since the end of the First World War, and Scotland's experience in those decades had been one of general decline and a gradual collapse in confidence. In the immediate aftermath of the conflict the economy had remained reasonably buoyant, mainly as a result of the wartime boom and the optimism generated by the end of the war, but by the early 1920s the alarm bells were ringing. Between 1921 and 1923 shipbuilding on the Clyde dropped from 510,000 tons to 170,000 tons as a result of cancellations, delayed orders and the effects of the Washington Treaty of 1921 which limited the size and extent of Britain's future warship construction.[3] Industrial unrest also added to the problems – a dispute with the boilermakers in 1923 and the effects of the general strike three years later affected production – but the Clyde was already beginning to pay for the artificial boom which had rescued it during the First World War. On 5 January 1931 the unthinkable happened when the last ship to be built at the huge Beardmore complex left the Clyde and the once-busy shipyard at Dalmuir was put up for sale.

Other heavy industries also suffered from the slump, with production at the North British Locomotive Company dropping off by two-thirds during the same period due to falling orders and a lack of confidence in the world markets.[4] The railway company mergers of 1923 also affected the industry when the London Midland and Scottish railway absorbed the Caledonian and Glasgow and South-Western, while the London and North-Eastern took over the North British and its subsidiary companies. Direction of both new companies was moved to London, and there was a resultant scaling down of engineering work in Glasgow and Kilmarnock. In the steel industry the huge conglomerate Stewarts & Lloyds relocated from Lanarkshire to Corby in Northamptonshire in 1932, forcing large numbers of the workforce to migrate south; its departure left a huge vacuum in the Clyde's industrial heartlands. But perhaps the most telling symbol of the decline was the looming bulk of Order Number 534 which occupied Number 4 berth at John Brown's shipyard at Clydebank. Work on the giant Cunard liner had been suspended on 11 December 1931 and for almost three years the gaunt, unfinished hull had been a sorry symbol of the economic decline and the consequent loss of almost 5,000 jobs. When work was resumed in the spring of 1934 it was greeted with wild enthusiasm, and the eventual launch of the 35,500-ton liner *Queen Mary* two years later seemed to herald a turnabout in the fortunes of the Clyde's shipbuilding industry. In the autumn of 1936 the keel was laid for another Cunarder, the *Queen Elizabeth*, and orders were received for the construction of twenty-two warships including the King George V class battleship *Duke of York*. Suddenly the good times seemed to have returned, as Clydebank prospered from the rapid re-armament of the Royal Navy with Admiralty work on hand in 1938 reaching 164,911 tons – almost as high as it had been in 1913.[5]

Other factors affected the decision to mount the exhibition. A new king, Edward VIII had come to the throne in 1936 and Cecil M. Weir, convenor of the Exhibition Committee and a leading banker, argued that 'coming so early in the reign of the King-Emperor it [the exhibition] would be a fine gesture to the world of the peaceful industrial confidence of the United Kingdom and the Empire overseas and of the undiminished courage, enterprise and resource of the Scottish people'[6] Although the country was shaken by the king's abdication later in the year and his succession by his brother, who reigned as King George VI, there was no slackening of enthusiasm or lack of optimism amongst the exhibition's organising committee. On the contrary, matters proceeded quickly and smoothly. Following a good deal of discussion and canvassing about the best location in Glasgow, Bellahouston Park was chosen as the venue as it was larger than Kelvingrove and enjoyed reasonable transport links with the city centre two miles away. (Against that, as the exhibition's historian has noted, 'the drive out through Tradeston and Plantation would bring the overseas visitor in the closest of contact with some of the worst housing in the Western world.')[7]

Despite the recent economic problems, money to fund the exhibition turned out not to be a major issue and in addition to civic contributions from Glasgow and Edinburgh, several Scottish firms proved to be equally generous, with five-figure sums from ICI, the engineering group G. & J. Weir, thread manufacturers J. & P. Coats of Paisley, Fairfield Shipping Company and the Distillers Company. By the time the appeal was launched on 20 October the committee had already raised £100,000, 20 per cent of its target.

From then onwards the planning proceeded apace. Thomas Tait, the designer of Sydney Harbour Bridge and St Andrew's House in Edinburgh, was appointed lead architect. He proved to be an inspired choice. Quite apart from his leadership qualities, he is best remembered for the construction of the great 300-foot-high Tower of Empire which dominated the park and which was known affectionately as 'Tait's Tower'. He also received unstinting support from a large team of young and up-and-coming architects which included Jack Coia, Basil Spence and Esmé Gordon. Throughout the project the idea was to showcase the best of Scottish industry and to produce a vision of what the future might hold for the country. All the buildings were unusually well designed and constructed (even though all of them, bar the Palace of Art, were destined to be temporary structures): there was a concert hall with universally admired acoustics, an Atlantic Restaurant which mirrored an ocean liner and had a menu (plus prices) to match, an amusement park with futuristic rides and even a clachan or model Highland village to hark back to a fondly imagined past. Glasgow city council also took the unprecedented step of allowing licences for the sale of alcohol during the exhibition, although this met with opposition from the Scottish Temperance Alliance which feared a mass outbreak of inebriation, 'a menace not only to the Exhibition but also the community'.

Equally noteworthy was the speed with which the project progressed. The Countess of Elgin formally turned the first sod in the spring of 1937, and just over a year later, on 3 May 1938, the exhibition was opened by King George VI at nearby Ibrox Stadium. From the outset the exhibition lived up to Lord Elgin's hope that it would represent 'Scotland at home to the Empire'. Visitors marvelled at the sweeping clean lines of the main pavilions, the bold use of glass and steel, the open avenues which added to the feeling of spaciousness and innovation. In later life the poet Maurice Lindsay, then a boy, remembered 'the shimmering cascades of floodlit water' and catching a glimpse of Mary, the Queen Mother, 'powdery and frail-looking as an Oscar Wilde heroine' as she made one of many visits to the event.[8] Three types of pavilion were on display – those devoted to the Dominions, those centred on various industrial activities and those mounted by private companies – and there were two distinctly Scottish pavilions which acted as showcases for the country. Fittingly for the west of Scotland, the largest and perhaps the most popular pavilion was the Palace of Engineering which contained large models of the ships which had made the Clyde famous. Pavilions were also given over to the BBC, the Post Office, the *Glasgow Herald* and *The Times*.

Even before the exhibition opened, 120,000 season tickets had been sold through a system of purchase by instalment, and by 14 May 1938 one million visitors had made their way to Bellahouston Park. Perhaps the most popular feature, because it was the most fun, was the amusement park which was run under the direction of Billy Butlin, a young Canadian impresario who had opened his first holiday camp at Skegness two years earlier. Here were gathered together the usual type of fairground attractions plus a variety of modern, even futuristic, rides such as a scenic railway with a top speed of 60 m.p.h., a Stratoplane and a huge dodgem track. For many visitors, including this correspondent from the *Evening Citizen*, the showground was what made the exhibition worthwhile: 'Everywhere were gadgets for turning you upside down, rolling you round and round, shaking your liver, in short, putting you in any position other than the normal one. Here man (and that means woman too) is twisted, thrown, bumped and shaken, and he likes it. If you doubt me go for yourself. Watch him come off the most fearsome-looking machine smiling and happy, and asking for more and getting it. No wonder that poets sing of the wonderful Spirit of Man.'[9]

For everyone who made the journey to the exhibition site it proved to be a time out of life which they would never forget, above all the floodlit edifice of Tait's Tower which seemed to symbolise the optimism which had prompted the event in the first place. But inevitably there were problems. The main drawback was the un-seasonable weather; the rainfall was the highest for thirty-five years, and only three summer Saturdays were free of downpours. As a result, attendances fell off with only 71,000 visitors on the last Saturday in July when 200,000 had been expected. Towards the end of the exhibition it was decided to open the exhibition to the unemployed free of charge, but the final tally was disappointing – 12,593,232 – and the event made a loss, which necessitated the making good of financial guarantees (three shillings and five pence in the pound). Other factors also explained the shortfall. Despite the best intentions of the orga-nisers the exhibition was viewed outside Scotland as a purely local affair. There was little mention of it in the English or national press, and further afield it received hardly any notice at all. In its leader of 31 October, at the conclusion of the exhibition, the *Glasgow Herald* commented somewhat sourly on the 'half-hearted support that was given by some of the Colonial Governments' and the lacklustre backing from London and Whitehall.[10]

Then there was the alarming and rapidly deteriorating international situation which contrasted uneasily with the innocent pleasures to be found inside Bellahouston Park. While thousands of people made their way to celebrate the British Empire and to gaze at its myriad wonders, things were beginning to fall apart in Europe; Nazi Germany had been threatening continental stability ever since Adolf Hitler had assumed the presidency on 2 August 1934, backed by the support of the country's rapidly expanding armed forces. A rash of sabre-rattling had quickly followed. The existence of the German air force (Luftwaffe) was announced in March 1935; the Rhineland was re-occupied in March 1936, thereby breaking the terms of the Versailles Treaty of 1919; and later that year Germany entered into treaties of friendship with Italy and Japan, the countries which would eventually form the wartime Axis powers.

But it was in 1938, the year of the Empire Exhibition, that Hitler's aggression increased with alarming intensity and rapidity. On 11 March German forces moved into neighbouring Austria to complete the *Anschluss*, a political union which was expressly forbidden by Versailles but one which Hitler declared to be a natural and popular *fait accompli*. Emboldened by the lack of any opposition from the other western powers, Hitler orchestrated another crisis in the summer by exploiting the demands of German-speaking Sudetens to cede from Czechoslovakia and to join the German Reich, as Germany had become. On 12 August the German Army was mobilised as Hitler demanded that the annexation should be allowed, claiming in passing that it would be his last territorial claim in Europe. For a while it seemed that a conflict was inevitable. It was what Hitler wanted, a limited military operation against the Czechs both to test his armed forces and to make good his intentions to dominate middle and eastern Europe, but against expectation Britain suddenly intervened in the crisis.

At the time Britain had no obligation to defend Czechoslovakia. It was not part of its sphere of interest, there was no treaty with the country and the prime minister Neville Chamberlain told parliament that there was no point in going to war against Germany 'unless we had a reasonable prospect of being able to beat her to her knees in a reasonable time and of that he could see no sign'. He knew that the re-armament programme begun in the previous year was not complete and he understood, too, that the country had no appetite for the kind of intervention that had taken Britain to war in 1914. But the claims of *realpolitik* also had to be addressed. France was in alliance with Czechoslovakia and would have to be supported if a wider European conflict broke out. As the situation deteriorated and became more precarious, Chamberlain decided to regain the initiative by flying to Germany to meet Hitler face-to-face at his summer retreat at Berch-tesgaden in the Bavarian Alps.

It was a parlous mission and it turned September into a worrying month for the people of Britain, who still had vivid memories of the previous conflict and were desperately anxious to avoid going to war again. As it turned out, it took two further meetings at Bad Godesburg and Munich for Chamberlain to come to an agreement which forced Hitler to back down. At a meeting on 29 September attended by delegates from Britain, France, Italy and Germany (but not Czecho-slovakia) the Sudeten Germans were given self-determination within agreed boundaries, and for the moment the crisis was over. It was a triumph for democratic principles over the threat of force, and Chamberlain was judged to be its architect. History's verdict has been less kind. Appeasement gradually became a dirty word and Chamberlain has been blamed for being naïve when he stated in the House of Commons on 3 October that 'under the new system of guarantees the new Czechoslovakia will find a greater security than she has ever enjoyed in the past'. That turned out to be wishful thinking, but Chamberlain did at least buy much-needed breathing space at a time when Britain was not in any position to wage a continental war. The overwhelming emotion was one of relief, and even his political opponents were grateful. During the same parlia-mentary session James Maxton, MP for Bridgeton, rose to thank the prime minister for doing 'something that the mass of common people of the country wanted done'. Earlier in his career Maxton had been one of the 'Red Clydesiders' and an ardent conscientious objector who spent time in prison in 1916 after being found guilty of sedition.

In September 1938 others felt the same way as Maxton did and many of those who trooped into Bellahouston Park also recalled the widespread relief that war had been averted. Even so, the tensions of Munich impinged on the event's dying days. Before the exhibition finally closed the army put on display some of its most modern military equipment and there was a mock bombing raid carried out by three RAF Hawker Hind light bombers of 603 Squadron from RAF Turnhouse near Edinburgh. With the defending searchlights and anti-aircraft artillery beating off the attackers it gave spectators a thrilling show, but it was also an eerie preview of things to come.

To the very end the rain was an ever-present theme and the 364,092 visitors on the last day, 29 October, were treated to relentless showers which failed to dampen their spirits. At midnight it was all over, and almost immediately the builders moved in again to begin the task of dismantling the pavilions and the buildings which had given so much pleasure to so many people. Some of the structures survived in other guises. The Palace of Engineering was moved to Prestwick airport where it is still in use; the South African pavilion was purchased by ICI for use at their works at Ardeer; and the Empire Cinema, designed by Alister MacDonald, son of former prime minister Ramsay MacDonald, was moved to Lochgilphead where it later became a travel lodge. The Highland clachan was shipped across the Atlantic to resurface in San Francisco. Most of the lumber and the remaining materials were simply auctioned off. As for Tait's Tower, the stately edifice which epitomised the exhibition and which could be seen from at least a hundred miles away, it was kept in place and was intended to remain as a memorial to the enterprise. However, it was not to be as the costs of maintaining the edifice eventually proved to be prohibitive, and although a few seaside towns offered unsuccessfully to purchase the tower it was demolished the following summer. Persistent rumours claimed that Tait's Tower was removed because it could have offered a navigational aid to enemy bombers, but that seems unlikely as the demolition took place in July 1939 before war had broken out. Today, only the 3,000-ton concrete base remains to show where the futuristic structure once stood on the ridge above the park.

And so it was all over. Scotland had enjoyed a long summer in which it had been at the centre of the empire, so to speak, and the visitors to the exhibition had been given a glimpse of what the future world might hold for them with broad open avenues and elegant visionary buildings constructed in concrete, steel and glass. For a brief few months it seemed that the future had arrived and that Scotland would prosper as a result, but ten months later the country and its empire were at war again, fighting for their survival. As for Bella-houston Park, it was quickly put on a war footing and became a temporary barracks for Polish troops who fled to Scotland after the Nazi invasion of their country in September 1939 (see Chapter 9). With the park covered in tents and huts, it was as if the exhibition and all its high ideals had never been.

1 Here We Go Again

In the summer of 1933 the poet Edwin Muir returned to Scotland with his wife Willa Anderson to spend some time in Orkney where he had been born on 15 May 1887 on the island of Wyre. It was a poignant moment. Ever since leaving the islands during his early teenage years, Orkney had transmogrified in his mind into a Paradise Lost, his childhood a Golden Age to which he could never return. To Muir's way of thinking it was little sort of banishment, and the change in his fortunes could not have been more dramatic. From the bucolic calm of a farming background he was plunged into grinding poverty in Glasgow where his parents and two brothers died and he was forced to work in a rendering factory, an experience which left deep mental scars. Absolution arrived when he married and escaped from Glasgow to live in Europe where he built up an enviable reputation as translator of writers such as Franz Kafka and Heinrich Mann, but always in his mind's eye he had been in exile from a remote but kindly world which had helped to fashion his poetry and the man he had become. Work was another impetus; he was after all a professional writer. Not only did the Orkney visit rekindle his love for the place of his birth and give him the opportunity to recapture the echoes of the past through his poetry, it also produced the impetus for writing *Scottish Journey*, an account of a personal peregrination through a country which he thought he knew intimately but by the mid-1930s he discovered that he hardly knew at all.

When Muir had left Scotland in 1919 the economy was still reasonably buoyant thanks to the artificial post-war boom which had benefited the shipbuilding and heavy industries in the west, and the resilience of coal in Lanarkshire and in the Lothian and Fife fields. As it turned out, though, the initial optimism of that first year of peace was mirage, and by the middle of the next decade and into the 1930s

Scotland had entered a difficult and challenging period. The official statistics provide stark evidence of a sharp economic decline: within the twenty years between 1913 and 1933 shipbuilding on the Clyde had fallen from a record 757,000 tons to a meagre 56,000 tons; the production of steel had fallen from 20 per cent of the UK output to 11.5 per cent; pig iron from 13.5 per cent to 5.5 per cent; and the fishing industry had seen its numbers fall from 33,283 fishermen to 26,344.[1] There had also been a worrying reduction in the numbers of people working on the land: in 1921 the census carried out by the Board of Agriculture showed that the number of male workers had dropped from 175,651 in 1911 to 169,984 ten years later.[2]

Politics too had changed the complexion of the country. The old Liberal hegemony which had held the country together for so many years had disappeared during the war. The main beneficiaries had been the Conservatives and Labour; the latter party won 34 seats and 35.9 per cent of the total votes cast in the 1924 general election. This allowed the first Labour administration to come into power under the leadership of Ramsay MacDonald, albeit with the support of the Liberals. A second election later that year returned the Conservatives under Stanley Baldwin with a total of 415 seats, 38 of them in Scotland. Labour dropped to 152, with 26 in Scotland, but the biggest losers were the Liberals who ended up with only 42 seats, 9 of which were in Scotland. When Labour won the next election with another minority government in 1929 it was the largest party in the House of Commons. However MacDonald's promising career ended sadly and messily in the summer of 1931 when he was forced into forming an unpopular National Government during a financial crisis which almost brought about the collapse of the pound. Viewed as a traitor by the left – most unfairly – MacDonald stood down four years later, a broken man.

It was against that background that Muir set out on his perambulation around Scotland, and the result is one of the sharpest pieces of analysis ever to have been written about the country and its people. He began his journey in Edinburgh where, like many others before him, he was made uncomfortably aware of the contiguity of the wealthy and the poor, as evidenced by the closeness, yet apartness, of the neighbouring New and Old Towns, the former the home of the wealthy professional classes, the latter a sordid slum. He also became conscious of the all-pervasive 'floating sexual desire' which he encountered in the city's streets and 'adjacent pockets and backwaters: the tea-rooms, restaurants and cinema lounges'. Conviviality and restraint seemed to march hand-in-hand in the capital, and the memory of Scottish history overlaid everything encountered in a city that Muir did not find to be particularly Scottish.[3] From Edinburgh he headed south to the Borders where he discovered, to his delight, that the small towns still had active lives of their own and retained a sturdy independence. This stage also allowed him to visit Abbotsford near Selkirk, the home of Sir Walter Scott, but Muir was unimpressed, likening the building to a 'a railway hotel designed in the baronial style' and its collection of relics to an arsenal reflecting 'violent and dramatic masculine action'.[4]

Another Scottish literary icon, Robert Burns, also received critical treatment when Muir moved on to Ayrshire by way of the south-west. Unlike Abbotsford, he found that the poet's cottage in Alloway was less a museum and more a place where 'a human being could live with decency and dignity', but he was contemptuous of the cult surrounding Burns, describing it as 'a vested interest, jealously preserved like all vested interests'.[5] From there Glasgow beckoned, and as he made his way towards the city he became aware that he was leaving the Scotland of myth and history and entering contemporary Scotland with its 'spectre of Industrialism'. This is the beating heart of *Scottish Journey*, and Muir's narrative produced the best set-piece descriptions of what most of the central belt of Scotland was like during the 1930s. Much of what he experienced was coloured by his sojourn in the city a dozen years earlier, but what struck him were the changes that had been brought about by unemployment at a time when 69 per cent of Glasgow's registered shipbuilding workers were out of a job:

> Thousands of young men started out a little over twenty years ago with the ambition of making a modest position in the world, of marrying a wife and founding a family. And thousands of them have seen that hope vanish, probably never to return for the rest of their lives. This is surely one of the most astonishing signs of our time: the disappearance in whole areas of society of a hope so general at one time that not to have it would have seemed unnatural. As for the generation of unemployed who have risen since the war, many of them are not even acquainted with this hope.[6]

In fact, by the time the book was published in 1935, the Muirs had decided to settle in St Andrews – the decision to return to Scotland having been cemented by *Scottish Journey* – and there were signs of a gradual recovery across the country. Government subsidies allowed work to begin again on the ship that would become the Cunard liner *Queen Mary*, and against the background of the worsening international situation a policy of re-armament benefited the shipbuilding, steel and heavy engineering industries. As had happened in the First World War, the need for sandbags came as a lifeline to the jute industry in Dundee, and under the terms of the Special Areas (Development and Improvement) Act of 1934, government funds were made available to areas where unemployment was 40 per cent of the insured workforce. This brought much-needed public sector projects and employment to Scotland's 'special area' which was identified as Clydebank and North Lanarkshire. Another interventionist measure was the creation of the Scottish Economic Committee which was formally recognised in 1936 as the main instrument for finding solutions to the country's economic problems. In a time of despair it provided a degree of hope, but many of its initiatives such as the creation of the Hillington Industrial Estate in Renfrewshire were largely palliative rather than remedial. As was noted at the time, Hillington only created 15,000 mainly menial jobs while the government's naval rearmament programme rejuvenated the Clyde by ploughing £80 million into orders for new warships.[7]

Muir ended his odyssey in Orkney after making his way north through the Highlands which predictably he found to be beautiful but empty and made a wasteland by the clearances of the previous century. It also allowed him the opportunity try to make sense of his experiences and to put them into a social, economic and political perspective. Generally speaking, his findings were gloomy both about the country and its people whom he found to be lacking a cause which they could support in order to get Scotland out of its slough of despond. He had little enthusiasm for the nationalist movement in general or for the National Party in particular which he reckoned was 'numerically so weak as to be negligible'.[8] It had come into being in 1928, becoming the Scottish National Party (SNP) six years later following amalgamation with the moderate Scottish Party, but, as Muir pointed out, its impact on Scottish politics was insignificant.

Sporadic attempts had been made in 1924 and 1927 to revive the home rule legislation which had been scuppered by the outbreak of the First World War in 1914, but the SNP was usually viewed as a minority party dominated by extremists or eccentrics. There might have been a good deal of nationalist sentiment within the country as a result of the dire economic conditions and a perception that not enough was being done for Scotland but this did not translate into votes, and at the 1935 election the SNP only contested eight seats, winning 16 per cent of the poll.

Outside the political spectrum, though, nationalism did have a number of powerful adherents amongst the intelligentsia, and none was more influential than the poet who wrote under the name of Hugh MacDiarmid. During the First World War Christopher Murray Grieve had served on the Salonika front with the Royal Army Medical Corps, and on demobilisation he had gone on, almost single-handedly, to lead a cultural revolution aimed at transforming Scottish literature. As his biographer put it, he had lost faith with the Independent Labour Party (ILP) and Fabian socialism which dominated the left in Scotland and 'he now held firmly nationalistic opinions about the economic state and inferior political status of Scotland.'[9] MacDiarmid began writing poetry in Scots, and from those early efforts he evolved the idea of a Scottish renaissance movement whose aim was to dissociate Scottish writing from the vernacular-based poetry of the late nineteenth and early twentieth century and to bring it into line with contemporary political thinking. Like W. B. Yeats, T. S. Eliot and Ezra Pound he was aware of the post-war exhaustion of English culture and of the need to explore a new means of self-expression. As a result he put his faith in the idea of a 'synthetic Scots', an etymologically based language which would 'adapt an essentially rural tongue to the very much more complex requirements of our urban civilisation'.[10]

Ironically, MacDiarmid was expelled from the National Party when its left wing was purged in preparation for the creation of the SNP. He then joined the Communist Party only to be expelled in 1938 for 'nationalist deviation'. Other literary figures who flirted with nationalist politics included a trio of novelists – Eric Linklater, who stood unsuccessfully for the National Party in the East Fife by-election in 1933, Lewis Grassic Gibbon, the author of the *Scots Quair* trilogy which lamented the break-up of the farming community, and Compton Mackenzie, a bestselling author and dramatist who had served in the intelligence services during the First World War. Of the three, Mackenzie was the most eccentric in his approach to nationalism but his literary prestige ensured that his ideas were given publicity. At heart he was a romantic and a sentimental Jacobite whose ideas were best expressed in the *Pictish Review*, one of the many publications edited by MacDiarmid: 'All the dreams that haunt us – the salvation of Gaelic, the revival of Braid Scots, a Gaelic University in Inverness, the repopulation of the glens, a Celtic federation, and a hundred other things, will only embody themselves when we have a Scottish Free State under the Crown.'[11]

It was an extreme view which managed to be parochial, even Brigadoonish, in its approach, but despite the fractures within the movement and the occasional dottiness which frightened off potential supporters the Westminster government took Scottish nationalism seriously. In 1926 the post of Secretary of State for Scotland came into being, thereby providing Scotland's senior politician with a permanent place in the Cabinet, and ten years later work began on the construction of St Andrew's House in Edinburgh which was built on the site of the old Calton Jail to enable the Scottish Office to have a centralised presence in Edinburgh. Until then its main departments – Health, Education, Agriculture and Fishery – sprawled over eighteen different locations, and the new building brought a sense of unity and centralisation when it opened in 1939 to a design by Thomas Tait, the leading architect of the earlier Empire Exhibition in Glasgow. True to form the plans for the new building had caused considerable controversy in Edinburgh – the resulting building has been likened to a Soviet-era railway station – and its function has also been queried. Although some historians such as James Kellas hailed its opening as a moment which 'accelerated the movement towards political separatism', Christopher Harvie noted that it only gave Scotland what Dublin had received at the time of the Act of Union of 1801, while Richard Finlay has claimed that 'administrative devolution provided the appearance of greater autonomy without compromising the existing political structure's ability to set the agenda and dictate policy.'[12]

While these events were unfolding it is easy to understand Muir's exasperation but his alternative solution was hardly more practical. He favoured a hundred years of socialism and the imposition of 'social credit', a fashionable economic system evolved by Major C. H. Douglas, a wartime aviation engineer of Scottish descent who based his theory on the observation 'that we are living under a system of accountancy which renders the delivery of the nation's goods and services to itself a technical impossibility'.[13] Douglas's thinking gathered considerable support but the concept was difficult to grasp, a fact ridiculed by Linklater in his novel *Magnus Merriman* (1934) in which the character Hugh Skene, a thinly fictionalised MacDiarmid, 'refused to explain the system because, as he logically declared, an explanation would be wasted on people still ignorant of its fundamental hypotheses.'[14] None the less, Muir was adamant that 'Scotland needs a hundred years of Douglasism to sweat out of it the individualism which destroyed it as a nation and has brought it to where it is.'[15]

There were a number of reasons for the prevailing political confusion which enveloped Scotland in the 1930s. First and foremost was the sense of defeatism caused by the depressed economy and its side effects – the high unemployment (at one stage never less than 23 per cent of the available workforce), the lack of investment, low wages and an alarming rise in emigration between the censuses of 1921 and 1931 which saw an annual loss of an average of 80 per thousand people (compared to 5 per thousand in England). Towards the end of the 1930s the deteriorating international situation was also a factor and encouraged the popularity of 'popular front' politics to oppose the policy of appeasement of Nazi Germany. As we have seen, throughout that period Hitler had made a succession of increasingly outrageous territorial demands, and the arrival of 1939 brought no cessation of his bellicose rhetoric. On 15 March German forces occupied Bohemia and Moravia, and Hitler was driven in triumph through Prague as Czechoslovakia fell into Nazi hands. At the same time he made threatening noises about Poland, a move which was countered on 1 April by Britain and France which jointly guaranteed Polish territorial integrity as a tripwire to deter further German threats.

War was now more or less inevitable and the mood of the country began to change. The euphoria of Munich became a memory, opposition to re-armament evaporated, appeasement became an unmentionable word and opposition to fascism hardened. The Committee of Imperial Defence began to plan for war: the first steps were taken to create an expeditionary force to serve in France, the Royal Navy moved onto a war footing and plans were laid to bomb German industrial targets. On 27 April there was a further escalation when conscription was introduced in peacetime for the first time in Britain with the passing of the Military Training Act which obliged men aged twenty and twenty-one to undertake six months' military training.

Attempts were also made to woo the Soviet Union into a pact which would be similar to the triple entente of the First World War. However these ended on 23 August when Josef Stalin entered into a non-aggression pact with Hitler who had already decided that Poland should be his next target and did not want to trigger Soviet animosity. Also known as the Molotov–Ribbentrop Pact, it was a cynical piece of diplomacy which divided Eastern Europe, including Poland, into Nazi and Soviet spheres of influence. As the month neared its end there was a sense that war was not only imminent but necessary, both to save the country and to check Hitler's growing domination of Europe. On the day before the pact was signed the German leader had convened his senior generals and told them that he wanted them 'to unpityingly and mercilessly send men, women and children of Polish descent and language to death. This is the only way to gain the *Lebensraum* [living space] we need.'[16] A week later, the Chief of the Imperial General Staff (CIGS) General Sir Henry Pownall noted in his diary: 'We must finish the Nazi regime this time, to compromise and discuss is useless, it will all happen again . . . we must have a war. We can't lose it.'[17]

In addition to the military and naval preparations the first civil defence measures began to appear across the UK, and the newspapers were full of advice about what should be done in the event of the expected air raids. On 24 August parliament passed the Emergency Powers (Defence) Act which gave it wide-ranging authority to do whatever was required to maintain the defence of the realm. The following day vulnerable points were taken over by soldiers of the Territorial Army. (The War Diary of 5th Highland Light Infantry recorded the fact: 'Cowlairs [railway] Tunnel occupied by 2/Lt G. R. Dunn, 8 NCOs [non-commissioned officers] and 24 Ptes [privates].'[18])

This, and subsequent legislation, effectively suspended all civil liberties for the war, and while the moves were broadly welcomed they did cause concern. When some criminal cases were held in camera in Greenock Sheriff Court, Arthur Woodburn, Labour MP for Clackmannanshire and East Stirlingshire made a complaint in parliament but was assured by the Solicitor-General that as these cases involved the movement of warships the powers conferred by section 6 of the Act had been invoked.

The whole question of curtailing liberties was discussed throughout the first parliamentary session of the war and the general feeling, as expressed by Sir Dingle Foot, Liberal MP for Dundee, was that the safety of the state had to come first. After apologising for using the word 'English' to describe the country's victory in the War of the Spanish Succession he said that the theory had been tested in Marlborough's time and it still held good in 1939: 'We think that once again, by the same methods and along the same lines, we can contradict the expectations of many people on the Continent of Europe, but it seems to many of us – and certainly to Hon. Members who sit in this part of the House – that this can be achieved only if, at a time of emergency and war, instead of trying to suspend our free institutions, we jealously preserve them.'[19]

In addition to the legislation other practical measures were announced. Reservists were called up to rejoin the armed forces, and Air Raid Precaution (ARP) wardens were put on standby to make sure that the rigorous blackout regulations would be enforced after nightfall. Calls were also made for volunteers to increase the size of Scotland's fire brigades from 21,000 to 300,000, and for the creation of 200,000 auxiliary policemen to augment the 70,000 officers already serving in Scotland. Gas masks had also been issued and tested, and newspapers carried poignant photographs of children standing in serried ranks with the cumbersome rubber masks hiding their faces. In the event of a gas attack they would have been useless, but that summer they were an important part of people's lives at a time when it was feared that the Germans would use gas or chemical bombs against the civilian population.[20]

As had happened in the previous conflict people remembered the summer of 1939 as being one of the best in living memory. In stark contrast to the rain which had made the previous summer months such a trial, Scotland enjoyed high temperatures and sunny skies. At the time the future poet and critic Maurice Lindsay was on holiday with his family in the Kyles of Bute on the Clyde and he could see that they were living on borrowed time. In the previous summer he had been commissioned in the 9th Cameronians, a Territorial Army battalion, and as a critic of appeasement he was perhaps better placed to see that 'reality demanded repayment': 'It was especially difficult to believe that the scent of the old-fashioned roses in the garden, the soft peach-down on the arms of the girls with whom we played idle tennis or gently dallied, and the cheerful phut-phut-phut-phut of the busy paddle steamers fussing over the glinting, sunny Clyde, was but a surface cover over the menacing march of distant soldiers bearing death and destruction on a scale we could not visualise but found it impossible not to fear. Yet so it was.'[21]

The balmy weather and holiday atmosphere only added to the sense of unreality as the situation became more tense in Europe, with Hitler increasing pressure on Poland by threatening to occupy the Baltic port of Danzig (Gdansk) which was a free city under the mandate of the League of Nations. As German forces began to assemble along the eastern border of Poland the people of Scotland went on with their business as if they were divorced from events which were not part of their lives. How could they not have done otherwise? On the last Saturday of peace, 2 September, there were full crowds at all the main football matches in the Scottish League where Rangers beat Third Lanark 2–1 in front of 30,000 spectators at Cathkin Park, Celtic defeated Clyde 1–0 in a close-fought game at Parkhead, Hearts overcame Motherwell 4–2 at Tynecastle, while Albion Rovers outclassed Hibernian 5–3 at Cliftonhill. They were the last official competitive football games to be played for seven years.

By then the fighting had already started. On the previous day, 1 September, in the early hours of the morning the first shots of the conflict had been fired when the aging German pre-Dreadnought battleship *Schleswig-Holstein* opened fire on the Polish naval base at Westerplatte in Danzig while making a courtesy visit to the port. At the same time a border incident was fabricated and four German divisions of Army Group North poured into the 'Polish Corridor', the disputed territory which provided Poland with access to the Baltic while cutting off Germany from East Prussia. Ahead of the advancing tanks flew strike aircraft such as the much feared Junkers Ju-87 (Stuka) dive-bomber which began pounding strategic targets and machine-gunning anyone on the ground. These were the tactics of *blitzkrieg* (lightning war) and from the outset it was apparent that they were both terrifying for those on the receiving end and hugely successful for those carrying them out. Close-range artillery fire was also useful in neutralising Polish defences as was the sheer weight of the infantry assault on Polish positions.[22]

In response to the German aggression, Lord Halifax, the British foreign secretary, sent a curt message to Hitler informing him that Britain would fulfil its obligations to Poland unless German forces withdrew, but the German leader was not in the mood to respond to firm words. There was a delay as the formal diplomatic response had to be finalised with France, and there was some last-minute wavering in Paris, but at nine o'clock on the morning of 3 September Sir Neville Henderson, Britain's ambassador to Germany, delivered an ultimatum stating that if hostilities did not stop by 11 a.m. a state of war would exist between Great Britain and Germany. Hitler did not respond and a quarter of an hour later Chamberlain went on the radio to announce to the British people that they were at war with Germany.

It was a moment which no one would ever forget. Although Chamberlain's broadcast had been trailed by the BBC earlier in the morning, many people were attending church services when the declaration of war was made. Bill King, a miner's son from Dalkeith, was with his family in St John's Church when the minister made the announcement from the pulpit, and he remembered that the effect on the congregation was 'just absolute stillness'. For Constance Ross, attending a similar church service in Buckhaven in Fife, the moment was even more dramatic. During the reading there was a knock on the main door which was answered by the beadle who then turned to the congregation to confirm their worst fears: 'That was Civil Defence to tell us that Neville Chamberlain the Prime Minister has just announced over the radio that we are now at war with Germany. You've to go home immediately, take shelter and wait for further instructions.' Years later, on the seventieth anniversary of the outbreak of the war Constance Ross still recalled a 'feeling of dread and uncertainty as we scuttled home, looking fearfully upwards, expecting an aerial bombardment at any moment.'[23]

No sooner had the declaration of war been made than the air-raid sirens sounded in Edinburgh, the result of an enemy aircraft reported off Berwick-on-Tweed. A few minutes later came the 'all clear' when it was found to be a false alarm. In the west of Scotland Chamberlain's announcement was followed by the onset of a late summer thunderstorm, the thunder and lightning providing another harbinger of the sound and fury of the years ahead. That evening the *Edinburgh Evening News* published a special edition announcing the declaration of war and carrying other pages of announcements including the news that 'from now until further notice the one o'clock time gun at Edinburgh Castle will not be fired'.[24]

While these were natural precautions, and steps had to be taken to put the country on a war footing, the initial excitement and momentum was followed by a curious lull. In the opening months of the war it became clear that the Germans had laid no immediate plans to attempt to invade Britain or to attack civilian targets. However, that exclusion did not extend to traffic on the sea, and as a result Scotland was to play a part in an incident which led to the first Allied civilian loss of life in the conflict. Two days earlier, shortly after midday on 1 September, the Glasgow-registered Donaldson Atlantic liner ss *Athenia* left Princes Dock in Glasgow bound for Montreal. (Some of the dockers booed the departure, claiming that the passengers were 'cowards' who were deserting the country.) En route she called at Liverpool and Belfast, and on the day that war was declared she was sailing to the north-west of Ireland, some sixty miles south of Rockall. So too was *U-30*, a type VIIA Atlantic submarine under the command of Fritz-Julius Lemp, one of twenty-seven long-range boats which had been ordered to put to sea on 22 August to patrol the area to the west of Britain as far south as the Straits of Gibraltar. On the outbreak of war all the boats had gone on a war footing which meant that they had to operate under the terms of the *Prisenordnung* (prize regulations) which permitted them to stop and search merchant ships and to ensure the safety of passengers and crew before sinking them.

At that point the Germans had no intention of waging unrestricted submarine operations as they had done in 1917. Not only was this outlawed under the London Naval Treaty of 1936, but Hitler was still hopeful of reaching a diplomatic settlement with Britain and France.

With that in mind Lemp and his fellow captains had been ordered not to attack Allied vessels of any kind. All that changed as dusk fell across the Atlantic when Lemp sighted a large blacked-out vessel sailing westward on a zigzag course. This was the *Athenia* under the command of Captain James Cook carrying its complement of 350 crew and 1,103 passengers, many of them Americans escaping the coming war. Unsure of what action to take – the vessel was sailing an unusual course and showed no lights – Lemp submerged *U-30* and began tracking his target. Clearly it was a medium-sized liner but it also seemed to be behaving suspiciously, and Lemp might have believed that it was either a troopship or an armed merchantman. At any rate he was taking no chances, and shortly after 7.30 p.m. he fired two torpedoes. One misfired, but the other slammed into the port side of *Athenia* and exploded in number five hold, smashing the bulkhead between the boiler and engine room and destroying the stairways in the third-class accommodation.

A huge column of spray shot skywards, and *Athenia* began settling by the stern as panic-stricken passengers thronged the decks. As preparations for evacuation were hurriedly put in place distress signals were sent from the radio room. These were picked up at the Malin Head receiving station, prompting a rescue operation involving three British destroyers (HMS *Electra*, HMS *Fame* and HMS *Escort*), a Norwegian tanker (*Knute Nelson*), a Swedish yacht (*Southern Cross*) and a US tanker (*City of Flint*). Despite mishaps during the operation when one of the lifeboats was crushed by *Knute Nelson*'s propeller, the casualty list was relatively small – ninety-eight passengers and nineteen crew. *Athenia* eventually sank the following day, and the first survivors began arriving a day later. Those taken to Galway by the *Knute Nelson* received a warm welcome, but there was chaos when the British destroyers arrived at fogbound Greenock on 5 September. The survivors found themselves on a quay where a sugar ship was unloading, and it took the initiative of Donald Maclean, Greenock's Inspector of Public Assistance to retrieve the situation. Two days later he informed the Scottish Office: 'Having visited the scene and witnessed the awful condition of the survivors I, with the concurrence of the Provost and Town Clerk, immediately secured from a large Drapery Firm in the town, sufficient new clothing, comprising Suits, Dresses, Boots etc, and all manner of underwear, both ladies, gents and childrens [sic] and within 1 hour of their arrival the survivors were all suitably clothed for their journey by buses to Glasgow.'[25]

The cost to the Corporation of Greenock was £733, and Maclean hoped that this would be made good by the government. Although there was an outbreak of local generosity with an appeal led by Glasgow's Lord Provost Patrick Dollan which raised £5,707, both the Scottish Office and the Treasury refused to make any funds available to cover the cost of the clothes given to the survivors at Greenock.[26]

By then British submarines had also been in action. Shortly after the outbreak of war HMS *Oxley*, a Dundee-based O-class submarine from the 2nd Submarine Flotilla was sunk by a sister boat HMS *Triton* while on patrol close to the Obrestad light on the Norwegian coast. Shortly before war was declared the flotilla had deployed to Dundee and this was their first offensive patrol which had in fact begun on 24 August. It ended in tragedy late at night on 10 September when *Triton*'s officer of the watch noticed another submarine, also on the surface, on the port bow. Although three warnings were given on the box lamp and a final warning was made by firing green flares by rifle grenade, there was no response. *Triton*'s captain, Lieutenant Commander H. P. de C. Steel, RN, concluded that it was a German U-boat, and ordered tubes 7 and 8 to be fired with a three-second interval. Less than a minute later, an explosion was heard: it was *Oxley* which sank almost immediately. Three survivors were found, including the boat's commanding officer, but one of them was drowned during the rescue operation. On the return to Dundee a Board of Inquiry found that Steel had done all he reasonably could in the circumstances. *Oxley* was out of position, *Triton* had acted correctly, and as a result the first Allied submarine casualty of the war was due to what later came to be known as 'friendly fire'.[27] At the time the loss of *Oxley* was attributed variously to an internal explosion or to a collision with *Triton*, and the truth was not revealed until the 1950s. As for *Triton*, it too was sunk a year later, in December 1940, while on patrol in the southern Adriatic.

It had proved impossible, though, to disguise the fate of the *Athenia*, and inevitably its sinking caused international outrage. Comparisons were made with the similar torpedoing of the *Lusitania* in 1915, but the Germans countered the anger with propaganda claims that the ship had been sunk by a mine or deliberately by a British submarine.

They also took steps to cover up the incident: Lemp did not note it in his log, his crew was sworn to silence, it was not mentioned in the war diary of German U-boat Command and the whole facts were not made available until after the war. A few days after the incident Lemp was in action again when he sank another Glasgow-registered ship – the merchantman *Blair Logie* – but only after he had permitted the crew to take to the lifeboats. Towards the end of *U-30*'s tour it was involved in a bizarre incident when it was attacked by three Blackburn Sea Skua dive bombers of 803 Squadron flying from the carrier HMS *Ark Royal*. Two of the aircraft were destroyed by dropping their bombs too early, and the surviving pilots were picked up by Lemp to become prisoners of war. One thing was certain: the submarine was back as a key component in naval warfare. A steady succession of further sinkings followed in Scottish and Irish waters, including the obsolescent aircraft carrier HMS *Courageous* which was torpedoed to the west of Ireland on 17 September.

As for Lemp, he did not survive long, succumbing to gunfire from the destroyers HMS *Broadway* and HMS *Bulldog* after his new command *U-110* was depth-charged to the surface south of Greenland on 9 May 1941. *Bulldog*'s commander, Captain Joe Baker-Cresswell, was initially intent on sinking *U-110* by ramming but pulled out at the last minute to take her into captivity intact. It was a judicious decision: on board the submarine the boarding party led by Sub-Lieutenant David Balme, RNVR, found a top-secret Enigma coding machine together with its code-books, a vital piece of intelligence which enabled British code-breakers to decipher signals sent between German warships and submarines and their home headquarters. For the British it proved to be a priceless discovery, and just as Lemp kept quiet about his part in the sinking of the *Athenia*, so was it never disclosed by the Royal Navy that his second command, the *U-110*, had fallen into enemy hands.

There was another grim homecoming on the Clyde involving the loss of civilian passengers when the destroyer HMS *Hurricane* docked at Gourock on 19 September 1940 carrying 105 survivors from the torpedoing of the Ellerman Lines passenger liner SS *City of Benares*. Once again the ship had fallen victim to a U-boat attack while crossing the Atlantic, on this occasion as part of the westbound Convoy OB-213 which had left Liverpool on 13 September heading for the Canadian ports of Quebec and Montreal. Although by then the country was becoming hardened to the losses of merchant and passenger ships to submarine attack, this incident was made worse by the fact that amongst the passengers on *City of Benares* were ninety children who were being evacuated to Canada under the terms of a scheme operated by the Children's Overseas Reception Board (CORB). This well-meaning organisation had been established with government sponsorship earlier in the year to co-ordinate the growing activities of wealthy families who were sending their children overseas to escape the increasing dangers of enemy air attack and the threat of German invasion. They were also responding to offers of hospitality from families in countries friendly to the UK, notably Australia, New Zealand, South Africa and the United States, to provide safe havens for children at risk, and whose parents could afford the necessary expense of travel. To co-ordinate the British response to these offers, an interdepartmental committee was established, chaired by the Parliamentary Under-Secretary of State for the Dominions, Geoffrey Shakespeare, and including representatives from the Ministries of Health, Labour, and Pensions, the Dominions, Home, Foreign and Scottish Offices, the Treasury and the Board of Education. As a result the committee formed CORB with the following terms of reference: 'To consider offers from overseas to house and care for children, whether accompanied or unaccompanied, from the European War Zone, residing in Great Britain, including children orphaned by the war and to make recommendations thereon.'[28] A special Board for Scotland with its own Advisory Council was also established, and while it followed the policy laid down by CORB, a Scottish Liaison Officer was appointed to keep the Scottish Office informed of daily decisions and progress being made.

Through organisations such as Barnardos, Quarriers and Fairbridge, Britain had a long history of organising juvenile emigration, sending children, mainly paupers and orphans, to live and work in the Dominions as farm labourers and domestic servants. Those involved thought that they had the best interests of the children at heart, but this was the first time that children had been evacuated in time of war, and the first time, too, that those involved came from mainly wealthy families. Perhaps because it was thought to be a temporary exile, CORB had been inundated with 200,000 applications between June and August 1940 when the scheme was suspended. The first to be chosen came from areas which were thought to be especially vulnerable to bombing, and in that initial period CORB selected 2,664 children for evacuation. Canada received the bulk of them – 1,532 in nine parties, while three parties sailed for Australia, a total of 577, a further 353 went to South Africa in two parties and 202 to New Zealand, again in two parties. During the selection process it was agreed that at least 10 per cent should be Scottish applicants, and each sailing party was selected with care to represent a cross-section of British society.

By the end of the summer a further 24,000 children had been approved for sailing in that time, and over 1,000 escorts, including doctors and nurses, had also been chosen. At a time when Britain was facing the very real danger of German invasion, CORB was considered to be a success story even though it was already becoming apparent that there would be insufficient shipping to transport the chosen children to their destinations. Fears were also expressed about the wisdom of risking children on the high seas at a time when the U-boat menace was growing – the Dutch liner *Volendam* was damaged off the west coast of Scotland on 30 August while carrying 320 children – and as a result of those concerns CORB decided that evacuee ships crossing the Atlantic should sail in convoy.

However even that sensible move could not save those who perished on the *City of Benares*. Launched at Port Glasgow in 1935, she was a fast and modern liner, and was made the flagship of the nineteen-strong convoy which was under the command of Rear Admiral E. J. G. Mackinnon, DSO, RN. In that position she was the lead ship in the centre column, but that made her an obvious target when the convoy was 600 miles off the west coast of Ireland in the gap between the extent of the Royal Navy's escort provision and the US neutrality zone. At that point, some 250 miles west of Rockall, Mackinnon was forced to lose his escorts, the destroyer HMS *Winchelsea* and two sloops which broke off to meet the eastbound Convoy HX-71, a move which gave Kapitänleutnant Heinrich Bleichrodt of the shadowing *U-48* his opportunity to attack. Although two torpedoes missed the *City of Benares,* a third hit the rear of the hull shortly before midnight on 18 September, and the liner quickly listed so that it was impossible to launch all the lifeboats. Of the 406 people on board the *City of Benares*, 248 perished, including the master (Captain

Landles Nicoll from Arbroath), the commodore, three staff members, 121 crew members and 134 passengers, including 77 of the 90 child evacuees.

Bad weather was the main problem – a force 5 storm was blowing – but there was also a fair degree of confusion. The rest of the convoy scattered and kept going as another ship, ss *Marina*, had also been hit. Without the naval escorts the survivors were on their own. The first help did not arrive until the following afternoon when HMS *Hurricane* (Lieutenant-Commander H. C. Simms RN) arrived from the north and picked up 105 survivors. Unfortunately, in the confusion one of the lifeboats was missed and was accidentally left behind when *Hurricane* steamed off to Greenock. The remaining boat contained forty adults and six children and was not picked up until eight days later. The sinking of the *City of Benares* was one of the worst civilian maritime disasters of the war, and the loss of so many children forced CORB to suspend operations. There were to be no more evacuations, and the loss of the children was to leave a long shadow over the whole programme. A quarter of a century later the novelist James Kennaway, whose father worked as a lawyer and factor in Auchterarder, could clearly summon up the thought of the whitening bones beneath the Atlantic swell of the wife of a local laird who had been lost with her son while 'doing her duty to protect' him.[29]

The submarine offensive confirmed suspicions that Germany would ruthlessly exploit its capabilities by attacking British shipping in the Atlantic where surface raiders would also be deployed. As a result the North Sea became Tom Tiddler's Ground, with both sides manoeuvring to gain control of the important Norway gap and its access to the waters south of Iceland. Because RAF Coastal Command's Avro Anson patrol aircraft lacked the range, the Dundee-based submarines maintained their patrols off the Norwegian coast but this could only be a stop-gap measure. Thought was given to repeating the 'Northern Barrage', a huge minefield bridging the gap between Shetland and the Norwegian coast which was put in place in the winter of 1917–18 to prevent German submarines from entering the Atlantic. It stretched for 250 miles, and of the 70,177 mines used in the defensive system, the US Navy's First Mine Squadron planted 56,571, working from bases at Invergordon and Inverness. Although a similar plan was prepared by Winston Churchill, who had been appointed First Lord of the Admiralty on the outbreak of war, the barrage was not created due to cost and concerns about the impact on neutral shipping. That being said, the pace of mine-laying in the North Sea did increase. In the opening months of the war the Royal Navy created a minefield between Orkney and Dover; in September 1939 alone, the minelayers HMS *Adventure* and HMS *Plover* planted 3,000 mines across the Dover Strait, and in the second half of the month the barrage was completed by 3,636 anti-U-boat mines. At the same time the navy created the East Coast Barrier, a mine barrage between twenty and fifty miles wide from Scotland to the Thames, leaving a narrow space between the barrage and the coast for navigation.[30]

As happened on the outbreak of the First World War, the Home Fleet made its way to Scapa Flow which was thought to be a safer option than the naval base at Rosyth. Initially it was very much a makeshift arrangement as the facilities were basic and the defences were inadequate. Although booms had been put in place to defend the three main entrances at Hoxa, Switha and Hoy, the air defences were modest, consisting of eight 4.5-inch anti-aircraft guns at Lyness, two 6-inch guns and one 4.7-inch gun at Stanger Head on Flotta, and two 6-inch guns at Ness. There was also a Royal Marine detachment equipped with machine-guns, and two TA companies from 5th Seaforth Highlanders and 7th Gordon Highlanders guarded the coastal defence batteries. At that point there was no RAF or Fleet Air Arm presence. That was not rectified until October when 804 Squadron formed at Hatston, one mile north-west of Kirkwall, equipped with Gloster Gladiators and Grumman Martlets. However, the naval presence was formidable, and at the time of the outbreak of war there were forty-four ships in the Flow including the carrier HMS *Ark Royal* and the battleships HMS *Nelson*, HMS *Rodney*, HMS *Resolution*, HMS *Royal Sovereign*, HMS *Ramillies* and HMS *Royal Oak*. Some were of First World War vintage, and there was a further reminder of that conflict when HMS *Iron Duke*, Jellicoe's flagship at Jutland, arrived as a floating administration block for the base's commander Admiral Sir Wilfred French. Stripped of its main turrets, it was anchored off Lyness.

On 15 September Churchill visited the naval base and found the occasion vaguely disquieting. Although the main warships provided solid evidence of British sea power, he disapproved of the renewal of the policy of 'distant blockade', which had been used in the First World War and which in the new conflict was revived by fitting out armed merchantmen to provide a Northern Patrol operating out of Scapa to interdict German traffic in the North Sea. He was also aware of the deficiencies in defence, especially the fact that there were insufficient destroyers to provide cover for the Home Fleet, and found his inspection 'a strange experience, like suddenly resuming a previous incarnation'. True to form, he also yearned for an offensive strategy, and told the First Sea Lord Admiral Sir Dudley Pound that 'the search for a naval offensive must be incessant'.[31]

So too did the Germans, who were intent on mounting a submarine attack on the British naval base. Shortly after the outbreak of war, Luftwaffe reconnaissance photographs suggested to Admiral Karl Dönitz, head of U-Boat Command, that there appeared to be a gap in the blockship defences in Holm Sound and that this could be exploited at flood tide. The task was given to Kapitänleutnant Günther Prien, the commander of *U-47* who had already accounted for one British ship, the Cunarder *Bosnia*. In mid-September he was recalled to Kiel to begin planning for the daring assault which was fixed for the night of 13/14 October. By then fears of an attack from the air had encouraged Admiral Sir Charles Forbes, commander of the Home Fleet, to remove his capital ships to Loch Ewe on the west coast of Scotland. Even so, Prien would have no shortage of targets, including the battleship *Royal Oak* which had been left behind because her top speed of 20 knots was inadequate to keep up with the rest of the fleet.

In the early morning of 13 October Prien arrived off Scapa, and after darkness fell he surfaced *U-47* and took her on a course to the north of Lamb Holm island and the mainland. A mistake almost forced him into the shallow waters of Skerry Sound but the navigator's skills corrected the course and he was able to thread his boat past the blockships *Seriano* and *Numidian*. Only the bright lights of the aurora borealis and the headlights of a passing vehicle discomfited him. Once inside the Flow, shortly after midnight, he headed west. Had he continued on that course he would have encountered the newly commissioned light cruiser HMS *Belfast* but instead he embarked on a reverse course, and 4,000 yards to the north saw the unmistakable outline of HMS *Royal Oak* with the elderly seaplane carrier HMS *Pegasus* anchored behind her.

Shortly before 1 a.m. he fired a salvo of four torpedoes from his bow tubes; one misfired, two missed the target but the fourth hit the bow of the *Royal Oak* causing minimal damage and triggering little concern amongst the battleship's crew. Prien then renewed the attack, and having missed with his stern tube, fired a salvo from the reloaded bow tubes, two of which struck home, hitting the battleship amidships and doing fatal damage. The explosions destroyed the starboard engine room, and as the lights went out the magazine caught fire, sending a fireball through the mess decks. The stricken ship started listing, and within thirteen minutes of Prien's second attack *Royal Oak* rolled over and sank. Lack of life-jackets and insufficient life-saving arrangements meant that the casualty list was high – 833 officers and men, many of them boy sailors aged fifteen to seventeen. Only the presence of the tender *Daisy 2* and rescue boats from *Pegasus* prevented further casualties amongst those who had managed to jump overboard.

As for Prien, he quickly retraced his course and by two o'clock in the morning *U-47* was back in the North Sea heading for home. In the confused aftermath it was thought that the battleship had succumbed to an internal explosion or had been hit from the air but divers sent down the following morning confirmed the torpedo attack. This was announced in the House of Commons on 17 October when Churchill conceded that the ship had been lost to 'a remarkable exploit of professional skill and daring'. He also had to face hostile questioning on the practice of using boy sailors in war zones and on the inadequacy of the defences. The former complaint was promptly resolved with eighteen becoming the minimum age, and steps were taken to improve the islands' defences after a Board of Inquiry identified nine possible access routes into the Flow.[32] The ships of the Home Fleet were also ordered to stay away from the base for six months.

Amongst the new measures was the strengthening of the air defences, including the construction of new fighter bases at Skeabrae, north of Stromness, and Grimsetter, south-east of Kirkwall. During the winter, work also began on the creation of the Orkney balloon barrage which consisted of twenty sites from which land-based balloons were flown (twelve on Flotta, four on Hoy and four on Fara) while a further eight waterborne balloons were flown from trawlers and covered the fleet anchorage. The sites were operated by 950 Squadron Auxiliary Air Force with its headquarters at Ore Hill on

Lyness, and its records show that the task was not for the faint-hearted: 'The chief impression of the first few months at Scapa were mud, deep clinging mud and wind, wind beyond the dreams of any Balloon Operator; and many and various were the "jury rigs" devised to protect the feeble fabric of the balloons from the raging storms.'[33] Inevitably there were occasions when balloons escaped their moorings and had to be shot down by fighter aircraft, and on one occasion a gale dragged a winch over the cliff at Cava and into the sea. In time the barrage proved its worth against air attack, but it was not yet in place when Scapa Flow was attacked by four Junkers 88 bombers on 17 October. During the raid HMS *Iron Duke* was holed and had to be beached, first in Ore Bay and then at Longhope. During the attack, one of the German aircraft was shot down by a Martlet from Skeabrae.

By then the first enemy aircraft had already been destroyed in Scottish skies.[34] On 8 October a Lockheed Hudson of 224 Squadron operating from RAF Leuchars shot down a Dornier Do 18 flying boat while patrolling twenty miles off Aberdeen.[35] (The same squadron has the distinction of the being the first to attack a German aircraft when a Hudson fired on a similar Dornier over the North Sea on 4 September.)[36] However, the aerial war in Scottish skies began in earnest on 16 October when two Heinkel 111 reconnaissance aircraft appeared over the Firth of Forth and were picked up by the radar station at Drone Hill near Cockburnspath. Having flown over Rosyth where they came under fire from an anti-aircraft battery – a 'first' for the gun crews of Anti-Aircraft Command – they were heading for home when they were intercepted near May Island at 10.21 a.m. by two Spitfires of 602 (City of Glasgow) Squadron (Auxiliary Air Force) from nearby RAF Drem. Although the aircraft managed to escape by heading into the clouds, the pilots Flight Lieutenant George Pinkerton and Flying Officer Archie McKellar became the first Spitfire crews to engage an enemy aircraft over the British land mass. It was also the prelude to a day of continuing and frequently bewildering action, and on the next occasion when Pinkerton was given the chance to open fire he got his kill.

That afternoon a larger force of Junkers 88 bombers was despatched to the area with orders to attack the battleship HMS *Hood* which German intelligence believed to be in the Firth of Forth. Before leaving his base at Westerland on the island of Sylt, the German commanding officer Helmut Pohle had received specific instructions from Hitler that the naval dockyards at Rosyth were not be to attacked to prevent civilian casualties, but as it turned out the intelligence was wrong and *Hood* was not there – the battleship refitting at Rosyth was HMS *Repulse*. However there were a number of capital ships in the Firth of Forth including the cruisers HMS *Southampton* and HMS *Edinburgh* which were lying off Inchgarvie, and these were legitimate targets. At 2.15 p.m. Pohle's aircraft approached the estuary over East Lothian but by then they had been picked up by the Royal Observer Corps as the ground tracking stations were temporarily out of action. The response was immediate. From RAF Turnhouse a section of three Spitfires of 603 (City of Edinburgh) Squadron (Auxiliary Air Force) took off, led by Flight Lieutenant Pat Gifford, and were immediately joined by another section which had attacked German aircraft as they flew over Threipmuir Reservoir near Dalkeith. As one of the Junkers flew towards the Forth it was intercepted by the second section and promptly shot down by a Spitfire piloted by Flight Lieutenant George Denholm. It crashed into the Forth where three of its four-man crew were rescued by the fishing yawl *Dayspring* from Port Seton.

It was not the end of the action. Pinkerton's section had been on patrol 20,000 feet above Dalkeith, and quickly joined the fray. As they headed towards the Fife shore they saw Pohle, who had just completed a bombing run on *Southampton*, which had the dubious distinction of being the first British warship to be attacked in the war. This time Pinkerton and McKellar were able to keep on the tail of the Junkers and shot it down, with Pinkerton, a Renfrewshire farmer in peacetime, getting credit for the kill. Despite Pohle's efforts at evasion the bomber crashed into the sea three miles off Crail where he was rescued, two of his crew having been killed in the attack.

Although the Germans had been beaten off they had succeeded in damaging the destroyer HMS *Mohawk* and killing sixteen seamen. They had also given a civilian population a grandstand view of what it was like to be under aerial attack – the entire raid lasted two hours, and people on the ground in Edinburgh, Fife and East Lothian were treated to the sight of Spitfires chasing and firing at enemy aircraft. There were casualties, fortunately minor. Two women were hit by flying glass in Davidson's Mains in Edinburgh, and as the German aircraft flew over the north of the city they machine-gunned targets on the ground. In Portobello two painters Frank Lynn and Joe McLuskie were working on the exterior of a house at 45 Abercorn Terrace when one of them, McLuskie, was hit and was rushed to Leith Hospital to have a machine-gun bullet removed from his abdomen. Other houses in the vicinity were damaged including 10 Hamilton Street (later Brunstane Road North), the residence of Lord Provost Sir Henry Steele who was reported to be 'very annoyed', not just because his house had been attacked and damaged – windows and internal mirrors had been smashed – but also because there had been no warning prior to the raid.[37]

If anything, the whole affair had been treated as a piece of exciting entertainment, with numbers of people, including a group of school-boys from Fettes College playing rugby at Inverleith, straining to watch the action. Some people claimed later that they thought it had been a training exercise, and the following day the *Scotsman* reported the incident under the headline 'Spectacular Sight for Population, Thought it Was a Practice'. It was fair comment: no air-raid sirens had sounded in Edinburgh to warn of any danger, and apart from the minor wounds to civilian personnel on the ground no great damage had been done. Four days later the bodies of two of the German aircrew were buried in Portobello after their swastika-draped coffins had been laid in St Philip's Church. When the funeral procession set off, thousands lined the streets, many of them members of 602 and 603 Squadrons, and pipers played the haunting tune 'Over the sea to Skye'. First blood had been drawn by RAF Fighter Command, and it was fitting perhaps that the kills had been made by part-time pilots of the Auxiliary Air Force whose squadrons had only recently converted to modern Spitfires. But it came at a cost. The operational books of 13 Group responsible for conducting air defence in eastern Scotland show that the squadrons expended a huge amount of ammunition – 603 Squadron alone fired 16,000 rounds – and those levels would be unsustainable in a lengthy war of attrition.[38] Equally, the experience had given a brief demonstration of what aerial bombardment would be like for the civilian population. On that sunny October day in Edinburgh, Fife and the Lothians, they had not been found wanting, and there was none of the panic that had been forecast by pessimists, but ahead lay sterner tests.

2 Phoney War

For the majority of the people living in Britain during the winter of 1939–40 there was a period which came to be known as the 'phoney war' or 'bore war'. It lasted from the outbreak to the early summer of 1940, when Hitler unleashed his forces to complete the invasion of France and the first serious enemy bomb attacks were mounted against the main cities of the United Kingdom. During that time neither the ground forces nor the air forces saw much action, the French did little to disturb the Germans in the Saar where there were possibilities of offensive action, and the only positive step taken to help the Poles militarily was the passing of the Franco-Polish Military Agreement on 9 September which allowed Polish forces to form and train in France. Otherwise the Poles were on their own, and following a short and sharp German onslaught they were soon forced to give up the unequal struggle. On 17 September, in support of the terms of the earlier Nazi–Soviet Pact but in breach of an even earlier non-aggression pact, the Red Army had crossed Poland's eastern border, thereby putting paid to any hope of further resistance. Those Poles who were able to escape fled south into Romania and Hungary, and as members of the Polish Free Forces many of their number eventually ended up in Scotland (see Chapter 9).

The Poles had paid a high price for their resistance – 65,000 casualties and 660,000 taken into German or Soviet captivity – but amongst their western allies there was still an air of unreality. An indication of the passivity of those early days of the war was given by the British Air Minister Kingsley Wood who responded to proposals that Germany should be bombed with the thought that 'there was no question of our bombing even the munition works at Essen, which were private property.'[1] Only at sea were hostile operations conducted by both sides, with German and British surface ships and submarines in constant action in the North Sea and the Atlantic. Following the sinking of HMS *Royal Oak* the Royal Navy gained a measure of revenge when the German pocket battleship *Admiral Graf Spee* was scuttled in the Uruguayan port of Montevideo on 17 December 1939 following a running battle with a joint Royal Navy–Royal New Zealand Navy cruiser force off the mouth of the River Plate. It was considered to be a triumph and was much applauded, but amongst the civilian population in general the prevailing lack of action diluted the feelings of determination and resolve which had accompanied the declaration of war. As a result large swathes of the population became bored with air-raid precautions and disillusioned by the constant emergency legislation which imposed restrictions on their daily lives.

In Scotland it was quite a different matter, especially on the east coast where warfare had quickly become a fact of day-to-day life and the phoney war was no such thing. For the rest of the year until the arrival of harsh winter weather curtailed operational flying, the broad expanse of the Firth of Forth seemed to act as a magnet for Luftwaffe bombers. Following Pohle's unsuccessful raid two more Heinkels were plotted off the Fife coast on 22 October 1939 and one of them was shot down by a section of 603 Squadron's Spitfires. Six days later another Heinkel was intercepted and hit while flying over Preston-pans and Tranent in East Lothian. Two of the crew were killed but the pilot Kurt Lehmkuhl kept control of the aircraft and managed to crash-land it near Humbie. He and the navigator Rolf Niehoff were captured and taken to Edinburgh Castle where they were entertained to lunch in the officers' mess before being sent to the Tower of London. Niehoff expressed considerable surprise at the excellent fare offered to him as he had been given to believe that there were serious shortages of food.

In addition to attempting to bomb the warships in the Forth estuary the Germans used submarines to sow magnetic and acoustic mines in the same waters and on the west coast. These were very different from the horned contact variety which floated on the surface, and initially they were extremely difficult to counter as they lay on the seabed and were detonated either by a ship's magnetic field or by its sound signature. They soon had victims, too, the first and most prestigious being the recently commissioned cruiser HMS *Belfast*. On 21 November while she was steaming towards the open sea to take part in gunnery practice in the company of the destroyer HMS *Afridi* and the cruiser HMS *Southampton*, *Belfast* was rocked by a huge explosion as she sailed between Inchkeith and May Island. A magnetic mine had exploded on the port side, destroying the boiler room and breaking the ship's back. One sailor was killed and twenty-one were injured, and it was a severe jolt to the navy's pride. Not only had the cruiser just entered service but a month earlier it had successfully intercepted the German liner *Cap Norte* which was attempting to get back to Hamburg under the guise of being a neutral vessel. At that stage of the war she was the largest enemy ship to fall into the navy's hands and her capture was a huge fillip for the North Sea blockade. Following the explosion in the Forth estuary tugs took *Belfast* in tow, but so great was the damage that thought was given to scrapping her. As it was, she did not return to fleet duties until November 1942. Another victim was the battleship HMS *Nelson* which was holed by a magnetic mine while approaching Loch Ewe on 4 December. The weapon was one of eighteen which had been laid by the submarine *U-31* during the night of 27/28 October, each one of which contained between 420kg and 560kg of explosives.[2]

However, by the time that *Nelson* had been damaged the menace posed by magnetic mines was close to being solved. Because the Luftwaffe was loath to use bombers to sow mines, the task was given to untrained aircrew flying seaplanes – one reason for the prevalence of Dornier aircraft in Scottish skies during the early months of the war. During an operation over the Thames estuary on the night of 24/25 November a modern magnetic mine was dropped onto the mud flats close to Shoeburyness where it was located and made safe by a naval team from HMS *Vernon*, led by Commander J. G. D. Ouvry RN. The discovery of the mine and its safe retrieval allowed scientists to develop counter-measures which included degaussing coils which reduced a ship's magnetism, as well as other ship-borne and airborne magnetic devices.

Despite the onset of unseasonable weather – the winter of 1939–40 was one of the coldest on record across Europe – the Luftwaffe continued to send hostile patrols to attack targets in eastern Scotland. Throughout December a number of fishing trawlers from Leith and Granton were sunk or damaged while operating in the North Sea, and both the Turnhouse- and Drem-based squadrons were kept busy, with a healthy rivalry being built up between the Edinburgh and Glasgow auxiliary pilots. They enjoyed a reward of sorts when the pilot of a Heinkel shot down over Fife Ness admitted that the German air crews had not expected to encounter Spitfires, and regarded the Firth of Forth as 'suicide corner'. In stark contrast to the deployment of the modern Spitfire fighters the RAF often had to resort to the use of older aircraft and more basic tactics. One of the strangest flights was provided by No. 1 Coastal Patrol of Coastal Command which operated out of RAF Dyce using slow-flying Tiger Moth training aircraft – in the event of ditching, each aircraft carried a car tyre's inner tube and two homing pigeons. Known as 'Scarecrow Patrols', these venerable un-armed aircraft flew over the North Sea to search for German submarines travelling on the surface, the reasoning being that any aircraft noise would be a deterrent. On 25 January 1940 the tactics seemed to work when a Dyce-based Tiger Moth sighted a trail of surface oil, and the crew (Flight Lieutenant Hoyle and Pilot Officer Child) was able to direct a destroyer to make a successful depth-charge attack.

However, not everything went the RAF's way. A month earlier, on 21 December 1939, 602 Squadron was scrambled to intercept an incoming flight of twelve bombers over Dunbar. Despite the poor visibility, the Spitfires made contact and attacked, shooting down two of them and killing one of the aircrew, only to find that they were not enemy aircraft but RAF Handley Page Hampden medium bombers of 44 Squadron returning from a sweep over the North Sea. The subsequent Board of Inquiry found that the bombers were well off course and were not flying with their under-carriages lowered in a defended area to signify that they were friendly aircraft, but it was still an unpleasant incident. When 44 Squadron left for their home base at RAF Waddington in Lincolnshire the aircrew made their feelings clear by over-flying the airfield at Drem and dropping hundreds of toilet rolls on their unwitting assailants.[3]

The approaches to the Tay estuary also became a battleground, with attacks being made on shipping by enemy submarines and bomber aircraft. On 2 December *U-56* managed to sink two mer-chantmen, first the Swedish-registered *Rudolf* and then the 3,829-ton steamer *Eskdene*, owned by the Dene Shipping Line. Although the crew abandoned ship and were rescued by an Admiralty trawler, *Eskdene* remained afloat, helped by her cargo of timber, and was towed into the Forth. Later she returned to service but was eventually torpedoed and sunk off the Azores in April 1941. The city of Dundee became the target of the first of a number of enemy raids when it was bombed on 2 August 1940, but the local newspaper reported somewhat derisively that the only casualties had been 'a cat and a flock of swallows'.[4] Heavier attacks were made later in that year with the first casualties being suffered on the night of 5 November, but there was an optimistic local hope that the city would be spared further damage on Hitler's orders because Dundee had failed to re-elect Churchill in the 1922 General Election. This myth was widely believed – after fourteen years as MP for Dundee, Churchill had lost out to Edwin 'Neddy' Scrymgeour, an Independent and the only prohibitionist ever to be elected to parliament. For his part, Churchill entertained little love for the constituency he had represented since 1908. After being defeated he vowed never to revisit Dundee, and in the summer of 1943 kept his word when he rejected the offer of being granted the Freedom of the City when it was offered to him by the council on a narrow vote of sixteen to fifteen.

Other parts of Scotland were also in the front line during the first winter of the war. At the beginning of December Scapa Flow became a Protected Area under Defence Regulation No. 13 which empowered the home secretary to prevent 'persons other than existing residents, Servicemen or police' entering the area with permit or permission.[5] This meant that the whole territory north and northwest of the Great Glen became a no-go area – a vast region which included Inverness-shire, Ross and Cromarty, Sutherland, the Western Isles and Orkney and Shetland. As if any additional evidence were needed following a succession of bombing raids, this put Orkney on the frontline, and throughout the autumn months the naval base at Scapa Flow came under frequent attack until the fleet dispersed to Loch Ewe. There were also raids on Shetland: on 22 November six Heinkels raided Lerwick harbour and succeeded in sinking an elderly Saro London flying boat of 201 Squadron which operated out of Sullom Voe. The short days of winter put a stop to this kind of hostile activity but the respite was only temporary. On 16 March 1940 Britain's first civilian casualty was caused when James Isbister, a 27-year-old workman was killed at the Bridge of Waithe on Orkney while watching a German air raid on the nearby Hatston air base.

Throughout this period the busiest army personnel were the gunners who manned the air defences in the Forth estuary and at Scapa Flow, most of whom were recently called-up members of the Territorial Army. On the wider front the build-up of the army was solid and unspectacular – in August and September 546,000 Territorials and Reservists were mobilised under the terms of the Reserve and Auxiliary Force Act of 1939. Following the peacetime call-up in June, all men aged from eighteen to forty-one became liable for conscription into the armed forces under the terms of the National Service (Armed Forces) Act, and it began with immediate effect. Shortly after his twentieth birthday, and three weeks after the declaration of war, Alistair Urquhart received 'the dreaded letter from the War Office' ordering him to report to The Gordon Highlanders' depot at Bridge of Don in his native Aberdeen. His father had served in the same regiment during the First World War, fighting with them at the Battle of the Somme in the summer of 1916, and the irony was not lost on young Urquhart when he arrived at the depot gates along with 'a mixed bunch, made up of farm-workers, plumbers, labourers, fishermen, apprentice engineers and plumbers'. At the time of his enlistment Urquhart had spent the previous five years working as an apprentice in Lawson Turnbull Ltd, an Aberdeen firm of plumbers' merchants and electrical wholesalers, and his one concern was that his job should be kept open for him.[6]

Although conscription avoided the 'volunteer craze' which had seen thousands of men sign up for service in the late summer of 1914, especially in Scotland, it did allow men to pre-empt the process by putting their names forward for service in particular arms thought to be glamorous such as the RAF. Amongst those who took that course of action was Bill King, who had been working as a coalminer at the Easthouses pit at Newtongrange in Midlothian, and volunteered immediately after he had passed his eighteenth birthday. With two friends he went to the recruiting office in the Music Hall in Edinburgh's George Street, and after a medical was accepted for service.

I don't think there was any specific reason I went to the Air Force rather than the army or navy, except the Air Force was needin' people an we thought we'd mair chance o' getting away. I think that was mair the reason we volunteered: we didna want tae go in the army. God Almighty! Just imagine yourself rushin' across a battlefield wi' a bayonet and a big six foot man comin' rushin' at ye! Ah'd ha' died o' fright! Up in the air everybody's the same size.[7]

The following spring King received his call-up papers and did his basic training at RAF Padgate near Warrington in Lancashire.

Volunteering was popular because it allowed an element of choice and provided the impression that despite the prevailing bureaucracy it was possible to control one's fate – an important consideration following the experience of the previous conflict, when the vast majority of Scotland's casualties had been infantry privates.[8] Eddie Mathieson from Edinburgh was turned down for the RAF because he lacked the educational qualifications, but he successfully joined the Royal Navy and served in the Royal Marines. Like many others of his generation who remembered the slaughter on the Western Front he did not want to be 'duffed into the Black Watch or Cameronians'.[9] There was another difference. Whereas the voluntary system in 1914 immediately brought huge numbers of recruits into the armed forces, conscription relied on registration, and initially it proved to be a slow and somewhat cumbersome business which began on 21 October with males in the twenty to twenty-three age group. Allowance was also made to exclude those in reserved occupations, such as farmers, medical workers, skilled tradesmen in war industries, firemen and policemen, who were considered essential to the war effort. Because registration was done through the Ministry of Labour, a Whitehall department, it makes it very difficult to assess the size of the Scottish response to the call-up, other than to estimate that it would not have been less than 10 per cent of the total UK population. There were other differences. Unlike the First World War there was less emphasis on immediately placing men in the infantry, and because men who joined up together did not necessarily serve in the same local unit there was no repetition of the 'pals' formations. While these had been beneficial in the earlier conflict by allowing men from the same localities to serve together, it meant that casualties would be concentrated on one area in the event of a high death toll. For example the two men who joined up with Bill King were not conscripted until later with the result he 'only saw them when we come home on leave'.

Even so, as far as the army was concerned Scotland's military
contribution to the war effort was not very different from what it had
been twenty-five years earlier. Men like Alistair Urquhart were called
up immediately – his parents had hoped that the initial of his surname
would delay the process – while others had to wait for their call-up
papers to arrive. There was seemingly no logic to the process. Most
of the conscripts would be bound for the army, then as now the
service which needed the greatest number of recruits. In the early
days at least, Scottish recruits joining the Regular Army tended to be
placed in one of the existing ten line infantry regiments, each of which
was composed of two regular battalions and an assorted number of
Territorial Army battalions.

Traditionally, all of the regiments recruited on a territorial basis so
that a man from the north-east like Alistair Urquhart would be
directed to The Gordon Highlanders while in all likelihood men
from other parts would also join their local regiment: The Royal Scots
(Edinburgh and Lothians); The Royal Scots Fusiliers (Ayrshire and the
south-west); The King's Own Scottish Borderers (the border counties); The Cameronians (Lanarkshire); The Black Watch (Angus, Fife
and Perthshire); The Highland Light Infantry (Glasgow); The Seaforth Highlanders (Ross and Cromarty, Sutherland and Western Isles);
Queen's Own Cameron Highlanders (Inverness-shire); The Gordon
Highlanders (north-east, Orkney and Shetland); and The Argyll and
Sutherland Highlanders (Argyllshire and Stirlingshire). There was also
a regiment of foot guards with two battalions (Scots Guards) and a
heavy cavalry regiment (Royal Scots Greys), both of which recruited
across the country.

All the Scottish regiments had long histories, some of which
stretched back to the seventeenth century, and all had fought with
distinction during the First World War when the numbers of the line
infantry regiments (but not foot guards or cavalry) had been swollen
by the creation of special service battalions of the New Army, raised
specifically for war service. One regiment, The Royal Scots, had
produced thirty-six battalions (Regular, Territorial and New Army),
which had served on every battle front except for the campaigns
against Ottoman forces in Mesopotamia and against German forces
and their local allies in east and west Africa. Six of its soldiers had been
awarded the Victoria Cross, the regiment had won 71 battle honours,

and over 100,000 men had worn the Royal Scots cap badge, but the price had been high in human terms. The Royals lost 583 officers and 10,630 men killed in action, an estimated 40,000 soldiers had been wounded and an unknown number of survivors succumbed to physical and mental wounds throughout the 1920s and into the 1930s.[10]

In the aftermath of that earlier conflict, in common with Scotland's other regiments, The Royals lost their New Army battalions to disbandment in 1919, and their Territorial battalions also suffered cuts as the army was reduced once more to a peacetime standing. In 1922 the 4th and 5th Battalions amalgamated as the 4/5th (Queen's Edinburgh) Battalion, and the 7th and 9th Battalions (the 'Dandy Ninth') amalgamated as the 7/9th (Highlanders) Battalion. All the other wartime Territorial battalions were disbanded, and the 3rd Battalion was placed in a state of 'suspended animation' which allowed it to continue in being without having an operational existence.

It was a similar story in the other Scottish regiments. As had happened throughout Britain's history the conclusion of hostilities brought an immediate reduction in the huge wartime armed forces and in most respects it was a case of 'business as usual' as regiments went back to the familiar patterns and routines of peacetime soldiering. Following the construction of the huge volunteer and conscript army, the post-war Regular Army returned to its position as an all-volunteer force, and horizons narrowed as regiments revived a way of life that all professional soldiers recognised and understood. A bottle-neck in promotion prospects also led to complacency and to a comatose condition which discouraged radical thinking and put a stop to reform. Pacifism, arising largely from the huge death toll from the war, was also a disincentive for change. All too often anti-war sentiments became anti-armed-forces sentiments, and the army suffered as a result. As the historian Correlli Barnett explained, the situation produced a time of stagnation when 'the professional horizon of regular officers shrank again from the complex management of technological war to the life of the regiment, to small wars in hot places and police duties in support of the civil authorities in India and Ireland'.[11]

Above all, soldiering remained the preserve of the regiment, especially in the infantry. Its structure had been fixed by a process which had begun over half a century ago in 1872 under the direction of the Secretary for War, Edward Cardwell, and was finalised nine years later by his successor Hugh Childers, whereby single-battalion regiments were linked with others of their kind to form new two-battalion regiments and provided with territorial designations. Driving the Cardwell–Childers' reforms was the theory that one battalion would serve at home while the other was stationed abroad, and would receive drafts and reliefs from the home-based battalion to keep it up to strength. As a result of these changes, regimental numbers were dropped and territorial names were adopted throughout the army but, as happens in every period of reform, the changes outraged older soldiers who deplored the loss of cherished numbers and the introduction of what they held to be undignified territorial names, some of which bore no relation to the new regiment's traditions and customs.

The two-battalion system allowed one to remain on home service while the second was garrisoned overseas, and to a large extent it worked. But there were drawbacks. The battalion serving overseas was inevitably fully manned as a result of receiving drafts from the home depot, and as a result there was a natural tendency for the home service battalion to be under strength. During the inter-war years and until the outbreak of war in 1939, the Scottish regiments were deployed at home and across the empire in the following locations:

The Royal Scots, 1st Battalion: India, home service; 2nd Battalion: Ireland, Egypt, China, India, Hong Kong.

The Royal Scots Fusiliers, 1st Battalion: India; 2nd Battalion: Ireland, India, home service.

The King's Own Scottish Borderers, 1st Battalion: India, Egypt, home service; 2nd Battalion: Ireland, Hong Kong, India.

The Cameronians (Scottish Rifles), 1st Battalion: Shanghai, Egypt, India; 2nd Battalion: India, home service.

The Black Watch, 1st Battalion: India, home service; 2nd Battalion: home service, Palestine.

The Highland Light Infantry, 1st Battalion: India, home service; 2nd Battalion: India.

The Seaforth Highlanders, 1st Battalion: home service, Palestine, Shanghai; 2nd Battalion: India, Palestine, home service.

The Gordon Highlanders, 1st Battalion: Ireland, India, Palestine; 2nd Battalion: home service, Singapore.

Queen's Own Cameron Highlanders, 1st Battalion: India, home service; 2nd Battalion: home service, Palestine, India.

The Argyll and Sutherland Highlanders, 1st Battalion: Egypt, home service; 2nd Battalion: Ireland, West Indies, Shanghai, India and Hong Kong.

During this same period Scots Guardsmen served in China, Egypt and Palestine while The Royal Scots Greys served in Palestine and were not mechanised until 1940. The men who served in all these regiments were volunteers, men who had joined the army as a career or who had been forced by economic or social circumstance to wear uniform. From contemporary recruiting literature it is clear that the army placed a high premium on the fact that its soldiers would have the possibility of serving overseas, perhaps in an exotic location, and the stations listed above show that the ambitious or adventurous soldier would stand a good chance of serving in India or in the Far East.

In addition to the Regular Army there was the Territorial Army (TA), a part-time force which had been raised originally in 1908 for home defence but which had served on the front line with great distinction in the First World War. It too had suffered from cutbacks, but as the Nazi threat developed in Europe in the late 1930s, belated steps had been taken to rectify the situation by providing more modern weapons and strengthening the TA's Anti-Aircraft Command. This consisted of five existing divisions and two projected divisions which would be responsible for manning the searchlight and anti-aircraft defences. To meet the needs for additional personnel, some existing infantry battalions were converted to other roles. For example, in The Argyll and Sutherland Highlanders the recently amalgamated 5th/6th Battalions resumed their previous separate identities – 5th and 6th – and were re-rolled as machine-gun battalions, but this was a prelude to a greater change. In 1941 the two battalions became, respectively 91st Anti-Tank Regiment (Argyll and Sutherland Highlanders), Royal Artillery, and 93rd Anti-Tank Regiment (Argyll and Sutherland Highlanders) Royal Artillery. Having been resurrected in Dumbarton in 1919 the 9th Battalion was also converted

to the artillery role, becoming 54th Light Anti-Aircraft Regiment
Royal Artillery. It consisted of 160 (Dumbarton) Battery, 161 (Alexandria) Battery and 162 (Helensburgh) Battery. The 7th and 8th
Battalions remained as infantry, as did their duplicates, the 10th and
11th Battalions, while the 12th, 13th, 14th, 15th and 30th served as
home-defence battalions for all or part of the war.[12]

On paper it was an impressive showing, but despite recent improvements the TA was still woefully under-equipped and under-
trained to fight a modern war. Partly, the reason lay in the structure of
the force which was still considered in many minds to be more of a
social club than a military formation. Soldiers were only obliged to
attend a small number of weekly drill nights and weekend camps, and
it was not obligatory to attend the annual two-week summer camp for
which there was the inducement of a £5 bounty. Although there was
a certain amount of weapons training and live firing, training was
often little more than basic drills using procedures which were usually
out of date and unsuited to modern warfare. It soon became apparent
that although the call-up produced the required numbers of men,
many of them had to be returned to reserved occupations while others
were underage or not of sufficient physical or mental calibre to
undergo active service. In December 1939 General Sir Frederick
Pile, commander-in-chief, Anti-Aircraft Command, reported that of
the twenty-five TA recruits in a 'fairly representative battery' who had
been called up before Christmas, 'one had a withered arm, one was
mentally deficient, one had no thumbs and one had a glass eye which
fell out when he doubled to the guns, and two were in the advanced
and more obvious stages of venereal disease'.[13]

The most important manifestation of the Territorial Army in
Scotland, and a source of great national pride, was the 51st (Highland)
Division which had been one of the leading British military formations of the First World War, with a reputation second to none. It was
also one of the four TA infantry divisions which had again been
earmarked for service in France as part of the British Expeditionary
Force (BEF). For many people in Scotland the Highland Division was
the upholder of the country's fighting spirit, and Territorial battalions
from all five kilted Highland regiments were represented in its order of
battle when it went to war in 1939 under the command of Major-
General V. M. Fortune, CB, DSO:

Divisional Armoured Reconnaissance Regiment
   1st Lothians & Border Horse (Yeomanry)

152nd Brigade: Brigadier H. W. V. Stewart, DSO
   4th Seaforth Highlanders
   6th Seaforth Highlanders
   4th Queen's Own Cameron Highlanders

153rd Brigade: Brigadier G. T. Burnet, MC
   4th Black Watch
   5th Gordon Highlanders
   6th Gordon Highlanders

154th Brigade: Brigadier A. C. L. Stanley-Clarke, DSO
   6th Black Watch
   7th Argyll & Sutherland Highlanders
   8th Argyll & Sutherland Highlanders

Royal Artillery: CRA Brigadier H. C. H. Eden, MC
   75th Field Regiment, Royal Artillery
   76th Field Regiment, Royal Artillery
   77th Field Regiment, Royal Artillery
   51st Anti-tank Regiment, Royal Artillery

Royal Engineers: CRE Lt Col. H. M. Smail, TD
   236th Field Company, Royal Engineers
   237th Field Company, Royal Engineers
   238th Field Company, Royal Engineers
   239th Field Park Company, Royal Engineers

Royal Corps of Signals: Lt Col. T. P. E. Murray 51st Divisional
   Signals Company

Royal Army Medical Corps: A.D.M.S., Lt Col. D. P. Levack
   152nd Field Ambulance
   153rd Field Ambulance
   154th Field Ambulance

Royal Army Service Corps: Lt Col. T. Harris-Hunter, TD
　Divisional Ammunition Company.
　Divisional Petrol Company Divisional Supply Column

Attached troops
　51st Medium Regiment, Royal Artillery
　1st Royal Horse Artillery (less one Battery)
　97th Field Regiment, Royal Artillery (one Battery)
　213th Army Field Company, Royal Engineers
　1st Princess Louise's Kensington Regiment (Machine-Gunners)
　7th Royal Northumberland Fusiliers (Machine-Gunners)
　6th Royal Scots Fusiliers (Pioneers)
　7th Norfolk Regiment (Pioneers)
　Sections of the Royal Army Ordnance Corps and the Royal
　　Army Service Corps[14]

It made a brave showing but in the early stages of the war equipment
was a problem. Uniforms were always in short supply, with the result
that some men had to train in civilian clothes, and riflemen were still
equipped with the old .303 Short Lee Enfield rifles and Mills grenades.
The standard machine-gun was the First World War Vickers and the
first .303 Bren gun did not appear until 1939. At the same time the
tracked Bren carrier began to be introduced, and supporting artillery
batteries were equipped with the new 25-pounder howitzer which
had a maximum range of 13,400 yards. Anti-tank measures were
provided by the Boys .55-inch anti-tank rifle, a bolt-action weapon
which was only capable of destroying the thinnest of armour, and then
only at close range. The division's armoured component, 1st Lothians
& Border Horse, arrived in April 1940 to replace 1st Fife and Forfar
Yeomanry, and was equipped with Bren carriers and Vickers Mark
VIB light tanks armed with a .50-inch Vickers machine-gun and a
.303 Vickers machine-gun. With a crew of three they had a top speed
of 25 miles per hour and a range of 130 miles, but their small size and
light armour meant that they were only really useful for reconnaissance duties.

On the other hand, morale in the division was high and this was
given an added fillip by the knowledge that the individual battalions
belonged to famous Highland regiments with proud fighting tradi-

tions. They also had a superb leader in Fortune, who had commanded 1st Black Watch in 1916 and enjoyed a well-deserved reputation as a fighting soldier. He was also keen to make his presence felt, and in the early months of the war while the division was training in England the divisional historian recorded that he was 'almost embarrassingly fond of the front area, keen to know what each platoon, what each section was doing, keen to take part in any action.'[15]

In February 1939 the Cabinet had taken the momentous decision to commit its armed forces to a continental role by forming an expeditionary force for service in France in support of the French Army. This would consist of four Regular infantry divisions, a mobile division and four Territorial divisions, but time was fast running out. Having been starved of funding there was much to be done to bring those formations up to strength and to find the necessary personnel and equipment. It was very much a race against time: by summer even the Regular divisions had only half of the required numbers of anti-tank and anti-aircraft weapons, and stocks of ammunition were completely inadequate to fight a protracted campaign. Nevertheless, plans were pushed ahead for the BEF to take its place on the left of the French Army in north-eastern France, with the Territorial divisions joining them as they became 'ready'. In fact the deployment was completed fairly quickly, and within five weeks of the outbreak of hostilities the four Regular divisions were in position under the overall command of Field Marshal Lord Gort VC, with I Corps (1st and 2nd Divisions) under the command of Lieutenant-General Sir John Dill and II Corps (3rd and 4th Divisions) under the command of Lieutenant-General Sir Alan Brooke. Including the Highland Division and the 52nd (Lowland) Division which landed in Normandy later in 1940 (see below), there were thirty-six Scottish infantry battalions in France, the others being (in order of precedence):

1st Royal Scots: 4 Brigade, 2nd Division
1st KOSB: 9 Brigade, 3rd Division
1st Black Watch, 12 Brigade, 4th Division
1st Camerons: 5 Brigade, 2nd Division
1st Gordons: 2 Brigade, 1st Division
4th Gordons: II Corps Machine-gun Battalion
6th Argylls: I Corps Machine-gun Battalion

In addition 1st Fife and Forfar Yeomanry served with 1 Light Reconnaissance Brigade (earlier it had been part of the 51st Division), and when 5th Infantry Division arrived as reinforcements in December it included 2nd Royal Scots Fusiliers, 2nd Cameronians (Scottish Rifles) and 6th Seaforths, which had previously served in 51st (Highland) Division.

Although there was inevitable grumbling from the reservists, especially from those who had only just settled down into civilian jobs, morale in the BEF was reasonably good. Three weeks after the declaration of war, 1st Black Watch crossed over to France after being inspected by the regimental Colonel-in-Chief King George VI and his wife Queen Elizabeth. Their one sadness was the order to hand in the kilt in place of battle-dress, a move which was explained by the operational reason to prevent the regiment being recognised by the enemy. It was not well received; one company sergeant-major being heard to remark, 'But damn it, we want to be identified.'[16] Lieutenant-Colonel Douglas Wimberley commanding 1st Cameron Highlanders was equally scornful, writing in his diary that:

> An attack has been made on the Highland Regiments as to their wearing their kilts in battle in Europe . . . the kilt as a battledress was being attacked from three angles. On the grounds of (unit) security, on grounds of its inadequacy in case of gas attack and on grounds of difficulty of supply in war. There was also the tinge of jealousy – why should the kilted regiments be given preferential treatment to wear a becoming kilt. The thickness of the kilt and its seven yards of tartan was extra protection. It was traditional in all highland regiments never to wear any garment in the way of pants under the kilt. But anti-gas pants were issued.[17]

Before embarking for France in January 1940, 5th Gordons went one further by mounting a symbolic parade at Bordon in Hampshire during which a single kilt was ceremonially burned. A stone memorial marked the spot inscribed 'We hope not for long'. The battalion was commanded by Lieutenant Colonel Alick Buchanan-Smith, a veteran of the previous war.

To defeat the western allies the German plan called for the invasion of the Netherlands, Belgium and Luxembourg, using two army groups to smash through the southern Netherlands and central Belgium while a diversionary attack was made through the Ardennes. The ultimate goal of this *Fall Gelb* (Plan Yellow) was control of the Channel ports as a prelude to invading Britain. However, Hitler prevaricated, the plans were subjected to constant change and there were delays in correcting the balance of ground forces. At the same time the French dithered and ordered an unnecessary move into the Saarland which did nothing to alter the strategic balance in the Allies' favour and introduced a sense of demoralisation and defeatism. As for the British, they eventually deployed thirteen infantry divisions (five Regular, eight Territorial) in France, but there was little armour and not much in the way of air cover. Compared to the Luftwaffe's 4,200 warplanes the Allies possessed only 2,000, half of which were fighter aircraft. In qualitative terms the German machines were also superior, and their air crews enjoyed better training and superior tactics; wisely the Royal Air Force held back its valuable Spitfire fighters for the defence of the British homeland.

Hitler had intended to launch the invasion of France as early as mid-November, but the onset of winter weather hindered armoured operations, and in January 1940 the plans had to be changed again when a copy fell into Allied hands. A new plan, code-named *Sichelschnitt* (Sickle Stroke), changed the weight of the attack to the south where Army Group A would attack through the rugged and supposedly impenetrable forests of the Ardennes before racing north to the Channel ports. To counter the threat, the Allied supreme commander General Maurice-Gustave Gamelin had produced Plan D which would see thirty-three British and French divisions moving eastwards to invade Belgium as soon as the German attack began. Once on Belgian territory they would take up station along the Dyle Line – a defensive position which ran along the River Dyle to Wavre. At the last minute it was extended north to Breda and the River Maas, the idea being to present the Germans with a defensive line which ran from Antwerp to the heavily fortified Maginot Line at Longuyon.

During this period 51st (Highland) Division was deemed to be 'combat ready', and crossed over to France at the beginning of January 1940, landing at Le Havre before moving by rail to a concentration area near the towns of Lillebonne and Bolbec. Unlike the experience of the First World War when military bands and excited crowds had greeted the arrival of the BEF, the soldiers of 51st (Highland) Division were given a muted welcome; one corporal in 4th Camerons remembered that the billets were barns shared with cattle and that the bedding amounted to 'a cart of evil-smelling hay'.[18] The division's first task was fairly agricultural too – digging an anti-tank ditch in the rear area, a thankless task which counted for little as the Allied plan was to move into Belgium once the Germans began their attack. This eventually happened in March when the division moved forward towards Bailleul. At the same time there was a change in the order of battle when it was decided to strengthen the division by adding three regular battalions to replace three TA battalions, one from each of the brigades. As a result 1st Black Watch replaced 6th Black Watch in 154 Brigade, 2nd Seaforths replaced 6th Seaforths in 152 Brigade, and 1st Gordons took the place of 6th Gordons in 153 Brigade.[19]

This was the prelude to another move which would influence the fate of the division in 1940. In April Gort decided to deploy the Highlanders in the Saar region of Lorraine where they were stationed on the Maginot Line, the huge French defensive system consisting of fortifications, underground shelters, block houses and anti-tanks ditches which had been constructed to deter German aggression. It was a highly sophisticated system with a network of railways and hydraulically powered gun positions, but much work still needed to be done to create associated trench systems, especially in the Metz region between Hombourg and Boulange. For the Highlanders this required further digging, but there were also opportunities to engage the Germans by mounting offensive patrols which allowed young and inexperienced soldiers like 2nd Lieutenant John Parnell, 7th Argylls, to discover the gulf between peacetime training and active service.

On patrol we wore the absolute minimum and just had our weapons and little else so that we could move quickly and get through fences. We didn't have sub-machine guns like the fighting patrols; the only weapons we had were the rifle and the Bren. I carried a revolver. It was only later, on the Somme, that I discovered how useless a revolver was and used a rifle instead. I don't think we blacked our faces or anything sophisticated like that, and we had no communications at all . . . We weren't exactly experienced soldiers at that stage.[20]

Battle patrols of this kind were a throwback to the infantry tactics which had been used in the previous conflict, but they proved their worth by gaining intelligence about enemy movements and by giving unblooded soldiers some idea of what lay in store for them.

There were also two other Scottish infantry divisions, both with equally famous histories – the 15th (Scottish) Division and the 52nd (Lowland) Division. Both had become inextricably linked by the sudden transformation of the Territorial Army in the summer of 1939. When the call had gone out from the War Office for the TA to be doubled in size, it was decided to form a second line division for the 52nd (Lowland) Division, and so the 15th (Scottish) Division was born, taking its numbering from the illustrious division of the same title which had built a formidable reputation in the First World War. It proved to be a difficult business. Not only was the new division scattered all over the country, with brigade headquarters in Glasgow, Hamilton and Edinburgh, there were few drill halls for training the men, and as the divisional historian remembered, equipment was mainly noticeable by its absence. For example the gunners 'may have heard of the 2-pounder A.Tk. [anti-tank] Gun – then the very latest – but had certainly never seen it.'[21]

However, by 15 September the new division had come into independent existence under the command of Major-General Roland Le Fanu, and started moving into its training areas in the Borders. Divisional headquarters was established at Jedburgh; 44 Brigade was based at Melrose, St Boswells and Earlston; 45 Brigade was based at Hawick; 46 Brigade was based at Galashiels; and the divisional artillery was based at Selkirk and Jedburgh. As happened so often during that time of turmoil, the division lost many of its first recruits when they were found to be essential workers or were declared unfit for further service. In October reinforcements started arriving from the English midland counties, and as happened throughout the conflict they quickly became perfervid Scots on donning the tam-o'-shanter bonnets worn by the Scottish regiments. The first order of battle was as follows:

44 Lowland Infantry Brigade, Brigadier B. C. Lake
  8th Royal Scots
  6th King's Own Scottish Borderers
  7th King's Own Scottish Borderers

45 Lowland Infantry Brigade, Brigadier D. S. Davidson, DSO, MC
6th Royal Scots Fusiliers
9th Cameronians
10th Cameronians

46 Lowland Infantry Brigade, Brigadier H. J. D. Clark, MC
10th Highland Light Infantry
11th Highland Light Infantry
2nd Glasgow Highlanders (Highland Light Infantry)

Machine-gun Battalion
1/7th Middlesex Regiment

Royal Regiment of Artillery, Brigadier John Scott
129th Field Regiment RA
130th Field Regiment RA
131st Field Regiment RA
64th Anti-Tank Regiment RA (Queen's Own Royal Glasgow Yeomanry)

Royal Engineers, Lieutenant-Colonel J. F. Gibson, MC, TD
278th Field Company RE
279th Field Company RE
280th Field Company RE
281st Field Park Company RE

Royal Signals, Lieutenant-Colonel V. D. Warren, MBE, TD
15th Scottish Divisional Signals

Royal Army Service Corps, Lieutenant-Colonel E. Doolan, MC
282nd Company RASC
283rd Company RASC
284th Company RASC

Royal Army Medical Corps, Colonel J. Gibson, DSO
193rd Field Ambulance RAMC
194th Field Ambulance RAMC
195th Field Ambulance RAMC
40th Field Hygiene Section RAMC[22]

The make-up of the division would change several times during the course of war, and more supporting arms would be added, but the original formation was a great example of improvisation and a will-ingness to work together. In December, 15th (Scottish) Division moved north into winter quarters, ostensibly to guard the Forth and Clyde approaches, but in reality to spend most of its time aiding the civil authorities during the bitter winter weather. During this period its brigades were scattered across Kilsyth, Kirkintilloch, John-stone, Hamilton, Kilmarnock, Strathaven and Glasgow, and the division did not return to the Borders until April 1940.

The fate of its parent division was rather different. The 52nd (Lowland) Division had a distinguished record, having taken part in the Gallipoli campaign of 1915 and the final fighting on the Western Front in 1918. Like its Highland counterpart it was com-posed of TA battalions which were drawn mainly, though not entirely, from the central belt and the Borders, and was had a good conceit of themselves. Divisional headquarters were located in Park Circus, Glasgow, with two brigades also located in Glasgow (Yorkhill Parade) and one in Edinburgh (Forrest Road). Following the urgent reform of the TA, each infantry brigade had been reduced from four to three battalions to enable the creation of new specialist formations – this resulted in 4th/5th (Queen's Edinburgh) Battalion Royal Scots becoming 52nd Searchlight Regiment Royal Artillery; 5th/8th Cam-eronians (Scottish Rifles) becoming 56th Searchlight Regiment Royal Artillery; and 7th (Blythswood) Battalion Highland Light Infantry becoming 83rd (Blythswood) Searchlight Regiment Royal Artillery. As a first-line fighting formation it did not take long for the reformed 52nd (Lowland) Division to be fully trained up for active service and moved south to Tidworth prior to deployment in France under the command of Major-General J. S. Drew, a Cameron Highlander. In June 1940 its order of battle was:

155 (East Scottish) Infantry Brigade – Brigadier T. Grainger-
Stewart, MC, TD
7th/9th (Highlanders) Royal Scots
4th King's Own Scottish Borderers
5th King's Own Scottish Borderers

156 (West Scottish) Infantry Brigade – Brigadier F. G. Chalmers,
   DSO, MC
4th/5th Royal Scots Fusiliers
6th Cameronians (Scottish Rifles)
7th Cameronians (Scottish Rifles)

157 (Highland Light Infantry) Infantry Brigade – Brigadier N. R.
   Campbell, MC, TD
5th Highland Light Infantry
6th Highland Light Infantry
1st Glasgow Highlanders (Highland Light Infantry)

Machine-gun Battalion
5th Argyll and Sutherland Highlanders

Divisional Troops
Royal Regiment of Artillery – Brigadier D. J. M. Campion, DSO
   78th Field Regiment RA
   79th Field Regiment RA
   80th Field Regiment RA
   54th Anti-Tank Regiment RA

Royal Engineers – CRE Lieutenant-Colonel R. E. Keelan, MC,
   TD
   240th Field Company RE
   241st Field Company RE
   241st Field Company RE
   243rd Field Park Company RE

Royal Corps of Signals – Lieutenant-Colonel T. M. Niven
   52nd Lowland Divisional Signals

Royal Army Service Corps – Lieutenant-Colonel F. R. Topping
   528th Company RASC
   529th Company RASC
   530th Company RASC

Royal Army Medical Corps – Colonel G. J. Linklater, OBE, TD
   155th (Lowland) Field Ambulance[23]

Of the three Scottish divisions the 52nd was destined to have the most unusual war history. As a frontline formation it moved south at the beginning of June and was earmarked to join the BEF, but the retreat to Dunkirk and subsequent evacuation changed all that (see Chapter 3). Instead, the division was despatched to Normandy between 7 and 12 June as part of the so-called Second British Expeditionary Force which was ordered to bolster the French forces in western France in the face of the continuing German invasion. From the outset the mission was doomed to failure, and as Captain Jack Lambert, 4th/5th Royal Scots Fusiliers remembered, the air of make-believe began when his battalion was ferried across the English Channel on a luxury liner which had been requisitioned for war service. Not only did all officers take a huge amount of luggage with them, including their blue patrol uniforms, but once on board they were treated to a superb lunch on a properly laid table 'with the appropriate wine for each course'.[24] Reality set in with the arrival of Lieutenant-General Sir Alan Brooke on 12 June. An experienced soldier and veteran of the Dunkirk evacuation, he could see that the French were in no condition to continue fighting, and from his first meeting with the overall French commander General Maxime Weygand at Le Mans he surmised that any further resistance would achieve nothing other than unacceptably high Allied casualties. Brooke's diary entry for 14 June is thoroughly dispiriting: 'Found him [Weygand] looking very wizened and tired looking with a stiff neck from a car smash on previous evening. He said he would speak very frankly. That the French Army had ceased to be able to offer organised resistance and was disintegrating into disconnected groups. That Paris had been given up and that he had no reserves whatever left.'[25]

Brooke had to act quickly, and he immediately contacted the War Office to order the bulk of his forces – 52nd (Lowland) and 1st Canadian Division – to make their way back to Brest and Cherbourg. To his astonishment he found himself talking to Churchill who seemed to have no knowledge that 52nd (Lowland) was under his command, and reminded him that he 'had been sent to France to make the French feel that we were supporting them'. (In his later comments Brooke simply noted that 'it was impossible to make a corpse feel and that the French army was, to all intents and purposes, dead'.)

Fortunately common sense prevailed, and the division began re-embarking at Cherbourg on 16 June. Despite the failure of French dock workers to offer assistance, most of the waiting warships and troop transports managed to get alongside, and most of the division was able to re-embark with their equipment intact. According to the War Diary of 7th/9th Royal Scots 'the Hun bombed the town blindly through the clouds in a mild and spasmodic way, but did the shipping little harm.'[26] Due to the exigencies of wartime censorship no news was released about the futile Normandy deployment, and nothing was released about the division's role until 1946 even though 157 Brigade had been involved in fierce defensive fighting during the retreat from Le Mans. In one action 5th HLI lost one officer and nine other ranks killed, and A Company of 5th KOSB had the distinction of being the last unit of 2nd BEF to engage the enemy when it ran into a German ambush in the last hours of the retreat. On its return to England, the division deployed in East Anglia where it trained in the anti-invasion role before returning to Scotland in October.

Although the 52nd (Lowland) Division had managed to escape relatively unscathed, others were less fortunate. On the day that they began their re-embarkation at Cherbourg, the liner HMT *Lancastria* was bombed off St Nazaire and sank with the loss of around 4,000 lives, many of them Scots, including remnants of 5th KOSB who were amongst the last to leave. (Due to the confusion and the need to get people on board as quickly as possible it proved impossible to compute the exact total.)[27] This was one of the worst tragedies of the war involving British troops as the casualty list was higher than the numbers lost in the Dunkirk evacuation. The ship had been built by Beardmore on the Clyde, and had started life as the *Tyrrhenia*, operated by Anchor Lines on the north Atlantic route to New York. On the outbreak of war she had been requisitioned as a troopship, seeing service in the earlier operations in Norway, and at the time of the Normandy evacuation while under the command of Captain Rudolf Sharp, a Shetlander, she was severely overloaded with passengers and military equipment. During a day of intermittent air raids *Lancastria* was bombed in the middle of the afternoon by Junkers 88 aircraft of II Gruppe/Kampf-geschwader 30. Three direct hits caused the ship to list, first to starboard, then to port, and she rolled over and sank within 20 minutes; around 1,400 tons of fuel oil leaked into the sea and was set partially ablaze, possibly by the German aircraft machine-gunning the survivors in the water. There were only 2,477 survivors.

Give the scale of the disaster, the government took immediate steps to prevent the news being given a wider circulation under the restrictions covered by the D-Notice system. Newspapers were banned from reporting the incident or from interviewing the survivors, and to all intents and purposes the story was to be buried; at the same time official papers relating to the sinking were restricted in the Public Record Office (National Archives) for 100 years. However, photographs of the tragedy were in existence in the US, and on 26 July 1940 the *Scotsman* took the momentous decision to publish a report of what had happened. Although the story was not entirely accurate, it did make use of first-hand accounts and painted a vivid picture of the terrible moments when the *Lancastria* began to succumb to the effects of the bombing: 'A cook told how he saw a soldier grab a young girl both of whose legs had been broken. He swam with her and both were picked up but she died later. Other survivors said that when the *Lancastria* heeled men clambered on the side in the belief that she would remain afloat, but within 20 minutes she sank suddenly and all the occupants were thrown into the water.'[28]

Because it was such an unusual occurrence for a national newspaper to break the D-Notice system, the *Scotsman*'s editor Sir George Waters published a trenchant editorial explaining why he had decided to break the rules – not for sensationalism but because the newspaper believed that its readers had a right to know what had happened.

The Government has given repeated assurances that it is not their policy to conceal news of losses and reverses since they know that the people of this country are not easily depressed by misfortunes. There is no reason to suppose that in general the Government are not fulfilling their undertaking of dealing honestly with the people in the publication of information and there may have been special reasons for delaying the announcement of the loss of the *Lancastria*.

Yet it is obvious that the belated release of news gives an opportunity for rumour to get busy and to embellish facts in a sensational form.

It also spreads suspicions that the Government's policy is to tell the public what they think is good for them to know and no more.

People with an itch for news are always prone to imagine that they are being kept in the dark and that much is happening behind the scenes. Frank and timely publication of information, good or bad, is the best antidote for gossip and distrust.[29]

The story did not become a public issue again until 2007 when the tragedy was debated in the Scottish parliament, and calls were made for the creation of a commemorative medal for those who had sailed on the doomed liner-cum-troopship.

Unfortunately it was not the last occasion when a liner would be sunk with numerous casualties and attempts made to cover up the real facts. On 2 July 1940 the former Blue Star luxury liner *Arandora Star* was hit by torpedoes off Malin Head and sank within half an hour. On board were 734 recently interned Italians, 479 German internees, 86 German prisoners of war, 200 military guards and 174 officers and crew. Of that number 446 Italians and 175 Germans perished; amongst them were 94 Italians of Scots extraction. Ironically, the commander of the German submarine was Gunther Prien, the so-called 'Bull of Scapa' who had been responsible for the earlier sinking of the battleship HMS *Royal Oak*. His decision to attack was influenced by the fact that the *Arandora Star* was armed with a 4.7-inch cannon and 2-pound anti-aircraft gun, and was sailing on a zig-zag course suitable for an armed merchantman. Several hundred Scottish-based Italians were on board the *Arandora Star* including Alfonso Crolla of the well-respected Edinburgh grocery firm of Valvona and Crolla, and Silvestro d'Ambrosio, a confectioner from Hamilton, who had lived for forty-two years in Scotland, and who had one son serving in the British Army and another serving in the Canadian Army. In an attempt to mitigate the incident the British government placed the blame firmly on Prien and encouraged the Scottish press to produce news stories which suggested that the death toll had been higher than expected because the Italian internees had panicked and started fighting with the Germans.[30] This was blatantly untrue. Most of the survivors were rescued by naval vessels and returned to Greenock where they were interviewed by the Admiralty Shipping Casualties Section, but the evidence about the sinking was not released until after the war.[31] In another incident which was hushed up at the time, it later emerged that one of the casualties, Antonio Mancini from Ayr, had become a British subject in 1938 and had been wrongly detained. As a result the Home Office paid compensation to his family and admitted that 'his detention from first to last was unlawful'.[32]

Why such a strange complement of passengers should have been making its way across the Atlantic is one of the sadder stories of a conflict in which human suffering was the norm. Shortly after the outbreak of war the government introduced stringent measures under Defence Regulation 18B to round up 'aliens' of German and Austrian extraction who might be considered security risks. These were divided into three categories: Class A who were considered high security risks and who numbered 596; Class B who were considered doubtful cases and numbered 6,742; and Class C who were considered no risk and numbered 66,002. At first only Class A aliens were interned, but by the summer of 1940 the rest had also been rounded up. When Mussolini entered the war on 10 June some 15,000 Italians were arrested immediately under Churchill's terse command 'collar the lot!' Given the sizeable Italian community in Scotland at the outbreak of the war, it was not surprising that many of that number, almost 2,000 males aged 17 to 60, were resident in Scotland, mainly in Edinburgh, Glasgow and the west of Scotland.[33] Under the government's catch-all legislation the Italians were then rounded up and despatched to internment camps in the Isle of Man, Northern Ireland and Orkney, prior to being forcibly evacuated to Canada.

What was surprising was the public reaction. There was a good deal of public anger about Italy entering the war as it smacked of opportunism in the wake of the British defeats in France and Norway, but politics also coloured the response. During the 1930s a Fascist Club had been established in Picardy Place in Edinburgh, and although it was mainly a social club and focal point for the city's Italian community, locals remembered that on occasions such as Armistice Day its 188 registered male members would parade in a uniform of black shirts, black fezzes and white gloves. In fact most of the internees had no allegiance to fascist Italy or to Mussolini, and were second-generation immigrants who had lived in Scotland since the main immigrations of 1913 and 1920. However that was no protection against the mob.[34] Edinburgh was the scene of the worst violence: a crowd of around 1,000 congregated in Leith and Stock-bridge to attack Italian businesses, mainly cafés, while similar attacks were launched in Govan and Maryhill in Glasgow. The Clyde coast saw similar incidents, with reports of anti-Italian violence in Port Glasgow, Greenock and Gourock.[35] One family in Raeburn Place in Edinburgh had their shop spared because one of their sons was a well-known follower of Hibs, and 'he used to call the Hearts supporters names'.[36]

In the aftermath, the government passed the Aliens (Protected Areas) (No. 5) Order, 1940 which prohibited designated enemy aliens from living within twenty miles of the coast on Scotland's east coast. Italian women were also prevented from travelling unaccompanied within a five-mile radius of their homes and, as happened to two women caught travelling from Dumfries before Christmas 1943, they could be fined £2 or imprisoned for fifteen days.[37]

The incidents involving the *Athenia*, *City of Benares*, *Lancastria* and *Arandora Star* were disastrous for the Allied cause in those early months, but there was one signal success which raised morale and gave a huge boost to the Royal Navy. During the campaign to sink the *Graf Spee* the German pocket battleship had been supported by the long-range tanker *Altmark* which had also been used to accommodate prisoners of war. When the loss of the *Graf Spee* left *Altmark* without a role, its skipper Captain Heinrich Dau attempted to get back to German waters by sailing north and skirting the Norwegian coastline. On 15 February 1940 he was sighted by three Hudsons of 224 Squadron from RAF Leuchars which alerted naval headquarters at Rosyth. Fortunately the Fourth Destroyer Flotilla was at sea, and one of its ships, HMS *Cossack*, a modern Tribal class destroyer under the command of Captain Philip Vian, was able to make contact with the *Altmark*. Although the German ship attempted to take refuge in Norwegian waters, Vian signalled the Admiralty and was promptly given permission to violate Norwegian neutrality. As a result on 16 February *Altmark* was boarded in Jossing Fjord, and 299 prisoners were liberated. *Cossack* arrived back in Leith the following day, and the incident received a huge amount of publicity, not least the stirring words used by the boarding party when they found the captured men on board. 'Any Englishmen here? Well the Navy's here! Come up out of it!'[38]

3 Defeat, Retreat and Making Do

War came to the BEF with a vengeance on 10 May 1940 when the Germans subjected France to the frightening tactics of *blitzkrieg*, using armour and air power to back a rapid ground assault into Belgium, Luxembourg and the Netherlands. The surprise was total, and the resistance was negligible. Early in the morning German airborne units of Army Group B began landing in the Netherlands to capture the capital The Hague and the vital crossings of the Meuse. Two days later all Dutch resistance was at an end as the country capitulated. In Belgium the fortress of Eben Emael was soon in German hands, even though it was thought to be impregnable. And as the Dutch forces fell back towards Rotterdam and Amsterdam, they left the Belgian left flank unprotected. At the same time seven German Panzer divisions of German Army Group A pushed through the Ardennes and began an unexpected move north towards the Channel ports.

While this was happening the BEF began its pre-arranged move into Belgium towards a defensive position known as the Dyle Line, passing such well-known battlefields of earlier wars as Waterloo, Ypres and Mons. Even at that stage the BEF's commander-in-chief, Field Marshal Lord Gort, was sure that the Germans could be held, issuing an order of the day on 13 May telling his troops that 'the struggle will be hard and long, but we can be confident of final victory'. One of the first Scottish battalions to go into action was 6th Gordons which came under machine-gun fire from enemy aircraft on 14 May. Two days later it had its first experience of artillery bombardment during which one officer and two soldiers were killed and five others were wounded. This was followed by a defensive action north of Brussels, but when the Gordons passed through the Belgian capital they were astonished to see signs of normality, with tramcars running and people going about their business as if there were no war. However, this unreal period was also remembered for the huge numbers of refugees on the roads. As the Gordons' War Diary recorded, 'There seemed to be little attempt at traffic control and the frequent jams and delays tried the tempers of everyone.'[1] By then Gort had decided to withdraw in stages to the River Escaut.

Taken aback by the ferocity and speed of the German advance into Belgium, the BEF began its long retreat back to the Channel ports, and the eventual evacuation from the beaches at Dunkirk. For 1st Camerons, fighting in 2nd Infantry Division, this meant engaging the enemy along the River Escaut where the BEF hoped to check the German advance by denying them crossing points. It was all too little and too late, and one incident recorded in the diary of Lieutenant-Colonel G. P. Miller, the commanding officer of 2nd Cameronians, gives a good idea of the confusion which surrounded this phase of the operation.

> During the day [18 May at Lessines], while we were preparing the bridge and crossings for demolition, refugees were pouring through us. The Belgian mayor came to me and stated that there were about two hundred wounded men in a convent, with only one girl to look after them. Could I supply transport to evacuate these wounded? My reply was that I was afraid I had not sufficient transport, but I would try to make them comfortable. During this conversation a man arrived at my headquarters informing me that there were some nuns amongst the refugees, who would be only willing to nurse the wounded. Later that night, when we withdrew, we were fired upon from the windows of the convent.[2]

By then Miller's battalion, the old Scottish Rifles, had endured its first experience of battle when it was attacked by German aircraft near Lemberg, and claimed its first kill when D Company shot down one of the enemy raiders. This was followed by orders to begin withdrawing again as the British and their French allies proved unable to halt the rapid tide of German military aggression. Lens was reached on 21 May and it soon became clear that the British position was becoming untenable. Hopes were pinned on a counter-offensive, as had happened in September 1914 at Mons, but the available forces were depleted in strength – 2nd Cameronians was reduced to a headquarter company and two rifle companies – and information was scant. On 28 May the battalion received orders to withdraw from Wytschaete, and to make its way with the rump of the BEF to the Channel coast. During the final embarkation 2nd Cameronians contrived to keep its heavy weapons, and returned almost intact to England. During the operations the battalion lost 360 casualties killed and wounded.

For another Scottish infantry battalion, 1st Royal Scots, first contact with the enemy was made on the River Dyle. In the face of a heavy German attack the battalion was forced to withdraw towards a new position near Calonne, and then further back towards Lys, scene of some of the fiercest fighting in 1918. Although the battalion was in continuous contact with the enemy it was also involved in a desperate rearguard action which quickly degenerated into a full-scale retreat. As their historian described the situation, 'to look back on these days and nights afterwards was to enter a nightmare world.'[3]

As the straggling remnants of the British Army fought their way back towards the Channel coast on 27 May, the Royals made their last stand at a position called Le Paradis, close to La Bassée Canal. In the company of elements of the 2nd Royal Norfolk Regiment, the Royals faced an overwhelming assault by superior German forces including armoured units, and within three days the battalion had fought itself to a standstill. Although some survivors managed to make their escape back to Britain, the 1st Battalion had ceased to exist as a coherent fighting unit. Amongst those who managed to escape was the commanding officer Lieutenant-Colonel H. D. K. Money, who said later that 'the Battalion did all that was asked of it; and the behaviour of all ranks was in the spirit of the highest traditions of the Regiment. Never once did the men fail to respond to their orders; never once did the Battalion give up a position until ordered to do so; and never did the men fail to respond to the old cry, "Come on, The Royals!"'[4]

Unfortunately it was not the end of the story. During the final attack on the Royals' position at Le Paradis, SS soldiers threw hand grenades into a regimental aid post, killing some of the wounded, and only the intervention of a German regular soldier prevented the rest being gunned down by machine-gun fire. Others were not so lucky: a party of over a hundred Norfolks was massacred after running out of ammunition and surrendering to the 14th Company of the

SS Totenkopf Division, under the command of Hauptsturmführer Fritz Knöchleinin. But the Scots had the last word. One of their sergeants survived the incident, and later gave evidence when the SS murderers were brought to justice after the war. During the fighting in Belgium 1st Royal Scots lost 141 dead and around 350 wounded, while 292 of their number went into German captivity.

Surrender was also the fate of 2nd Royal Scots Fusiliers, which retreated from its positions on the Charleroi Canal back towards the old First World War battleground of Vimy Ridge and then back towards Arras. The battalion counter-attacked on 22 May along the River Scarpe, and came under sustained aerial bombardment which caused the first substantial casualties. Three days later the battalion was positioned to the south-west of Ypres between Hollebeke and Zillebeke where it came under renewed German attack. The fusiliers' last stand was made on 28 May at a defensive position on the east bank of the Ypres-Comines Canal which they had been ordered to defend until they were relieved. However the expected counter-attack failed to materialise, and with ammunition running out and casualties mounting the commanding officer Lieutenant-Colonel Willie Tod had no alternative but to order his men to surrender. Most of the survivors, including Tod, went into captivity but around 250 managed to break out and make their way to the coast and safety before re-assembling at Blackdown near Aldershot. Before being taken to a prisoner-of-war camp Tod was ordered to appear before General (later Field Marshal) Walther von Reichenau, who told him: 'I wish to congratulate you. I am told your troops fought magnificently. I hope you will have lunch with me . . . I promise you that you will be home with your family by Christmas.'[5] Later still, Tod became the senior British officer at Colditz Castle, the secure prisoner-of-war camp for what the regimental war history called 'unregenerate and incurable escapers among the Allied prisoners-of-war'.[6]

By then the Germans had swept aside the French Ninth Army and were heading rapidly towards the Somme. Faced by the possibility of encirclement, and knowing that his lines of communication to the Channel were no longer secure, Gort prepared plans to pull the BEF back towards the port of Dunkirk. As the month drew to a close, 6th Gordons had reached Poperinghe where the men were ordered to dump all unnecessary equipment, and to disable their lorries and carriers before heading for the Dunkirk perimeter. Under cover of dark the battalion reached the beaches on 1 June to begin the evacuation back to England. The last unit to leave was the anti-tank company commanded by Major L. G. Murray. Also fighting its way back to the coast was 4th Gordons, which took part in a spirited defensive action along the canal between Comines and Ypres. Under fierce German aerial bombardment the battalion reached the Dunkirk beaches on the morning of 1 June when it received orders to make a last stand. That dire command turned out not to be necessary, and the battalion was evacuated the following day.

For another Scottish battalion on the beaches at Dunkirk, 1st Highland Light Infantry (HLI), the war had begun in Elgin where it had first mustered on its foundation in 1778 as the 71st Highlanders. Mobilisation and re-equipping took a fortnight to complete, and it was not until 21 September 1939 that the battalion entrained for Aldershot where it was informed that it would be a pioneer battalion in II Corps as part of BEF in France. (1st HLI was one of two home service battalions which had not been brigaded prior to the outbreak of war.) Although this was taken as something of an insult – pioneers were the work horses of any large formation, and were liable to be broken up into smaller units – the battalion, under Lieutenant-Colonel J. D. Russell, buckled down to the task in hand. Once in France, though, the battalion joined 127 Infantry Brigade as part of 42nd (East Lancashire) Division where it came under the command of Brigadier Sir John Smyth. A winner of the Victoria Cross in the previous conflict, Smyth had a high opinion of the HLI – the 2nd Battalion was present at the action in which he won his medal at Ferm du Bois in 1915 – and, as he revealed in his autobiography, he asked specially for the regiment to come under his command in 1940, noting that they produced the kind of soldiers he admired: 'The battalion set just the example for which I had hoped and were at all times co-operative, efficient and as tough as could be. They had a wonderful tradition, a very fine crowd of young officers, and the men, though they groused vociferously, as is the custom of the British soldier, got better as things got worse.'[7]

In the brigade were two Territorial battalions – 4th East Lancashire and 5th Manchester – and despite the differences in their backgrounds they quickly formed a close relationship with their regular counterparts from Scotland. During the advance into Belgium following the German assault on 10 May, 127 Brigade held the sector between Tournai and Pecq where they set about constructing defensive positions. A week later, the collapse of the French Army and the German invasion of Holland obliged the BEF to withdraw towards the Escaut Line. During the operation 1st HLI formed part of 'Macforce', a rearguard formed by 12 Brigade and two regiments of artillery to protect the exposed right flank. (The force was named after its commander, Major-General Noel Mason-McFarland, the BEF's Director of Military Intelligence.) For 1st HLI this resulted in a deployment along the River Scarpe where the battalion came under prolonged attack from the air. On one day alone the brigade managed to shoot down eleven German aircraft by small-arms fire, a remarkable achievement.

On 21 May the brigade rejoined 42nd Division, which was based at Lille, covering the rear of the BEF's retreat towards the Channel coast. In one action near Rexpoede the battalion lost twenty-five casualties killed or wounded, while others fell into enemy hands; for one officer, Major H. A. Adams it was a repeat of his experiences in 1917 when he was taken prisoner by the Germans. For a time it seemed that the battalion might be surrounded but the intelligence officer Lieutenant Philip Kindersley succeeded in getting through to divisional head-quarters, and then returned with the order to retire to the coast. Just as the 71st Highlanders had done at Corunna in the Peninsula War, their descendants in 1st HLI fought their way to the beaches at Dunkirk where the men embarked the destroyer HMS *Fidget* and landed at Ramsgate on 31 May.

All told, 338,226 soldiers made good their escape from the Dunkirk beaches, thanks mainly to solid discipline (the retreat never became a rout), the gallant defensive battle fought by French forces at Lille and indecision on the part of the German high command. Amongst the others which escaped was 1st King's Own Scottish Borderers (KOSB) which had crossed over to France under the command of Lieutenant-Colonel E. E. Broadway, and joined the British forces in positions near Lille on the border with Belgium. It found itself in good company: the divisional commander Major-General Bernard Law Montgomery (later Field Marshal Viscount Montgomery of Alamein) referred to the formation as the 'International Brigade', as 9 Brigade was composed of English, Irish and Scottish battalions – 2nd Lincoln-shire Regiment, 2nd Royal Ulster Rifles and 1st KOSB. When the German attack began in May the division moved immediately into Belgium to take up positions along the River Dyle to the east of Brussels but, as recorded, this was only a prelude to a steady with-drawal as the BEF fell back under the weight of the German assault. On the third day 1st KOSB was deployed on the River Escaut close to the old battlefield at Oudenarde, and with each passing day the British formations found themselves on the back foot as they started pulling back towards the Channel ports. Once at Dunkirk the only alternative to a last stand was evacuation, and as resistance would have resulted in the destruction of the British Army, the BEF was able to pull out using an incredible mixture of naval craft, merchant vessels and civilian pleasure boats. A Borderer, Henry Bridges, captured the mood in his poem 'Dunkirk' which paid tribute to the armada of little ships taking part in the operation.

> The sands were black with soldiers, and the skies were black with
>   planes,
> But the Monarchs and the Skylarks and the little Saucy Janes
> Undaunted by their danger set their course through the attack
> And from that hell of bloody death they brought our soldiers back.
> And women wept in England then with happiness and joy,
> And many an English mother ran to welcome home her boy.[8]

Once back in Britain 1st KOSB re-assembled at Shepton Mallet near Wells in Somerset. The new commanding officer was Lieutenant-Colonel D. C. Bullen-Smith, a future commander of the 51st (High-land) Division.

While the bulk of the BEF was involved in the great escape at Dunkirk, on 1 June a different fate awaited the 51st (Highland) Division which was deployed along a defensive line to the south-west of Abbeville near the mouth of the River Somme. Sixty miles away to the south-west lay the small port of St Valéry-en-Caux, with the road via Dieppe forming a southern boundary. As Brigadier Bernard Fergusson put it in his history of The Black Watch, 'all the ordeal of the next twelve days was to take place within that modest rectangle'.[9] As we have seen, the division had started the war under

French command in the Saar region, but following the initial German onslaught they had been compelled to withdraw towards the fortified positions in the French Maginot Line. In the first phase of the German attack on the division's flanks between 10 and 13 May, 4th Black Watch lost six killed and twenty-five wounded, with a further thirty being taken prisoner.

The speed of the German Army's armoured assault meant that the division was cut off from the rest of the BEF, and its fortunes were now tied firmly to the French Third Army under the command of General Antoine Besson. During this difficult period it became clear to the British high command that some elements in the French Army were considering suing for peace. As these included the commander-in-chief General Maxime Weygande and Marshal Philippe Pétain, the renowned commander of the First World War, the threat had to be taken seriously. Churchill was determined to keep France in the war at all costs, and that necessity was to play a part in determining the fate of Fortune's division. If the French were to sue for an armistice, as had been threatened, it would allow their powerful navy to fall into German hands, and make an invasion of Britain more likely. At the same time Churchill wanted to withdraw the bulk of the BEF through Dunkirk, even though that decision gave the impression to the French that their principal ally was withdrawing and leaving them to their fate. As the 51st (Highland) Division continued to pull further back into Flanders the political thinking in London was to have a decisive effect on what happened to them in the days ahead. Basically, Churchill's policy was to retain the 51st (Highland) Division in France for as long as possible as a means of keeping up pressure on the French to stay in the war.

On 4 June the division supported a French attack made by the remnants of the French armoured and artillery forces along the Mareuil ridge to the south of Abbeville, but although the French fought with great determination they were outnumbered and out-gunned. This was the last full-scale Allied attack of 1940 but even as it took place the last of the BEF was being picked up from the Dunkirk beaches. Whatever the outcome of the attack on the Mareuil ridge, the 51st (Highland) Division was now on its own in France, together with the remnants of the 1st Armoured Division. The following day the Germans launched a fresh offensive along the line between the

Somme and the Aisne, and the overwhelming power of their attack sealed the division's fate as it withdrew to the coast. It was a time of desperate fighting and confusion when men were exhausted both by the need to retreat and to fight a rampant enemy. To the end Fortune hoped to pull his division out through the port of Le Havre, but after almost two weeks of hard fighting, on 12 June he was forced to surrender to his opponents, the German 7th Panzer Division led by General Erwin Rommel. One of the last formations to fight to the end was 1st Black Watch which was surrounded by two German divisions at Houdetot where the Scots were supported by some remnants of the French cavalry. For the commanding officer Lieutenant-Colonel Eric Honeyman the order to surrender was difficult to accept – the moment was remembered by 2nd Lieutenant (later Brigadier) Angus Irwin, who commanded the Carrier Platoon: 'As the final attack was coming in, Colonel Honeyman was standing near me and said, "I never thought this would happen. Certainly not that I would ever have to chuck the can in but I'm afraid we're going to have to give up to save lives because we're completely surrounded." He then sent some runners to give the orders to cease-fire.'[10]

Just as the battalion was one of the last to surrender, so too were its men amongst the last casualties. An hour after the surrender Captain Neil Grant-Duff, commanding C Company, was killed leading his men in a brave but doomed counter-attack. His father had been killed in the First World War while commanding the same battalion. In a last gesture of defiance, 5th Gordons was ordered to make one final effort to clear the cliff-top positions outside the town, but this was forestalled when the French started surrendering in the face of a German tank attack. For one young officer, 2nd Lieutenant Donald Ritchie, who had earlier won the Military Cross, it was a harrowing moment: 'I was completely overcome by emotion. Tears rolled down my cheeks. I was keyed up to attack this bloody ridge and then the reversal. I'll never forget Platoon Sergeant Herbie Forsyth giving me a wallop on the back and a bottle of brandy to swig from and saying, "It's not your fault, sir." It was a terrible thing and we were completely unprepared.'[11]

Across the battlefield there were other isolated tragedies. During the fighting at Franleu, A and C Companies of 7th Argylls were quickly over-run, communications collapsed, and the other rifle companies were unable to offer supporting fire. With casualties mounting it quickly became clear that the battalion was incapable of creating a structured defence, and that it had ceased to exist as a fighting entity. The battalion War Diary described it as 'the blackest day in the history of the battalion', and this was reflected in the casualties – 23 officers and 500 soldiers killed, wounded or taken prisoner.[12] Amongst them was the commanding officer Lieutenant-Colonel E. P. Buchanan. Only D Company made it to safety, joining up with A and C Companies of the 8th Battalion which had reached the coast at Ault. Together with other survivors they formed part of a new breakout group known as 'Arkforce', after the village of Arques-la-Bataille in which it was formed. Most of the units involved in the operation lacked the carriers and weapons used by the rest of the division, but Arkforce was helped by the Germans' decision to bomb the fuel tanks in Le Havre, and created a huge smokescreen. On 15 June the Argyll survivors were evacuated, appropriately enough on board the ss *Duke of Argyll*, an LMS railway ferry which normally operated the Heysham to Belfast route. Others also managed to escape against the odds. Amidst the carnage and the despair the only other bit of good news for the division was the escape of 4th Black Watch and 6th Royal Scots Fusiliers which had fallen back on positions on the River Bresle near Dieppe. Having defended it for three days under heavy German fire, they were able to pull back towards Cherbourg where they were picked up and returned to England.

Later (see Chapter 10), a new 51st (Highland) Division came into being, made up of replacement battalions which took the numbers of those that had been lost at St Valéry. Few families in the Highland counties were left unaffected by what had happened, and for all the regiments this was depressing, yet as the days wore on there came the heartening news that substantial numbers had managed to escape. Amongst them was Captain (later Brigadier) Bill Bradford, the adjutant of 1st Black Watch who slipped away and cycled to the Pyrenees with the intention of breaking into Spain. Arrested by the Vichy French authorities, he escaped again and stowed away on a ship bound for Algiers. From there he and two others crossed the Mediterranean in a small yacht and reached Gibraltar even though none of them had any sailing experience. On his return he joined 5th Black Watch in the reconstituted 51st (Highland) Division.

Even luckier was Captain Derek Lang, 4th Seaforths. Despite being wounded he melted into the French countryside where the French resistance helped him to get to Marseilles. From there he managed to board a ship bound for Beirut, and crossed over into Palestine at the end of the year. He returned to his regiment and after the war was knighted and promoted to lieutenant-general in command of the army in Scotland. Another prominent escapee was 2nd Lieutenant Chandos 'Shan' Blair, 2nd Seaforth Highlanders, who spoke later about the sense of shock and disgrace he felt at being forced to surrender. Determined to escape at the earliest opportunity, he eventually absconded from the notorious Oflag VB camp at Biberach in Baden Württemberg, Germany. While outside the perimeter with a working party he managed to make good his escape, and walked the seventy-five miles to the Swiss border. From there he was given a passport and money which he used to travel to Madrid, and then crossed over to Gibraltar. Like the others, Blair returned to fight another day, and later, like Lang, as Lieutenant-General Sir Chandos Blair he became the senior army commander in Scotland and Governor of Edinburgh Castle.

For the rest, though, the war meant five long years in camps in Germany and Poland where the men were given agricultural work or laboured in coal mines, a dispiriting fate for professional soldiers. Even after the war had long ended a belief lingered that the 51st (Highland) Division had been 'sacrificed' unnecessarily, and in 1994 this was the subject of a book written by the historian Saul David. While his contention that the division 'paid a heavy price for the miscalculations of the Government' by leaving it under French command is correct, it is also true that General Fortune had little option but to remain with the French Army even when it became clear that the BEF would be withdrawn.[13] At the beginning of June his division was at the point of honour, and any precipitate retreat would have been a brutal betrayal of Britain's main ally. Besides, the 51st (Highland) Division was also undone by the speed and aggression of the German armoured divisions as they swung towards the coast to cut off any escape through Le Havre, and nothing could have prepared them for that.[14]

One positive thing came out of the experience. Shortly after the soldiers arrived at their prisoner-of-war camp at Oflag VIIC at Laufen, a group of officers devised a dance which became known as 'The Reel of the 51st Division'. Its dance steps and movements were smuggled back to Scotland where the reel became immensely popular and was danced throughout the country to show solidarity with the imprisoned Highland soldiers. Devised by Lt Jimmy Atkinson, 7th Argyll and Sutherland Highlanders, the key formation of the dance replicates a St Andrews Cross, the Saltire being the division's shoulder flash. The reel was soon published by the Perth section of the Scottish Country Dance Society, with funds being raised for the Red Cross. It then entered the society's repertoire, and it is still danced to this day at ceilidhs and balls, not just in Scotland but also across the world. As it turned out, though, St Valéry was not the only place where Scottish regiments were forced to surrender to the enemy. It also happened in the Far East.

When war broke out in Europe, Japan declared her neutrality even though she had signed an Anti-Comintern pact with Nazi Germany in 1936. However, the country entertained territorial ambitions in China and the western Pacific, and it possessed modern and competent armed forces which were fully capable of realising those ambitions. Throughout the 1930s extreme nationalists had come to play an increasingly important role in Japanese political life as the country's armed forces became more deeply involved in attacks on China. Following the fall of France, Japan signed the Tripartite Agreement with Germany and Italy, and began making serious preparations for entering the war by occupying the northern half of French Indo-China. By the following year, July 1941, the southern half had been occupied, as was much of southern China. This territorial aggrandisement was met with US demands for moderation but by then it was too late to exert any diplomatic pressure. By October Japanese policy, formulated by Minister for War General Hideki Tojo, had put the country on a war footing, and plans were finalised for launching an offensive which would attack the Allied nations, subdue China and create a Japanese Co-Prosperity Sphere incorporating Indo-China, Thailand, Malaya, Burma and the East Indies.

Japan entered the war on Sunday 7 December 1941 with a pre-emptive air strike on the US Pacific Fleet's base at Pearl Harbor in Hawaii, an attack which President Franklin D. Roosevelt denounced as a 'day of infamy'. This was followed in quick succession by further

Japanese assaults on the islands of Guam, Wake and Midway, while the Japanese Second Fleet escorted General Tomoyoku Yamashita's Twenty-Fifth Army to attack the north-west coast of the Malayan peninsula. For the British this was a valuable asset as it produced almost 40 per cent of the world's rubber and 58 per cent of the world's tin; it was also the key to Britain's major naval base at Singapore. The Japanese forces were outnumbered two to one, but the poorly trained defending British and Indian forces were ill-equipped to cope with the speed and ferocity of the Japanese advance, and by 14 December northern Malaya had been over-run. Within a further fortnight the Slim River defensive line had been breached, leaving Singapore at the mercy of the attacking Japanese forces. This was to be one of the biggest setbacks for the Allies at any stage in the war. Too late, the garrison in Singapore had been reinforced, but mostly by raw and untried troops. In 1941 command had been assumed by Lieutenant-General Arthur Percival who had divided the island into three sectors: the southern was held by two Malay and one Straits Settlement volunteer brigades; the western by 8th Australian Division and 44 Indian Infantry Brigade; and the north by 9th and 11th Indian Divisions. Shortly before the Japanese attack, 18th British Division arrived but it took little part in the fighting. There was virtually no air cover and most of it was provided by obsolescent aircraft.

Arrogance also played a part in Singapore's downfall. There was a generally accepted (though wrong-headed) belief that the base was invincible, and the colony's social life remained unaffected by the outbreak of war. When Alistair Urquhart arrived from Aberdeen with a draft for 2nd Gordon Highlanders his eyes had been opened to the reality of colonial life in its heyday. Private soldiers were treated with the same casual contempt the British settlers reserved for the Malay and Chinese residents; the prevailing feeling seemed to be that provided you were white and well-connected, social life still went with a swing. Above all, as Urquhart argued in his memoirs, no one believed that the Japanese would have the temerity to attack this invincible bulwark of British interests in southern Asia: 'The regular soldiers never dreamed that there would be a war in the East. I used to shudder when I thought about it because I knew it would be a calamity. Our officers were in a situation beyond their understanding and our training lacked both skill and urgency. We had no tanks because in its wisdom High Command believed that they were not suited to the terrain.'[15] Urquhart was not exaggerating. Some idea of the problems facing 2nd Gordons can be found in an order forbidding them from using their Bren carriers for more than 150 miles a month in case the tracks wore out. The battalion was also obliged to send drafts back to Britain, thereby losing experienced men, and the make-up of the battalion was in a state of constant flux.[16]

Although Singapore has become a byword for catastrophe in the history of the British Army, some regiments behaved better than others, and gave a good account of themselves during the fighting. Amongst these was 2nd Argyll and Sutherland Highlanders which had arrived in August 1939 to form 12 Indian Infantry Brigade with 4/19th Hyderabad Regiment and 5/2nd Punjab Regiment. Before the out-break of the Second World War the Argylls had begun training for jungle fighting in earnest, and this was intensified in 1940. Not that their efforts were always appreciated by their superiors. In his memoirs Captain A. J. C. Rose remembered being assured by a staff officer in Malaya Command that 'if we were not drowned in the seasonal rains we would be decimated by malaria'.[17] Fortunately, the commanding officer, Lieutenant-Colonel Ian Stewart, was a tremendous enthusiast, and his men were quickly nicknamed 'Jungle Beasts' on account of their ability to survive and thrive in the enervating conditions of the Malayan jungle. They also mastered the art of manoeuvring the elderly Lanchester armoured cars equipped with two Vickers machine-guns.

For the battalion the story of the fall of Singapore is soon told. During the initial invasion of Malaya, 2nd Argylls was involved in delaying operations as part of the rearguard for 11th Indian Division, and did not engage the Japanese until 17 December at Titi-Karangan where Colonel Stewart ordered Pipe-Major McCalman to play the tune *Gabaidh sin an rathad mhor* ('We'll take and keep the highway'). Later, Stewart recorded that not only was the tune appositely named but that it had been first played after the involvement of the Appin Stewarts at the Battle of Pinkie which was fought in 1547 as part of Henry VIII's attempt to force a marriage between his son and the infant Mary Queen of Scots. During the fighting at Titi-Karangan the Argylls lost 11 casualties but killed at least 200 enemy soldiers thanks to the Japanese tactics of attacking in 'human waves' against superior and disciplined firepower – according to Stewart 'the perfect answer to a machine-gunner's prayer'.[18]

As the Allied forces began their retreat there followed equally bruising encounters at Lenggong, Kota Tampan, Gopeng Dipang and Telok Anson which left 2nd Argylls exhausted and badly depleted. The fiercest fighting took place on the River Slim where the Lanchester armoured cars were no match for the heavier enemy armour. At one stage the battalion was reduced to ninety-four effectives under the command of Major David Wilson. As stragglers came in, the number increased to 250 men who were given the responsibility of guarding the causeway into Singapore. Many of those taken prisoner were either bayoneted or marched into captivity and, given the Japanese attitude to prisoners of war, they faced an uncertain future. At the end of the month Stewart returned to the battalion after a short spell in charge of 12 Brigade, and the battalion was reinforced by 210 Royal Marines who had managed to escape from the earlier sinking of the battleships HMS *Prince of Wales* and HMS *Renown*.

Thus was born the composite infantry battalion which was christened the 'Plymouth Argylls', a pertinent title given the regiment's associations with Plymouth, the city in which the marines were based. (The local football team is called Plymouth Argyle and its name could have been derived from the founders' admiration for the style of football played by The Argyll and Sutherland Highlanders when it was based in Plymouth in the 1880s. Another clue is that the team's dark-green and blue strip mirrored the regiment's tartan, but an alternative derivation could have been the name of the public house in which the founders first met.) Stewart renewed intensive training but time was running out for the exhausted and demoralised remnants of the Allied armies. On 8 February the Japanese started crossing from Johore into Singapore territory, and within three days had gained a substantial foothold as Percival's forces moved back into the perimeter. During this period the Plymouth Argylls moved north up the Bukit Timah Road towards the airfield at Tengah. Two days of intense fighting followed during which the Argylls and the marines came under heavy aerial bombardment, and attack by Japanese medium tanks. On Friday 13 February the Japanese intensified their assault by shelling the civilian areas, a move which caused great damage and created large numbers of casualties. By then it had become clear to Percival that further resistance was futile: water supplies were running low, and a defensive battle would only cause unacceptable numbers of civilian casualties.

The order to surrender was given on 15 February, and the remaining members of the Plymouth Argylls were marched into captivity in Changi Prison. Led by Piper Charles Stuart, they marched along streets lined by hundreds of Allied soldiers who, to salute their courage during those last desperate days of fighting, stood to attention as they passed. In his report, Field Marshal Sir Archibald Wavell added his own words of praise: 'There was one battalion – a battalion of the Argyll and Sutherland Highlanders – commanded by a remarkable commanding officer – which he trained most intensively in jungle fighting. There was no doubt whatever that this battalion was as good as and better than any of the Japanese, and naturally this battalion did quite magnificent work until they were practically wiped out in the battle of the Slim River on 8 January after a gallant fight.'[19]

Some of the survivors managed to escape on board naval vessels or Chinese junks – fifty-two Argylls and twenty-two marines made it to Ceylon; amongst their number was Colonel Stewart, who had been unwillingly evacuated and was later promoted to command 144 Infantry Brigade. Of those who went into captivity many were sent to work on the notorious Burma Road railway in Thailand. All told, the Argylls suffered 244 casualties killed in action, and 184 as a result of disease and deprivation while in Japanese captivity. Astonishingly, two soldiers in the battalion remained at large in Malaya where they helped to train Malay and Chinese resistance fighters.

For the rest of the Singapore garrison, ahead lay a season in hell as they went into Japanese captivity and slave labour. Amongst them was 2nd Gordons which had mounted a counter-attack at Bukit Timah village near the Alexandra Barracks before being forced to give up the unequal fight against superior numbers. With them went 14,000 Australian, 16,000 British and 32,000 Indian troops. Ahead lay long and painful years of slave labour on the Burma-Siam railway where the sickness rate and death rate quickly soared although, with a touch of regimental pride, the Gordons' war historian noted that 'in the Highlander abode a tough pride – almost arrogance – which no indignity devised by an Asiatic could subdue.'[20] In his memoirs Alistair Urquhart provides chilling descriptions of the barbarities inflicted by the Japanese as they took control of the city. While marching into captivity in the notorious Changi prison the men of the Gordons were confronted with 'a thicket of severed Chinese heads speared on poles on both sides of the road.' Broken bodies bore witness to massacres where people had been machine-gunned at will, and every scene spoke of devastation.[21] During the Singapore operations and the years in captivity 2nd Gordons lost 380 officers and men; their sacrifice is remembered on a memorial plaque in the Presbyterian Church in Singapore. Amongst those who eventually returned home after the war was Urquhart who survived the Burma railway, as well as being torpedoed while being transported to Japan as a slave labourer.

Equally devastating was the retreat from Burma which followed when it was invaded by the Japanese from Raheng in Thailand. Originally the Japanese had not been interested in occupying the whole country, and believed that their strategic needs would be served by taking the port of Rangoon and the airfields on the Kra isthmus. However their minds were changed by the realisation that the Allies could use Burma as a springboard to attempt to retake Malaya, and also by the threatening presence of the Chinese 5th and 6th Armies to the north along the lines of communication known as the Burma Road.

The Japanese plan to rectify the situation was based on a three-pronged attack – on Rangoon, the Salween River and the Sittan River – and, as had happened in Malaya, they relied on speed and aggression to accomplish these objectives. On 11 February they crossed the Salween. The retreating 17th Indian Division blew the bridges across the Sittang three days later, and by 18 March Rangoon had fallen. Although the British and Indian forces counter-attacked in the Irrawaddy Valley at the end of the month, they were outflanked to the east and to the west where the Japanese drove General Chiang Kai-shek's army back towards the Chinese border. Short of supplies, exhausted and demoralised, the two armies went their separate ways, and the British and Indian forces began what came to be known as 'the longest retreat in British military history'. Following a march of 900 miles, the survivors crossed over the border into India on 19 May: of the original 30,000, 4,000 were dead and another 9,000 were missing.

While these disastrous events were unfolding, three Japanese divisions had begun moves to invade the British colony of Hong Kong in southern China. This vital port and trading centre had been in British hands since 1842 when it was ceded by the Treaty of Nanking as an open port. In 1860 further territory was acquired on the mainland at Kowloon, and under the Peking Convention of 1898 the New Territories were taken over from China under a ninety-nine year lease. As a British Crown Colony, Hong Kong prospered as it offered a secure and dependable base during a period of upheaval which included the fall of the Manchu dynasty and Japanese intervention in China's internal affairs in the 1930s. It was, though, something of a strategic backwater, and at the outbreak of the Second World War its defences were pitiful. In the event of enemy attack the civil and military authorities had simply been told to hang on for as long as possible as there was no hope of any immediate help or reinforcement. The question of Hong Kong's position was put into stark relief by Winston Churchill on 7 January 1941 when he rejected the idea of sending reinforcements as 'there is not the slightest chance of holding Hong Kong or relieving it . . . we must avoid frittering away our resources on untenable positions.'[22]

As a result, in the summer of 1941, the land forces element of the Hong Kong garrison was extremely meagre: two British infantry battalions, 2nd Royal Scots and 2nd Middlesex Regiment (a machine-gun battalion); and two Indian battalions, 5/7th Rajput Regiment and 2/14th Punjab Regiment. These were supported by local artillery and volunteer defence units, but they were modestly equipped and trained. Two raw Canadian militia battalions were added in November, but apart from adding numbers and increasing morale their arrival only added substance to Churchill's warning about frittering away resources. The naval and air forces were also modest: one destroyer, eight motor torpedo boats, four gunboats and seven obsolescent reconnaissance aircraft. In short, 'Hong Kong was a "hostage to fortune" and it fell before the Japanese onslaught on Christmas Day 1941.'[23] However, that bald and historically accurate statement does not tell the whole story of the valiant attempt to defend an impossible position, and the suffering which was visited on those who survived the short but fiercely fought battle for Hong Kong.

The 2nd Royal Scots had arrived in the colony in January 1938 following a lengthy deployment in India, and the men quickly felt at home in a place where Scottish voices were familiar in the trading community, and where 'they could hear that most familiar of noises of the Auld Reekie [Edinburgh] of that time – the clank of jolting tramcars.'[24] The scenery, too, was pleasing, and the atmosphere within the colony was vibrant and exotic. For officers and men alike, Hong Kong was an ideal posting with its sporting and social opportunities, and a climate which provided hot summers and mild, refreshing autumn and winter days. As for training, it was pursued enthusiastically, but as Hong Kong was low on the army's priorities it proved difficult to keep the battalion up to scratch. Unit cohesion was not helped by the fact that the men were spread over four separate barracks, with some elements operating on the mainland. During those difficult early days of the war it was also impossible to hold on to key personnel: all too often experienced officers, warrant officers and non-commissioned officers were posted out of Hong Kong to serve in other units or training establishments elsewhere. As a result, when 2nd Royal Scots went to war it had only four pre-war regular officers, and the commanding officer Lieutenant-Colonel S. E. H. E. White only took over command a matter of weeks before the Japanese attack began.

To add to the difficulties in retaining personnel there had been a last-minute revision of the defence plan occasioned by the arrival of the two Canadian battalions. Already there had been a number of proposals ranging from manning a secure defensive 'inner line' on the mainland to a more limited plan to deploy mobile forces on the mainland before pulling back to the island. Shortages of manpower and equipment meant that the defence of the mainland positions was always going to be a problem, and by the outbreak of hostilities its pill boxes, weapons pits and trenches had been largely abandoned.

However, for all that the defence of the mainland was considered a non-starter, it was put into effect by the colony's new garrison commander, Major-General C. M. Maltby, General Officer Commanding, China Command. Under his revised plan three battalions would form a new brigade which would be responsible for defending the positions on the mainland. These would be the Royals, the Rajputs and the Punjabis, while the Canadians and the Middlesex took up defensive positions on the island of Hong Kong. Right up to the last minute, Maltby believed that the inner lines on the mainland could be held for up to seven days, even though intelligence reports revealed that the attacking Japanese forces would number up to 20,000 troops. The thinking behind Maltby's plan was plain – to provide a first line of defence which would give the colony some breathing space and the opportunity to destroy key installations – but it failed to take into account the enfeebled state of the physical defences and the fact that the positions were supposed to be held by a full infantry division. Unhappily, like many other senior army officers of his generation, Maltby had a low regard for the military abilities of the Japanese, and held to the view that they would be unable to compete against western soldiers – among the many absurd misapprehensions was a widely accepted belief that they were incapable of fighting at night due to their allegedly poor eyesight. There was even optimism that the Japanese were bluffing, and that the expected attack on Hong Kong would fail to materialise. During the weekend, when war broke out in the east, no one saw any reason to cancel parties or dances in Hong Kong, and church parade was held as usual on the day that Pearl Harbor was attacked.

For the Royals the move into Lo Wu Camp on the mainland had come as an unpleasant surprise. Not only was the change ordered a bare three weeks before the Japanese attack began, but the defenders soon discovered that many of the positions were 'at best, makeshift'.[25] As described by Captain David Pinkerton of D Company, the Royals' sector lay to the north-west of Kowloon and from the left, it:

> . . . ran from the sea across the valley between the Tai Mo Shan and Golden Hill ranges up to the Shingmun Redoubt, a miniature fortress of pill-boxes and concrete trenches communicating with each other by underground passages. The redoubt stood on the forward slope of a knife-edged ridge, overlooking a reservoir, on the far side of which the middle slopes of Tai Mo Shan rise up to its summit. From this point, the Inner Line slanted backwards, so that the redoubt was the apex of an angle facing the enemy, and obviously a key point.[26]

The general lie of the land would have been known to many of the men as the mainland was used for annual training exercises but the battalion was now forced to put itself onto a war footing in a tactical position which was unfamiliar to them. For a start the positions had to be renovated. Pill boxes had to be cleaned out and new trenches had to be dug. Wiring had to be replaced, communications enhanced and minefields created, although the latter activity was hampered by an acute shortage of anti-personnel mines. One fact stands for many: the key position was thought to be the Shing Mun Redoubt yet it was manned by forty-two soldiers consisting of A Company headquarters (one officer and nine soldiers), an artillery observation post (one officer and four soldiers) and one officer and twenty-six soldiers of 8 Platoon. All told, the Royals were expected to hold a defensive line which stretched over five thousand yards, five times the recommended minimum. The only artillery support came from sixteen howitzers and from the six-inch guns of the elderly Insect Class gunboat HMS *Cicala*. Other than the name of the defences – Gin Drinker's Line – there was not much to smile about, although with typical resolve, Pinkerton noted his belief that on the eve of battle 'we felt we were quite prepared to receive the Japanese'.

The battalion's war began at dawn on 8 December on what many soldiers remembered as a perfect Hong Kong winter's morning, crisp and sunny. As the Japanese air force flew missions to attack and destroy the RAF base at Kai Tak airfield, the Japanese army's 38th Division, commanded by Lieutenant-General Sano Tadayoshi, crossed the Sam Chun river into the Leased Territories, and by the following day had reached the main Allied defensive line. Despite determined resistance from the Royals, the Shing Mun Redoubt quickly fell into enemy hands, and its loss made the already over-extended defensive lines untenable. Much to Maltby's anger and disappointment there was no option but to order withdrawal from the mainland, and the operation was completed on 13 December. During this initial phase of the battle the Royals lost ninety-nine casualties, most of them in D Company which had begun the battle with seventy men, and had lost sixteen killed and seventeen wounded. Amongst the survivors was 2nd Lieutenant James Allan Ford, who remembered that 'after all the Battalion had come through we left the battlefield in buses, as if we were going back to the barracks after an exercise in the hill.'[27] Later still, after the war, Ford became a distinguished writer, and his novel *The Brave White Flag* is his own comment on the tragedy of the fall of Hong Kong.

Once back on the island of Hong Kong the options facing the defenders were limited, although, once again, the resistance was determined and whole-hearted. In the opening rounds the Japanese bombarded defensive positions and launched air attacks on Victoria, the central business district. During this phase 2nd Royal Scots was deployed in the north-east sector until 16 December when the battalion handed over to the Rajputs and went into reserve. Two days later the Japanese landed in strength between North Point and Aldrich Bay. They moved quickly to bisect the island and split the defending forces. To do this they had to take possession of the strategically important Wong Nei Chong Gap on the slopes of Mount Nicholson which guarded the main north-south road at the narrowest point in the island, but the importance of the feature was overlooked by Maltby. Later this failure to reinforce the position meant that 2nd Royal Scots found itself caught up in some of the fiercest fighting on the island. Despite determined attempts to clear Japanese positions, on 19 December the Royals were forced to withdraw from a hopeless situation, and one subaltern spoke for everyone in the battalion when he said: 'That was the worst day my men had in all the Hong Kong fighting, and as an officer in battle the worst day I experienced.'[28]

The determination displayed by the defenders forced the Japanese to halt temporarily to regroup but by then the end was already in sight. Casualties had been high on the Allied side, and with food, water and ammunition running low it was obvious that the ability to resist had been eroded. By 23 December Colonel White was left with barely 180 men under his command, and was unable to maintain contact with garrison headquarters other than by runner. And yet, in spite of all the difficulties, some sparks of hope remained. On Christmas Eve the arrival of 200 pairs of brown gym shoes allowed the battalion to mount night patrols with some hope of success, Pinkerton noting that 'by now it had become obvious that our patrols could do little useful work at night on roads or the stony hillsides in ammunition boots.'[29] By contrast the 'un-soldierly' Japanese had worn rubber-soled boots to good advantage. That proved to be the final piece of resistance. In the afternoon of Christmas Day Maltby gave the order to surrender, and to fly the white flag. For the Royals this came as shattering news as they had been preparing themselves to fight to the last man; instead Colonel White was forced to go forward to the Japanese lines through Wanchai Gap to give his surrender to the Japanese at the Hong Kong Tramway Depot at North Point. When the roll-call was taken it was found that in the course of 17 days' fighting the Royals had lost 12 officers and 95 soldiers killed, and 17 officers and 213 soldiers wounded.

The fighting for Hong Kong was over but it was not the end of the war for the survivors – 22 officers and 608 soldiers, who went into Japanese captivity. For them, the four years as prisoners of war was to be a terrible experience, and three officers and fifty-nine soldiers died whilst in Japanese hands. The treatment meted out to Allied prisoners of war has been well documented – for example, the high casualties on the Burma-Siam railway or the Bataan death march – but the Royals had further reason to be shocked by Japanese barbarity. After the fall of Hong Kong, 1,816 British prisoners of war were transported to Japan on board the elderly freighter *Lisbon Maru*. As happened on many other 'death ships', they were packed into the holds where the average space for one man was one square yard which meant sleeping in shifts and limited availability of latrines. On the night of 30 September 1942 the *Lisbon Maru* was attacked and torpedoed in the China Sea by the submarine USS *Grouper*. Although the ship did not sink immediately, the British prisoners of war were battened down in the holds while most of the Japanese crew and guards were taken off. Two days later, with conditions worsening and the ship in danger of sinking, there was a mass breakout which ended in tragedy. Men who jumped into the sea were drowned or were used as target practice by the rescue ships, and the rest failed to escape before the *Lisbon Maru* sank. Of the 1,816 who set sail for Japan only 970 survived and were taken to Japan where they endured further misery in Japanese camps. It was not the worst incident – a fortnight earlier 5,620 Allied prisoners had been killed when a British submarine sank a larger freighter – but it does mean that the name *Lisbon Maru* occupies an unhallowed place in the regiment's history.

One other incident stands out from that desperate period. Many of the surviving Royals were placed in a camp at Sham Shui Po on the mainland where they were commanded by their senior officer Captain Douglas Ford. Early on he managed to make contact with Chinese collaborators who managed to smuggle in badly needed medical supplies. Plans were also made for a mass breakout, although the weakened condition of the men inside the camp made this something of a non-starter. In any case, as Ford's brother, James Allan Ford, has pointed out, 'the outward messages contained little, if anything, more than the International Red Cross would have learned, if Japan had been a signatory to the Geneva Convention.'[30]

But it was always a high-risk gamble, and when the Japanese discovered the extent of the communication, reprisals were inevitable. Along with others, Douglas Ford was arrested on 10 July 1943, subjected to sadistic torture, and held in solitary confinement on starvation rations. Throughout the experience he refused to give anything away, despite receiving agonising treatment from his captors, and continued to accept sole responsibility for his actions. As a result two sergeants implicated in the plot received prison sentences instead of the death penalty when the trials for espionage were held in December, but after perfunctory proceedings Ford and two other officers were condemned to death for committing an act of espionage. On 18 December they were shot by firing squad, but even in those last dreadful minutes Ford's courage and resolution never wavered. Although weakened himself, he gave assistance to his brother officers, and as the junior of the three took his place on the left of the line. In acknowledgement of Ford's courage the Japanese officer in charge of the firing squad insisted that the condemned man, a gallant Royal Scot, should stand on the right. After the war, Ford received the posthumous award of the George Cross 'in recognition of his most conspicuous gallantry while a prisoner-of-war in Japanese hands'.

The ruinous defeats of the British Army in France and the Far East could have had a damaging influence on the people of Britain but the opposite seemed to happen. For the next eighteen months Britain was on her own, supported only by the forces of the Dominions and by the forces of free Europe which had managed to escape the Nazi and Soviet invasions. It was a parlous period but within weeks of the defeats at Dunkirk and St Valéry there was renewed hope when RAF fighters overcame their German opponents in the skies above southern England and gained sufficient superiority to persuade Hitler to abandon plans for a cross-Channel invasion. By any standards the Battle of Britain was a glorious and hard-fought victory, and the author George Orwell was right to compare it to Trafalgar or Salamis. It has also created its own mythology. Quite apart from the fillip to the national psyche, it gave substance to the defiant decision to fight on against Nazi Germany, and to refuse all overtures to make any bargain with Hitler. History generally records it as an English victory which was won over the counties of Kent and Sussex – often in full view of those living below – but amongst the air crew were squadrons and aircrew representing the Dominions, Poland, Czechoslovakia, the United States and Scotland, which was represented by its two auxiliary air force squadrons.

In the middle of August 602 Squadron left Drem for Tangmere to replace 145 Squadron's Hurricanes, and were first in action against enemy aircraft on 16 August. A fortnight later 603 Squadron left Turnhouse, and replaced 65 Squadron at Hornchurch in Essex. It too was soon in action, losing three Spitfires and two crew on 28 August, a fact recorded by one of the pilots Richard Hillary, who watched the squadron returning with 'smoke stains along the leading edges of the wings showing that all the guns had been fired.'[31] Before the war Hillary had been a noted athlete at Oxford and had served in the University Air Squadron. On the outbreak of war he had joined 603 Squadron whose B Flight was operating from RAF Montrose. No sooner had the squadron moved south than Hillary had five kills to his name, and had also experienced his first crash on 29 August when he crash-landed in a field near Lympne. Four days later during a dogfight over the Channel, Hillary's Spitfire was hit by a Me 109 and he only just managed to escape from his cockpit after the canopy jammed. Horribly burned during the descent, he landed in the sea off the Kent coast, and after three hours in the water was picked by the Margate lifeboat.

From there, after treatment at Margate and in London, he was sent to the Queen Victoria Hospital in East Grinstead where his severe burns were treated by the distinguished plastic surgeon Archibald McIndoe, who was responsible for treating aircrew who had been badly burned, mainly in the face and limbs. Like most members of the 'Guinea Pig Club' – the treatment was in its infancy and largely experimental – Hilary survived, and eventually returned to flying duties. Having used his influence to persuade the authorities to agree to this move – his memoir *The Last Enemy* had become a bestseller – he was posted to 54 Operational Training Unit at RAF Charterhall near Greenlaw in Berwickshire. It was clearly a mistake as Hillary was physically incapable of handling an aircraft and the inevitable happened: on the night of 8 January 1943 he was killed together with his navigator Sergeant Wilfred Fison when he lost control of his Bristol Blenheim V light bomber which crashed in heavy fog near Crunklaw Farm.

Hillary's squadron fought for the remainder of the Battle of Britain, and returned to Scotland in December, as did 602 Squadron. Both of the Scottish auxiliary squadrons saw out the rest of the war and were disbanded in the summer of 1945 having seen active frontline service in the UK, Europe and Malta. Their record speaks for itself: both were first to see action against the Luftwaffe, and first to shoot down German bombers over the UK mainland. In New Zealand-born Flying Officer Brian Carbery, 603 Squadron had one of the RAF's five top-scoring aces in the Battle of Britain, and the squadron itself had the honour of being the highest scoring squadron, with 58 kills in return for the loss of 30 aircraft, while 602 Squadron's record was 35.5 kills for the loss of 17 aircraft.[32]

4 Frontline Scotland

In common with the rest of the UK, Scotland was put on a war footing as soon as hostilities with Germany began. At that early stage defence of the homeland was a priority, and even before the outbreak, as the international situation worsened, steps had been taken to establish an administration to deal with civil defence issues. On 26 August, a week before the declaration of war, Tom Johnston, Labour MP for West Stirlingshire, was appointed Regional Commissioner for Civil Defence in Scotland (one of twelve commissioners created for the United Kingdom), a powerful post which gave him a wide range of responsibilities not just for co-ordinating measures for the protection of the civilian population, but also for taking over the administration of Scotland in the event of the collapse of central government.[1] His appointment came against a background of existing constitutional changes to the way the Scottish Office operated: under the terms of the Reorganisation of Offices (Scotland) Act of 1939, all the Scottish government departments had been effectively abolished as legal entities and made subject to the direction of the Secretary of State for Scotland.

Initially, as a Labour MP, Johnston had been chary about accepting the commissioner's post as he believed that it could have implicated him in the Chamberlain government's policy of appeasement, but as soon as he took up the position he emerged as the ideal choice, with a rare gift for understanding the threat posed by enemy aerial bombardment and the need, as he put it in his memoirs, 'to prepare for the worst and hope for the best'.[2] His political associate was David Ogilvy, 12th Earl of Airlie, a prominent Angus landowner who was also Lord Chamberlain and a committed public servant. Working with them were a number of talented individuals including Johnston's chief of staff Norman Duke and his press officer Alastair Dunnett, later to become a distinguished editor of the *Scotsman* newspaper.

Johnston proved to be the right person for such an exacting job which required not only political skills of the highest order but also a good deal of tact and discretion. In all those respects he was no stranger to the demands that would emerge once he took up office in Edinburgh. Indeed, it could be said that there was no other candidate who could have brought so many talents to public life during wartime, even though he had a history of being a thorn in the flesh to the authorities during the previous conflict. Born in Kirkintilloch in 1881, as a young man Johnston had embraced socialism, joining first the Fabian Society and then the Independent Labour Party (ILP). With the help of a modest inheritance he founded a weekly magazine *Forward* in 1906, and quickly developed it as a significant campaigning publication with a strong emphasis on self-help and political integrity, and imbued with a distinctly humanitarian outlook. At the outbreak of the First World War the magazine's tone was sceptical of the war effort and at the end of 1915 it was closed down under regulations 2, 18 and 27 of the Defence of the Realm Act after Johnston broke the censorship rules by reporting the opposition of Glasgow munitions workers to David Lloyd George's 'dilution' plans (the system by which men were replaced by women in skilled jobs). The order was rescinded in February 1916, but from that point onwards Johnston was under increasing scrutiny by the authorities, not least because of his political associations and the robust editorial stance he adopted in his magazine's editorials. As a result he was investigated by the Lord Advocate but no further charges were brought against him or *Forward*.[3]

Through his journalism and his own political leanings Johnston had become associated with the group of ILP politicians known as the 'Red Clydesiders', men such as James Maxton and Willie Gallacher. who were opposed to the war and who were imprisoned for their support of the wartime strikes in the Clyde's shipbuilding yards. In 1922 Johnston was elected ILP MP for West Stirlingshire, and although he lost the seat two years later he was quickly returned for Dundee at an early by-election. When Labour returned to office in 1929 he gave up Dundee and was returned as MP for his old seat of West Stirlingshire. During the 1920s and early 1930s Johnston's political career was marked by an interest in the colonies, regarding the empire as a means of encouraging social and political progress and the needs of the unemployed.

Never a strict party man, he began to believe in the importance of consensual politics, and enjoyed friendships across the spectrum, including the Scottish Conservatives Walter Elliott, later a Scottish Secretary, and the novelist and historian John Buchan. Opposed to the formation of Ramsay Macdonald's National Government Johnston lost his West Stirlingshire seat in 1931 but re-won it four years later. He also supported the League of Nations, was opposed to re-armament and held a number of ministerial posts including Under-Secretary of State for Scotland and Lord Privy Seal. Although a pacifist by inclination, he was also a realist and when war with Germany became inevitable in 1938 he was ready to admit that while he was saddened by the turn of events at Munich, something had to be done to stand up to the Nazi menace. At the time he made his feelings clear in an editorial in *Forward*: 'I confess I found it difficult to clarify my emotions about the events of last weekend. Relief, almost gratitude, that our generation has had another escape – however temporary – from war. Shame and humiliation at the way the Czechs were egged on and "guaranteed", and then left in the lurch! And finally apprehension that every ally we abandon, every friend we betray, leaves us the weaker for the day when the goose-stepping gangsters will order us in turn to put up our hands.'[4]

As a principled socialist and humanitarian Johnston was opposed to the concept of war but by 1938, having recognised its inevitability, he quickly came to the conclusion that preparations had to be made to protect the civilian population. When he was asked to become a Regional Commissioner that same year he agreed in principle but asked to be allowed to make his final decision when the country was at war or 'the selection will be deferred until the occurrence of an emergency'. Such was the importance the government placed on his acceptance of his post, this condition was agreed by the House of Commons.[5]

Once appointed he set to work with a will. At the time there were complaints that the twelve Regional Commissioners would simply become 'dictators' in the event of government collapsing or a German invasion, and there were even hostile comments that the system replicated the regional associations created by Oliver Cromwell in 1655, the period known as the rule of the major-generals, 'the most intolerable experience England ever had'.[6] However, those protests missed the point that the Regional Commissioners were supposed to act as facilitators and enablers and not, as was often claimed, as 'janissaries' or even as 'Nazi Gauleiters'. At the time the threat posed by enemy bombers was well enough known and understood but government measures were still inadequate and piecemeal, and Johnston had been highly critical of the lack of urgency shown by Sir John Anderson, the Lord Privy Seal, who was responsible for the United Kingdom's air-raid precautions policy. In short, Johnston saw it as his duty to correct the shortcomings and to ensure that the people of Scotland were not only protected but were fully aware of the dangers they faced.

Amongst his concerns was the haphazard way in which plans for the evacuation of children had been drawn up by the Department of Health in Edinburgh (see Chapter 8). In particular he was disappointed by the low take-up in pre-war trials for evacuation and the apparent lack of urgency in getting the message across to the public. He was also much vexed by practical matters such as ensuring the proper provision of accommodation and fresh food for the evacuees. In Scotland the problem had been made worse by the fact that not only was there a lower standard of housing but the Department of Health found itself working with a smaller margin of available rooms, and even before evacuation began there was a marked degree of opposition to the whole concept of making accommodation available for what had been called the 'dregs' of the big cities.[7] It had already been agreed that Scottish children would not be sent to England or English children sent to Scotland.

In the event, when war did break out, the evacuation of large numbers of Scotland's children was only a mixed success – as was the provision of air-raid defences which was Johnston's main preoccupation when he took office. During the First World War a policy of strategic bombing had been utilised by the main combatants using airships and heavy bomber aircraft, and in the 1920s and 1930s it was assumed that 'the bomber would always get through'. One prophet of air power, the Italian General Giulio Douhet even suggested that the ferocity of unrestricted bombing of civilian targets would encourage the population to give up the will to continue, and demand that the fighting come to a stop. While many of the predictions about the destruction of civilian morale were so apocalyptic that many people

believed that mass bombing would never be carried out, the theory
had already been put into practice by the British in Mesopotamia
(Iraq) in the early 1920s and by the Germans during the Spanish Civil
War in the following decade. Mindful of the dangers posed by
unrestricted enemy aerial bombing, the Cabinet turned its attention
to the problem at a meeting on 7 November 1938 which considered
the response both from a military and a civilian point of view. It was
recommended that the fighter construction programme begun under
the re-armament policy should be accelerated, that 20 escort vessels
should be laid down for the Royal Navy, and that the army should be
provided with 1,264 new anti-aircraft guns 'of all types'. This latter
policy would have 'absolute priority'.[8]

In the wake of the Munich crisis the mood of the meeting was
obviously sombre, and it was recognised that 'it was Germany's
strength in the air and the relative weakness in this sphere of the
other Powers which was the main factor causing the unrest and
anxiety which existed in the world to-day'. Consideration was also
given to extending and enhancing air-raid precautions including the
construction of blast-proof shelters and strengthening existing buildings against bomb attack. In all instances this would be a devolved
responsibility under the direction of the Air Raids Precaution Department which had been founded in 1935, and the Cabinet's first
recommendation spelled this out: 'That the duty of organising air raid
precautions should be left to the local authorities, but that powers
should be taken in the forthcoming Air Raid Precautions Bill [15
November 1937] to deal with an authority which is clearly neglecting
its duties, and also to strengthen, in quality and numbers, the regional
inspectorate of the Home Office.'[9]

It had been against that background that Johnston had taken office,
and he quickly accepted the view that there had been a fair degree of
neglect in organising Scotland's air defences, especially with regard to
safeguarding the civilian population. Glasgow had been particularly
tardy, virtually ignoring the government's instructions, and providing
only £4,617 for precautionary measure in the 1938–9 financial year.
(At the same time almost four times that amount was voted for
expenditure on the city's parks.)

Pacifism was one reason as many Labour councillors believed
that preparations of this kind were 'warlike' and would encourage

militarism. For example, on 28 May 1936 a meeting of Glasgow Corporation 'moved as an amendment that the Corporation do not proceed with a scheme of Air Raid Precautions but calls upon the Government to take the lead in securing the abolition of aerial bombing, believing as we do that this would prove the most effective way in safeguarding the citizens of this and other cities.'[10] Lack of informed opinion was another: there was still a widespread belief that little could be done against the power and aggression of sustained aerial bombardment, and that measures to contain the threat would be too expensive and time-consuming.

As war became inevitable in 1939 attitudes did change and, by the end of 1941, prompted by Johnston, Glasgow had provided shelters for 835,055 people, leaving a balance of 76,784 persons still without access to private or communal shelters. The protection was made up of the following types of construction:

1. Steel (Anderson) each providing accommodation for six persons.
2. Individual surface shelters (brick), accommodating six persons.
3. Communal domestic surface shelters accommodating from 12 to 48 persons.
4. Adapted basements giving accommodation for 50 persons per basement.
5. Morrison indoor shelters accommodating 4 or more persons.
6. Strengthening of tenement closes by strutting.
7. Special structural works to provide accommodation for invalids.[11]

The blackout of buildings during hours of darkness proved also to be a problem. Because so many Glaswegians lived in tenement buildings there were issues about turning off stair lighting because it was linked to external street lighting. Roof lights and gas-powered close lighting also caused problems – the Corporation estimated that there were some 3,300 closes in the city, and that the lack of lighting would create severe inconvenience and danger to those living in tenement flats. There were also difficulties with tenement buildings in Edinburgh where the Chief Constable attempted to resolve the issue by ordering that back green doors should be kept open and unlocked at night to enable wardens to inspect premises. Even so, a detailed reconnaissance carried out by the Royal Air Force in the days following the outbreak of war showed that little was being done, and that 'generally speaking, lights were visible throughout the whole city, and vehicles in particular were clearly visible.'[12] With a population of approximately 470,000, Edinburgh eventually required 7,175 ARP wardens, and a total of 30,000 public air-raid shelters were constructed including a number which were dug in Princes Street Gardens.

Advertisements also abounded in local newspapers extolling the benefits of 'government approved lightproof cloths and papers, wood and steel shutters, blinds and curtains' to ensure that no chinks of light were made visible to enemy bomber crews overhead. As a result of the regulations vehicles had to drive with dimmed lights, and had their bumpers and tyre sidewalls painted white, but as fuel rationing was in place and there were fewer private cars on the road this was not really an inconvenience, even though there were a number of minor accidents in the early days.

However, in Scotland difficulties with the blackout were exacerbated in 1941 when 'double summer time' was introduced to give an extra two hours of daylight during the normal one-hour advancement ahead of Greenwich Mean Time (GMT). During the winter months there was no return to GMT but instead a single hour's advancement was applied. The move was introduced both as an energy-saving measure and to provide additional daylight for the farming community, especially during the harvest period. It also brought the UK into line with the rest of Europe, but while the move did benefit the war effort it caused problems in Scotland, especially in the north, where summer daylight was already long and winter daylight already short. According to James G. Pittendreigh, at the time a pupil at Skene Street School in Aberdeen, it was a dislocating time for all concerned.

When we got to school at 9 a.m., which was when we usually started, it was really only 7 a.m. and still pitch dark in winter. Before we could switch on the lights in the classroom we had to put up the black-out panels. As the windows of our classroom were rather large this took up a bit of time. Of course when it became daylight at about 10 a.m. this process was reversed using up more time. In summer time if we went to bed at 9 or 10 p.m. it was really only

7 or 8 o'clock at night and it was difficult to get to sleep. In fact in
midsummer it was daylight until midnight! What this did to our
biorhythms can only be imagined but we managed to live with it
somehow.[13]

Young James carried a small torch with a dim light to give him a
modicum of light when out in the evening, and remembered the
wardens going round as darkness fell to enforce the blackout. Responsibility for ensuring those regulations was in the hands of 1.5
million Air Raid Precaution (ARP) wardens – men and women –
who checked that the blackout was in place, maintained air-raid
shelters and assisted rescue work following bomb attacks. Most were
unpaid volunteers, and although the presence of the ARP warden was
not always welcomed by those who failed to maintain a complete
blackout, these officials did provide a vital service as they had to have
good local knowledge both to assist the people in their areas and to
direct rescue services after bomb attacks.

Another important measure was the creation in August 1941 of the
National Fire Service (NFS) which provided a nationwide service
consisting of existing local authority fire brigades augmented by a new
force of part-time auxiliaries. A separate service was formed for
Northern Ireland in 1942 but Scotland remained part of the NFS
throughout the war, and this proved to be a drastic change for the 228
fire brigades which operated across the country. As a result of the
emergence of the NFS the country was divided into six fire areas, with
a Fire Force Commander who was responsible to the Secretary of
State for Scotland. It was a fully integrated system: within each fire
area, divisions and sub-divisions were formed with senior officers in
command, and at each level there was a fire control room, reporting to
the level above, until the last link was made with the major control for
the UK in London. The creation of the NFS was intended as a
wartime emergency measure with a restoration to the status quo once
hostilities ended. By and large the legislation worked, and although
there were familiar complaints that the auxiliaries were simply avoid-
ing military service, the NFS came into its own during the Clydebank
blitz of 1941 (see Chapter 6).

Perhaps the most obvious manifestation of the mobilisation for the
defence of the UK homeland was the creation of the Local Defence

Volunteers (LDV), or as they were better known, the Home Guard. The organisation was formed on 14 May 1940 when, just as the situation was deteriorating in France, the Secretary for War Anthony Eden broadcast to the nation appealing for volunteers to come forward to provide a part-time volunteer defence force whose primary task would be to counter the threat of invasion posed by German airborne forces. Volunteers, aged from seventeen to sixty-five, would not be paid, but Eden promised that they would be armed and would receive a uniform, and that 'these duties will not require you to live away from your home'.

In the confusion of May 1940 when the heavens seemed to be falling, it was a drastic step. Militias of this kind had been formed before in time of war whenever invasion was a threat or national security endangered, and Eden's request for able-bodied men to come forward was quickly heeded across the country. This was especially true in Scotland where the volunteer and militia forces had been enthusiastically supported in the latter part of the nineteenth century. On the day following Eden's announcement 1,200 volunteers arrived at police stations in Glasgow to register. Edinburgh was similarly overwhelmed with large numbers of volunteers drawn from all levels of society, and in Aberdeen 600 also registered their interest on the first day. A week later the *Glasgow Herald* reported that a former provost of Greenock had come forward to offer his services despite being eighty years old.[14] By the end of the war some 250,000 had served in its ranks, and the organisation itself had undergone several changes of role.

In an attempt to bring some order to the announcement, the War Office produced a chain of command which formalised the basis of the LDV's structure and its relationship to the Regular and Territorial forces. At Scottish Command headquarters in Edinburgh Castle the responsibility for the new organisation was put in the hands of a General Officer Grade II (GSO II), a relatively senior staff officer, and below him at the three area headquarters was a GSO III to co-ordinate administration with local unpaid LDV organisers further down the chain of command. Less easily fixed was the provision of uniforms and weapons. The first issue was considered essential if the volunteers were not to be considered as fifth columnists, and therefore liable to be shot out of hand by invading German soldiers. Eventually a simple uniform of denim overalls was supplied, and while field caps were also worn, Scottish LDV units were permitted to wear a tam-o'-shanter bonnet provided that it was uniformly worn.[15] Later still, LDV units were allowed to wear the cap badge of their local regiments so that those in Edinburgh could sport a Royal Scots badge while those in the north-east wore the stag's head badge of The Gordon Highlanders. This practice was followed across Scotland with heartening results, and while it encouraged the gradual militarisation of the LDV it made the volunteers feel that they were an integral part of the larger regimental family.

The second issue was more contentious. If the volunteers were to have any realisable military role they needed to be armed, but in the early days modern infantry weapons were in short supply even for the regular forces. In some desperation, mixed with the eternal optimism that suffused the LDV throughout its existence, some units simply used whatever weapons came to hand. In rural areas shotguns and sporting rifles were ruled to be legitimate weapons by the War Office, and some older .303 rifles from the First World War were also made available. Eventually the government was able to import 500,000 US Springfield rifles, again of First World War vintage, but these were not universally popular as they used .300 calibre ammunition and had to be degreased on arrival.

So great was the enthusiasm for the new project that the government was forced to suspend recruiting at the end of July, by which time the LDV had attracted 1.3 million volunteers across the UK. Although the force was supposed to be strictly egalitarian in nature – initially there were to be no officers and no saluting – many of the group and zone organisers were retired officers, and the extant records reveal a sense of cohesion and soldierly discipline which helped the volunteers to believe that they were doing a useful job. In his record of the service of the 6th Perthshire Battalion, Lieutenant-Colonel A. D. Hunter made it clear that his men were no lambs to the slaughter but soldiers who believed that they would give a good account of themselves.

Reports had led the country generally to believe that the Germans of 1940 were better trained, better equipped, tougher and even more ruthless than counterparts of the first Great War. The veterans of 1914–18 did not altogether believe this, but they did believe that they would almost certainly be called upon to meet a very formidable enemy, who so far in the war had proved invincible, and that they would have to face and kill him under handicap of insufficient arms, very little training and none of the benefits of being a cohesive fore. Not least, they had known war at first hand and knew all war's savagery and terror.[16]

In keeping with a tradition begun in the First World War when many Scottish Territorial battalions were formed from work or club associations – 15th Highland Light Infantry from the Glasgow Tramways Department, for instance – many LDV units had similar connections, notably with railway companies, the post office and industrial work places. Quite early on, there was also a change in title. Prompted by Churchill, on 31 July 1940 Eden agreed that the LDV should be known by the alternative title of Home Guard, and the appellation stuck. So, too, did another title, Dad's Army, which was later to become the name of an immensely popular and successful television comedy series about a fictional English Home Guard unit in Walmington-on-Sea. On returning from the ineffectual intervention in Normandy, on 29 June 1940, Lieutenant-General Sir Alan Brooke wondered why 'we in this country turn to the old men when we require a new volunteer force?'[17] Later, when he was appointed Chief of the Imperial General Staff (CIGS) in November 1941, Brooke changed his mind about their effectiveness but he continued to hold to the view that wars were not won by militias. As the historian of the Home Guard in Scotland has pointed out, there was a fair degree of pragmatism at work in creating the force, and as a result different areas produced different characteristics. Rural areas tended to attract larger numbers of retired officers, many of them quite senior and drawn from the landowning classes, while industrial areas in the central belt tended to be more egalitarian, at least in the early days. He also recorded the unusual fact that the 3rd Edinburgh Battalion, based at the Braid Hills Golf Club, included a judge, Lord Fleming, who 'found himself on patrol one night with a fellow volunteer whom he had last seen in the dock before him in the High Court.'[18]

Fleming was later commissioned in the same battalion, another sign of the inevitable militarisation of the organisation. In November the government overturned its original plans for the Home Guard by announcing that 'His Majesty has therefore been pleased to direct that King's Commissions shall be granted to all approved commanders in the Home Guard, and that the Force shall also have a suitable complement of warrant and non-commissioned ranks. The commissioned, warrant and non-commissioned officers will bear the traditional titles of their ranks.' Although the innovation was deprecated by those who had hoped that the Home Guard would remain an egalitarian 'people's army' it was perhaps inevitable that it would be gradually subsumed into the structure of the armed forces. There was a catch, in that those commissioned were officers in name only, and to all intents and purposes they were still private soldiers who only held command and authority within Home Guard units.

Even so, the use of ranks gave rise to stock characters such the figure of the bumptious Captain Mainwaring in the television series *Dad's Army* but as often as not there was some truth behind the caricatures. In the summer of 1940 the novelist Compton Mackenzie left his home in the south of England to return to Suidheachan, his house on the island of Barra which he had built a few years earlier. On his arrival he found a letter from Sir Donald Cameron of Lochiel, the Group Organiser for Inverness-shire, who invited him to take over command of the LDV in Barra, later part of the Hebrides Battalion, Home Guard. During the First World War Mackenzie had served as a staff officer and intelligence agent, and his position as a well-known author and local personality made him an ideal choice. Good novelist that he was, it also gave him some prime material for his novel *Keep the Home Guards Turning* (1943) which is a thinly disguised account of the doings of the Barra volunteers. He was not spoiled for choice in garnering his material; communications with headquarters in Inverness on the Scottish mainland 150 miles away were primitive, orders often took up to two weeks to arrive, and there was a stream of misunderstandings including the unexpected arrival of modern weapons including Lewis guns which promptly had to be returned.[19]

Set on the fictional islands of Great and Little Todday, the novel featured the absurd character of Hector Macdonald of Ben Nevis who had already appeared in the earlier *The Monarch of the Glen* (1941), and introduced the figure of Captain Paul Waggett who would resurface in similar guise as an officious English Home Guard officer in

Mackenzie's later and hugely successful novel *Whisky Galore* (1947). Such as it is, the plot of *Keep the Home Guards Turning* is thin – it involves an exercise in which Ben Nevis invades the Toddays to recapture a left boot which belongs to his own company – but Mackenzie had in fact based it on a real-life escapade in June 1941. At the time the Western Isles had been designated a Protected Area in which all movements were subject to possession of a military permit, and at the beginning of 1940 there had been a further restriction which required a separate permit to visit Barra. This arrangement allowed the Home Guard on South Uist to mount an exercise to test their neighbours' security by mounting an 'invasion' across the five-mile stretch of water which separated the two islands. Although the invading force was supported by a platoon of Royal Engineers, Mackenzie's Home Guardsmen successfully fought off the interlopers, allowing the novelist to boast to his friend Christopher Stone that 'they tried a surprise landing' but were defeated at their landing grounds at Eoligarry, Bruernish and Castlebay.[20]

Amusing though Mackenzie's account was, it cannot disguise the fact that the Home Guard units took their responsibilities very seriously throughout their existence, and this was particularly true during the first year of operation when it seemed all too probable that Hitler's forces might attempt to invade the country by crossing the English Channel. There was also a much more serious side to their activities. From the outset the LDV and Home Guard acted as cover for top-secret Auxiliary Units whose task was to go underground and 'stay behind' to organise resistance in the event of an enemy invasion.

Fittingly for their objectives, not much was known about these shadowy units, and their personnel were encouraged not to discuss the nature of their covert activities. The units were the brainchild of two exceptional officers, Major (later Major-General) John 'Jo' Holland and Major (later Major-General) Colin McVean Gubbins, both of whom had had extensive experience of irregular warfare, most recently in Norway where independent companies had been formed to organise resistance against the invading Germans. A handful of the officers involved in this operation were consequently employed by a new organisation called Military Intelligence (Research) or MI(R) which had been founded by Holland in March 1939. Designated as Intelligence Officers (IOs) they set about recruiting members of the

Auxiliary Units from within the communities where the units would operate. A high premium was placed on local knowledge and field craft (gamekeepers and poachers both served in numbers) but according to a War Office directive to Home Guard commanders the main attribute required was an ability to remain tactful at all times: 'Only reliable men of discretion are enrolled, and I am therefore to request that every assistance may be given by HG Commanders to Officers of Auxiliary Units in securing the right men for this duty though it is realised that it may mean the loss of a good man to the local Home Guard unit.'[21]

Three battalions of these secret units were formed across the UK, with 201 Battalion covering Scotland and Northern England. Individual units usually consisted of an officer and up to twelve men, and they operated with the assistance of their designated IO. In Scotland the organisation's headquarters was at Melville House, the seat of the Earls of Leven, near Ladybank in Fife, which was chosen by the senior IO for Scotland Captain Eustace Maxwell, brother of the writer Gavin Maxwell. Not only was the house centrally situated but it also contained ample grounds for training including a secluded small arms range. Units were brought here for training in demolition, signals work and close-quarter combat, but all this activity had to be carried out without any fanfare. By the very nature of their duties members of Auxiliary Units tended to be a close-knit group, most of whom came from the same neighbourhood or workplace, and not even their families were allowed to be told what they were doing. On one occasion those under training tested the security of Scottish Command and managed to leave behind a timed thunderflash in the GOC's private lavatory. Other exercises were held with Auxiliary Units operating against the Polish forces who were guarding Fife's coastal defences.

The grounds of Melville House also housed a model Observation Post which was built by Welsh miners brought up to Fife and returned immediately to their homes in order to maintain secrecy. This was the standard base from which patrols operated, and which, in the event of an invasion, would provide lairs varying in size and design. Situated in remote areas, usually underground, these positions contained basic living facilities and arms caches, and were considered to be so secret that construction workers were never told their real purpose. Around

100 were thought to have been constructed in Scotland. Some were purpose-built by tunnelling companies of the Royal Engineers to a design by Lieutenant-Colonel Colin Field: Nissen huts made of corrugated iron were placed in trenches and buried with ventilation shafts camouflaged as rabbit burrows, but these proved to have condensation problems which made explosives unstable. Other hide-outs were built into badger setts; still more were simply basements in houses or the ruins of buildings. There were even hides in castle dungeons or in underground chambers, the most famous being the souterrain or earth house on the machair at Ness on the Isle of Lewis. A natural hiding place, it had been built with a long underground passage leading to a circular central chamber. Unfortunately it had to be cleared out, and the IO responsible for the area Captain A. G. Fiddes-Watt (an artist and picture restorer in civilian life) was appalled by the unnecessary destruction of priceless Iron Age shards.

Perhaps the most dramatic secret location for use by the Auxiliary Units was a large underground bunker constructed on the flanks of East Lomond Hill above the village of Falkland in Fife. The brainchild of General Andrew 'Bulgy' Thorne, who had become General Officer Commanding-in-Chief in Scotland in April 1941, it was planned as the nerve-centre for the Scottish resistance, and with its superb location overlooking the Howe of Fife it would have been a difficult position to dislodge. Thorne, a Grenadier Guards officer from Moray, knew what he was talking about: before the war he had served as military attaché in Berlin where he learned that East Prussian landowners were training their estate workers as irregular 'stay-behind' units, and he believed that the idea had merit. Although the threat of invasion had lapsed, Thorne also believed that the Germans were still capable of launching a successful attack against the Scottish mainland, using airborne forces to capture Fife and create a lodgement while a twin-pronged seaborne attack would be made against the Forth and Tay estuaries. Having established a hold in the east he expected that the German panzer forces would then drive westward to cut the country in half. Thorne's main concern was to integrate the Auxiliary Units into the home defence structure of Scottish Command, especially the last line of defence known as the Scottish Command Line, a series of defensive blocks to protect the Tay, the Forth and the Clyde. The East Lomond–Melville House nexus was central to those plans. Local people in the area knew nothing about this; the bunker on East Lomond was constructed by Canadian Army tunnellers, and once the job was completed they were posted elsewhere. The position itself was filled in after the war, and for many years only a heavily padlocked ventilation shaft revealed its existence.[22]

Some idea of the secret nature of the work of the Auxiliary Units in Fife can be found in the experience of Tom Wilson, a farmer at Carslogie near Cupar, who was a lieutenant in 1st Fife Home Guard. At the age of thirty-six and in a reserved occupation, he was telephoned shortly after the fall of Dunkirk by Eustace Maxwell. He was informed that he had been recruited into a new top-secret unit and that no one, not even his family, was to be told what he was doing. On the 50th anniversary of the founding of the Auxiliary Units Wilson finally broke cover and told his story, summing up his experiences with a terse comment: 'We were to work behind enemy lines, sabotage was to be our business.' Wilson's squad comprised six men, all locals known to him. There was a shoemaker, a roadman, an electrician, a butcher and a barber. As happened elsewhere, none knew which of the others had been chosen from their battalion until their first meeting at an empty house on his farmland at Carslogie. 'We knew the country and that was the point,' he explained in an interview later in life. 'We could move about freely in the countryside.'[23] So good was the security that long after the war many units thought that they were unique, and that there was no overall command structure. The IO for Fife and Angus was Captain W. D. Clark; at one stage he had 121 men under his command, and 25 secret hideouts were constructed in his area.[24]

In addition to the protection of the civilian population, the Scottish Office had also laid plans for safeguarding the country's treasures. The most important of these were the Crown Jewels, the so-called 'Honours of Scotland', consisting of the Crown, Sceptre and Great Sword of State. Last used in 1651 to crown Charles II, they had been in danger before, having been hidden in Dunottar Castle and then in Kineff Church in Perthshire during the Cromwellian occupation of Scotland. Although they had been restored in 1660 they went missing after the Act of Union in 1707, and were not recovered from their sealed case in Edinburgh Castle until the novelist Sir Walter Scott engineered a much-publicised 'discovery' in February 1818. Clearly they were still of symbolic importance, and on the outbreak of war the decision was taken to remove them from public display in the Crown Room in Edinburgh Castle and to place them in a locked case which was then removed to a vault. Two years later they were moved once more and placed in two zinc-lined cases which were sealed and placed in separate concealed locations in the nearby Half Moon Battery. Four sealed envelopes contained the exact location, and one bore the instruction that the regalia were to be destroyed in the event of an enemy invasion.

Scotland's main art treasures and other irreplaceable objects were also moved from their collections in Edinburgh – from the National Gallery of Scotland, the National Portrait Gallery of Scotland, the Royal Scottish Museum and the National Library of Scotland. In conditions of great secrecy, 418 paintings and 609 portraits were removed in 12 wagon-loads on 31 August 1939. On 12 October an official of the National Galleries of Scotland was able to inform the Scottish Office that 'the Collections of the National Gallery, Portrait Gallery and Museum of Antiquities have been moved to six mansion houses, 3 in Peeblesshire, 1 in Berwickshire, 1 in East Lothian and 1 in Selkirkshire'. To oversee them in their new locations a gallery attendant was placed in each house where he was given basic accommodation and paid an additional fourteen shillings per week. As a concession they were also allowed to take with them a few items of personal furniture.[25] Although precise details were kept secret at the time, it transpired that for the safekeeping of these treasures the Scottish Office requisitioned accommodation in a number of country houses, mainly in the Borders: The Glen at Innerleithen, Glenmoriston at Innerleithen, Leithen Lodge at Innerleithen, Fernilee at Galashiels, Manderston at Duns and Winston Castle at Pencaitland. A number of other country houses were requisitioned to store valuables from other Scottish cultural institutions. The full list reads as follows:

Borthwick Castle, Middleton, Midlothian
    National Library
    Royal Scottish Museum
    Registrar General
    Geological Survey

Morinish Lodge, Killin
   National Library
   General Register House

Blackness Castle, West Lothian
   Royal Scottish Museum

Torwoodlee, Selkirkshire
   Royal Scottish Museum

Crookston House, Midlothian
   Royal Scottish Museum[26]

Throughout the period of the evacuation there were problems in
guarding the various locations and maintaining the correct levels of
humidity. By December 1940, after the invasion scare had died down,
the National Galleries re-opened two of its rooms for an exhibition
of photographs to raise money for the Polish Relief Fund. All the
collections were returned and the operation was concluded on
18 July 1945

In retrospect, and with the benefit of hindsight, the Germans'
ability to mount a cross-Channel invasion was vastly over-rated, but at
the time the threat was taken very seriously indeed. It also suited
Churchill's purpose to unite the nation behind him to act in common
cause, both through his own rhetoric and by the rapid expansion of
measures to stem any enemy assault on the British mainland. Following the rapid fall of Norway and France there was a need to rebuild
national confidence and morale, and that necessity accounts for the
enthusiasm and determination which suffused the national mood in
the summer of 1940. That being said, Hitler's ambition to mount an
invasion was not entirely make-believe but rooted in military reality.
With Poland and Western Europe in his hands it seemed inconceivable that the German leader would not turn his attention to
Britain. His commanders were cock-a-hoop following their easy
victories, and the litter on the Dunkirk beaches told them all they
needed to know about Britain's plight. Such was the disarray in the
defending forces that the 1st (London) Division, responsible for
defending the Channel coast from Sheppey to Rye, had only eleven

modern 25-pounder field guns, as well as four obsolete 18-pounders and eight 4.5 howitzers which had been used in the previous conflict. In the whole of the United Kingdom there were only 80 heavy tanks, all incapable of engaging modern German panzers with any hope of success, and 180 light tanks used largely for reconnaissance purposes. For the fifteen divisions available for combat after the fall of France on 31 May there was insufficient transport, and contingency plans had to be put in place to use civilian buses.

It was a curious time. Throughout the summer the possibility of invasion remained a potent threat, and the southern counties along the Channel coast became a huge armed camp. However, no precise plans had ever been laid to counter an invasion of the UK, as the last serious attempt had taken place in February 1797 when a small French force had landed at Fishguard in Wales during the war against Revolutionary France. Commanded by Colonel William Tate, an American who had fought the British during the war of independence, it was the precursor of a larger invasion force but it was quickly subdued and rounded up. The Irish rebel Wolfe Tone who supported the action described Tate's men as 'unmitigated blackguards', and in one instance a dozen French soldiers surrendered to a Welsh woman armed only with a pitchfork, in the mistaken belief that her traditional red cloak denoted that she was a soldier. Half a century later, during the reign of Napoleon III, there was another scare but the possibility of any invasion actually taking place was so remote that it had never been considered by the army's Staff College.

It was at that juncture when a German invasion might have succeeded that Hitler hesitated. He still hoped that the British government would sue for peace, enabling him to turn his attention to Eastern Europe, the real object of his territorial ambitions. There was also a very real possibility that a seaborne invasion would fail through lack of specialist equipment, and Hitler was far from certain that his navy and air force would be able to gain the tactical superiority for such a venture. In addition, accurate intelligence about British resistance was in short supply, leading the German leader to complain to his generals: 'We are divided from England by a trench 37 kilometres wide and we are not even able to get to know what is happening there.' However, despite those misgivings the Germans continued with their plans for an invasion. The army tested new equipment such as amphibious and submersible tanks, and logistics experts began assembling the shipping that would convey the invasion forces, the basic units being large commercial barges used on the Rhine. The head of the Luftwaffe, Herman Göring, began to make fanciful claims that his aircraft would destroy the RAF in the air and smash their bases in Kent.[27] Only the navy's commander-in-chief, Grand Admiral Erich Raeder, was sceptical, telling Hitler on 11 July that an invasion had to be an operation of last resort, and could only be carried out once German aerial superiority had been established. Nevertheless, five days later Hitler issued Directive No. 16, 'Preparations for the Invasion of England', which gave the go-ahead for the operation to commence in the first half of September when conditions would be favourable – a dark passage and a rising tide on arrival. The operation was codenamed Sealion.

Throughout August the German thinking underwent several modifications, and at the same time plans were also laid for controlling the country once the invasion had succeeded. Prepared under the direction of Heinrich Himmler's Reichssicherheitshauptampt, the central security office ran by Reinhardt Heydrich, second-in-command of the secret police (Gestapo), they envisaged the immediate creation of Gestapo headquarters in London with five *Einsatzgruppen* working in Bristol, Birmingham, Liverpool, Manchester and Edinburgh, the main purpose being 'to combat with the requisite means all anti-German organisations, institutions, opposition and opposition groups'. The man given responsibility for the operation was SS Standartenführer Dr Franz Six, and he had a formidable array of assets at his disposal. Indeed, from the archival material relating to the German invasion it is possible to build up a detailed picture of what the UK would have looked like under Nazi control.[28] One handbook contained 174 photographs, mostly taken from the air and culled from publications such as the *Illustrated London News* and *Country Life*. For the Scottish section there was even a glossary of words in Gaelic.

Central to Six's policies was the arrest and liquidation of leading figures and the elimination of organisations which might oppose German authority such as churches, trades unions, schools and the police. All suspects were listed in the *Informationsheft GB* (Special Wanted List), and the Scottish content contained some curious bedfellows. The Scottish Farm Servants Union was to be closed down because it was of 'Marxist persuasion', and for different reasons the Scottish Boy Scouts Association was on the list because it was such 'an excellent source of information for the British intelligence service'.[29] At the time Jim Brown was a nineteen-year-old Rover Scout with the Edinburgh Craiglockhart troop. For him and countless others scouting meant the simple pleasure of camping at nearby Bonaly or tramping the Pentland Hills; it certainly was not about working covertly for the intelligence services. 'The Germans may have come to conclusions about [Robert] Baden-Powell's activities but they were wide of the mark as far as we were concerned,' he claimed in 1990. 'If anything, the Boys Brigade was more militaristic than us. We all came from different backgrounds, religious and social, and we all went to different schools.'[30] Nevertheless Brown would have been one of the many Scout leaders rounded up by the Gestapo had Scotland been invaded in 1940.

The Scottish Unionist Association would also have been raided, and there were plans to close down every local office of the Transport and General Workers' Union from Aberdeen to Stornoway and Barrhead to Methil. The principal Scottish freemasons' lodges were also on the hit-list, along with two major and long-established Scottish businesses – publishers William Blackwood and Sons Ltd and J. & P. Coats, the Paisley cotton manufacturers. Both were unusual selections for attention by the Gestapo. The Edinburgh publishing house of William Blackwood had been founded in 1805, and had recently published the work of John Buchan and Hugh MacDiarmid as well as a wide range of well-known English authors including George Eliot, Anthony Trollope, Edward Bulwer-Lytton and R. D. Blackmore. According to the *Informationsheft*, Blackwood's only fault had been the publication in 1936 of *Tales from Tyrol*, a run-of-the-mill collection of short stories by Olga Watkins, a member of a leading Anglo-Austrian family who gained fame as a prominent member of the legislative council in Kenya. A fluent German speaker, as a young woman during the First World War she had attracted the attention of the notorious British spymaster Richard Meinertzhagen. No one knows why the Paisley 'cotton kings' were included on the list although by the outbreak of the war J. & P. Coats was one of the largest commercial concerns in Scotland, employing 28,000 workers at their Anchor and Ferguslie mills in Paisley.

Heydrich's headquarters also produced the *Sonderfahndungsliste GB* (Special Search List, also known as the Black Book) which included the names of 2,820 British politicians, writers, artists and intellectuals, as well as European exiles resident in London, all of whom would have been taken into custody by the Gestapo: 'All persons enumerated in the Special Search List will be seized.'[31] On the evidence of what happened in the rest of Europe, and in view of Dr Six's infamous record in Moscow two years later when large numbers of prisoners were executed on his orders, that would have meant arrest, interrogation, torture and almost certain death in a concentration camp. Most of the names on the list are fairly obvious (Winston Churchill and Anthony Eden), others less so (Noël Coward and Virginia Woolf) but the Scots on the list make a variegated group. Listed for arrest by the foreign department of the German security forces were the Duchess of Atholl who had raised funds for humanitarian relief during the Spanish Civil War, the scientist J. B. S. Haldane, Professor R. W. Seton-Watson, the novelists Naomi Mitchison and Rebecca West and the MPs Robert Boothby, James Maxton and Mannie Shinwell. A different fate awaited Willie Gallacher, Communist MP for West Fife, who was wanted for immediate imprisonment by the Gestapo, and the writer and historian Robert Bruce Lockhart who was wanted by Walter Schellenberg's counter-espionage department.

It is not difficult to see why the politicians were included, even though the list is eclectic. Haldane, brother of Naomi Mitchison, was a pioneering geneticist who was also a Communist while the Duchess of Atholl was considered a dangerous liberal, and Lockhart was on the list on account of his connections with British intelligence. In 1918 he had been implicated in a plot to assassinate the Soviet leader Lenin, and had been sentenced to death in absentia by the Russians who were still Hitler's allies in the summer of 1940. His interest in Balkans politics may also have told against him. It certainly accounted for the most wanted Scottish name on the list – Robert William Seton-Watson of London University's School of Slavonic Studies, who was a vociferous opponent of appeasement. The Nazis were particularly interested in his papers 'for the German-Balkan politics, especially for Hungary and Jugoslavia'. If these were not found at his London address, paratroopers were to raid his Scottish home at Kyle House on the Isle of Skye.

Seton-Watson was Britain's foremost Balkanist, and had built up an international reputation for his outspoken views on the Slavonic nationalists and for his role in settling the borders of Yugoslavia at the Paris peace conference in 1919. A quiet, diffident man, he seemed to be in closer touch with the realities of central European affairs than many members of the British government, and he had been quick to point out the dangers posed by Hitler's territorial ambitions. In 1940 he was employed in the political intelligence department of the Foreign Office where he enjoyed a close relationship with Dr Edward Benes (also on the list) who was head of the provisional Czech government in London.

Also included on the list were the names of every Jewish refugee who had made their home in Scotland in the 1930s: they would have been easily traced by cross-reference to the index, which contained the main towns and cities of Britain, so that under Glasgow can be found M134 – Dr Lorenz Michaelis, born in 1902 and wanted by the inland security services whose Einsatzgruppe D, led by the notorious SS murderer Otto Ohlendorf, was responsible for the deaths of 90,000 Jews in Russia between June 1941 and July 1942.

The existence of the Black Book only became known after the end of the war when details were published in the press. Some of those listed regarded their presence as a badge of honour; Noël Coward recorded in his memoirs that after the war was over and the details had been revealed he received a telegram from Rebecca West which read: 'My dear – the people we should have been seen dead with.'[32] Others were less sanguine because even though the existence of the *Sonderfahndungsliste GB* had not been generally known it was clear from what had happened in Europe that the Nazis would target politicians and intellectuals, especially if they were on the left or had been opponents of appeasement. That description would have applied to the Haldane family which had two members of the list – J. B. S. Haldane and his sister Naomi Mitchison, both of whom were prominent socialist thinkers and opponents of Nazism. At the time Naomi was living in the family home at Carradale in Kintyre which was being used as an evacuation centre for children from Glasgow. While recalling those days on the 50th anniversary of the invasion scare she admitted her fear that she would be targeted if the Nazis ever came to Scotland.

I remember hearing that both my husband [Labour politician Richard Mitchison] and myself were on the Gestapo death list. It was deeply upsetting. I kept wondering what would happen to all my Glasgow kids if the Nazis came in and took over. At first I thought I would try to convince them I really loved Germany, but that would never have worked, so then I thought I might be able to shoot one or two of them before I was shot myself.

I recall telling one of the local fishermen that I knew quite well and he said, 'Och well, we will just have to get a boat and take you over to America if the worst happens.[33]

While the German invasion of Scotland was only a remote possibility, it is also probable that not everyone in the country would have been dismayed by the outcome. From the evidence of what happened in the rest of occupied Europe, including the Channel Islands which was occupied in the summer of 1940, the Nazis would have attempted to enter into alliances with those friendly, or at least not unfriendly, towards them. While there would have been mass round-ups of the kind of people represented in the Black Book, the German administration would have looked for the same kind of co-operation they had found in the Channel Islands, Vichy France and other parts of occupied Europe. In pursuit of those aims the Nazis established 'Radio Caledonia', which was part of its 'Concordia' propaganda network of short-range stations which purported to be broadcasting from within the UK, and in this case made appeals to Scots to make a separate peace with Hitler. Its main broadcaster was Donald Grant, a Hoover salesman from Alness who had joined the British Union of Fascists before the war, but the station ceased broadcasting in August 1942, having failed to make any impact within Scotland.[34]

However, from the evidence of the research undertaken by Schellenberg's department, the Nazis would have expected (but would not necessarily have received) support from a number of sympathetic organisations including the Anglo-German Fellowship which had been established in 1936 to foster links with Nazi Germany, and which contained several prominent supporters of appeasement. Many were establishment figures, and amongst the fellowship's Scottish membership were the Duke of Hamilton, Lord

Arbuthnot, Lord Lieutenant for Kincardineshire, and Sir Thomas Moore, Unionist MP for Ayr Burghs.[35] Similarly, The Link, another influential pro-German group founded in 1937, had several Scots amongst its membership, as did the Right Club, a secret society which had been founded in 1939 by Captain Archibald Ramsay, Unionist MP for Peebles and South Midlothian, a well-known appeaser and anti-Semite. Although these far-right groupings had been closed down or infiltrated by the beginning of the war they still attracted interest from the security services, and Ramsay was arrested on 23 May and interned under the provisions of Defence Regulation 18b.

In addition to these pro-fascist organisations, most of which were relatively harmless if extremely wrong-headed, the Nazis would probably have looked for support from those members of the SNP who were vociferous supporters of home rule and disapproved of the continuation of the union. The poet and classicist Douglas Young was chairman of the Aberdeen branch at the time, and as a prominent opponent of conscription (see Chapter 5) he was frequently vilified as being a Nazi sympathiser. That was not the case, but he did advise Roland Muirhead that Scotland should seek a separate peace if an invasion were successful, and that prominent Scots should be prepared to take part in the new form of governance under Nazi rule: 'The Germans will look around for aborigines to run Scotland, and it is to be wished that the eventual administration consist of people who have in the past shown themselves to care for the interests of Scotland.'[36] There were other prominent members of the nationalist community who were also potential Nazi sympathisers. Amongst them were the writer Ronald Macdonald Douglas, who was briefly interned, and Arthur Donaldson who had been expelled from the SNP on account of his extreme views. Having founded his own pro-independence party, United Scotland, Donaldson became a leading opponent of conscription, and was eventually arrested in 1941.

At the time his supporters believed that his arrest was due to his views on conscription but it was later revealed that he had been targeted by MI5. Donaldson had reportedly told one of its agents that he anticipated a German invasion and that he would be prepared to establish an independent but pro-Nazi Scottish government similar to the administration established by Vidkun Quisling after the fall of Norway. The agent reported these findings to his superior officer

Richard Brooman-White, an artillery officer from Dumbarton who had been forced to leave the army due to ill health, and was working at the time for a new section of MI5 devoted to scrutinising 'Celtic movements': 'The movement in Scotland must then be able to show the German government that it is organised and has a clear-cut policy, that it is not with England in the war. The German government will give them every possible assistance in their early struggle, and when fire and confusion is at its height in England the movement can start in earnest.'[37]

As a result of Donaldson's discussions with the MI5 agent, his arrest was ordered by the Lord Advocate Thomas Cooper with the backing of Lord Rosebery, who had succeeded Johnston as Regional Commissioner for Civil Defence on the latter's promotion to Secretary of State for Scotland (see Chapter 5). However, after spending five weeks in Barlinnie Prison in Glasgow Donaldson was released on Johnston's orders either because the evidence was too flimsy or, more likely, because MI5 could not afford to jeopardise its position if the incident ever became public property. Donaldson survived the war and later became the SNP's chairman in the 1960s.

Other leading Scots who flirted briefly with the idea of dealing with Nazi Germany were the poets Hugh MacDiarmid and George Campbell Hay (Deorsa Mac Iain Deorsa), a Gaelic speaker who lived in Edinburgh having been educated at Fettes and Oxford. Writing to fellow poet Sorley MacLean (Somhairle MacGill-Eain) on 5 June 1940, MacDiarmid put forward the idea that while 'the Germans are appalling enough and in the short-term view more murderously destructive, they cannot win – but the British and French bourgeoisie can, and is a far greater enemy'.[38] Within this same period (but a year earlier) Hay would have been quite content to see southern Britain overrun by the Nazis, writing to Douglas Young in May 1939 that it would be history's revenge: 'Of course there will be starvation – in England. It will be an interesting thing for Ireland to watch.'[39]

Donaldson, and to a lesser extent, Young and Hay, clearly believed that there was little difference between government from Westminster or Berlin, and that Scotland had much to gain following the confusion of an invasion and the establishment of Nazi rule, but their thinking was never put to the test. On 17 September Operation Sealion was postponed, and the Germans began returning their invasion barges to the Rhine. By then the Battle of Britain had been fought, and the German failure to win air superiority had put paid to any immediate thought of a cross-Channel invasion. By then, too, Hitler's strategic goals had also changed: on 18 December he issued a new Directive No. 21 in which he ordered his forces to be prepared to 'crush Soviet Russia in a rapid campaign'.

5 Scotland's Conscience, Moral and Political

By the 1930s most of the political optimism generated by the end of the First World War had evaporated. Scotland entered the Second World War with recent memories of the economic depression and a fractured political system which seemed to be incapable of grappling with the country's manifold problems. In the aftermath of the First World War the Liberal party had begun its long and painful decline, and as it did so, a pattern began to emerge in Scottish politics. Both the Conservatives and Labour had picked up support from the Liberals but each benefited in different ways. Increasingly the middle classes were seen as the preserve of the Conservatives who worked hard to build up core support in country areas and amongst young people who wanted to 'get on in life'. Labour continued to look for support from the industrial working class, especially in the central belt but also got backing from moderates and free-thinkers who saw them as the coming party and an engine for social change.

During that inter-war period Scottish politics remained largely unionist in complexion but that did not mean that nationalist or home rule sentiments had been eclipsed, even though one of the first political casualties of the First World War had been a bill aimed at producing a measure of political devolution for Scotland. In May 1914 a Home Rule Bill had passed its second reading in the House of Commons, mainly as a result of the promptings of the Scottish Home Rule Association and the Young Scots Society, a radical-minded grouping within the ruling Liberal Party who described themselves at the time of their inception in 1901 as being in favour of free trade, social reform and what they called 'the unquenchable and indefinable spirit of nationalism'. They were also pro-Boer, much to the ire of unionist newspapers such as the *Scotsman*.[1] The bill had envisaged the creation of a devolved Scotland within the framework of a new federal structure for the United Kingdom or, as prime minister H. H. Asquith put it, the new union would have a peculiarity: 'that while for common purposes all its constituent members can deliberate and act together, none of them is at liberty to deal with those matters which are specially appropriate and necessary for itself without the common consent of all.'[2] The Liberals had supported the concept of home rule since the 1880s when it seemed that Ireland would be granted a measure of independence as part of William Ewart Gladstone's desire to settle the 'great moral issue of Ireland' and that in the process Scotland would lose out. In 1894 and 1895 Scottish home rule bills had gained parliamentary majorities but had not been passed due to lack of parliamentary time. The Liberals had also been responsible for the creation in 1885 of the Scottish Office under the leadership of a secretary for Scotland who had specific responsibilities in a number of areas including education, agriculture and fisheries.

This latest bill was swept away by the great tide of war in the summer of 1914 but the notion of home rule or devolution was not entirely dead. In 1918 the Scottish Home Rule Association was revived by Roland Muirhead, a radical businessman from Lochwinnoch who was also a prominent nationalist, and it attracted the support of many other leading ILP members including James Maxton and Tom Johnston. During that same period both the Scottish Council of the Labour Party and the Scottish Trades Union Congress passed resolutions in favour of home rule and for Scotland to be represented at the Versailles peace negotiations as an independent country. In the following year, 1920, the Executive of the Scottish Council of the Labour Party adopted a draft bill which stated that 'a determined effort should be made to secure Home Rule for Scotland in the first session of Parliament, and that the question should be taken out of the hands of place-hunting lawyers and vote-catching politicians by the political and industrial efforts of the Labour Party in Scotland which should co-ordinate all its forces to this end, using any legitimate means, political or industrial, to secure the establishment of a Scottish Parliament'.[3] However, the proposal failed to find any backers, as did two later efforts in 1924 and 1927 when Scottish Home Rule bills were unsuccessfully introduced, respectively, by George Buchanan, ILP MP for the Gorbals, and the Rev. James Barr, ILP MP for Motherwell.

However, it was not all a lost cause. Through Buchanan's and Barr's efforts interest in nationalism had been given a boost, and on 23 June 1928 the National Party of Scotland was founded in Stirling. Its membership was variegated – a mixture of intellectuals, idealists, students and disenchanted former ILP members – and its first chairman was Muirhead, while its secretary was John MacCormick, a young Glasgow lawyer with a talent for public speaking. Six years later it joined forces with the Scottish Party to become the Scottish National Party (SNP) but by then membership of the party was in a parlous state, having dropped to 2,000 in September 1939.[4]

The coming of war could have been a body blow to the new party – a planned all-party convention on home rule had to be cancelled – but there was a new rallying call. Two years earlier, during the 1937 party convention, the SNP passed a resolution which declared that it was 'strongly opposed to the manpower of Scotland being used to defend an Empire in the government of which she has no voice', a move which committed its members of military age to refuse to be conscripted until a separate Scottish government had been formed. The same meeting stopped short of attempting to secure Scottish neutrality in the event of war but the decision to oppose conscription gave a clear indication of the strength of the party's anti-war sentiments. An Anti-Conscription League founded by Wendy Wood, a radical and somewhat unortho- dox political activist, defended the 'constitutional right' of Scots to avoid military service while the Scottish Neutrality League argued that Scotland should be allowed to demand neutrality in the event of a war. As it happened, the SNP dropped the measure on the outbreak of war but that decision was hotly contested and did not imply a complete willingness to support the wartime Westminster government. In April 1940 the SNP broke ranks when it put up a candidate to fight a by- election in Argyll. Although an electoral truce had been instituted by all the main parties on the outbreak of war the SNP did not feel bound to accept it and fought a doughty campaign in which the candidate was its leader William Power, a noted poet and journalist. As might have been expected, the Conservatives retained the seat (Major Duncan McCallum, 12,317 votes) but Power did well to garner 7,308 votes, or 37.2 per cent of the poll, and might have done better had not the Germans invaded Norway two days before polling day, a move which underlined the parlous nature of the country's war effort.

Power was an interesting character. Born in Glasgow in 1873 he came from farming stock, originally from Angus, and was well versed in his country's history and literature. Largely self-taught – he left school aged fourteen and worked in the Royal Bank of Scotland for twenty years – he began writing as a young man, and his contributions to the *Glasgow Herald* led to a permanent position as a leader writer and political commentator. All the while his interests were widening, and in the 1920s he became associated with Hugh MacDiarmid's Scottish Renaissance movement, fully supporting its credo that nationalism and internationalism could co-exist and were not mutually exclusive. An autobiography *Should Auld Acquaintance* (1937) is notable for his shrewd comments on the contemporary scene and the personalities who fashioned events during the inter-war period. However, at the time of the Argyll by-election Power was sixty-seven and his authority was waning. A fresh row was also about to erupt within the party about its attitude to conscription, and this was destined to plunge the SNP into fresh disarray.

The emergence of the new fault line was caused by the poet and academic Douglas Young who had already emerged as an outspoken opponent of the conflict by recommending that Scotland should attempt to broker a separate peace in the event of Germany winning the war. In the summer of 1940 he decided to capitalise on the SNP's earlier opposition to conscription by refusing to be called up for National Service, and began a lengthy legal defence of his actions. It was a high-profile case, not least because Young had made no secret of his beliefs – at a May Day rally in Aberdeen in 1939 he had answered a heckler by pointing out that the British government had no jurisdiction to conscript Scots against their will under the terms of the Act of Union of 1707.

No court in Scotland would uphold the view that the legislation allowed Scots to refuse conscription but Young was both a determined and a resolute fighter who was absolutely certain of the rightness of his cause. He was also instantly recognisable, being a tall rangy man with a distinctive black beard, and he possessed the intellectual capacity for a lengthy tussle with the legal profession. Born in 1913 in Tayport in Fife, he spent part of his childhood in Bengal before being educated at Merchiston Castle School, the University of St Andrews and New College, Oxford where he studied classics. At the time of his protest he was teaching Greek at King's College, Aberdeen where he had become involved in nationalist politics, becoming chairman of the local party branch. As to the conduct of the war, his opinion was unequivocal: Scotland should be granted Dominion status with 'no acquiescence in the unconstitutional conscription, either for military purposes or, as was soon imposed, for industrial work.'[5] This did not make Young an all-out pacifist but he remained true to his principles as far as conscription was concerned, and his position is made clear in a poem, 'Auntran Blads', which was written at the time of his refusal to be conscripted.

> Instans tyrannus—But och, why fash
> for the waesome war, that doesna inspire us,
> nae me oniewey, wi onie rowth o pleasure,
>   as weel warssle wi the Antinoe papyrus [Antinoöpolis, situated in
>   Middle Egypt].[6]

When he did make enquiries about his personal position in 1940 the official response was that Young was in a reserved occupation and would not be called up for National Service, but this changed in the spring of 1942. Having been 'de-reserved' (as he put it) and having received his call-up papers Young promptly refused to attend the obligatory attestation and medical examination. (Ironically, because he did not enjoy robust health this would probably have found him unfit for service.)

As had happened during the First World War there was a system for conscientious objectors to register their refusal to serve, but this time round it was a much fairer process. Once their objection had been registered, they had to appear before a tribunal whose members had to include a trade union representative and a lawyer but no longer required the presence of a serving officer from the armed forces. Objectors were also allowed to produce letters of support, and were encouraged to bring a character witness to speak on their behalf, but it was still a daunting process. Having failed to convince his tribunal Young was allowed to take his appeal to an appellate tribunal chaired by a sheriff who was clearly sympathetic but still refused to grant him any leeway. In the words of Young's friend and fellow writer Compton Mackenzie, the situation almost became farcical: 'Douglas

Young, six feet and six inches tall, thin and bearded, argued with an elderly Sheriff that the Treaty of Union had conveyed no power to the Parliament of the United Kingdom to conscribe the Scots for foreign service. The Sheriff, who must have thought that he had something like a totem pole before him, congratulated Douglas Young on the able presentation of his case and then, expressing regret, sentenced him to twelve months' imprisonment.'[7]

Having been sentenced, Young immediately gave notice that he would appeal, and it was at this stage that the SNP began imploding. In April 1942 their good showing in Argyllshire was not repeated at a similar by-election in Glasgow Cathcart where their candidate William Whyte only polled 1,000 votes, coming a poor fourth behind the Labour candidate and two independents, one of which was the Hon. William Douglas-Home, a well-known and successful playwright and son of the 13th Earl of Home, who had already come to prominence by opposing Churchill's policy of seeking Germany's unconditional surrender as a pre-condition of ending the war.[8]

Two months later, by a small majority (thirty-three to twenty-nine), Power was ousted from the leadership of the SNP by Young, and at the same time MacCormick left the party with his supporters to establish the rival Scottish Convention. This marked the climax of a long-simmering row which had been triggered by a clash of rival political ideologies. MacCormick believed in consensus politics in which he sought to unite people of any political persuasion to support the common cause of home rule. Others, notably Arthur Donaldson and Dr Robert D. McIntyre, put their trust in the emergence of the SNP as an independent party fighting to gain an electoral mandate for home rule and the creation of a Scottish parliament. This latter view was supported by the majority of the younger members, and it was their support which provided the impetus for Young's victory. Some idea of the animus created by this confrontation can be seen in an open letter written by Donaldson to MacCormick after the latter claimed that Young's supporters had plotted against him in the offices of the pacifist Socialist Party in Burnside Street in Glasgow. This was denied by Donaldson: 'It would seem in fact that, far from there having been a successful conspiracy to unseat you, the result was as big a shock (but more pleasant) to your opponents as it was to you. It would appear to have been due, first to a general realisation within the

Scottish National Party that a continuation of your dominance, however disguised, meant an early demise of the Party; and, second, to the ineptitude, petulance and, latterly, vindictiveness shown by you at the Conference.'[9]

Although many members deplored this fatal tendency to schism, the split did determine the future direction of the SNP. McIntyre, a public health doctor from Hamilton, became secretary, and bent his considerable energies towards reforming the SNP's strategies with the aim of making it electable. As for the new chairman, Young's appeal failed when it was heard in the High Court in Edinburgh, and he spent the next nine months in Saughton Prison.

Alone of the British political parties the SNP made conscientious objection an issue for public debate, but there were a number of other groups which either opposed the war or established networks to help those who wished to object to conscription. The No-Conscription League had branches throughout Scotland, and on Sunday 19 November 1939 organised a packed meeting in St Andrew's Halls Glasgow where one of the speakers was Guy Aldred, a leading pacifist from the previous conflict. During the course of the Second World War some 60,000 men and 1,000 women registered as conscientious objectors across the UK, and the figures were particularly high in Scotland. In Britain as a whole the average rate of refusal was 19 per cent, whereas the figures for Scotland were: South-West Scotland, 41 per cent; South-East Scotland, 34 per cent; North of Scotland, 50 per cent; and North-East Scotland, 22 per cent.[10]

Those whose objections were upheld were offered a variety of alternatives. As in the First World War, the tribunals had the power to allow full exemption from military service, without conditions; or exemption conditional on doing alternative civilian service; or exemption only from combatant duties in the army.[11] Otherwise they could dismiss an application altogether and the applicant would have to do National Service or face prosecution. Under legislation provided by Emergency Powers (Defence) No. 93 there were four local tribunals in Scotland – South-Eastern (Edinburgh), South-Western (Glasgow), North-Eastern (Aberdeen) and Northern (Inverness). Each was chaired by a sheriff or sheriff-substitute, with four members appointed by the Ministry of Labour and four impartial members, at least two of whom were women. By July 1947 the tribunals in

Edinburgh and Aberdeen had been wound up, with Glasgow remaining for the whole of Scotland to deal with young men who objected to being called up for post-war National Service.[12]

Throughout the Second World War those who refused to serve in the armed forces but were not wholly opposed to participating in the conflict were usually offered the alternative of serving in the Non-Combatant Corps. This was another relic from the First World War which had been revived in August 1940, and permitted those who served in it to work on projects 'not involving the handling of military material of an aggressive nature'. All told, 6,766 conscientious objectors took this course of action, and served with considerable courage as unarmed soldiers, mainly as medical orderlies with the Royal Army Medical Corps (RAMC), while 465 men volunteered to serve as bomb-disposal operatives with the Royal Army Ordnance Corps (RAOC). One of the Scots who took that route was Edwin Morgan from Glasgow, later to be a fine poet, who served as a non-combatant medic in North Africa with 42nd General Hospital, RAMC. Later in life he recorded some of his memories and impressions in his collection *The New Divan*.

> I dreaded stretcher-bearing,
> my fingers would slip on the two sweat-soaked handles,
> my muscles not used to the strain.
> The easiest trip of all I don't forget,
> in the desert, that dead officer
> drained of blood, wasted away,
> leg amputated at the thigh,
> wrapped in a rough sheet, light as a child,
> rolling from side to side of the canvas,
> with faint terrible sound
> as our feet stumbled through the sand.[13]

After the war Morgan returned to teach at Glasgow University and emerged as a brilliantly innovative poet who became Scotland's first 'Makar' or poet laureate in 2004.

Another reluctant Scottish soldier-poet in the Middle East was George Campbell Hay who had earlier expressed considerable diffidence about the possibility of a German invasion. In December 1938 he had joined the activist Wendy Wood's Comunn airson Saorsa na h-Alba (League for the Independence of Scotland) which argued for a plebiscite on Scottish independence, and which led Hay to believe that at long last 'Scotland is awakening'. At the outbreak of war he had started training as a teacher in Edinburgh with the aim of getting a position in the Highlands but in April 1940 he was eventually called up for National Service. His appeal failed, and when ordered to attend a medical examination he took himself off to hide in the Argyll hills rather than be conscripted. Predictably, he was quickly arrested, and after a brief period of imprisonment he joined the Royal Army Ordnance Corps and saw service in North Africa as part of Operation Torch at the end of 1942.

Other Scottish writers who also registered as conscientious objectors were the poet Norman MacCaig, the short story writer Fred Urquhart and the novelist and journalist Cliff Hanley. Another poet, James King (J. K.) Annand, also toyed with the idea of declaring his objections but when the time came to be conscripted he changed his mind 'because I felt that I really ought to be involved in what was happening in Europe.'[14] Annand had been taught in his native Edinburgh at Broughton School where one of his teachers had been George Ogilvie, an early influence on Hugh MacDiarmid, and other contemporaries or near contemporaries were fellow poets A. D. Mackie and Roderick Watson Kerr. Having graduated from Edinburgh University he was teaching when war broke out. When he was called up he volunteered to serve in the Royal Navy, and saw service on the Arctic convoys before being commissioned in 1943. Like Morgan, his war experiences influenced later poetry such as 'Atlantic 1941' which offers a bleak perspective of life on a convoy escort.

> And little I thocht to be lockit in
> A magazine like a jyle,
> Or end my days in the choking clart
> O a sea befylt wi ile.[15]

After the war Annand returned to teaching, as did his fellow Edinburgh poet Norman MacCaig, but there was a difference. Born in Edinburgh in 1910, MacCaig had decided quite early in his life that he was not going to do anything which involved using weapons: 'I just refused to kill people; simple as that.'[16] When war broke out he was working as a primary school teacher in Edinburgh, and his call-up papers arrived in the winter of 1941. At the tribunal he explained his reasons for objecting to military service, not on the grounds of religion or politics, but on the grounds of his refusal to wilfully take life. As a result he was sent to a Non-Combatant Corps company at Ilfracombe in Devon which was linked to the Royal Pioneer Corps. However MacCaig refused the order, and was arrested and held in the guardhouse at Edinburgh Castle where he was eventually sent under military escort to Ilfracombe. For a while it worked well enough, and MacCaig remembered being involved in fire-watching and basic farm work, but in 1944 his company was detailed to work in a tank depot and he refused because 'if I'm working in a tank depot I might as well drive a tank'.[17]

As a result of his decision MacCaig faced trial by court-martial in Aldershot, and was sentenced to ninety-three days in prison, the time being spent in Winchester Prison and Wormwood Scrubs in London. On release he was sent back to Edinburgh where he worked as a jobbing gardener for the rest of the war. That should have been that, but there was an unfortunate corollary. MacCaig returned to teaching in the city but throughout his post-war career he was consistently refused any promotion, being turned down on ten occasions for the post of deputy headmaster. Later, at a civic reception, by which time he was a well-known poet, he met the Lord Provost who had chaired the Education Committee and asked him outright if it was true that his applications had been blocked because of his background as a conscientious objector. The Lord Provost admitted as much, and revealed that MacCaig's applications had been resolutely opposed by a Church of Scotland minister sitting on the committee. On the other hand, noted MacCaig, throughout his war service there was 'never a word of abuse from the armed forces – just the civilians'.[18] That was a widely held perception, and it was generally the case that 'conchies', as they were disparagingly known, were better treated in the Second World War than they had been in the previous conflict. Even so, that judgmental term remained in regular use: when appointments were being made to appellate tribunals a scribbled note on a Scottish Home Department memorandum of 24 May 1940 read: 'I believe that Lord Fleming is accepting the conchy post [as chair of an appellate tribunal].'[19]

In addition to sending men to the Non-Combatant Corps, tribunals could also enforce essential civilian work in areas such as agriculture or forestry, hospitals and social service. Inevitably, this was seen by many civilians as a soft option, hence the abuse which was frequently heaped on conscientious objectors. For that reason tribunals often recommended that applicants should be posted to other areas of the country to work away from home so that in some small measure they were making similar sacrifices to those serving in the armed forces. Female applicants were given the choice between the women's military services (provided that weapons were not involved), civil defence, or work in industry, often in armaments factories. For an unhappy few who either refused point blank to accept any kind of service or fell foul of the military authorities, there was no option but a custodial sentence. By the end of the war, about 5,000 men and 500 women had been charged with offences to do with conscientious objection, and most of them were sent to prison. A further 1,000 or more were court-martialled and given prison sentences for refusing to obey military orders. At least 10 per cent of those involved would have been Scots.

Looking back at the cases involving Scottish writers who were also conscientious objectors it is hard to avoid the impression that there was a fair degree of official spite involved in the actions against them. This seems to have been the case with Douglas Young. Having been released from Saughton where, by his own account he had been treated reasonably well – he continued work on a commentary on the Greek poet Theognis and was allowed to possess the relevant texts – he was soon in trouble again after bring released. In February 1944 the SNP contested a by-election in Kirkcaldy Burghs with Young as their candidate and, thanks largely to McIntyre's efforts, he came close to causing a major upset, polling 42 per cent of the votes, as opposed to the government candidate's 52 per cent. What is more, not only was he known as a conscientious objector but the main plank in his campaign was a promise to introduce a bill to give Scotland Dominion status similar to the British North America Act of 1867 which established the Dominion of Canada. Even an establishment newspaper like the *Scotsman* was forced to concede that Young and the SNP could not be dismissed as a flash in the pan: 'There is here something which the Government and the Scottish Office must take note of. Mr Douglas Young is a fervid Scottish nationalist who refused from conviction to obey the law of a Government whose authority to conscribe Scotsmen he denied. Kirkcaldy Burgh electors, instead of ridiculing his constitutional claim, went to the polls and voted for him in very large numbers.'[20]

Instead, the authorities took a different tack, and in the summer Young was conscripted once more, this time by the Ministry of Labour to undertake non-military service. Once again he was forced to appear before an appellate tribunal where he was sentenced to a statutory three months in prison. Once again he appealed, this time on the grounds that conscription was a violation of Clause XVIII of the Act of Union of 1707 which seemed to safeguard Scots from being sent abroad by a Westminster government. This stood or fell on the interpretation of the wording that 'no alteration be made to laws which concern private right, except for evident utility of the subjects within Scotland' and it was doomed to fail. Young received a good deal of public sympathy and support but he was sent back to Saughton for a second term where the prison authorities again allowed him to continue his academic work. Even so, he continued to stand up for his rights and requested provision of additional electric light and the use of a typewriter. His fellow prisoners were not forgotten, and in one complaint he claimed that inmates at Saughton were not receiving their allotted rations, for example criticising the 'duffs' (steamed or boiled flour puddings) which 'have their raisins few and far between & are soggy & unpalatable'.[21]

He was released on 7 December 1944, and after the war returned to teaching, firstly in Dundee and then in St Andrews. As a poet he was prominent in the post-war debates about the use of Scots or 'Lallans'; however, in politics he left the SNP and rejoined the Labour Party after the former rejected the common cause policy and voted in favour of banning members from joining other political parties.

However, despite those high profile cases the issue of conscription did not give the SNP the political leverage which its fundamentalist members might have wanted. It was, though, a useful stick with which to beat the government, and another opportunity came in 1943 when the party campaigned to prevent the unpopular conscription of 13,000 unmarried Scottish girls to work in munitions factories in the English Midlands. The scheme had attracted widespread criticism across Scotland, especially as it seemed to involve a degree of coercion, with the girls being locked in reserved railway compartments, and was being overseen by female supervisors during the journey south. Even though the Ministry of Labour backed down, the SNP did not gain all the credit from the decision as the trades unions had also been involved. Worse (from their point of view), the protest failed to cover over the split caused by the leadership contest which had only succeeded in weakening the party by producing 'two competing sets of losers' at a time when the SNP had already been weakened, and there is little doubt that the party's leadership quarrels left it badly hamstrung for the remainder of the war.[22]

The self-destruction within the SNP also coincided with the growing strength and authority of the rule of central government from Westminster. On coming to power in May 1940, Churchill had created an all-party coalition with a War Cabinet of thirty-five ministers which included Labour leaders Clement Attlee (Deputy Prime Minister), Ernest Bevin (Minister of Labour and National Service) and Hebert Morrison (Minister of Supply); as well as Conservative allies Anthony Eden (War Office) and Lord Beaverbrook (Aircraft Production). In the initial months of his leadership Churchill was preoccupied with the threat of German invasion which had been ended by the failure of the Luftwaffe to gain supremacy during the Battle of Britain, and it was not until the beginning of 1941 that he visited Scotland, travelling first to Edinburgh on 3 January and then again on 17 January when he met Tom Johnston and visited civil defence services in Glasgow. The latter visit was supposed to be a secret but when Churchill's train arrived in the city his private secretary Sir John Martin recalled that 'a mob of hundreds if not thousands was waiting at Queen Street Station and we had to fight our way to the cars and then into the City Chambers'.[23]

Afterwards Churchill made an impromptu speech, and that evening dined with Johnston and Lord Provost Dollan before returning overnight to London. It turned out to be a momentous occasion. In the official party was Harry Hopkins who acted as US President Franklin D. Roosevelt's special emissary, and was in the country to assess Britain's position before deciding whether or not to offer any American support to the war effort. After the dinner several informal speeches were made and Johnston invited his American guest to address the gathering, having ascertained earlier that Hopkins was proud of his Scottish ancestry and his antecedents from Perthshire. As Johnston recorded at the time, Roosevelt's envoy's words were not mere pleasantries but could be read as an emotionally charged signal to his hosts.

> Mr Chairman, I am not making speeches here. I am reporting what I see to Mr Franklin Delano Roosevelt, my President, a great man, a very great man. But now that I am here and on my feet perhaps I might say in the language of the old book to which my grand-mother from Auchterarder, and no doubt your grandmother too, Mr Chairman, paid so much attention, that (and here Hopkins paused and looked straight down the table at Churchill) Where-soever thou goest we go, and where thou lodgest we lodge, thy people shall be our people, thy God our God, even unto the end.[24]

Hopkins was indulging in theatricality, but for Churchill, who was easily moved by any display of sentimentality, it seemed to be the first indication that the US would support the Britain in the war. The prime minister's 'eyes welled up in tears' because this was an outcome which he earnestly desired.

It was also a moment which changed Johnston's political career. Churchill was determined to strengthen his War Cabinet, and was equally determined that it should include Johnston. Although he turned down the first offer of Health, on 9 February he accepted the position of Secretary of State for Scotland which had been previously held by Ernest Brown and Sir John Colville. It was an astute appointment. Johnston was a well-respected Labour politician and proved to be a capable administrator with an appetite for hard work and an ambition to get things done. Churchill also realised that with such an important Labour member in the Scottish Office there would be little chance of history repeating itself on the Clyde, which remained relatively strike-free throughout the war.

The perception of Johnston as a strong man who could manage Scotland on his own gave him considerable benefits. Not only did his Cabinet colleagues generally bow to his wishes or leave him to his own devices, at least as far as Scotland was concerned, but it created the freedom to evolve his own way of doing things. He was also in a position to name his own conditions before accepting the post. The first was personal in that he asked to work without his ministerial salary, just as he had done while serving as Regional Commissioner, thereby underlining his own independence. ('My resources are adequate to my needs but I don't want to make a song and dance about it.') The second condition was equally shrewd. He told Churchill that he wanted to establish 'a Council of State for Scotland – a council composed of all the living ex-Secretaries for Scotland, of all parties; and whenever we were all agreed upon a Scottish issue, I could look to you for backing!' Although the prime minister could see that this would be a kind of shadow Scottish national government whose decisions would be difficult to countermand, he agreed to both conditions.[25]

The council came into being in September, and it was composed of five of Johnston's predecessors in office, all of whom had contributed significantly to political life in Scotland and the UK. Lord Alness, as Robert Munro, had held the position as a Liberal between 1916 and 1922, and was one of the longest-serving secretaries; amongst other matters he had been responsible for suppressing Tom Johnston's magazine *Forward* in 1915 while serving as Lord Advocate. Archibald Sinclair, a Liberal and a friend and confidante of Churchill, held the post between 1931 and 1932, and became Secretary of Air in 1940; after the war he was ennobled as Viscount Thurso. Walter Elliot was Conservative Secretary of State for Scotland between 1936 and 1938, and had proved to be an innovator and interventionist responsible for the creation of the Hillington industrial estate and a firm supporter of the Empire Exhibition of 1938. John Colville had occupied the post in Chamberlain's government at the beginning of the war, and was later appointed governor of Bombay; after the war he was ennobled as Baron Clydesmuir. Ernest Brown, Johnston's immediate predecessor, had become Secretary of State for Scotland in Churchill's 1940 government, and was unusual in being an Englishman.

From the outset the new body showed that it meant business by instituting a series of inquiries which would investigate areas of regeneration and renewal. It held its first meeting at the Scottish Office in London on 29 September 1941, and boldly set out its immediate ambitions which the council members thought would be for the long-term good of Scotland after the war: 'The Council would consider Scotland's post-war problems, set up enquiries as necessary (deciding their priority) and survey the results. While the responsibility for any action taken remained with Ministers, the advice and support of the Council would be of the utmost value. The object was, of course, that at the end of hostilities the Government should have available authoritative advice on the questions considered and should be in a position to act at once.'[26]

At that first meeting twelve main areas were identified for further investigation: hydro-electric development, the herring industry, hill sheep farming, gas grids, regionalisation of water supplies, unification of hospital services, housing, health services, food production, dairy farming, the white-fish industry and industrial development. Although most of them were imbued with revivalist, even messianic, intentions (a good example being an ill-fated scheme to introduce citizenship in schools) they also helped to point the way to the country that Scotland would become in the post-war world.[27]

Perhaps the most successful of those initiatives was the first committee of inquiry into the development of hydro-electric power in the Highlands which was chaired by Lord Cooper, the formidably energetic and resourceful Lord Advocate. It helped that he was of scientific bent and combined a keen intellect with a forensic mind, and his committee worked quickly and efficiently to produce the report which Johnston, a keen proponent of hydro-electric power, wanted. The idea of harnessing Scotland's water assets to produce electricity was not new: following a number of small private attempts to use hydro-electric power at Fort Augustus and Strathpeffer, the system came into its own in the 1930s with the development of the aluminium smelter at Kinlochleven before the First World War and the first major integrated hydro-electric complex at Tongland in Kirkcudbrightshire.

There was a snag. Although these had shown that hydro-electric power was technically and economically viable, many of these pioneering innovations had either been squandered or scandalously neglected. One reason was the influence of the coal lobby, which feared that the industry's pre-eminence and profitability would be challenged by the introduction of a new and potentially dangerous system. The other main opposition came from landowners who argued that the arrival of dams, pipelines and pylons would ruin the essentially primitive nature of the Scottish Highlands and its indigenous wildlife. As a result of their objections six hydro-electric projects had been turned down at Westminster in 1940, largely as a result of well-organised landed opposition to their introduction. Johnston was keenly aware of what was happening. Likening those groups to 'corbies' (hooded, or carrion, crows) who were driven by self-interest and had little or no concern for the good of the country, he promised he would personally 'inform the 51st Division when it returned after the war of the names and addresses of the saboteurs.'[28]

Fortunately Cooper and his committee were objective and pains-taking in their approach, and during the collection of evidence they spread their net widely. When he finally reported on 15 December 1942 his paper carried a stinging rebuke to those who had attempted to stymie the introduction of hydro-electric power in the Highlands, claiming that 'all major issues of policy, both national and local have tended to become completely submerged in the conflict of contend-ing sectional interests'.[29] Not only would the continuation of such attitudes have a deleterious effect on the future economy of the Highlands, but the Cooper Report stated bluntly that any regenera-tion could not be dependent purely on prohibitively expensive thermal power stations. This was music to Johnston's ears, and the main recommendations were incorporated in the Hydro-Electric Development (Scotland) Bill which became law the following year.

To all intents and purposes the act nationalised the development of Scotland's natural water assets in the Highlands by creating the North of Scotland Hydro-Electric Board. This became responsible for the construction of the necessary infrastructure and also for ensuring that the Highlands as a whole benefited from the introduction of afford-able and environmentally friendly power. This latter point was central to Johnston's political viewpoint, namely that there was a social welfare aspect to the legislation – a key point in section two of the act insisted that profits from the scheme should be used for 'the economic development and social improvement of the North of Scotland'. This was seized upon by Conservatives as socialism, or worse, and Johnston had to fight extremely hard to ensure that the legislation passed through parliament unscathed by its main oppo-nents. Quite apart from his own innate parliamentary abilities, he was helped by the support of eight Cabinet colleagues, notably the

Chancellor of the Exchequer Sir Kingsley Wood, and by the board's first chairman, the Earl of Airlie who was frequently vilified by his fellow landowners. To these attacks Johnston responded that he would not be dissuaded by 'a few shameless twelfth of August shooting tourists, who themselves took care to live in the electrified south for eleven months of the year [and] moaned about the possible disappearance in the Highlands of the picturesque cruisie [open boat-shaped lamp with a rush wick]'.[30]

The creation of the hydro board (as it quickly became known) was one of the high-water marks of Johnston's tenure as Secretary of State for Scotland, and he was justly proud of the achievement. Although there would be problems in implementing the scheme in the post-war world, and many of the wartime objections returned to haunt the board, it was still a hugely altruistic innovation, and one which pointed the way to later policies which depended as much on social vision as on economic good sense. It also proved the capability of the Council of State, as it was the first occasion when a piece of specifically Scottish legislation reached the statute book without a division.

The success also prompted Johnston to extend the reach of his activities in Scotland by encouraging a more inclusive approach to politics and by putting Scotland first wherever possible. Here he was only partially successful. An attempt to rejuvenate the Scottish Grand Committee foundered due to lack of general interest amongst Scottish MPs who believed, probably rightly, that it was only a talking shop and a poor one at that. First formed in 1907, it was established to provide Scottish MPs with the opportunity to consider the committee stage of Scottish bills, but although Johnston saw it as a means of rectifying the democratic deficit by reinforcing the committee as a forum for Scottish affairs, its few meetings were badly attended. Robert Boothby, the outspoken Conservative MP for East Aberdeenshire, was probably not far wrong when he dismissed it as 'a pretty dismal fiasco', and was scornful of its pretensions to resemble an alternative 'Scottish National Parliament'.[31] It certainly did not meet Johnston's hopes for the introduction of a form of Scottish self-government.

More successful and certainly more to the point was the creation of the Scottish Council on Industry which was chaired by Sir William Young Darling, Lord Provost of Edinburgh and a director of the

Royal Bank of Scotland. Representatives came from the Chambers of Commerce, the Scottish Trade Union Congress, the Scottish Development Council, the Scottish Office and local authorities. Under existing wartime legislation most of Scotland's social and economic life was largely governed by Whitehall departments such as the Ministry of Labour and the Board of Trade and their agencies, leaving law and order, the health service, agriculture and education in the hands of the departments of the Scottish Office. This meant that there was little Scottish input into wartime production, economic planning and industrial investment, with the result that Scottish industry missed out on the increased production levels and was largely used for storage. Indeed, the Cabinet noted at the time that there was a distinct reluctance for Scottish firms to take advantage of existing and new schemes for wartime expansion even though funds had been made available on a UK basis.[32] Johnston was determined to change that and outlined his thinking at the fifth meeting where he claimed that 'the stage was now set for all possible preventive action to stop, save in cases where good cause was shown, the drift south of industry, particularly peace-time industries'.[33] In short, Johnston wanted Scottish industry to get a fair share of wartime contracts both to maintain production and to retain employment.

There was still a lot of leeway to be made up following the downturn of the economy during the Depression years. The poor housing stock, especially in the west of Scotland, prevented mobility and led to large-scale emigration to England – the relocation of Stewarts & Lloyds to Corby in Northamptonshire being a prime example. During the 1920s an estimated 400,000 people left Scotland as a direct result of poor housing conditions or unemployment; in Dundee alone the rate in the jute industry rose to over 70 per cent in 1931 and 1932. Steps had been taken to rectify the situation through regional assistance schemes but it is noticeable that Scotland missed out on many of the opportunities produced by wartime growth, either because there had been no diversification or because the available workforces were ill-equipped to meet the new challenges. Notable exceptions were the Rolls-Royce factory at Hillington, which began producing engines for Spitfire fighters in 1940, and the Ferranti facility at Crewe Toll in Edinburgh which produced gyro gunsights for the same aircraft. Within three years of arriving in the west of Scotland

Rolls-Royce was producing 400 Merlin engines a week while Ferranti came north as a result of the expansion of its defence electronics business and a lack of available labour in Manchester.

During the same period only thirty-two government-sponsored factories opened in Scotland, mainly for aircraft and vehicle production, but some things remained the same, with shipbuilding and its associated trades remaining prominent in the Scottish economy and employing over half of the available workforce.[34] Ironically, this had been foreseen by the Council of State at its third meeting on 8 December 1941 when members bemoaned 'the fact that expansion of industry in Scotland was ephemeral, being almost entirely confined to munitions and war industries, which would, from their very nature, decline rapidly after the end of hostilities, while more permanent industries were attracted to England'.[35] Even so, towards the end of the war, in July 1944, unemployment fell to 16,199 from its 1940 high of ten times that number, thanks largely to the exploitation of wartime opportunities and the stemming of the tide of workforce removals to similar factories in England.[36]

Johnston also turned his attention to agriculture and fisheries, both devolved issues with their own department in the Scottish Office. Both were central to the war economy, and it soon became apparent that there were anomalies which did not always favour Scotland's interests. From the outset Johnston favoured the introduction of a uniform milk price across the UK because Scottish milk producers had been missing out by almost one penny a gallon, a loss which was exacerbated by the heavier costs in road transport. In an effort to ameliorate the latter problem the War Cabinet decided on 1 October 1942 to authorise the Milk Marketing Board and the Scottish Milk Marketing Board (as the sole purchasers from producers) to pay for supplies at collection centres instead of, as was done previously, at consuming centres.[37] While this did not completely resolve the issue for Scottish farmers, it was considered to be an equitable outcome as milk producers in the west of England and Wales faced similar problems, and the cost of levelling out the Scottish returns would have amounted to £300,000 a year. Hill sheep farming was also an issue. In addition to the uncertainty traditionally present in rearing upland sheep, the exigencies of wartime brought fresh problems such as coping with the bracken when labour was short and the cumulative effect of two bad springs in 1940 and 1941. Fluctuations in market prices added to the feelings of insecurity, and in 1943 the government increased the subsidy per head to eight shillings. As a result the earned net income for Scottish hill sheep farmers rose that year to £760, a threefold rise from the position at the start of the war.[38] In addition to the increased subsidy, the farmers had been helped by a Scottish Office innovation whereby surplus stock was taken to government-owned hill-grazing parks for fattening up before going to market. This came about as a result of another of Johnston's committees of inquiry, in this case chaired by Lord Balfour of Burleigh.

Another problem was the perennial lack of a decent housing stock in rural areas. In 1917 a Royal Commission on Housing in Scotland had revealed that the average farm worker's house 'has too often been selected not for its suitability as a site but for economy of land and the convenience of the farm worker. The result is that the site is often a contributing factor in the prevailing dampness of the houses, and aggravates the difficulties of water supply and drainage.'[39] Although it had been agreed that this was a matter of scandal, little had been done to resolve the issue which Johnston described as 'appalling'. In a belated attempt to make things better, in 1943 subsides were made available of £200 per house which resulted in the immediate construction of eighty cottages for farm labourers' use. As workers tended to move every six or twelve months from one farm to the next, legislation was passed in 1941 under the Essential Work (Agriculture) (Scotland) Order to prohibit the cancellation of contracts unless permission was given by the local National Service office. This was more often honoured in the breach but it did at least bring some order to the traditional movement of farm servants and the accommodation that was available to them. During the war the full-time labour force in Scotland's farms increased from 72,000 to 96,000, but this reflected the need to increase food production and the use of prisoners of war (see Chapter 9). Johnston was also justifiably proud of the first steps that were taken in fish farming at Loch Sween where marine biologists made rapid strides in the cultivation of flat fish as a means of easing the nation's food-supply problems.

It would not be unfair to claim that in managing his role as Secretary of State for Scotland Johnston regarded the country as his personal fiefdom. The robust way in which he promoted Scottish industry, agriculture and fisheries in Cabinet meetings is evidence of his concern for Scotland's best interests and his own abilities as a politician. He was also a good team player, and amply rewarded Churchill's willingness to bring him into the heart of the war government. While Johnston never warmed to the Westminster way of doing things, and disliked the constant journeying between Scotland and London, he played a full role in formulating policy. In particular, he was hugely supportive of moves to implement the Beveridge Report of 1942. Officially known as the Report of the Inter-Departmental Committee on Social Insurance and Allied Services, this ground-breaking initiative was one of the main fruits of Labour's coalition agreement with the Conservatives; it was intended to investigate and provide suggestions for thoroughly overhauling 'the existing national schemes of social insurance and Allied services, including workmen's compensation, and to make recommendations'. It was chaired by the economist Sir William Beveridge, and when it was published in December 1942 it was clear that by addressing five identifiable threats to society – want, ignorance, disease, squalor and idleness – it provided the blueprint for the implementation of a 'welfare state' once the war was over.

The central plank of the report was the provision of a national health service which would produce 'cradle-to-grave' services which would be paid for by weekly financial contributions; in return, benefits would be provided for the unemployed, the sick, the retired and the widowed. It was a ground-breaking set of reforms, and its implementation depended on a huge amount of political goodwill and a willingness to work collectively for benefits which would only become available once the war was over. The concept was dear to Johnston's heart, and from 1943 onwards he worked closely with the Minister of Health Henry Willink, Conservative MP for Croydon North, who was responsible for drafting the White Paper, *A National Health Service*, based on the recommendations of the Beveridge Report.

Another impetus behind Johnston's support for the creation of a national health service came from innovations which had been introduced to the hospital services in Scotland. At the outbreak of war thought had already been given to dealing with the expected casualties from enemy bombing attacks, and steps had been taken to increase the number of hospital beds that would be needed under the emergency powers. In Scotland that authority was given to the Scottish Department of Health which was not only responsible for administering the scheme but, unlike England and Wales, ran the participating state hospitals. Seven new hospitals were also introduced at Raigmore (Inverness), Stracathro (Angus), Bridge of Earn (Perthshire), Killearn (Stirlingshire), Law (Lanarkshire), Ballochmyle (Ayrshire) and Peel (Selkirkshire). Under the same programme new annexes were built at existing hospitals, and in total the Emergency Hospital Service (EHS) scheme in Scotland eventually produced an additional 20,500 beds, an increase of some 60 per cent on Scotland's pre-war provision.

However, although this was encouraging and demonstrated what could be done when emergency services were directed by the state and funds were made available, the expected take-up in beds never materialised. Scotland was certainly bombed, and in 1941 huge numbers of casualties were caused during the blitzes of Clydebank and Greenock (see Chapter 6), but by the end of 1942 the numbers of raids had diminished. As a result it soon became apparent that the beds were lying empty, and could therefore be put to better use, or as Johnston put it in his memoirs: 'It was obviously foolish to have the well-equipped hospitals often standing empty and their staffs awaiting Civil Defence casualties – which, thank God, never came – while war workers could not afford specialist diagnosis and treatment.'[40]

Because the Scottish Department of Health was responsible for running the EHS scheme, it was in a position to admit patients directly from the waiting lists held by the voluntary hospitals. In January 1942 hospitals with long waiting lists were allowed to refer patients who were not war casualties to the EHS hospitals, regardless of how long their treatment would last. By the end of the war 32,826 patients had been treated in this way; many of them had been on waiting lists for three months or longer.[41] By the standards of the day Johnston's policy was radical in that it made good use of existing facilities, and in so doing helped to ease the lengthy waiting lists that accumulated in the pre-war system of local authority and voluntary hospitals. It was also unique to Scotland as the Department of Health did not enjoy similar powers to its opposite number in Scotland, and in any case the English and Welsh hospitals were opposed to any introduction of this 'curious arrangement' north of the border.[42]

Cognisance also has to be made of the pioneering Highlands and Islands Medical Service (HIMS) which had been established in 1913 with a Treasury grant of £42,000 to bring basic medical care to more than 300,000 living in an area which amounted to half the Scottish land mass. Although it was not strictly free, the fees were set at minimal levels, and the scheme was operated centrally from Edinburgh where the Scottish Office worked in co-operation with local health committees. By 1929 there were 175 nurses and 160 doctors in 150 practices covering some of the most remote areas of the Highlands and Islands where doctors and nurses worked for the first time in tandem to provide the necessary care. Funds were also found to allow specialist surgeons to work in the more isolated hospitals, with the result that comprehensive health care suddenly became universally available in areas which had been previously deprived.

In 1933 when Edward Cathcart, Professor of Physiology at Glasgow University, was appointed to lead a committee of inquiry into the existing health services in Scotland, he and his colleagues concluded that HIMS produced good results because it put the general practitioner at the centre of health care: 'The Highlands and Islands Medical Service has been an outstanding success and is universally approved. On the basis of the family doctor, there has been built up by flexible central administration a system of co-operative effort, embracing the central department, private general practitioners, nursing associations, voluntary hospitals, specialists, local authorities and others, to meet the medical needs of the people.'[43] The report was published in 1936, and although it concluded that the cost of health services should be met from an extension of existing insurance schemes, many of its broader principles were embraced in the planning for the post-war National Health Service.

Even more enterprising was Johnston's introduction of the Supplementary Medical Service which from its locus was also known as the 'Clyde Basin Experiment'. Launched at the beginning of 1942, it was originally limited to workers under the age of twenty-five whose health was poor and required treatment but by the end of the year it was extended to war workers of all ages. Basically, the scheme was led by general medical practitioners who were encouraged to refer suitable patients to Regional Medical Officers for examination by a panel of suitable experts. Those requiring further treatment were admitted to EHS hospital wards or were sent to auxiliary hospitals for rest. No fees were charged, and the intended purpose of the experiment was to treat patients and to prevent further breakdowns in health 'by investigating and removing the physical, psychological or social causes.'[44] In all, by 1945 11,000 patients had been treated in this way, and Johnston received plaudits from his Cabinet colleagues both for the Clyde Basin Experiment and for the useful lessons which had been learned in preventive medical treatment in Scotland.[45] Equally successful was an ancillary scheme to provide respite and convalescent care for recovering industrial patients. Several large hotels were requisitioned for this purpose, including the opulent railway hotel at Gleneagles, where a wing was made available as a fitness centre for recuperating miners requiring physiotherapy or occupational therapy in a residential setting. Johnston was reported to be delighted by the fact that miners were being treated in this luxurious and beneficial way.

The success of the Clyde Basin Experiment and the use of EHS hospitals would help to fashion the emergence of the future National Health Service in Scotland after the war, and in so doing it would evolve somewhat differently than England and Wales (see Chapter 12). It was not perfect, and the numbers of admissions were relatively small but the bed spaces had been provided, and it had been proved that a centrally administered service could work in Scotland. The drawbacks arose from the perception of the benefits provided by the scheme. Many general medical practitioners were wary of anything which seemed to threaten their independence of action and smacked of state control, while many patients did not always want to be hospitalised or thought they were not sufficiently unwell – this applied most to the preventive measures. Finance, or lack of it, was also a factor. While the scheme was well funded, and those treated received travelling expenses and small subsistence allowances, there was no provision for compensation for loss of wages. That was clearly a factor which had to be considered by workers who had family responsibilities, and probably accounts for the low take-up in referrals for respite care. Nevertheless there is no doubt that during the war Scotland led the way in introducing fresh thinking to public health care, and it is not surprising, perhaps, that when Johnston looked back at this period in his life he regarded it as a time of innovation and enterprise when optimism was in the air: 'Meanwhile, and emanating from the activities being stirred up under what was the Council of State umbrella, there was arising a new spirit of independence and hope in our national life. You could sense it everywhere, and not least in the Civil Service. We met England now without any inferiority complex. Our tails were up. We were a nation once again.'[46]

Johnston's confidence came about as a result of all the hard work he invested in making Scotland work during the war, and it raises the question of how much he valued the idea of devolution. In his younger days he was certainly a supporter of home rule and could be described as a nationalist and patriot in a non-party political sense. As a minister in Churchill's wartime Cabinet he was not above playing the Scottish card when necessary, and was always intent on getting the country's fair share of available funds. However, he was also aware of the potency of the threat allegedly posed by extreme nationalism; at one stage in 1943 he told John Reith, Minister of Works and founding father of the BBC, that the SNP could provide the basis for a Sinn Fein-type of separatist movement should there be increased agitation for home rule.[47] Herbert Morrison, wartime Minister of Supply, told a similar story, and while Johnston may well have feared trouble from the SNP, it also suited his purpose that the concern should be aired at a time when he was consolidating his own power in Scotland.

Throughout Johnston's period at the Scottish Office there is no evidence that he ever pushed for home rule during or after the war, but that did not stop him from pursuing Scotland's best interests at a time when the realities of economic and social life were governed by Whitehall ministries. In 1944 William Leonard, Labour MP for St Rollox, published a memorandum in association with MacCormick's Scottish Convention, proposing the establishment of a Scottish government which would have authority to deal with industrial development, as well as some powers relating to Scotland which were then held by the Ministry of Labour and Ministry of Transport. Although Johnston was sympathetic, he rejected the proposal, largely because he had already tried without success to reach a similar agreement, only to be told by Treasury officials that it would add immeasurably to his own workload and would 'merely reproduce work which might without difficulty have covered Scotland as well as England in the first place'.[48] Johnston tended to agree with that assessment, and placed his faith instead in the presence of a strong Secretary of State who would argue for Scotland's fair share and ensure that UK ministries understood that point of view when directing their policies. And it has to be remembered that Johnston was above all a socialist, albeit always a gradualist, who valued the possibilities of consensus and working in a common cause. That was what was needed in wartime Scotland, and that was what he provided.

6 Total War

On a clear moonlit night on 13/14 March 1941 the terrors of modern warfare were visited on Scotland. A German bomber fleet of 236 aircraft arrived over Clydebank from three different directions to drop 270 tons of high explosive munitions and 1,700 incendiary bombs on the densely populated area below. Amongst their intended targets were the Clydebank shipyards and the complex at Hillington, but the bombers and their lethal payloads were indifferent to the fate of 50,000 civilians who lived under their flight path. (Due to the influx of workers into the area the real figure was closer to 60,000.) Shortly after 9 p.m. the air-raid sirens began to wail, first on the east coast as the raiders passed over South Queensferry, and then in Glasgow and Clydebank as the German pathfinder force, flying ahead of the main fleet, dropped green marker flares and incendiary bombs.

Their task was made easier by the use of target photographs taken by reconnaissance aircraft before the war, and also by the use of a crude radio directional navigation system known as *X-Gerät* (X apparatus). By directing a series of radio beams across the British mainland the Germans were able to direct specially fitted pathfinder aircraft towards their destinations. In this way key targets were criss-crossed and located along the route, while stop-clocks on board the aircraft accurately measured the time between them. Later in the war British scientists developed counter-measures to 'bend' the radio beams, but in 1941 *X-Gerät* was still the primary means for German bombers to find their targets.

During the Clydebank raid the pathfinder aircraft were Heinkel IIIs of Kampfgeschwader 100 which was based in north-west France. The operation was made much simpler by the clear weather conditions and by the explosions of the first incendiary bombs. These began an inferno which gave the best marker for the attacking bombers flying behind them from bases in northern France, the Netherlands and Norway. As the west of Scotland housed several strategic targets amongst the heavy industries in the area, it was no stranger to hit-and-run raids – the first had taken place a year earlier on 19 July, and another on 18 September had destroyed the cruiser HMS *Sussex* refitting at Yorkhill Dock – but it soon became obvious that the German attack on Clydebank was something different. Not only did it involve a large fleet of bombers, but they arrived at intervals in three waves between 9 p.m. and 3 a.m. the following morning.

It was a carefully planned and calibrated operation based on sound intelligence, and it followed in the wake of similar German raids on English cities such as London, Liverpool and Coventry. The attack came from the south, with the bomber fleet flying up the west coast, and the first wave veering eastwards towards Edinburgh before flying across the central belt to follow the distinctive line of the River Clyde. Towards midnight the second wave arrived, having hooked westwards, and began its attack from the north to fly in over Loch Lomond. Finally, a third wave attacked directly from the south, flying over Glasgow.

By that time the whole Clydeside conurbation was ablaze due to the intensity and accuracy of the German incendiary bombs. Casualties were caused almost immediately during the first wave when a bomb destroyed a tenement at 11 Queen Victoria Drive in Scotstoun, killing sixteen people. This was followed by direct hits on Beardmore's Diesel Works at Dalmuir, but this was only a prelude to the destruction wrought by the main force of the first wave when it arrived over the area at 9.30 p.m. Wartime censorship prevented any immediate reporting of the raid, but a month later an anonymous piece appeared in the local press describing the reaction of a family in a tenement who had taken shelter in the stairwell.

Incendiary bombs rained down, flashing up the brilliant sky, shells from the guns lit the heavens, loud reports echoed fearfully and over all, menacingly, hovering like many ghoulish, mechanical birds of prey, droned the bombers scattering death and desolation. Amid shouts and frantic gesticulations, we all cowered low as the whistling sound of a bomb was heard near at hand. Then followed a deafening explosion and the falling crash of falling masonry, and clouds of choking dust and the cries of women and children. Miraculously, in that dark hell of horror caused by brutish man, not one of our party was killed.[1]

They were lucky. The intensity of the German raid soon overwhelmed the rescue services which were further hampered by the fact that the burning buildings provided a perfect target for the bomber crews in the following waves. In the confusion, communications quickly broke down, water mains were broken, the electric power failed, streets were blocked by falling buildings and many fires burned out of control.[2]

Before the raid Clydebank possessed ten basic and twenty-one supplementary rest centres to shelter those made homeless, but owing to the extent of the bomb damage only seven were still in use after the first raid and four after the second. To make matters, worse, if that were possible, the lull between the raids gave hope that the danger had passed. Although the first wave had cleared the area by 11.30 p.m., the second force arrived from the north half an hour later and the third and final wave reached the target at three o'clock in the morning.

The all clear did not sound until 6.30 a.m. when the people of Clydebank and the surrounding areas – Glasgow, Renfrewshire, Dunbartonshire and Lanarkshire – started assessing the damage. Because Clydebank had been the epicentre of the attack it was the worst affected, but due to the 'creep back' effect which saw German bomber crews dropping their loads ahead of the intended target there was a huge radius of damage which stretched from Barrhead in the south to Balloch in the north-west and Cumbernauld in the east.[3] Parachute mines added to the terror. Not only did they leave a plethora of unexploded bombs which had to be disposed of after the raid, but by exploding at roof level they produced a hugely destructive blast. In the worst incident involving such a weapon, in Tradeston, 100 people were killed when one exploded above Nelson Street, including 11 in a passing tram. The resulting photograph of the wreck amid the rubble of buildings became one of the iconic images of what quickly became known in government circles as the Clydebank blitz: 'Clydebank, relative to its size, was "blitzed" to an extent which no other town in the country had yet suffered. Hardly a house was left undamaged, several housing schemes were completely wiped out, and by Saturday evening more than half the population had left the town. Naturally, all the public utility services were seriously damaged and completely disorganised.'[4]

In addition to the extensive damage and the sheer carnage produced by the bombs there was a huge human cost. While the raids did not produce panic, they did induce an instinct to get away from the stricken area. Around 12,000 people had been made homeless during the first night, and they were sent to rest centres in Renfrewshire, Dunbartonshire and Lanarkshire.[5] It was as well that they were evacuated because the German bombers came back the following night, and this time their task was made even easier by the guidance provided by the blazing fires. Once again the damage was extensive, and once again the rescue services were almost overwhelmed by the relentless nature of the attack and the steady build-up of casualties and destroyed buildings. At Old Kilpatrick the concentration of Admiralty fuel supplies exploded sending flames leaping into the night sky, and direct hits on Denny's Shipyard at Dumbarton destroyed the keels of two ships. When the Regional Commissioner visited Clydebank a day later he could only report that the town had 'suffered a major disaster'.[6] Three fire stations had been put out of action, many fire tenders failed to get close to the worst fires due to bomb damage in the streets and attempts at co-ordination quickly broke down in the mayhem, one example being the failure to connect hoses of different sizes and patterns.

In the immediate aftermath of the blitz, assessing the extent of the damage and the size of the casualty list proved to be no easy matter. For a start there had been a mass evacuation from Clydebank as people struggled to get away from the town. A situation report by the Department of Health revealed the extent of the evacuation and showed the lengths which the inhabitants of Clydebank were prepared to go to escape the damage: 'Considerable numbers of people went of their own accord to other areas, some to friends by means of travel warrants, some to friends finding their own transport and some finding their own transport but requiring rest centres or billeting accommodation on arrival. Reports have come in from areas as far apart as Dumfries Burgh, Bridge of Allan and Dunoon of the last class above.'[7] Mainly this was due to the fact that those fleeing the scene had been made homeless, but there was also an atavistic desire to get away from the scene of the disaster and join those who had already escaped. Amazingly, during the evacuation mass panic did not materialise.

> On the second day a large number of homeless persons estimated to amount to at least 25,000 left of their own accord, proceeding by such transport as they could find, or on foot. Thus, by the evening of Saturday the 15th March probably over 40,000 persons or more than two-thirds of the population had left the town. They left, however, in a quiet and orderly manner. At no time during the ordeal through which the town had passed or afterwards was there any sign of panic: all accounts agree that public morale was magnificent.[8]

By then first attempts had been made at assessing the death toll, and in the first few days following the raid the numbers fluctuated wildly, mainly because it proved to be difficult to retrieve bodies from the wreckage. The situation was exacerbated when the local greyhound stadium, designated as a temporary mortuary, was destroyed, and emergency centres failed to cope. Eventually, at the end of April the toll was fixed at 1,063 dead, 1,602 seriously injured, 1,727 slightly injured. This was the total for the whole of the affected areas – Glasgow, Clydebank, Renfrewshire, Dunbartonshire, Lanarkshire and Stirlingshire – with the highest numbers being in Glasgow (647 dead, 390 seriously injured, 1,290 slightly injured) and Clydebank (358 dead, 973 seriously injured, 166 slightly injured).[9] The records of Blawarthill Hospital in Clydebank tell their own story: over the two nights it treated 1,061 people, of whom 122 died, 304 were detained and 635 were treated and released.

However, although the cost to the civilian public had been enormous, with an estimated 12,000 houses destroyed or damaged, the Regional Commissioner was able to report that 'damage to industrial premises and plant was much less than expected. The shipyards, docks and factories situated in Clydebank – key points such as John Brown's, Singer's and the Royal Ordnance Factory – are of such importance that if they had suffered anything like the damage done to the houses a few hundred yards away from them the war

effort would have been dealt a heavy blow.'[10] One warship managed
to retaliate: during the raid the Polish destroyer *Piorun* was in dry dock
at John Brown's yet its crew under the command of Commander
Eugeniusz Pawski managed to man the ship's anti-aircraft guns to
return fire to the bombers overhead.

At the time a news blackout was imposed, and all reporting omitted
actual names and any description of the damage and casualties. Partly
this was done for security purposes to prevent the Germans from
gaining useful intelligence about the outcome of the raid, but other
factors were also involved, most notably the need to maintain civilian
morale at a time when there were fears that industrial unrest could
return to the Clyde's shipyards. In addition to addressing the threat
allegedly posed by extreme nationalists, the intelligence services were
also concerned about the response of the left, especially members of
the Communist Party in the west of Scotland. A few weeks earlier in
the Dunbartonshire by-election the Communist vote had been 3,862
to the Labour candidate's 21,900 (Adam McKinlay) and this had
generated fears that the vote presaged a return to the 'Red Clydeside'
strikes and agitation of the First World War.

At the time of the raids 12,000 engineering apprentices were
already on strike for higher wages but they returned to work on
the Monday and according to a Scottish Office intelligence report
most workers exhibited 'a sense of relief at having been able to stand
up to the ordeal'. The same report commented on a public meeting
held in Clydebank on 6 April involving Joseph Westwood MP,
Under-Secretary of State for Scotland, Sir Steven Bilsland, Civil
Defence Commissioner for the Western District and David Kirkwood
MP for Dumbarton Burghs. (During the First World War Kirkwood
had led a strike at Parkhead Forge while acting as convenor of shop
stewards, and had been arrested and sent into internal exile in
Edinburgh.) About 900 attended, mainly men, and although there
was some criticism of the rescue services, the Scottish Office's official
observer thought that given the circumstances of the raids the atmosphere was reasonably upbeat: 'The meeting indicated that there was
still plenty of fight in Clydebank and the audience was composed of
people whose morale did not require any stimulating but who had
some pertinent questions to which they asked for answers.'

In fact the main grievance was the shortage of time allowed for questions at the end of the meeting, but this was resolved in time-honoured fashion: 'Mr Kirkwood dealt rather vigorously with the interrupters and stimulated an even more vigorous response. This argument was continued in the street in the best traditions of Clydebank and its MP.'[11] Paradoxically, the day before the report was written, Clydebank and other targets across central and western Scotland were attacked once more, but this time the casualties were much lower – 29 killed, 71 seriously injured and 253 slightly injured.[12] Raiding continued throughout the month of April, and the last blitz-type attack took place on the nights of 5/6 May and 6/7 May when the target was Greenock. Once again the Luftwaffe used the tactics which had served them so well over Clydebank, attacking in waves using pathfinders ahead of the main bomber force and illuminating the area with flares and incendiary bombs.

Once again, too, Greenock was a valid strategic target as it was home to shipyards, the Royal Naval Torpedo Factory and a seaplane maintenance base (RAF Greenock). It was also an assembly point for the Atlantic convoys at the Tail of the Bank, and there were always resident warships from the Royal Navy and Free French Navy. Like Clydebank it was heavily populated, with workers' housing sitting alongside the various industrial and military installations. Given the circumstances, Greenock could have provided a grim repetition of the Clydebank blitz, but on this occasion there were several important differences. The first was that people took the warnings seriously and, having learned the lessons of the earlier blitz, the civil defence services were better prepared. It helped that shelter was provided by a network of tunnels at the east end of the town, and for many people these proved to be life-savers.

The second factor was the availability of a squadron of Boulton Paul Defiant night fighters of 141 Squadron based at RAF Ayr which managed to shoot down three enemy aircraft during the course of the raids. First constructed as a bomber interceptor with a crew of two, the aircraft was unusual in having a rear-ball turret as its armament. Initially successful in action against German pilots, who mistook it for the similar-looking Hurricane, its lack of forward-firing weapons proved to be its Achilles heel, and following a high loss rate it was withdrawn from frontline interception duties and converted to the night-fighter role. Although their success rate was limited during the

Greenock blitz, the presence of the Defiants in the night sky caused confusion amongst German bomber crews, frequently causing them to offload their bombs before reaching the target.

Deception also played a part on the ground. On the moorland behind Loch Thom, a reservoir two miles to the south in the hills above the town, the Air Ministry had constructed intricate decoy positions under a system known as Starfish. Using lights and various specially manufactured artifices the position resembled a built-up area, and during the second night of the raids prepared positions were set ablaze to replicate a successful bomb attack. It worked too. The 'blitz map' for Greenock and the evidence of bomb craters show that the Loch Thom Starfish site had succeeded in diverting bombers from the second waves into attacking the burning positions.[13]

If anything, the second night produced a heavier raid due to the larger size of the German bomber fleet (155 aircraft) and the still-blazing target area. The worst incident was the bombing of the Ardgowan whisky distillery where 3 million gallons of spirit ignited and proved almost impossible to bring under control. Parachute mines also proved to be lethal, not just over the intended target but also at other nearby locations including Kingswood and Drumchapel. Some 246 people died in the Greenock blitz during the two nights of raiding and 626 were injured, 290 of them seriously. A further 52 were listed as 'missing', believed killed in the town. Further afield 74 died in Port Glasgow; of that total 30 people perished while taking refuge in an air-raid shelter in Woodhall Terrace.[14]

As had happened in March, criticisms were levelled at the rescue services, and there were accounts of fear turning to panic in some areas as people tried to escape from the town – 5,575 were evacuated by the authorities – but the final finding was that vital experience had been gained at Clydebank, and that as a result the death toll was lower than had been anticipated.[15] Also on the credit side, much of Greenock's industrial capacity remained reasonably intact despite a number of direct hits on several sites including Scott's shipyard. As it turned out, the Greenock blitz was the last concerted effort by the Luftwaffe to bomb Scottish targets in great numbers.

Raids continued along the east coast throughout the year and for much of 1942, but the last recorded bomb attack on the Scottish mainland took place on the night of 21/22 April 1943 when fifteen

German aircraft attacked targets in Aberdeen, Fraserburgh and Peter-head. Amongst the buildings hit were the Gordon Barracks at the Bridge of Don, tenement buildings on the north side of Aberdeen and on railway property and tracks in the Kittybrewster area. Later it was found that 125 people had been killed on the ground.[16] The final tally for the air war over Scotland shows that the total civilian casualties for the period 1939–45 was 8,245 – 2,250 killed, 2,167 seriously injured and 3,558 slightly injured. The bulk of these were suffered in the Western District which comprised the city of Glasgow and the counties of Argyll, Ayr, Bute, Clackmannan, Dumfries, Dumbarton, Kirkcudbright, Lanark, Renfrew, Stirling and Wigtown (2,112 killed, 1,792 seriously injured and 2,578 slightly injured); the smallest numbers were in Northern District which comprised Inverness and the counties of Caithness, Inverness, Ross and Cromarty and Suther-land (21 killed, 9 seriously injured and 38 slightly injured).[17]

Tragic though these losses were, they are relatively modest compared to the greater intensity of the German blitz on England; whereas Clydebank was raided four times, Liverpool was 'blitzed' on twenty-four occasions and London on seventy-two.[18] Even so, according to internal intelligence reports, people in Glasgow and Clydebank recognised that they too were part of the national effort and that the experience of being 'blitzed' had provided a new sense of national solidarity; they were 'bearing their full share of Britain's difficulties and bearing it just as well'.[19]

The figures also pale into insignificance when compared to those from the Allied bombing campaign against Germany, especially between 1941 and 1945. Exact figures of German casualties vary, but the final estimate of the United States Strategic Bombing Survey gives the following figures for German casualties in the European theatre: 305,000 killed and 780,000 severely or slightly wounded, with 485,000 residential buildings totally destroyed by air attack and 415,000 heavily damaged. This represents a total of 20 per cent of all dwelling units in Germany, although the report also shows that in fifty cities that were primary targets of the air attack, the proportion of destroyed or heavily damaged dwelling units is about 40 per cent. The result of all attacks was to render homeless some 7,500,000 German civilians, although the researchers conceded that the figure might have been higher.[20]

However, coming on top of the earlier air raids on Scotland's east coast towns and cities in 1939 and 1940, the Clydebank blitz was a bitter reminder that in modern warfare there were many frontlines and that they were occupied by civilians as well as service personnel. Because the naval war was fought largely in the distant wastes of the north Atlantic and the Arctic Ocean, it was out of sight and often out of mind, but ports on Scotland's west coast, notably on the Clyde estuary, provided safe havens and gathering points for the main convoys. From the outset of the war the 'Atlantic Bridge' was essential for bringing in supplies and military *matériel* from north America. Canada was an important ally, providing personnel and equipment, while under the lend-lease scheme the US was a vital arsenal, and after 1942, increasingly the main force within the Allied camp. Gourock and Greenock became used to the sight of huge convoys assembling and the arrival and departure of once-elegant liners such as the Cunarder 'Queens' bedecked in wartime grey camouflage for their roles as fast transatlantic troop carriers. Throughout the war the Clyde was also the main assembly point for military convoys bound for the Middle East and Far East. Following the blitzes of 1941, when it seemed that Glasgow and Liverpool faced destruction from enemy bombing, special deepwater military ports were constructed on the west coast at Faslane and Cairnryan.[21]

The Battle of the Atlantic, as it came to be known, was the most hard-fought and dangerous campaign undertaken by the Allies, and it was one of the costliest in crews and ship losses. By the war's end 5,150 Allied and neutral merchant ships had been sunk and over 30,000 British Merchant Navy crew members had been lost; added to this figure was the loss of surface warships, especially convoy escorts, and aircraft. It was a heavy price for keeping the sea lanes open, and Churchill was correct in stating that 'the only thing that ever really frightened me during the war was the U-boat peril'.

Perhaps the most unusual consignment involving the Clyde ports was the emergency export of Britain's gold bullion reserves and securities, then worth £2 billion, which were shipped from Gourock to Halifax in Nova Scotia in October 1939, with a second convoy sailing from Greenock the following summer. All the cargo, code-named 'Fish' reached the final destination in what has been described as the biggest financial transaction in history. Another curious consignment was the cargo of the ss *Politician*, a fast merchant ship belonging to the T. & J. Harrison line which ran aground off Eriskay on 5 February 1941 after Captain Beaconsfield Worthington committed a navigational error while entering the north Atlantic through the Hebrides on a voyage to Jamaica. Amongst its cargo was a consignment of 264,000 bottles of malt whisky, many of which were salvaged by the islanders. The incident was turned into a novel *Whisky Galore!* (1947) by Compton Mackenzie and later still (1949) a memorable Ealing comedy film.

The use of the Western Approaches for convoy work encouraged the Germans to deploy submarines and long-range Condor aircraft, and from 1940 to 1944 there was a steady enemy presence in Scottish home waters and in the skies above the Western Approaches. Incoming convoys were attacked with grim regularity – seventeen ships of Convoy SC7 were sunk off Rockall in October 1940 – and fishing vessels and other inshore craft were regular victims of enemy attack. In response, a new Coastal Command base opened on Tiree in 1941 to provide air cover, with other aircraft flying out of Oban, Islay and Benbecula. On the Kintyre peninsula the Royal Naval Air Station at Machrihanish became an important training facility, and it was from there that Corsair and Barracuda aircrew trained for the carrier-based attack on the German battleship *Tirpitz* in April 1944.

Those operations properly belong to the overall Allied direction of the war against Germany but there was one aspect of the convoy system which had a distinctly Scottish contribution – the Arctic Convoys which took much-needed supplies to the Soviet Union and which were considered essential for encouraging the Soviet war effort. Following Hitler's decision to attack the Soviet Union in the summer of 1941, Joseph Stalin put immediate pressure on the United Kingdom to supply him with war *matériel* to sustain his war effort. The tonnage delivered helped to assuage his demands for the creation of a second front.

In the first operations the convoys assembled at Reykjavik in Iceland but from September 1942 inbound and outbound convoys sailed directly from the deep waters of Loch Ewe. The first of these was PQ18 which left on 2 September and arrived at Archangel nineteen days later. It was also the first to have air cover provided by the carrier HMS *Avenger*, a converted merchant ship equipped with three Swordfish and six Sea Hurricane aircraft. Although thirteen ships were lost, mainly to German air attack, the convoy was counted a success and gave much-needed experience to the accompanying pilots on board *Avenger*. Convoy JW51B sailed from Loch Ewe on 22 December 1942 with fourteen merchant ships heavily laden with tanks, aircraft, aviation fuel and ammunition. To meet the possibility of attack, it was protected by a huge escort force which consisted of the destroyers HMS *Achates*, HMS *Orwell*, HMS *Oribi*, HMS *Onslow*, HMS *Obedient* and HMS *Obdurate*; the Flower-class corvettes HMS *Rhododendron* and HMS *Hyderabad*; the minesweeper HMS *Bramble*; and two trawlers, *Vizalma* and *Northern Gem*. The overall commander was Robert St Vincent Sherbrooke on board *Onslow*. Although the threat from German aircraft did not fully materialise, the convoy was threatened by enemy surface ships led by the heavy cruiser *Admiral Hipper* and the pocket battleship *Lützow*, but this was beaten off on 31 December by the British destroyer screen. During the action *Onslow* was hit and Sherbrooke was badly wounded, although he survived and was awarded the Victoria Cross.

The action came to be known as the Battle of the Barents Sea, and it was followed a year later by the Battle of North Cape which saw the German battle-cruiser *Scharnhorst* sunk by a Royal Navy force led by the battleship HMS *Duke of York*. The final convoy JW66 left the Clyde on 16 April 1945, and the final inbound wartime convoy RA66 arrived off the Tail of the Bank in time to celebrate the end of the war in Europe on 8 May – a second convoy RA67 arrived at the same destination on 30 May with all ships burning their navigation lights, mirroring the street lights in Gourock and Greenock. Altogether seventy-eight convoys sailed to the Soviet Union through some of the worst sea and weather conditions in the world, around the north cape of Norway and through the Barents Sea to the northern Russian ports. Throughout the voyage they had to face the threat of attack by German submarines, surface ships and bombers, and paid a heavy price for the 4.43 million tons of supplies which reached their destinations – 104 merchant ships, 20 Royal Navy warships, a submarine and two armed whalers were lost in the convoys, with Germany losing 31 submarines.[22]

Between 1941 and 1943 the poet J. K. Annand served on board the Scapa-based Tribal class destroyer HMS *Tartar*, and in his recollections he claimed that the convoy experience was 'very dull and unexciting in a way' where 'our worst enemy was the weather'.[23] Later, though, the scenes came back to inform his poetry, and his poem 'Arctic Convoys' tells the modern reader all there is to know about conditions aboard a Scottish-based destroyer on the Murmansk run.

> Caulder the air becomes, and snell the wind.
> The waters, splairgin as she dunts her boo,
> Blads in a blatter o hailstanes on the brig
> And geals on guns and turrets, masts and spars,
> Cleedin the iron and steel wi coat o ice.[24]

In April 2010 thirty surviving Scottish veterans of the convoys were presented with special medals by the Russian government to mark the part they played in the Arctic convoys.

During that same period Scottish soldiers were also taking the war back to Germany and Italy as and when they could, fighting on faraway battle fronts in North Africa, Somaliland, Madagascar, Syria and Burma. All too often those campaigns were not just an offensive necessity but a means of preventing a total Axis victory. Although the fighting in Europe had been ended by the collapse at Dunkirk, and would not be resumed again until the D-Day landings in June 1944, there were several other theatres of war in which Scottish military formations made a signal contribution to the national war effort at a time when Britain was fighting for its life, virtually alone, together with the forces of its Dominions and the free forces of various European powers-in-exile.

The first Scottish unit to see action in the wake of the Dunkirk withdrawal was 2nd Black Watch which had begun the war on internal security duties in Palestine. In May 1940 it left for Suez where it was picked up by the Royal Navy for 'an unknown destination' which turned out to be the port of Aden in Yemen. From there the battalion moved into British Somaliland (later Somaliland) which had come under attack from a huge Italian army based in Abyssinia (later Ethiopia) at the beginning of August. Not only did the enemy forces possess overwhelming superiority in armour and air power, but the five defending British and Indian battalions were all under-strength and modestly equipped. The Italians were also helped by the French decision to sign an armistice on 22 June following the collapse of France. This move took their forces of seven battalions in French Somaliland (later Djibouti) out of the defensive equation and made life more difficult for the defending Allied forces.

Reinforcements were rushed into British Somaliland, including 2nd Black Watch, the whole force coming under the command of Major-General A. R. Godwin-Austen, but it was already a lost cause. On 11 August the Italians began their main attack on the Allied positions at Tug Argen. Overwhelmed by the superior strength of the opposition, Godwin-Austen ordered the retreat on 13 August to save his forces from a potentially disastrous defeat and possible annihilation. As the units made their way back to the coast to be picked up by the Royal Navy at Berbera, their retreat was covered by 2nd Black Watch. At one stage in the operation a determined bayonet charge led by Captain (later Lieutenant-Colonel) David Rose held up the Italian advance through the Barkasan Gap but it was not enough to save the situation. During the fighting retreat the British force lost 38 killed and 222 wounded. Of that number, 7 Black Watch soldiers had been killed and 16 were wounded, one of the latter being Rose who was hit in the shoulder.[25]

From Berbera the battalion was taken to Egypt where the next imperative was the country's defence against the possibility of Italian attack. Already in the country was another Highland battalion, 2nd Camerons, which had recently arrived from its last posting in India. On arrival in Egypt the battalion was brigaded with 4/7th Rajputs and 1/6th Rajputana Rifles in 11th (Indian) Infantry Brigade, 4th Indian Division, as part of the hastily organised Western Desert Force which consisted of 4th Indian Division and 7th Armoured Division and which was commanded by Major-General Richard O'Connor, a distinguished Cameronian officer. In the uneasy period before Italy entered the war on 11 June 1940, the Allied forces in Egypt spent the time training for the expected onslaught from Libya where the Italians had deployed 250,000 troops. It was an anxious period as Italy was in a position to threaten Britain's control of the Mediterranean and its vital lines of communication with India and the Far East.

The Italian attack began in the middle of September, and they moved quickly into Egyptian territory by capturing Sidi Barrani. In response, O'Connor decided to counter-attack before the Italian advance gathered any momentum, and 2nd Camerons was involved in the first part of the offensive on 22 October against Italian positions at Maktila. The battalion also played a role in the attack on Nibeiwa Camp which resulted in the capture of 2,000 Italians and was the prelude to the retaking of Sidi Barrani on 10 December. Taken by surprise by the determination and ferocity of the British offensive, the Italians quickly capitulated to O'Connor's much smaller force of 30,000 soldiers.

As a result of this first Allied land victory of the war, 38,000 Italians, 237 artillery pieces and 73 tanks fell into British hands, and the only remaining sign of the Italian presence was at Sollum, Fort Capuzzo and Sidi Omar. Following the easy victory and the lack of any Italian response, General Sir Archibald Wavell, GOC Middle East, decided to move 4th Indian Division from Egypt to East Africa where the Italian commander, the Duke of Aosta, had opened his campaign by invading Sudan. Another formation, 5th (Indian) Division, was sent to reinforce the local garrison which consisted of the Sudan Defence Force and three British infantry battalions, including 2nd Camerons. In the face of these aggressive Allied measures the Duke of Aosta started withdrawing his forces back into Ethiopia through Eritrea, a land of desert plains and high rocky mountains. The main battle of the campaign was fought at Keren where the Italians occupied positions on high ground overlooking the main road through the Ascidira Valley. It was an imposing obstacle of razor-like ridges and peaks which rose to over 6,000 feet, and the initial attacks at the beginning of February failed to make any impression on the Italian defences.

Despite the difficulties, on the first day of the battle, 3 February, the men of 2nd Camerons succeeded in taking their objective which was subsequently renamed Cameron Ridge and was used as a jumping-off point for further attacks. The fighting resumed on 15 March with the overall commander General Sir William Platt issuing a stark warning to his men: 'It is going to be a bloody battle against both enemy and ground. It will be won by the side that lasts the longest.' Twelve days later the issue was decided by the grit and determination of the two Indian divisions. Some of the hardest fighting involved 2nd Camerons during the attacks on the enemy positions on Mount Sanchil and Brig's Peak. The battalion War Diary provides a good idea of the conditions facing the men when they went into the attack: 'Zero hour arrived and the artillery opened. B and C Companies advanced over the brow of the hill, with D Company following C. A Company, for the moment, was kept back. The enemy put down a hail of mortar and machine-gun defensive fire, but it was quite impossible to see the result on either side owing to dust and smoke, though it was afterwards learnt that a large number of our casualties were sustained during the first two hundred yards of this advance.[26]

The victory at Keren persuaded the Italians to withdraw from Asmara, and the capture of the port of Massawa on 8 April signalled the end of Italian resistance in Eritrea, but it came at a price. The British suffered 3,767 casualties killed or wounded, and amongst that number were 209 men of 2nd Camerons.

As a result of the successful outcome of the campaign, Wavell was able to return 4th Indian Division to North Africa where Egypt was under a new threat following the arrival of German forces, the Afrika Korps, under the command of General Erwin Rommel. A series of successful assaults had retaken all the ground won by the Allies in the previous year, and Cyrenaica was in danger of falling into Rommel's hands. By the beginning of April 1941 the vital port of Tobruk was under threat, and Churchill ordered that it had to be held at all costs. His directive also ordered the Western Desert Force to counter-attack and engage all enemy forces between Tripoli and El Agheila, and in so doing to regain ascendancy in Libya. It was easier said than done. Rommel renewed his attack at the beginning of May, and as the Allies withdrew Tobruk was left isolated. Despite offering stout resistance the garrison was forced to surrender on 21 June. Amongst them was 2nd Camerons which continued fighting for a further day before the commanding officer Lieutenant-Colonel C. S. Duncan ordered all able-bodied men to break out and attempt to reach safety in Egypt. For the rest who were unable to escape it was a bitter moment, but Duncan insisted that he and his men should be allowed to march into captivity with pipes playing and all the honours of war. Later in the year, on 20 December, a new 2nd Battalion came into being by re-designating the regiment's 4th Battalion, a Territorial Army formation which had been reformed after the earlier surrender of 51st (Highland) Division at St Valéry-en-Caux. One other Scottish regiment was involved throughout this stage of the fighting – 2nd Scots Guards which served as part of 22 Guards Brigade and took part in the successful defence of Halfaya Pass in May 1941.

While these events were unfolding during the spring of 1941, 2nd Black Watch moved from Berbera to Egypt where it was transported immediately to Crete whose defence was considered to be vital to Britain's interests in the Aegean and the Mediterranean. The island's defence became even more imperative when the Germans moved rapidly into Yugoslavia and then into Greece, forcing the retreat of all British and Commonwealth troops. Many of these were shipped to Crete but they arrived without their equipment, including artillery and ammunition which had been left behind in Greece. By the end of April there were 30,000 troops on Crete under the command of General Bernard Freyburg, a New Zealander whose plan centred on the need to defend the key points – the airfields at Heraklion, Retimo and Maleme and the main port at Suda Bay. The 2nd Black Watch was part of 14 Brigade which was entrusted with the defence of the Heraklion sector in the north of the island, including its vital airfield. The German attack began on 19 May 1941, and by the end of the day 5,000 German airborne troops had landed on Crete, either by parachute or by gliders towed by Junkers 52 transport aircraft.

For a while the defenders put up spirited resistance – the Germans had underestimated the size of the British garrison – but the lack of air cover soon became apparent. On 21 May the airfield at Maleme fell into German hands, and four days later Freyburg informed Wavell that 'our situation here is hopeless'. Fearing another calamity, Churchill agreed to a withdrawal, and the evacuation began on the night of 28/29 May. In the Heraklion sector 2nd Black Watch covered the brigade's retreat to the harbour and the Royal Navy ships, including the cruisers HMS *Dido* and HMS *Orion* which were waiting offshore ready to take the men. During the operation they lost one of their company commanders, Major Alastair Hamilton, who had vowed earlier that 'the Black Watch leaves Crete when the snow leaves Mount Ida'. Six destroyers conveyed the men from the mole to the cruisers, but while this was happening there was a near-disaster when the steering gear on the destroyer HMS *Imperial* jammed and she started slewing around. On board were a number of Black Watch soldiers who managed to escape by leaping on another destroyer, HMS *Hotspur*, which had turned back to offer assistance. Worse followed the next morning when the retreating ships were attacked by German bombers as they struggled towards Alexandria. Both *Dido* and *Orion* received direct hits and casualties were high on both ships – 260 killed and 280 wounded on *Orion* and over a hundred on *Dido*, many of them killed when a bomb exploded in the canteen which was packed with troops. Of those killed, 103 were 2nd Black Watch. When the convoy reached Alexandria a Black Watch piper climbed onto the bridge of HMS *Dido* and played the battalion in as the ships made their way into the harbour and safety. A searchlight picked him up in its beam and, as many survivors remembered, it was a moment when grown men wept.

During this same period perhaps the most bizarre and least heralded campaign was the fighting against Vichy French forces on the island of Madagascar, which involved three Scottish battalions: 1st and 2nd Royal Scots Fusiliers and 6th Seaforth Highlanders. Initially, the governor of the island had thrown in his lot with the Free French forces under the command of General Charles de Gaulle, but he changed his mind and resigned his post after the destruction of the French fleet by the Royal Navy at Mers-el-Kebir in July 1940. The operation had been ordered by Churchill to prevent the French warships being used by the Germans during the proposed invasion of Britain, and it sharply divided French opinion after it became clear that 1,300 sailors and marines had been killed in the bombardment. Following the governor's resignation he was replaced by a representative of the Vichy government, General Armand Leon Annet. That altered the strategic balance in the region, as the Vichy government collaborated with the Germans, and in March 1942 the British received intelligence that Germany had persuaded Japan to occupy Madagascar as a means of gaining naval superiority in the Indian Ocean, a move that would threaten strategic supply routes. To prevent that happening a British invasion force, Force 121, was put together under the command of Major-General Robert Sturges, Royal Marines, consisting of 17 and 29 Brigades (with 13 Brigade as a strategic reserve) and No 5 Commando. (At the time the force was bound for India before being diverted to take part in the operation, which was codenamed Ironclad.) In the first major amphibious operation of the conflict and the first offensive landings since Gallipoli in 1915, Sturges's primary task was to capture the northern naval base at Diégo Suarez with support from a naval task force under the command of Rear-Admiral Neville Syfret. Both the infantry brigades contained Scots Fusiliers – the 1st Battalion served in 29 Brigade while the 2nd Battalion was brigaded in 17 Brigade with 2nd Northamptonshire Regiment and 6th Seaforth Highlanders.

With air cover provided by aircraft of the Fleet Air Arm flying from the carriers *Indomitable* and *Illustrious*, the first assault was made against Diégo Suarez on 5 May. Although Operation Ironclad achieved complete surprise, the resistance was surprisingly strong, and the fighting for the port and the town of Antsirane (later Antseranana) lasted for three days before the French capitulated. During the attack 1st Royal Scots Fusiliers made an eighteen-mile forced march before running into heavy defences to the south of Antsirane, consisting of pill-boxes and an anti-tank ditch. Much of the fighting ended up being close-quarter combat involving generous use of the bayonet. In his account of the battle, Jim Stockman of 6th Seaforths provided a graphic account of the moment when bayonet practice was translated into the reality of battle.

As I kept going, I suddenly came across this huge Senegalese coming at me. For a moment I panicked, hesitated. Then, on thankful impulse, stopped him in his tracks by thrusting forward and shoving the bayonet right through him until it emerged on the other side.

At first, I did not realise the ferocity with which I had struck him and then found to my horror that I could not pull it out again. I had to fire a round, twist savagely and pull in order to disengage it from his body.[27]

The Seaforth charge succeeded in taking the Vichy French position and Antsirane fell overnight. It was not the end of the struggle, as the French governor retreated to the south of the island with the rump of his forces. In the original plans for Ironclad the capture of the naval port had been deemed to be sufficient, but following its capture the South African prime minister General Jan Smuts insisted that the whole island and its 900 miles of coastline should be captured.

During a lull in operations, 2nd Royal Scots Fusiliers was moved to

India on 11 June when 17 Brigade resumed its deployment to the sub-continent to join 5th Division for the defence of India following the Japanese invasion of Burma; these forces were replaced by 22 East African Brigade, 7 South African Motorised Brigade and 27 North Rhodesian Infantry Brigade, which arrived during June and August. The campaign reopened ahead of the rainy season on 10 September when 29 Brigade and the East African forces landed at the ports of Majunga in the north-west and Morondava on the west of the island. Although progress was slow, the capital Tananarive fell two weeks later, and 1st Royal Scots Fusiliers was also involved in the operations to take the eastern port of Tamatave. The last major action was at Andriamanalina on 18 October. Annet surrendered near Ilhosy, in the south of the island, on 5 November. By then 1st Royal Scots Fusiliers had withdrawn from Madagascar for rest and recuperation in South Africa. At the beginning of the following year it moved with 29 Brigade (now part of 36th Division) to Poona in India for training in jungle warfare in preparation for deployment on the Burma front.

In the Far East the fall of Hong Kong and the later collapse of Singapore had been followed by the Japanese invasion of Burma and the consequent threat that India itself might be invaded. In July 1942 the Japanese high command made plans for 'Operation 21', a three-pronged attack from Burma towards Ledo, Imphal and Chittagong. It was over-ambitious in concept as the terrain in northern Burma was not suited to rapid offensive operations, but the fact that India was threatened was enough to concentrate British minds about the precariousness of their position. Allied to increasingly strident demands from Indian nationalists for Britain to quit India, there was an immediate need to restore British standing by taking the offensive back to the Japanese and retrieving lost ground in Burma. The first of these initiatives was the first Arakan campaign, which opened in September 1942 and was aimed at capturing the Akyab peninsula following an advance from Chittagong by way of Cox's Bazaar and Donbaik. It did not achieve the desired result. By the following May the Japanese had retrieved all the ground won during the advance; for the British it was not only an expensive failure which cost over 5,000 casualties, but it inculcated a belief that the Japanese were unbeatable jungle fighters.

Amongst those taking part in the operation was 1st Royal Scots, which fought in 6 Independent Brigade Group, together with 1st Royal Welch Fusiliers, 1st Royal Berkshire Regiment and 2nd Durham Light Infantry. Originally, the formation's role was to attack Akyab from the sea, an undertaking that involved the Royals in their first experience of combined operations, but shortages of landing craft necessitated a change of plan to more conventional operations. As a result the Royals went into the line on 6 March 1943 for the attack on Donbaik, and the subsequent fighting gave them their first experience of taking on the Japanese who had created heavily fortified positions in 'chaungs', river beds or deep tidal creeks. The Royals' commanding officer, Lieutenant-Colonel R. W. Jackson, originally a Sherwood Forester, provided a telling description of these obstacles in an article written after the war in conjunction with the battalion's Intelligence Officer, Captain J. S. Purves.

> The position held by the Jap here [near Donbaik] was a small strong-point made out of the main chaung (or river bed) stretching from the sea to hills 500 to 800 feet high. These hills overlooked the chaung and were held by the Jap. The chaung itself was well dug, revetted [strengthened] sufficiently to withstand shelling from 25-pdrs or 3.7 howitzers. It also included some tanks sunk into the ground. Our lines approached in places as close as forty yards and gave the Battalion an inkling of what trench warfare used to be like, as part of the Battalion perimeter ran through a narrow chaung.[28]

The description presaged the kind of fighting which followed. Despite facing heavy incoming fire, the Japanese showed that their positions were well defended and, as Jackson and Purves confirmed, 'a period of trench warfare set in'. One Japanese pill-box, known as 'Sugar 5', proved to be particularly impervious to attack, and for a time the Royals were involved in an attempt to dig a mineshaft underneath it. An order to 'straighten the line' put paid to their efforts when 6 Brigade pulled back and 'angry and disgusted, the miners left their work uncompleted'. On 27 March the Brigade Group was ordered to move back to the north along the coastal plain, and during fierce fighting at Indin on 6 April, 1st Royal Scots suffered heavy casualties in an action which one officer described later as 'utter pandemonium'. During the Japanese attack on the brigade headquarters Brigadier R. V. C. Cavendish was killed, and crucial documents including code-books fell into enemy hands. There was no option for the Royals but to withdraw towards Kyaukpandu where there was a chance to regroup. By then the first rains of the monsoon had begun and marching was difficult, with the result that 'most of us were sleeping on our feet . . . we looked like ragamuffins'.

The loss of the Buthiadaung-Maungdaw defensive line and the subsequent withdrawal were counted as victories for the Japanese, whose forces commanded by Lieutenant-General Takeshi Koga had shown dash and determination in their counter-attack. However as the battalion moved back towards the frontier Captain Purves remembered that many of the men thought that 'we should have been going SOUTH against the Jap and not NORTH'. Nevertheless the retreat continued and the battalion moved back into India on 24 May. In the aftermath of the failure of the operation the British high command criticised many of the frontline units for the lack of fighting spirit and their willingness to surrender when facing heavy odds. During the latter stages of the campaign a staff officer at the headquarters of Lieutenant-General N. M. S. Irwin reported that most of the infantrymen were 'either exhausted or browned off or both', and were 'obviously scared of the Jap and generally demoralised by the nature of the campaign'; or 'hate the country and see no object in fighting for it, and also have the strong feeling that they are taking part in a forgotten campaign in which no one in authority is taking any real interest'. The report was written after a visit to the brigades fighting on the Maungdaw Front in the second week of May, but the author of the report made an exception of 6 Brigade 'who had had a hammering, but were still staunch'.[29] During this first Arakan campaign the Royals' casualties were 6 officers and 26 soldiers killed, and 10 officers and 117 soldiers wounded. Another 500 had fallen victim to malaria, with the result that when 1st Royal Scots finally reached Chittagong it only numbered some 400 soldiers.

Another Scottish battalion was also taking part in the defence of Burma at this time: this was 2nd King's Own Scottish Borderers (KOSB), which had spent the opening months of the war fighting in a little-known campaign to put down an uprising led by the Faqir of Ipi in India's North-West Frontier Province. Following a deployment in Razmak which lasted over a year the battalion joined the Fourteenth Army in August 1943 for the second phase of the Arakan operation. Its eventual destination was the Arakan peninsula, but before then it trained with the rest of 7th Indian Division between Peshawar and Rawalpindi. This was followed by specialist jungle training at Singhori near Chindwara in the Central Indian Province (today Madhya Pradesh) where the battalion was joined by training teams made up of soldiers who had already experienced the vastly different conditions of fighting in Burma. According to the regimental war historian it was a steep learning curve for all the Borderers.

> These courses of instruction, ranging from divisional level down to companies and platoons, gave every man in the division a chance to learn quickly and thoroughly all that could be taught to make him fit for battle in the jungle. The individual training was carried out in company jungle camps where the men spent five days, returning to Singhori for two days and then back to the jungle camp. The Borderers were shown how to use bamboo, how to navigate in dense jungle and elephant grasses, and how to live on the land; in brief, how to conquer the jungle as a necessary preliminary to beating the human enemy, the Japs.[30]

This was very much the credo which was later adopted by the British and Allied armies in Burma: the jungle need not be a hostile place but approached differently it could be an environment which offered a measure of protection. And above all, the Japanese opposition were not supermen but ordinary soldiers who were capable of being beaten. Training also included live-firing and other toughening-up exercises which were carried out in all weather conditions to make sure that the troops were readied for whatever the shock of battle would throw against them.

The chance to put theory into action came at the end of August when 2nd KOSB moved by train from Ranchi to Madras, where they boarded the troopship *Ethiopia* for a four-day voyage across the Bay of Bengal to land in Chittagong on 20 September 1943. By that stage of the war this formed the southern front of the Allied operations against the Japanese, the other two being the central front with its main battlefields at Imphal and Kohima, and the northern front bounded by Yunnan and Ledo. By the time the Borderers reached the Arakan the monsoon had arrived, and both sides were more than content to sit it out until the weather improved. As a result 2nd KOSB saw little of the enemy as they settled into their positions between the Mayu Hills and the Naaf River which was described as 'a waste of flooded fields with hillocks covered in jungle scrub'. Although the hills were not particularly high they had steep precipices, and the ravines were deep and threatening with their fair share of insects and snakes. As was the case on other fronts in Burma, rations and ammunition had to be carried in by mule trains.

As the weather began to improve, 2nd KOSB was able to send out fighting patrols to engage Japanese ration parties, and scored a first success on 8 October when an ambush succeeded in killing thirty of the enemy who came from an Imperial Guards regiment. This was followed by a similar encounter a few days later on a position known as the 'horseshoe' in which the Japanese had unwisely advertised their presence by flying their national flag on the high ground. However, on the debit side it soon became apparent that casualties would not just be caused by enemy fire; sickness, too, was a problem. In the first months in the Arakan the battalion's casualty rate was 120 sick men (mainly malaria and dysentery) to every man killed or wounded by enemy action. Gradually better standards of hygiene were introduced and by 1944 the ratio had fallen to six to one.

Following a period of recuperation, the battalion moved south by way of the Ngakyedauk Pass (known throughout the Fourteenth Army as 'Okedoke' Pass) to new positions opposite the Japanese lines at Tatmin Chaung. The aim of the commander of XV Indian Corps, Lieutenant-General Sir Philip Christison, a Cameron Highlander, was to recapture Akyab so that its vital airfields could be used to operate against Rangoon. This phase of the operations provided the Borderers with their first set-piece battle against the enemy, but it was preceded by a lengthy game of cat-and-mouse. At that stage of the fighting the British and Indian armies in Burma lacked detailed intelligence about their opponents, and a high premium was placed on reconnaissance patrolling with the objective of bringing in a live prisoner. (To add a sense of competitiveness to the process there was a reward of 250 rupees and 28 days' leave.) Although 2nd KOSB failed on that score – a raiding party did bring in one prisoner but he was found to be dead on arrival following a blow to the head as he tried to escape – the deployment did bring a successful engagement with the Japanese at the beginning of 1944. This took place on a position known as Able Hill where the objective was to cut the Japanese lines of communication with Mungdaw, and it was conceived, in its first stages, as a night operation. With 1st Queens on the right and 4/5th Gurkhas on the left, 2nd KOSB attacked in the centre towards Ledwedet Hill and immediately ran into fierce enemy fire which killed the commanding officer Lieutenant-Colonel W. G. Mattingly. After two weeks in the line the battalion was relieved by the Gurkhas and returned to the start line, where the men were treated to comforts such as warm food, clean clothes and blankets, and rum and cigarettes.

After a short period of rest the battalion moved to a new position in Wet Valley where it relieved 1st Queen's and then prepared to move again – north towards Taung Bazaar, which had been occupied by 4,000 Japanese troops. This was a difficult and demanding operation which had to be carried out in unknown territory, and as the regimental war history explains, it involved a night march, something that most soldiers fear and dislike: 'There were no guides, no maps, and this stretch of the country was unfamiliar. A course was set on a compass bearing and the column set out. A mule column is not easily kept quiet, but the animals seemed to sense the danger. The eerie march in the misty moonlight took four hours, and the column was duly navigated to the rendezvous. The mules by a mischance had acted as the spearhead of the brigade on this move, but the column had luck on its side.'[31]

On arrival at its new position at Allwynbin, four miles south of the Ngakyedauk Pass, 89 Brigade constructed its 'Admin Box', the main centre for communication, and in reality shaped more like a bowl than a box in the lea of a position called Sugar Loaf Hill. There the brigade was joined by 33 Brigade and 114 Brigade, all three of which were now fenced in by the opposition. Air supply became imperative; here the brigade was helped by the fact that the RAF enjoyed air superiority, and its Spitfires were more than capable of shepherding the Dakota transports to their targets. The arrival of food, cigarettes and other comforts came as a much-needed relief to the men of 2nd KOSB who had gone five days without a square meal. Expectancy turned to disappointment in one instance where the containers were full of ammunition, but this was balanced by others which were replete with 'food and smokes'. This provision from the skies was a real morale-booster while fighting in difficult terrain and facing an unyielding enemy. Not only did it bring much-needed provisions to the beleaguered men in the Admin Box but it produced solid evidence that others knew about their plight and were doing their best to help them. Bucked by that kind of support, battalions like 2nd KOSB always rediscovered the urge to take the fight back to the enemy. Despite the difficult conditions morale rarely slumped, and in the pages of the SEAC (South-East Asia Command) newsletter there were glimpses of the kind of humour expressed by an anonymous Borderer about fighting in the Arakan (to be sung to the tune of a popular, if vulgar, rugby club song).

> Japs on the hilltops
> Japs in the Chaung
> Japs in the Ngakyedauk
> Japs in the Taung
> Japs with their L of C [lines of communication] far too long
> As they revel in the joys of infiltration . . .[32]

Re-supplied and suitably refreshed, 89 Brigade took the initiative and reopened the battle for the Admin Box in the first week of February. It quickly proved to be an intensive period of combat, often at close quarters and with quarter neither given nor expected. At one stage the Japanese broke into the medical dressing station and massacred those being treated. The nights were made hideous by howls and shrieks from the attacking Japanese, but despite the determination of their assaults the enemy attack was soon running behind timetable. The Admin Box remained secure, Ngakyedauk Pass was reopened with 2nd KOSB in the vanguard, and after a grim eighteen days of heavy fighting the British and Indian positions in the Arakan had been secured.

For the Borderers there was one more action on the Maungdaw–Buthidaung road where a massive artillery barrage preceded their attack on Japanese positions at Tatmin Chaung. In one chilling incident on the Horseshoe position, the Japanese were seen to be pegging out a body in the hot sun as a lure. Although 2nd KOSB suspected that the unfortunate victim was a Borderer, the position could not be attacked until nightfall, by which time the body had disappeared. During the mopping up operations a position was found with 126 dead Japanese soldiers, all of whom had been ordered to commit suicide after losing the battle.

On 26 February the Japanese called off their attacks in the Arakan; for the first time in the war British and Indian troops had managed to stave off a major Japanese offensive, and the commander of the Fourteenth Army, General Sir William Slim, was suitably effusive in his appreciation of the British and Indian battalions which had brought the fighting in the Admin Box to a victorious conclusion: 'British and Indian soldiers had proved themselves, man for man, the masters of the best the Japanese could bring against them.'

7 The Arsenal of War

Whichever way the topography of Scotland is examined, it makes ideal territory for the training of service personnel. Firstly, much of the terrain is rugged high land which offers challenging conditions for adventurous training, while the low land is open and reasonably flat with good internal communications. Secondly, the surrounding waters provide a variety of sea conditions, and thirdly, and perhaps most importantly, most of the land and coastal waters, especially those on the western side of the country, are beyond the prying eyes of a European enemy. From the military point of view, therefore, Scotland has always provided defence planners with a number of possibilities and opportunities. The land mass sprawls over a large area – just over 7.7 million hectares. One-third of the UK, it consists largely of high land and rough grazing; less than two million hectares is made up of pasture or arable land. Some idea of the size of the area can be gauged by super-imposing Scotland upon England: Scotland then stretches from Aldershot in the south to the Borders in the north, and from Liverpool in the west to Scarborough in the east, even before the western and northern isles have been taken into account.

But there is one problem with the lie of the land: physical barriers like the Mounth (the mountain massif which includes the Cairngorms) and the Southern Uplands make north–south and east–west communications difficult. Historically, the high lands provided a refuge in time of danger and helped, therefore, to preserve Scotland's independence. Invaders from the south were forced to use the eastern coastal route to bypass the Cheviots or the difficult upland terrain in the west through Annandale. Other problems are posed by the length of the coastline which is the longest in the UK – over 0.4 million hectares of foreshore – and much of this consists of long sea lochs and broad open firths. Most of the high ground is sparsely populated or uninhabited, and the weather conditions are often harsh and unpredictable. Rivers and inland lochs also provide barriers, and the pattern of north–south roads was determined by the presence of glens and mountain passes, some of which, like the Pass of Drumochter on the main route between Perth and Inverness, rise up over 450 metres. In short, from a military standpoint Scotland offers most advantages to its defenders and provides a serious test to those intent on invasion. By its very nature, it is a terrain which was made for demanding military and naval training.

To utilise that topography during the Second World War, Scotland was home to the necessary service structures which made the country a vital cog in the homeland defences of the UK. The Royal Navy had two naval commands which covered Scotland: Rosyth Command, formerly Coast of Scotland Command, and Western Approaches Command. Although the Flag Officer of the latter command (Rear-Admiral J. S. M. Ritchie) had his headquarters in Liverpool, there were important Scottish presences at Glasgow where the Flag Officer Vice-Admiral James Troup had his headquarters at St Enoch's Hotel (HMS *Spartiate*) and at Greenock (HMS *Orlando* and HMS *Monck*) where the Flag Officer was Vice-Admiral Bertram Watson, followed by Rear-Admiral Richard Hill. There were other significant naval presences under Western Approaches Command at Dunoon (HMS *Osprey*), Largs (HMS *Monck*), Inverary (HMS *Quebec*), Lamlash (HMS *Orlando*, later HMS *Fortitude*), Campbeltown (HMS *Nimrod*), Ardrossan (HMS *Fortitude*), Oban (HMS *St Andrew*, later HMS *Caledonia*), Lochalsh (HMS *Trelawney*), Stornoway (HMS *Mentor*), Aultbea (HMS *Helicon*) and Tobermory (HMS *Western Isles*).[1] By the end of the war in 1945, the Royal Navy possessed 29 bases in Scotland, some 25 per cent of its global total.[2]

The army in Scotland was equally well established and entrenched within the fabric of Scottish society. Scottish Command had its headquarters at Edinburgh Castle, and the GOC-in-C at the beginning of the war was General Sir Charles Grant, a Coldstream Guards officer, but he gave way in 1940 to Lieutenant-General Sir Harold Carrington, who had been commissioned into the Royal Field Artillery in 1901 and had served in the Boer War and the First World War. The command was divided into two areas: Highland with two nominal Territorial Army divisions, 9th and 51st, and Lowland with two nominal divisions, 15th and 52nd. Both areas also contained supplementary reserve units and various supply and service formations. The teeth arms were composed of 2nd Royal Scots Fusiliers at Redford Barracks in Edinburgh, 1st Highland Light Infantry at Fort George in Inverness-shire, 2nd Seaforth Highlanders at Maryhill Barracks in Glasgow and the Royal Artillery's port defences at Leith, Gourock and Orkney.[3]

Carrington did not last long in his posting. In June, under circumstances which are far from clear, he was replaced as GOC-in-C by Lieutenant-General Sir Andrew Thorne who had previously commanded XII Corps, responsible for home defences in south-east England, and who remained GOC-in-C Scotland for the rest of the war. An experienced Grenadier Guardsman, he brought an air of quiet authority, and proved to be an energetic and inspiring holder of the post. It had been largely due to him that Scotland's home defences had been stabilised in the summer of 1940. In other circumstances he might have considered the move a demotion, as he left an operational command for an administrative command, but if he did feel any personal disappointment he never showed it. For his services in Scotland he was promoted full general in February 1945, and as Commander-in-Chief Allied Forces Norway was given responsibility for returning Crown Prince Olav to Norway (see Chapter 12).

All frontline RAF aircraft came under the control of Number 13 Group whose headquarters were at RAF Newcastle, with Sector Airfields at RAF Acklington in Northumberland, RAF Dyce in Aberdeenshire, RAF Turnhouse outside Edinburgh, RAF Unsworth in Northumberland and RAF Wick in Caithness. The fighter airfields were at RAF Catterick in North Yorkshire, RAF Drem in East Lothian, RAF Grangemouth in West Lothian, RAF Kirkwall on Orkney and RAF Sumburgh on Shetland. The Group was also responsible for the long-range early-warning Chain Home Stations at RAF Anstruther, RAF Bamburgh, RAF Danby Beacon, RAF Doonies Hill, RAF Drone Hill, RAF Hillhead, RAF Nether Button, RAF Ottercops Moss, RAF Shotton, RAF St Cyrus and RAF Thrumster. The Chain Home low-level stations were RAF Cockburnspath, RAF Cresswell, RAF Douglas Wood, RAF Fair Isle, RAF Rosehearty and RAF School Hill.

Immediately war was declared all three service commands in

Scotland faced urgent demands in preparing their regular and part-time units for service, and in making plans for the defence of the homeland. A year earlier the Royal Navy had decided that Rosyth could not be used as a main base as it was too far south to guard the vital northern gap between Shetland and Norway, and the bulk of the Home Fleet was moved to Scapa Flow and then to Loch Ewe (Aultbea). Almost immediately the sinking of HMS *Royal Oak* and the aerial attacks on Orkney and the Firth of Forth forced the Admiralty to re-assess its bases in Scotland to counter the threat of attack from the sea and the air. As a result the Firth of Clyde was also taken into account because it was on the western side of the country and enjoyed deep-water approaches, but it was finally decided to return to Scapa Flow once its anti-submarine and anti-aircraft defences had been strengthened. This led to a rapid expansion of the base's infrastructure to guard and defend the Home Fleet, and huge numbers of service personnel made the long journey by train to the Pentland Firth crossing. To meet the need for suitable catering on trains between Perth and Thurso, the London and Midland Scottish (LMS) railway provided luxurious pre-war Pullman cars which were operated by members of the Salvation Army.[4] Ahead lay the uncertain waters of the Pentland Firth to Orkney, and according to the historian of the North of Scotland, Orkney and Shetland Shipping Company, the company carried over 300,000 passengers over the Firth between 1939 and 1945, in addition to 176,000 sheep, 35,000 cattle and 4,500 pigs.[5] At the height of its activities the Orkney garrison was some 60,000-strong.

For the first time, too, many of them were women serving in the Women's Royal Naval Service (WRNS), the Women's Royal Army Corps (WRAC), the Women's Auxiliary Air Force (WAAF) or the various nursing and volunteer services. The waters of the Flow itself were home to a variety of headquarters ships, mainly obsolete warships or liners which had been reprieved from the breakers' yards, but the shore areas of the mainland, Hoy, Flotta and South Ronaldsay were soon covered with a variety of hastily constructed buildings, notably the ubiquitous Nissen huts which were made of pre-cast corrugated iron, and which came in three different sizes. Gradually some leisure facilities began to appear including a large canteen, a garrison theatre and a 1,500-seat cinema, but due to its remoteness Orkney was not always a popular posting. True, some warmed to its big skies, fantastic seascapes, the local bird life and the long days of summer, but for many it was a dismal place which gave rise to one of the best-known pieces of doggerel about the vagaries of life on active service during the Second World War.

> This bloody town's a bloody cuss,
> No bloody trains, no bloody bus;
> And no one cares for bloody us
> In Bloody Orkney.[6]

And so it continues for several amusing verses. Under the title 'In Bloody Orkney' it was purportedly written by a certain Captain Hamish Blair, and it appeared in the pages of *The Orkney Blast*, a newssheet founded by the novelist Eric Linklater who responded to a request made for such a publication by the local GOC Major-General G. C. Kemp.

The poem proved to be immensely popular, and soon gained a wide currency throughout the armed forces, where it was quickly adapted to reflect dismay at other equally unpopular postings. Its authorship has also been questioned – Blair was almost certainly a *nom de plume* – but the publication in which it appeared was real enough and equally well received. Linklater had strong local links with Orkney, and had served as a soldier in The Black Watch during the First World War before becoming one of the most popular and successful writers of his day. Shortly after the outbreak of war he had been commissioned in the Royal Engineers, and following acceptance of Kemp's invitation to found a newspaper, he took on the Ministry of Supply to gain sufficient amounts of rationed newsprint by arguing that Orkney's remote position made it a special case. He also secured the services of two remarkable soldiers, Private Gerry Meyer and Gunner Geoffrey Halton, who together edited the paper's first editions after Linklater had been posted away from the islands. Eventually the circulation was 6,000, but as Meyer pointed out, its readership was probably ten or twenty times larger, perhaps even more, before it ceased publication on 24 November 1944.[7]

In the period between 1941 and 1944 Scapa Flow was integral to naval operations in the Atlantic and the Norway coast (see Chapter

10), and it was also home to some of the largest capital ships in the Royal Navy. Amongst them was the new battleship HMS *Prince of Wales* which left the base on 21 May 1941 to join the battle cruiser HMS *Hood* in the Denmark Strait between Iceland and Greenland. Earlier that day aircraft of RAF Coastal Command had spotted the German battleship *Bismarck* and heavy cruiser *Prinz Eugen* refuelling in a fjord south of Bergen in Norway, evidently preparing to break out into the north Atlantic to attack Allied convoys. It seemed an equal fight, but for all that the heavily armed 'mighty *Hood*' was the pride of the Royal Navy between the wars, she possessed old-fashioned armoured protection which made her vulnerable to long-range fire, while *Prince of Wales* was so new that she had not been fully worked up and still had contractors on board. When the ships made contact, an accurate shot from *Bismarck* annihilated *Hood* which exploded with the loss of all but three of her 1,415 crew, one of whom was Midshipman William Dundas whose family lived at Muthill in Perthshire. In the aftermath of the sinking *Prince of Wales* made good her escape. The loss of *Hood* prompted a massive retaliation operation which included the carrier HMS *Victorious* from Scapa whose Swordfish torpedo bombers were able to locate and hit *Bismarck* on the night of 24/25 May but, unfortunately, without disabling her. Following a protracted hunt the German battleship was eventually sunk by superior British naval forces two days later.

The decision to concentrate assets on Scapa Flow had two knock-on effects for the navy in Scotland. Rosyth, so vital to North Sea operations in the First World War, became an important refitting and repair port which eventually had a workforce of 7,096 men and 2,204 women overseen by a staff of 21 naval officers and some 500 civil servants. With a sizable influx of workers from England, accommodation became a problem, and new houses had to be built at Rosyth and Dunfermline, with around 3,000 other workers being forced to travel by rail from outlying areas including Edinburgh and Falkirk.[8]

The other change was in submarine operations. At the outset of war both Rosyth and Dundee had been designated as submarine bases, along with Harwich and Blyth in England. As the problems of air raids increased in 1940, Rosyth became a fulcrum of naval activity, and over-crowding became a problem with three depot ships operating in the Forth estuary. Eventually it was decided to explore options on the west coast, and on 21 June the depot ship *Cyclops* left Rosyth to anchor in the Holy Loch. At the end of August she moved to Rothesay Bay and was replaced by the depot ship *Forth*. A further move in October saw the depot ship *Titania* move from the Forth to the Holy Loch, with the result that by the end of the year the Clyde had become the main operational and training base for submarines of the Royal Navy, with twenty-five boats making up the Second, Third and Seventh Flotillas, thus beginning a relationship with the area which lasted throughout the post-war years and into the twenty-first century. At the same time the Ninth Submarine Flotilla remained on the east coast for operations in the North Sea, with its headquarters in Dundee (HMS *Ambrose*).[9]

By far the best use of the Scottish land mass was made by what came to be known as 'special forces' – mainly commandos and operatives of the Special Operations Executive (SOE). This had come into being in the summer of 1940 and been given the task, in Churchill's dramatic phrase, 'to set Europe ablaze' or, in the more prosaic words of its founding document, 'to co-ordinate all action by way of subversion and sabotage, against the enemy overseas.'[10] In fact SOE had its origins in an initiative taken by the Secret Intelligence Service (SIS, or MI6) in September 1938 to investigate sabotage tactics against Germany in the event of war. Out of this came a shadowy organisation within the War Office which was first named General Staff (Research) and then Military Intelligence (Research) or MI(R). Its duties were to study the dynamics and tactics or guerrilla or irregular warfare and to interview and train the necessary personnel. This was the organisation which had produced the Auxiliary Units under colonels Holland and Gubbins, and they quickly extended the remit to operate overseas in enemy-held territory.

Norway presented the first opportunity, and MI(R)'s response to the German invasion in April 1940 was to despatch a number of small teams to operate behind enemy lines and to make contact with the Norwegian resistance movement. Although they returned without achieving any of their objectives, one six-man team, Operation Knife, laid the foundations for MI(R)'s next move. Amongst its members was a Scottish landowner, Captain William Stirling of Keir, who had served earlier with 5th Scots Guards, a specialist ski unit hurriedly trained for winter warfare during the Norway campaign. With his cousin Simon Fraser, Lord Lovat, Stirling proposed that a special training school should be established within the Scottish Protected Area, and this led to the War Office requisitioning the house and estate at Inverailort as Special Training Centre Lochailort in May 1940. Situated in the mountainous territory of Arisaig, off the road that runs from Fort William to Mallaig, it provided the perfect setting for the kind of secretive training proposed by MI(R). It was the first step in a process which would see large numbers of Allied military and naval personnel being given unorthodox training in the wilds of Highland Scotland, where for the most part they were out of sight and largely out of mind.

Their story remained untold for many years, largely due to restrictions on reporting SOE's activities and the withholding of official papers, but it is now clear that those training facilities played a major role in Scotland's contribution to the war effort.[11] The remote fastnesses of Arisaig and Morar proved to be ideal territory for training purposes, and through Scottish Command SOE added to its holdings by requisitioning other remote country houses and shooting lodges including Arisaig House, Camusdaroch, Garramor, Glasnacardoch Lodge, Inverailort, Inverie House, Meoble Lodge, Rhubana and Traigh House, all of which were located within the Protected Area and were therefore out of bounds to anyone without the relevant passes. Recruits and training staff were a mixed bunch, and they reflected the tough, no-nonsense yet frequently bohemian and eccentric approach adopted by many who were attracted to the special forces. One of the instructors at Glasnacardoch was Captain Gavin Maxwell of The Scots Guards, a grandson of the Duke of Northumberland who went on to write *Ring of Bright Water*, the classic account of his otter colony at Sandaig on the Sound of Sleat (named Camusfearna in the book). Another was Admiral Sir Walter Cowan, aged sixty-nine and a veteran of the Battle of Omdurman in 1898 (Kitchener's defeat of Islamic fundamentalists known as Mahdists in Sudan), who served with No. 11 Commando and who helped with the handling of small boats.

In June 1940, with the support of the Royal Navy and the Royal Marines, the British Army began using the term 'commando' to describe specially trained forces which would be raised for conducting raids in Nazi-occupied Europe. First used in the previous century by the Boer republics of Transvaal and the Orange Free State to describe the military system by which men had a requirement to do national military service, it became associated with low-intensity guerrilla warfare tactics. Boer commandos elected their own officers, provided their own horses and weapons, and were adept at field craft. Gradually the term became synonymous with any troops involved in irregular warfare, and the new force was originally designated as Special Service troops whose members wore a distinctive dark green beret after completing their rigorous basic training. (The unfortunate and potentially lethal acronym SS was dropped from badges in October 1944, being too similar to the German SS or *Schutzstaffel*.) An army 'commando' consisted of some 400 soldiers who were all volunteers, and of the original units drawn up, No. 10 and No. 11 Commando were formed from units within Scottish Command. (The latter reinforced its Scottish identity by wearing the tam-o'-shanter bonnet with a black hackle.)

From the outset great reliance was placed on attaining a high standard of physical fitness and creating resourcefulness, the objective being to inculcate an offensive spirit within all units. Courses were held at Lochailort, but individual commando units were supposed to operate as self-contained entities, and the island of Arran with its rocky coastline and hilly terrain was favoured as a training area by the two Scottish commandos. No. 8 Commando, recruited mainly from foot guards regiments, also trained on the island. By 1944 the army had twelve commandos including No. 10 (Inter-Allied Commando) which consisted of men from a variety of European countries, including some Germans, and No. 14 Commando which had been trained in the winter warfare role. Initially commando training was carried out in the area of the Clyde estuary at two main locations: the first in the grounds of Kellburn Estate, just south of Largs, and the second around Inveraray on Loch Fyne, the home of the Duke of Argyll. By then too the Royal Navy had established eight Royal Marine Commandos, and in 1942 training was centred at Achnacarry Castle in Inverness-shire, in a remote glen about fourteen miles from Fort William. The ancestral home of Cameron of Lochiel, it soon attracted a well-deserved reputation for the rigour and thoroughness of its training programmes which were conducted by Lieutenant-Colonel Charles Vaughan, nicknamed the 'Rommel of the North'.

The west coast of Scotland was also home to several establishments belonging to Combined Operations Command which had been established in 1940 under the direction of Admiral Sir Roger Keyes to plan and train for amphibious operations against enemy targets in occupied Europe.

The commandos, both army and Royal Marine, all saw meritorious war service, mainly in the Middle East and Mediterranean theatres, but there was one special forces group which took the war back to the enemy from Scottish territory – No. 1 Norwegian Independent Company, also known as *Kompani Linge*, named after its commanding officer Captain Martin Linge who was killed in a badly planned raid in December 1941. Originally based at Henley-on-Thames, the Norwegians moved north in 1940 to three shooting lodges (Drumintoul, Glenmore and Forest) in the Cairngorms close to Coylumbridge, where they operated as Group 26. The terrain was ideal for winter warfare training, having similarities with Norway, and under SOE direction the Norwegians quickly built up a reputation for their professionalism and toughness. They also had to learn how to melt back into their native Norway while it was under Nazi control because the group's main purpose was to operate behind enemy lines. This posed obvious risks, not just to the members of *Kompani Linge*, but also to any Norwegian civilians who gave them assistance and then fell into the hands of the Gestapo. At the time the Germans operated a policy of unrestricted retaliation against Norwegian civilians who were thought to have helped undercover agents.

Around 350 recruits passed through the group's training courses and then took part in missions in Norway, most of which were mounted from Scotland. In addition to dropping by parachute, always a risky business, members of *Kompani Linge* were flown to Norway by Catalinas of 333 Squadron from its base on the Tay estuary or by submarine from the same location, while others made the equally dangerous journey by small vessels, usually fishing boats, from bases in Shetland. Manned by Norwegian sailors and operated under the aegis of SOE, these were all-volunteer units, and the most famous, the Norwegian Independent Naval Unit, was known as the 'Shetland Bus'.[12] Operating firstly from Lerwick and Lunna Voe, and latterly from Scalloway, the unit mounted forty-three operations during the winter of 1941–2. Of these thirty were counted as successes, but three boats were lost and fourteen crew members were killed, while a serious storm in November destroyed equipment and hampered planning. The following winter season was more disappointing, largely due to the fact that the Germans were better prepared, and the unit lost six boats and thirty crew members.[13] In 1943 the situation was eased when the US Navy provided three fast submarine-chasers which operated under the names of *Hitra*, *Hessa* and *Vigra* and offered higher speeds and greater firepower. Another Norwegian operating base was established at Burghead on the Moray Firth but it mounted only five operations, and was shut down after a fatal sailing accident damaged its security.

Given the nature of the operations which had to be carried out over difficult terrain during the short days of winter, there were several setbacks, and the relationship between SOE and Milorg, the Norwegian resistance movement, did not always run smoothly. Bad luck also played a part – the Dundee-based submarine *Uredd* disappeared with all hands in February 1943 while landing a group to attack the pyrite mines at Sulitjelma in the north. However it was not all losses; at the same time another Norwegian group mounted a spectacular and hugely successful operation against a 'heavy water' plant at Vemork in the Hardangervidda. At the time this was considered to be a key component in the quest to harness atomic energy, but because the plant was heavily defended and beyond the range of RAF bombers the attack had to be made overland by ski, the members of *Kompani Linge* having been dropped by parachute. An earlier glider-borne operation had ended in disaster, but at the end of February 1943 six Norwegians mounted a *coup de main* assault on Vemork and succeeded in putting the plant out of action.[14] It was the high point of the Norwegian war effort, and the exploit was later turned into the film *The Heroes of Telemark* (1965).

Around a quarter of a million Allied soldiers received special forces training in Scotland during the war – they included US Army Rangers and Polish parachutists – and the remoteness of the West Highlands made it a perfect place to hone their skills. It also helped that most of the facilities were in a Protected Area which meant that their activities could be carried out far from the eyes of prying outsiders. Local people were asked to use their discretion, and soon became accustomed to the presence of soldiers and the sound of realistic training. Natural reticence helped in this respect, as did the long reach of history. One trainer at Lochailort remembered ordering a boatman on Loch Morar not to discuss what was happening and received the reply 'Aye, we kept Prince Charles secret here.'[15] (The reference was to Prince Charles Edward Stuart's escape following the Jacobite defeat at Culloden in 1746.)

There were other secrets, and in one instance the creation of a sensitive no-go area in the West Highlands meant exactly what it said. In the summer of 1942 Gruinard Island between Gairloch and Ullapool was deliberately contaminated with a highly toxic strain of anthrax called Vollum 14578. The intention was to test the use of anthrax spores as a weapon of war on a flock of eighty sheep by exploding a small chemical bomb, which succeeded in killing the animals. However, later tests showed that the island had been lethally contaminated, and it had to be placed in indefinite quarantine. Gruinard Island was placed out of bounds and remained so until 1990, after it had been decontaminated by spraying it with 280 tonnes of formaldehyde solution diluted in seawater.[16]

While the west coast and the Western Highlands were used extensively for training purposes by special forces and commandos, regular forms of warfare were not ignored by the armed forces. Following the brief foray into France in June 1940, 52nd (Lowland) Division returned to Britain where it was employed on home defence duties, first in eastern England and then in the central belt of Scotland where it guarded the Scottish Command Line which had been established to protect the Tay, Clyde and Forth estuaries. At the same time the battalions within the division started branching out into areas other than anti-invasion training. A sniping school was established in Glen Etive, and battle schools were set up at Forres and Edzell for realistic training, including the use of new commando tactics. But the biggest change came in September 1942 when it became known that training was about to start for a new and specialised role as mountain warfare troops prior to an anticipated invasion of Norway. Beneath the familiar cross of St Andrew worn on the shoulder, the men of the 52nd (Lowland) Division wore a new badge – MOUNTAIN. As the British Army's only specialist mountain warfare division, the 52nd was given a number of privileges: its manpower levels were sacrosanct, new specialist equipment was always forthcoming, it was expanded to include the Norwegian Brigade, and its Reconnaissance Regiment was equipped with tanks as well as armoured cars. In return it had to work extremely hard.

From autumn 1942 and throughout the following year, the division was involved in a series of arduous training exercises in the Cairngorms which involved the men living in the hills for weeks at a time. Instruction was also given in fighting in snow conditions, skiing and handling of loads on horses and, with the help of Sikh handlers, mules. Throughout the training cycle conditions were as close as possible to the anticipated reality of Norway. Exercise Goliath I took place in November 1942 and lasted sixteen days in the northern area of the Great Glen, while Goliath II lasted three weeks in the hills of Perthshire. For the men of $7^{th}/9^{th}$ Royal Scots it was an entirely new kind of training: 'This had been arduous and exhausting, involving as it did the carrying of enormous loads over the peaks of the Cairngorms. All will remember Exercise "Edelweiss", conducted in a two-day blizzard, and "Goliaths I and II", which lasted two and three weeks respectively. On returning from our advanced training base at Derry Lodge it was a pleasant change to undergo training in combined operations at Inverary.[17]

Although the soldiers in the division would not have been aware of it at the time, their presence in Scotland contributed to a deception plan aimed at keeping the Germans guessing about Britain's policy towards Norway. The training for mountain warfare was in deadly earnest – in 1941 plans had been laid for Operation Jupiter, a direct invasion of Norway which Churchill hoped would take some pressure off the Soviet Union. Although these were shelved when it became obvious that any invasion would be doomed to failure, they were revived in late 1943 when General Thorne was asked to draw up plans for a force which would be capable of liberating Norway following the invasion of Europe through Normandy. Two options were chosen: Operation Rankin B which envisaged the Germans withdrawing forces from Norway to help counter the Allied invasion of France, and Operation Rankin C which assumed that the Germans in Norway would stay in place and offer determined resistance. During the summer of 1944, as events moved swiftly in France, Thorne was ordered to plan for Operation Apostle which would create Force 134 for the eventual liberation of Norway.[18]

As it turned out, Scottish Command was destined not to finalise plans for the planned invasion of Norway and the Rankin operations were shelved, but Scotland did play a vital role in Operation Overlord, the plans to invade Europe through Normandy in the summer of 1944 (see Chapter 11). Many of the amphibious warfare techniques perfected in Scotland were adapted for the regular forces which would be used in the invasion of Europe. One of the assault formations was 3rd Infantry Division, and its training began in south-west Scotland in the winter of 1943–4. With its divisional battle school at Moffat, it then moved to the Combined Training Centre at Inveraray where it was able to practise beach landings on Loch Fyne and further afield on the inner Hebridean islands of Eigg and Rhum, as well as the beaches on the island of Arran. As the training intensified and further realism became essential, the division moved to the Moray Firth area where the seaward areas near Forres and Nairn were similar in topography to the landing beaches in Normandy. The final full-scale exercise took place on the night of 17/18 March 1944 before the division moved to the Channel coast to begin preparations for the D-Day landings. By that stage the tempo had increased to include live firing and the use of innovative weapons such as amphibious armoured vehicles, and to meet the need for absolute security civilians and livestock were removed from the immediate area.

Despite tight security, the Germans knew that an invasion was imminent but they could not work out where the landings would take place, and inevitably this caused an element of confusion in their own thinking. Their task was also complicated by the Allied deception plans, which had been codenamed Operation Fortitude, and which had come into being as a result of a conference of Allied senior commanders at Combined Operations headquarters in Largs between 28 June and 2 July 1943. Chaired by Mountbatten, its agenda was dominated by the invasion plans, and so many high-ranking officers were present that, with a nod to history, it was nicknamed the Field of the Cloth of Gold.[19]

Central to the thinking of the planners was the need to make the Germans believe that the main attack would come at the Pas de Calais and that any other attack would be a feint. To that end a number of deceptions were organised to convince the Germans that the area north of the River Seine had to be heavily defended at all costs. Allied air power was used to good effect to instil the idea that the Pas de

Calais was the real target. For every reconnaissance flight over Normandy, two were flown over the Pas de Calais, bombing missions were twice as heavy over the same area, and interdiction raids were increased on targets north and east of the Seine. According to the BBC war correspondent Chester Wilmot, 'the British played upon the notorious tendency of the German Intelligence Officers to approach problems with a card index mind, indefatigable in collecting information, but incompetent in assessing it.'[20] By far the most important subterfuge was the creation in Kent of the fictitious First United States Army Group (FUSAG) which consisted of large quantities of decoy equipment – mainly aircraft and landing craft – and a web of communications units which broadcast messages simulating the creation of a huge force about to mount a cross-Channel invasion. The Germans fell for the deception, not least because they learned that FUSAG's commander was General George S. Patton whom they had come to respect during the fighting in North Africa and Sicily. Despite being warned by Hitler to be wary of landings in Normandy, von Rundstedt continued to be obsessed with the Pas de Calais.

At the same time, a separate deception operation was planned for Norway and the rest of Scandinavia where the German garrison numbered 250,000 troops. Known as Operation Fortitude North, its purpose was to convince the Germans that an invasion of Norway was still an Allied intention and that a large force, the British Fourth Army, was being assembled for the purpose in Scotland. As Thorne did not have the necessary forces under his command, a fictional army with fictional headquarters in Edinburgh was established with the following equally fictional order of battle:

British II Corps (fictional – Headquarters Stirling)
    55th (West Lancashire) Infantry Division (Northern Ireland)
    58th Division (fictional, Aberlour)
    113th Independent Infantry Brigade (garrison for Orkney and
       Shetland Islands)

British VII Corps (fictional – Headquarters Dundee)
    52nd (Lowland) Infantry Division (Dundee)
    US 55th Infantry Division (fictional, Iceland)
    Three US Ranger battalions (fictional, Iceland)

United States XV Corps (Northern Ireland)
   US 2nd Infantry Division
   US 5th Infantry Division
   US 8th Infantry Division[21]

To maintain the illusion, Thorne established a staff to create increased fake radio traffic amongst the divisions, reconnaissance flights were stepped up over Norway and dummy aircraft were placed on existing RAF bases. For a short period the Firth of Forth was made a Protected Area, suggesting that it would be the assembly point for the invasion force, and 52nd (Lowland) Division moved its headquarters to Dundee. There was also a change in the division's training cycle in June when it moved to Inverary to be schooled in amphibious operations on Loch Fyne.

Although it has been suggested that Operation Fortitude North did not wholly deceive the Germans, as their attention had been diverted by a build-up of Soviet forces along Norway's northern border and they therefore did not investigate the Fourth Army's radio traffic, it is a fact that they did not move troops out of the country at the time of the D-Day invasion. While being interrogated after the war, the German head of operational planning, General Alfred Jodl, admitted that Hitler had feared an invasion of Norway and had maintained the garrison as 'insurance' against such an attack.[22]

Shortly before the D-Day operation, the fictional Fourth Army was removed and the deception operation was concluded. As for its only operational component in Scotland, there was another change of role for 52nd (Lowland) Division. Following the exercises at Inverary it was given a new role as an air transportable formation. The idea was to use the mountain-trained division in support of airborne operations in Europe by landing the division with its own transport (jeeps and trailers) after parachute troops had secured the ground. It was a bold concept, and a number of potential targets were identified including the Brest peninsula and the forest of Rambouillet south of Paris, but the speed of the Allied advance after D-Day put paid to any of the plans being put into effect. A more ambitious plan to use the 52nd (Lowland) Division as air-landing troops in support of the 1st Airborne's ill-fated operations at Arnhem in September also failed to materialise following the failure of Operation Market Garden, the ambitious but ultimately unsuccessful plan to capture the Rhine bridges by Allied airborne forces in September 1944. Eventually the division was employed in a regular infantry role in Belgium and north-west Europe (see Chapter 11).

Although Scotland's main military and naval contribution to the war effort was measured largely in terms of its isolated land mass, and the Orkney and Shetland islands to the north, the country also provided a more traditional response through its heavy industries, most of which were situated in the central belt. In the First World War the Clyde had deserved its appellation of the workshop of the nation's war effort: it was there that 90 per cent of Scotland's shipbuilding capacity was concentrated, producing the bulk of Britain's biggest commercial and naval warships. Glasgow and the west of Scotland also expanded their heavy industries to meet the need for the construction of weapons and ammunition, with peacetime firms diversifying their efforts into building new weapons of war such as warplanes, tanks and field guns. As a result the workforce prospered. The same was true in the other industrial centres on the east coast where Edinburgh (engineering and light manufacturing), Dundee (jute and shipbuilding) and Aberdeen (engineering and shipbuilding) all made contributions to the industrial war effort and once again the war came as a lifeline to the working communities. And just as the pattern of industrial specialisation mirrored what had happened in the First World War, so too was the major part of Scotland's industrial infrastructure still situated in the traditional areas of the central belt.

Shipbuilding and its associated trades remained pre-eminent, with the Clyde taking the lion's share of the Admiralty's warship orders. By 1938 the total tonnage under construction, 164,911, was not dissimilar to the figure in 1913, 167,286.[23] Fairfield had orders for one battleship, one aircraft carrier, two cruisers and four destroyers, while John Brown at Clydebank had received orders for one battleship, one cruiser, three depot ships and four destroyers. Four other firms – Scott, Stephen, Denny and Yarrow – were equally busy with orders for more than 10,000 tons of naval and merchant shipping.[24] In Dundee the Caledon yard constructed 'Empire' merchant ships to the specification of the Ministry of War Transport, as well as a number of warships including the convoy escort aircraft carrier HMS *Activity* which was based on an Empire merchant ship. On the outbreak of war one of the main preoccupations had been the presence of major ships under construction which were thought to represent tempting targets for German bombers, especially on the Clyde. These included the Cunard liner *Queen Elizabeth*, the battleship HMS *Duke of York* and the aircraft carrier HMS *Indefatigable*, but it was not until 12 July 1940 that the area was raided by German bombers. By then, in grey livery and under conditions of great secrecy, *Queen Elizabeth* had sailed to New York without benefit of trials or even an escort, a remarkable achievement.

Almost immediately, though, Clydebank was hit by a number of labour problems, and while these were never as serious as those that had flared up during the First World War when strikes on 'Red Clydeside' were commonplace, they did cause problems to the management. Despite the introduction of legislation – the Emergency Powers Act and the relevant Defence Regulations (Order 1305) – which banned strikes in wartime, there were over 900 stoppages across the UK during the first months of the war. Most of them were short-lived and settled by conciliation, but they gave notice that the labour force was still determined to protect workers' interests.

By far the most serious outbreak of trouble on the Clyde came in February 1941 when apprentices in the shipbuilding and related industries went on strike over a pay dispute which had first emerged in 1937. Although there had been a settlement, there was still resentment over the low wages paid to apprentices. The 1941 dispute broke out originally at the Glenfield & Kennedy engineering works and then spread to the Clyde. With the coming of war the passing of the Essential Work (General Provisions) Order in 1941 permitted the introduction of dilution, which allowed less skilled workers known as dilutees to be employed in jobs previously reserved for time-served men. While this made sense from a war production point of view, it created anomalies in pay scales with the result that a senior apprentice could find himself being paid under one pound a week while a dilutee would be paid four times that amount after a basic training programme which lasted only six weeks.

As it turned out, the government acted with reasonable haste to resolve the issue – by fixing the apprentice's pay at a percentage of the journeyman's wage according to his age – and the apprentices went back to work following the Clydebank blitz, but there was an unpleasant incident when the leader of the apprentices, John Moore of John Brown's, had his reserved status removed and was called up for National Service.[25] Only the threat of further industrial action put a stop to this unnecessary aggravation, and following an inquiry, Moore's status was restored, allowing him to return to his reserved occupation.

Following Hitler's invasion of Russia and the subsequent Allied alliance with the Soviet Union, there was a temporary cessation of serious incidents of striking – the exceptions being major incidents in Kent in 1942 and Liverpool the following year – but by 1944 there were over 2,000 stoppages across the UK involving the loss of 3,714,000 days' production. With a war still to be won, this led to the imposition of Defence Regulation 1AA, supported by the Trades Union Congress (TUC), which made incitement to strike unlawful. For the most part, and compared to what happened during the First World War, relationships between workers and management remained mainly quiescent on Scotland's industrial front for the rest of the conflict. All shipbuilding work was counted as a reserved occupation, and for most of the war the Clydebank yards worked round the clock, including Sundays, and ended up producing 994 warships and 503 merchant vessels. To put this in perspective, in the five years before the war the total tonnage launched on Clydeside was 322,000 tons, but the average annual tonnage launched from 1940 to 1944 was 493,000 tons.[26]

As ever, shipbuilding depended on its ancillary and related industries, and, above all, on the production of steel. Once again the war came as a lifeline to the latter industry, and production in the west of Scotland averaged 1.9 million tons throughout the conflict. The main producers were Bairds (Gartsherrie); Frederick Braby (Glasgow); Clyde Alloy Steel (Motherwell); Colville's (Bellshill, Glasgow, Glengarnock and Motherwell); Dixon's (Glasgow); Lanarkshire Steel (Motherwell); Smith & McLean (Gartcosh and Glasgow); Steel Company of Scotland (Cambuslang); Stewarts & Lloyds (Mossend); and John Williams (Wishaw). In addition, the industry also supported a variety of heavy metal works such as ferrous tubes, forgings and stampings; iron and steel casting; wire and wire ropes; and sheet-metal work. Iron production also rallied and managed to produce an average of 500,000 tons throughout the war years. Considering that the immediate pre-war output had been 409,000 tons, this was a significant improvement.[27]

Mention should also be made of Scotland's role in the development and production of aluminium which was helped greatly by the rapid strides made in hydro-electric power in the Highlands. Following the formation of the British Aluminium Company in 1894, initial production from bauxite was based at Larne in Northern Ireland. However in 1913 it was switched to Burntisland in Fife where demand quickly outstripped the plant's ability to supply alumina, so much so that a second factory had to be built at Newport in Monmouthshire. At the same time production from alumina by reduction was started in the Great Glen at Foyers, Fort William and Kinlochleven, which all benefited from the provision of hydro-electric power. Before the war all fabrication was completed in England and Wales, but in June 1944 the Ministry of Aircraft Production opened a new rolling mill for aluminium alloy sheet at Falkirk, and by the end of the war it had become one of the largest installations of its kind in the world.[28]

The other great staple of Scotland's heavy industries was coal, but it enjoyed mixed fortunes during the war. Although there was a critical national need for coal, both for industrial and domestic use, production was a problem, and in the first twelve months the impact of war soon became obvious. Production across the UK's coalfields fell from 4,485,000 tons in September 1939 to 4,095,000 tons in August 1940. By the following year, 1941, the situation had deteriorated further when annual production fell from 231,337,900 tons in 1939 to 206,344,300 tons in 1941. It was to be the beginning of a worrying downward trend.[29] In Scotland matters were even worse. In 1939 the output had been 30.5 million tons, but by the end of the war this had slumped to 21.4 million tons; in the first half of 1942 productivity in Scotland had fallen to 12.99 per cent, the lowest in the UK, whereas in Yorkshire during the same period it was 20.58 per cent. Even more worryingly, the Scottish workforce had declined by 10 per cent from its pre-war high of 88,000 men.[30] When the figures were published the public was reported to be 'profoundly shocked', and because the drop in production threatened Britain's war effort, the Ministry of Fuel and Power began an investigation into what was described by the *Official History* as 'one of the remarkable features of the economic history of the war.'[31]

The main problem was diagnosed as a drastic fall in the output per miner employed in the industry; in Scotland this was found to be particularly severe – from 345 tons per man per year in 1939 to 266 tons in 1945. At first absenteeism was thought to be the main reason, as it had been a perennial problem since the strikes of the 1920s, but this was balanced by the fact that there had been no appreciable reduction in the number of shifts being worked. The hard winter of 1941–2 was probably another factor, as was industrial unrest, especially in Lanarkshire, which resulted in only three weeks in the whole of 1941 being free of industrial disputes. However, further investigation revealed that the principal factor in the declining output was the fact that the mining population had been denuded by men being called up into the armed forces. Miners who were reservists or served in the TA put on uniform in 1939, and between then and July 1941, 80,000 coal-related workers in the vital twenty-one-to-forty age group had been called up into the armed forces. After that date, in an attempt to staunch the flow, their occupation was given reserved status. An appeal was made to miners in the services to return to their former occupation through a radio broadcast by Ernest Bevin in June 1941, but only 500 responded, mainly in England and Wales. A year later came the Mining Optants Scheme which allowed men aged under twenty-five to remain in mining as an alternative to military service, but this only produced 2,750 applicants.[32] By the end of 1943 only 50,000 miners had returned to the industry.

The outcome of the shortages in personnel led to the conscription of the 'Bevin Boys' which partially solved the problem (see Chapter 8), but it is not difficult to understand why coalmining had become such an unpopular industry. From being a relatively well-paid and influential job before the First World War – especially after the introduction of the minimum wage in 1912 – it had been emasculated by the strikes and lock-outs of the 1920s, and in consequence the miners felt that they had been humiliated. Wages had slumped compared to many other occupations, there was more mobility and choice in the workplace, industrial relations were poor, and working conditions were often dangerous; as a result, fathers did not want their sons to follow them down the pit. To exacerbate the situation the industry was still mainly in private hands and little had been done to attract new entrants.

It took time for the wartime government to intervene in any meaningful way. To begin with the industry was put under the control of the Mines Department within the Board of Trade, but in 1942 the department was abolished and all functions relating to coal production were transferred to a new Ministry of Fuel and Power. The wartime work of the ministry was mainly of an executive nature; it included responsibility for overseeing coal production, controlling the price of coal and regulating the health, safety and training of all mine workers. However despite that intervention, the *Official History* concluded that 'the war finished with gloomy prospects [for the industry].'[33]

It was not all pessimism on the Scottish industrial front. War, the great bringer of technological change, created opportunities for diversification in Scotland, and to a limited extent these were accepted. With war production coming under government control there was greater scope for smaller firms to participate in major construction programmes. This was especially true of aircraft production, which was the responsibility of the Air Ministry. On 7 February 1940, during a House of Commons debate on the granting of building contracts, Sir Kingsley Wood confirmed that of his ministry's list of 100 new contracts, 45 had been given to Scottish firms.[34]

The largest contribution was made by the Rolls-Royce factory at Hillington where Merlin engines were manufactured for Hurricane and Spitfire aircraft, the RAF's frontline fighters. Initially developed in the 1930s, the Merlin was to become the mainstay of RAF operations during the war, and all told around 150,000 examples were built in several variations for use by a wide variety of aircraft. To meet the expected demand Rolls-Royce had to expand its operations from its main base at Derby, and moved the bulk of production first to Crewe and then to Hillington in June 1939. With its pre-war industrial development site, a workforce in waiting and access to local steel and forgings, the site proved to be an ideal choice, and it was fully operational by the summer of 1940, eventually employing 160,000 workers. Most had little previous experience of engineering work and had been recruited to meet the needs of war production, with the result that it took Rolls-Royce until the following year to get into full production. In the early stages of the operation only 4 per cent of the male workforce were said to be skilled, and training was made an immediate priority.[35] Other centres of aircraft construction were at Dumbarton, Greenock and Prestwick.

Following the Munich crisis in 1938 there had been a concerted drive to increase the production of warplanes, and by September 1939 the monthly average had increased from 200 a month in the first six months of 1938 to 780 a month.[36] Priority was given to five existing main types: Wellington, Whitley and Blenheim bombers, and Spitfire and Hurricane fighters. At the same time work continued in the development of Halifax, Manchester (later redesigned as the Lancaster with four, instead of two, engines) and Stirling heavy bombers which were due to come into service in 1941. More powerful Merlin engines were also required to boost the performance of improved Hurricane, Beaufighter and Defiant aircraft for service in the night-fighter and ground-attack roles.[37] Work was directed by the Ministry of Air Production and Ministry of Supply through individual manufacturers such as Hawker, Avro and Supermarine, with companies such as Rolls-Royce supplying the main components, of which the most vital was the Merlin, in all its many variants.

As a result of this wartime expansion, Hillington became a vital cog in the British war machine and one of the largest industrial operations in Scotland, with an output of 400 Merlins a month by March 1942. However, the creation of the Rolls-Royce complex was not without problems. In the early days there were difficulties with accommodation for the workforce as the surrounding area had little in the way of available housing. This was addressed early on by the construction of 1,500 houses at Penilee by Glasgow Corporation and the Scottish Special Housing Association, a Treasury-funded organisation which had been formed in 1938 under the Housing (Scotland) Act. Under the terms of the arrangement the houses would revert to council ownership for letting once the war was over.[38] There were also problems with the engineering innovations within the factory, and the pace of the work led to outbreaks of absenteeism. Not only were workers, including women, expected to work an 82-hour week with only one Sunday half-day per month as holiday, but in the early days there was continuous interruption from air raids and air-raid warnings which created a tense atmosphere. Eventually the pattern of work was cut back to 54 hours a week, but as Ken Milne, one of the workforce remembered in 2010, although Hillington was a modern factory it was

What Scotland's future looked like in the summer of 1938. One of the most popular attractions at the Empire Exhibition in Glasgow's Bellahouston Park was the Palace of Engineering, exhibiting large models of the ships which had made the Clyde famous. (The Mitchell Library, Glasgow City Council)

Hawker Hart light bombers of 603 (City of Edinburgh) Squadron above the Forth railway bridge in 1934. Re-equipped with Supermarine Spitfire fighters the part-time auxiliary squadron claimed its first kill, a Junkers 88, over the same area on 16 October 1939. (© Museum of Flight, National Museums Scotland. Licensor www.scran.co.uk)

First casualties of war: survivors from the sinking of SS *Athenia* arrive at fog-bound Greenock on 5 September 1939. The unarmed passenger liner had been sunk the previous evening by the *U-30* under the command of Kapitänleutnant Fritz-Julius Lemp.

Mathematics class in progress at Broomlee evacuation camp near West Linton. Before the war plans had been laid to evacuate women and children from the Central Belt to escape the expected air raids. In addition to the camps most evacuees were billeted in private houses. (National Archives of Scotland)

The threat of enemy bombing was taken seriously throughout the conflict. Although the anticipated chemical warfare attacks failed to materialize, people were encouraged to carry gas masks and to practise wearing them, as these telephonists are doing.

Kilbowie Road in Clydebank after the first intensive enemy bombing attack on the night of 13 March 1941. Known as the Clydebank Blitz, most of the damage was done to housing, and 35,000 people were made homeless while 528 were killed. (West Dunbartonshire Council)

A section of local defence volunteers on patrol by Loch Stack in Sutherland. Better known as the Home Guard, the force came into being in May 1940 to provide a part-time defence force whose primary task would be to counter the threat of invasion posed by German airborne forces.
(Imperial War Museum H 7323)

General Władysław Sikorski and King George VI inspecting Polish troops at Glamis Castle. With their smart uniforms and the romance of their recent fighting experiences the Poles were well received in Scotland; many married Scottish girls and settled in the country after the war. (Imperial War Museum H 7755)

Tom Johnston acted as Churchill's Secretary of State for Scotland between 1940 and 1945 and used his authority to protect Scotland's interests. A 'Red Clydesider' in the First World War, Johnston launched numerous initiatives to help the war effort and to create jobs.

Two foresters from British Honduras (Belize) cutting timber for pit props and wood pulp in East Linton. They were an important part of the war effort, but their treatment by the authorities ranged from callous indifference to off-hand cruelty. (Imperial War Museum ZZZ 12724 D)

A working party of 'Lumber Jills' of the Women's Timber Corps, formed in 1942 to train young women for war work in Scotland's forests. After basic training 4,900 of their number worked as foresters, mainly in the Highlands, freeing up men for service in the armed forces.

Fairfield drillers at work on a gun-shield for the battleship HMS *Howe* prior to commissioning in August 1942. At the outbreak of war the Clyde yards had 164,911 tons of ships under construction including the Cunard liner *Queen Elizabeth* and the aircraft carrier HMS *Indefatigable*. (The Mitchell Library, Glasgow City Council)

Having been conscripted for war work in 1942 the poet Hugh MacDiarmid worked as a lathe-turner at Mechan's Engineering Company in Scotstoun in Glasgow.

Women played in a key role in war work, and after 1941 were liable to be conscripted. A group of workers is preparing ration packs of tea, milk and sugar at the Scottish Co-operative and Wholesale Society (SCWS) factory at Shieldhall in Glasgow in 1942. (The Mitchell Library, Glasgow City Council)

Commandos cross a toggle bridge at the Commando Training Depot at Achnacarry in Inverness-shire. Simulated artillery fire gave some realism but the most potent factor was the rugged terrain. The western Highlands proved to be ideal training ground for operations in occupied Europe.

Men of the 2nd Argyll and Sutherland Highlanders engaged in jungle training in Malaya in 1941. Nicknamed 'Jungle Beasts' on account of their ability to survive in the enervating conditions they were one of the few battalions to emerge with credit following the surrender of Singapore the following year.

Blindfolded survivors from the *Scharnhorst* are led ashore at Scapa Flow after the German battle-cruiser was sunk by a naval force led by HMS *Duke of York* on 26 December 1943. During the Battle of North Cape only 36 of *Scharnhorst*'s sailors survived from a crew of 1,968.

Two of the four-man crew of the X-class midget submarine HMS *Extant* (*X-25*) prepare to dock in the Holy Loch. Just over 50 feet in length the boats were designed for stealthy penetration of enemy harbours to attack individual targets such as the battleship *Tirpitz*.

A line of Allied merchant ships makes its way around the north cape of Norway to the Russian ports of Murmansk and Archangel. Altogether 78 Arctic Convoys assembled at Loch Ewe for the dangerous voyage in which they endured attack by enemy surface ships, submarines and aircraft. (National Archives of Scotland)

The pipes and drums of the 51st Highland Division play in the main square of Tripoli on 28 January 1943, following a review by General Bernard Montgomery, commander of the British Eighth Army. The division played a key role during the Battle of Alamein in October the previous year. (Imperial War Museum E 21969)

Led by a piper, soldiers of the 2nd Argyll and Sutherland Highlanders move up to the attack during Operation Epsom on 26 June 1944 to outflank Caen. The initial assault was made by the 15th Scottish Division and the ground they fought over came to be known as the 'Scottish Corridor'. (Imperial War Museum B 5988)

Major-General T. G. Rennie, commander of the 51st Highland Division in Rouen in September 1944. He had recently taken over the division after it had been badly mauled in Normandy and had quickly restored morale and fighting spirit. In the following year he was killed during the crossing of the Rhine. (Imperial War Museum BU 1518)

A De Havilland Mosquito VI fighter-bomber of 143 Squadron fires rockets at German merchant ship during an attack by the Banff Strike Wing on the harbour at Sandefjord in Norway. Formed in 1944 the wing operated out of Banff and Dallachy in the North-east. (Imperial War Museum HU 93037)

Soldiers of 10th Highland Light Infantry come ashore after crossing the Rhine at the end of March 1945 as part of the final push into Germany. The exploit was commemorated in a memorable march, '10th HLI Crossing the Rhine', composed by Pipe-Major Donald Ramsay and Corporal J. Moore.

Victory parade in Bremerhaven on 12 May 1945 led by the pipes and drums of the 51st Highland Division which was then under the command of Major-General Gordon Macmillan. The salute was taken by Lieutenant-General Brian Horrocks, the commander of XXX Corps. (Imperial War Museum BU 6560)

Even before the war ended preparations had been made to celebrate the end of the fighting. The Scottish Office was keen 'to avoid the hooliganism which may develop amongst an excited crowd with nothing to do', but crowds still gathered to celebrate in Princes Street Gardens in Edinburgh. (Scotsman Publications)

hard and enervating work: 'There was the constant noise of machin-
ery. It was pretty much working 24 hours a day. The only time they
were silent was during lunch and the short tea breaks which you had
to take standing by your machine.'[39]

There was also an issue with rates of pay. Amongst the Hillington
workforce were 20,000 women who were expected to work under
the same conditions as male workers. From the outset of the operation
the Amalgamated Engineering Union (AEU) reached an agreement
with management that women would receive equal pay with men
after thirty-two weeks in post, but this was evaded by management
which claimed that the machines had been simplified for use by
women. Because this did not apply to men who received a larger
wage, the AEU mounted a challenge at the beginning of 1943.
During the subsequent inquiry which was headed by Lord Wark, a
new grading system came into being, and this was accepted by the
AEU. However, when it was introduced it was found that it applied
to only 80 per cent of the female workforce, leaving large numbers of
women on the lowest grades. As a result, 16,000 workers went on
strike for a week in October 1943. This led to a new agreement which
listed every machine in the factory, the work done on it, and the rate
for the job, regardless of who was operating the equipment. On
average it was calculated that the mean weekly wage for a 47-hour
week would be £4 3s, a result that satisfied the bulk of the workforce.[40]

In the aftermath of the walkout passions continued to run high at
Hillington, and the AEU took the unusual step of accusing the strike
committee (Clyde Workers' Committee) of being anti-war and
Trotskyite in its approach by misrepresenting the deal on offer. In
so doing, claimed the anonymous author of an article in the AEU
magazine *New Propeller* (later called *The Metal Worker*), they simply
played into the hands of the 'capitalist Press' which had accused
workers of entertaining pacifist tendencies: 'Unfortunately, wild
rumours were deliberately fostered by anti-war elements in the works,
whose declared policy is to hold up vital war production, the effect of
which is to help Hitler . . . In order to hide their Fifth Column
disruptive role they attempted to cover up this disruption by dragging
in the Communist Party so that workers would be diverted by the
"Red Bogey" so beloved by Goebbels.'[41]

This was strong language, but it reflects the unions' need to protect their members' rights at a time when strikes were illegal and any manifestation of stoppages or walkouts were thought to be unpatriotic. In this instance, too, AEU negotiators believed that the management of Rolls-Royce had not fully explained the outcome of the Court of Inquiry and had been economical with the facts by producing grading cards which gave the impression that women would remain on the lowest grade of pay. By then, too, women had become an integral part of the workforce. In 1942 women had been admitted to membership of the AEU and dilution had become an accepted part of the war effort. Indeed the Rolls-Royce plant at Hillington could not have operated without the huge input made by female workers who had demonstrated that they were the equal of the mainly male workforce.

It was a delicate balance: on the whole unions had signed up to the no-strike legislation and were supportive of the war effort, not least because the Soviet Union was an ally. At the same time, though, industrial relations were not always easy, strike action continued throughout the war and workers, such as the Hillington women, were not always inclined to accept second best if they felt that their rights were being infringed or they were being worsted over rates of pay. Memories were still alive of the problems caused during the inter-war years when trade unionism was in decline and management was in the ascendancy. This was especially true in the coalmining industry, but it was also rife in all sectors of manufacturing where shop stewards had been victimised and there had been a noticeable decline in working conditions. It took some time for employment levels to rise as government policies began to take effect across the industries involved in the war effort. As a result, membership of the trades unions increased from 4.5 million to 7.5 million over the course of the war, and this was accompanied by the spread of recognition agreements to industries which had previously been neglectful of any involvement with the TUC.[42]

There was a price to be paid for Scotland's failure to benefit fully from the huge increases in wartime production. By the end of 1946 unemployment in Scotland had crept up to 5 per cent, and although this was to fall as world markets rallied to meet the need for replacement equipment, especially in shipbuilding, Scotland's heavy industries were still rooted in the Clyde valley just as they had been earlier in the century. Worryingly, there had been little diversification during the war when only thirty-two government factories had been built in Scotland, and this was clearly regarded as a lost opportunity.[43] As a result, there had been little improvement in Scotland's infrastructure. A list of engineering projects on the railways shows that only one line in Scotland had been improved – between July 1942 and March 1943 £95,000 was spent on four passing loops on the Ayr–Stranraer line, built as a result of the construction of the modern deepwater port at Cairnryan. In the munitions sector, a key employer in Scotland during the previous conflict, the three existing Royal Ordnance Factories at Bishopton and one at Irvine were refurbished as part of a national programme undertaken by the Ministry of Supply. Elsewhere, a new nitro-glycerine works was built in 1940 at Dalbeattie by Sir Robert McAlpine for the Royal Naval Armaments Depot, and was in constant use throughout the war. As for other wartime emergency factories, most closed after 1945, the notable exception remaining open for business being the Rolls-Royce engine factory at Hillington which survived until 2005, before moving to nearby Inchinnan.[44]

8 Home Front

For the first time in the history of modern warfare, civilians across the UK discovered that they too might find themselves on the front line or that they were required to make substantial and valuable contributions to the nation's war effort, not just in the armed forces but also in the civilian support services. That had been true to a lesser extent during the previous conflict, but in most respects the Second World War proved to be all-embracing as far as the population was concerned. Very few British people, even children, escaped being caught up in what was taking place, and while that inclusiveness helped to democratise the war, it also meant that civilians had to share many of the dangers and privations that had previously been the lot of service personnel. Certainly, no one in Scotland, even in the most remote or under-populated rural areas, escaped the reality of modern total war. By the same token, just about every family contributed members (male and female) to undertake some form of service under the various National Service Acts which harnessed the energies of the bulk of the population.

The idea of universal effort and combined hardship was so rooted within the national consciousness that when the BBC broadcast loyal messages to the king during the celebrations for the end of the war in Europe, the words of the civil defence services took pride of place immediately after the tributes offered by the armed forces: 'We are ordinary citizens, men and women, old and young, weak and strong; and most of us are part-timers. Our battle was fought around our homes, in the villages, the towns and the cities of our country, among our people and our own kin. For us, the sounding of the Alert was a summons to face the danger, and to face it without the satisfaction of being able to hit back.'[1]

Those sentiments were given voice in May 1945 at a time when the war had been won and there was some reason to express satisfaction, but they give a good indication of the sense of common cause which had guided Britain's war effort throughout the conflict. By then, too, the hardships facing the civilian population had been revealed and people wanted their suffering to be recognised as part of the communal war effort. Enemy bombing had destroyed buildings and made people homeless, and the death toll in the main cities had been considerable, but this was balanced by an understanding that it was part of the price that had to be paid. In fact, even before hostilities had broken out, preparations had been put in place for children and vulnerable adults to be evacuated in advance of the anticipated bombing campaign against major cities. On 24 May 1938, the Home Secretary Sir Samuel Hoare had set up a commission under the chairmanship of Sir John Anderson, MP for the Scottish Universities, which outlined the need for evacuating children from potential target areas and to provide billeting for them with families in parts of the country considered to be safe. In Scotland detailed planning began as early as the first half of 1939 to take children from the main centres of population in the central belt and to move them to safer areas in the countryside.

Within the Scottish Office, responsibility for organising the evacuation was put in the hands of the Department of Health which identified the following areas for immediate evacuation: Edinburgh, Rosyth, Glasgow, Clydebank, Greenock, Port Glasgow, Dumbarton and Dundee. Following German bombing raids against targets in the Firth of Forth area in October, North and South Queensferry and Inverkeithing were added to the places requiring evacuation. The reception areas were to be towns and villages in the Borders, the North-East and the Western Highlands, and the relevant powers were vested in Regulation 22(1) of the Defence Regulations 1939.[2]

From the evidence of the planning papers produced by the Scottish Office a great deal of effort was put into the exercise to ensure its smooth operation once hostilities had broken out, although it has also to be said that the public response was muted. As early as March 1939 Glasgow Corporation's Evacuation Officer had circulated a letter to parents and guardians advising them of plans to evacuate children. In Edinburgh a similar survey of 33,150 households was held but it attracted little interest, with only 12,462 families registering, only 30 per cent of the total. Unlike similar schemes in England, Wales and Northern Ireland where school classes were the focus for children being moved, Scottish evacuees would be kept together in family groups. The first trial involving 200 children was held in Cupar, Fife in June but overall the national registrations proved to be disappointing. Glasgow followed Edinburgh's example with only 106,000 children being signed up for the scheme, less than 50 per cent of those expected.

However, the arrival of war seemed to concentrate minds. When the order arrived 'implement forthwith' on 3 September, 118,833 children in Glasgow arrived at the city's main railway stations where 388 special trains had been organised to remove them to designated safe areas.[3] Clyde steamers were also pressed into service, and the Royal Scottish Automobile Club organised private cars for transport. The Scottish Special Housing Association also made available a number of camps at Broomlee (West Linton), Middleton (Gorebridge), Glengonnar (Abington), Aberfoyle and Belmont (Meigle). Responsibility for billeting arrangements was left in the hands of the local councils, and by the end of September the total figures for evacuees in Scotland were:

Unaccompanied schoolchildren:	62,059
Mothers and accompanied children:	91,170
Expectant mothers:	405
Blind persons, cripples and other special cases:	1,787
Teachers and helpers:	13,465[4]

For everyone it was a traumatic experience. Many of the children had never left their homes or neighbourhoods before, and on arrival there was frequently confusion in getting mothers and children to their final destination. This caused added difficulties for the billeting officers, especially in areas where housing was sub-standard – the Anderson report had indicated that children over the age of fourteen should be given single rooms and those under the age of fourteen would have to share. All evacuations had to be completed before nightfall, and in Scotland there were problems with late-arriving trains and transfers from the stations to the billets, especially in rural areas. Religion also intruded, with reports of Catholics from Glasgow being made unhappy because they had been billeted in 'strong Presbyterian homes in the south-west'.[5] Problems of perception also abounded. Two Glasgow children billeted in Dumfries-shire were sent to a comfortable middle-class home and given a bed with clean white sheets. When the householder went to bid them good night she found them cowering in a corner. 'We're no' goin' there,' they said, 'that's the bed for the deid folk.'[6]

Almost immediately there were other tensions between the evacuees and those providing the billets. Middle-class hosts were confronted with families who had been brought up in overcrowded tenement flats with basic toilet facilities and a rudimentary grasp of personal hygiene. A story told by Tom Johnston summed up the problem. A party of 'ragged and smelly' evacuee children was billeted on the Countess of Elgin who asked her housekeeper to fill a bath with hot water so that they could be washed, but one little boy screamed at the sight and refused to be immersed, shouting all the while in an unintelligible accent. Eventually Lady Elgin asked her housekeeper to tell her what the boy was saying, only to receive the reply: 'He's saying, madam, that it's ower fuckin' deep and ower fuckin' hot.'[7]

Enuresis, or uncontrolled urination, proved to be a particular problem, with a leading medical journal reporting that 'every morning every window is filled with bedding hung out to air in the sunshine. The scene is cheerful but the householders are depressed.'[8] A report showed that one-third of the children were verminous – impetigo was also a recurring problem – and although local education authorities had statutory powers to provide clothing and boots through Section 6 of the Education (Scotland) Act of 1908, a large proportion of the children arrived ill-shod and badly clothed. In Auchterarder in Perthshire the Kennaways were one of many local families who provided billets for children from Dundee, and as the future novelist James Kennaway remembered, it was a bewildering time for everyone (his father was a wealthy lawyer and factor and they lived in a large and comfortable house). On getting back from church the Kennaways found waiting at the front door 'some extraordinary people . . . dirty, dark and real . . . half a dozen keelies with their mother . . . the woman is awful, highly painted yet dirty, small with too much hair, tired and oddly silent'. No sooner were they admitted to the

Kennaway's house than two of the boys urinated on the front doorstep and one of them merely remarked, 'it trickles a' the way doon'.[9]

Another novelist, Robin Jenkins, was also involved in the process as a boy, in his case as a participant, and later wrote about it in *Guests of War* (1956) which was based on his own experience. In the novel he traces the fortunes of a group of evacuees from Gowburgh (Glasgow) after they arrive in the douce Borders town of Lanrigg (Moffat). Almost immediately, one of the mothers, Bell McShelvie, questions her motives for escaping with her son while leaving the rest of the family in danger back at home. In the novel's opening pages she accepts a neighbour's reproach that she is being selfish. 'Here indeed was her battlefield: the enemy she had to fight was despair at the ugliness shutting her in, at the inevitable coarseness and pitiable savagery of many of the people shut in with her, and above all at her inability to keep her own family healthy, sweet, and intact. She was weary of fighting. Even soldiers in war were given relief . . . The battle was at its height, therefore, and she had made up her mind to desert.'[10]

There is a sub-text: Bell has spent most of her life in a rundown tenement and yearns to return to the countryside which she remembers leaving as a six-year-old girl. As she and many others discovered, it was a fraught time, and although for some it turned out happily enough, in general, evacuation was a dislocating experience which led to a great deal of unhappiness and loneliness. By January 1940 at least two-thirds of those evacuated had started returning to their homes, and the count showed that the exodus had been uniform across the country. Amongst them is the fictional Bell McShelvie, who fails to overcome her feelings of guilt and decides to return to Gowburgh with its 'age and grime' and its many faults.[11] The figures for those who decided to remain were:

Unaccompanied schoolchildren:	37,600 (61 per cent)
Mothers and accompanied children:	8,900 (9 per cent)
Expectant mothers:	40 (10 per cent)
Blind persons, cripples and other special cases:	160 (9 per cent)
Teachers and helpers:	3,100 (23 per cent)[12]

It was not always the evacuees who failed to adapt. There is also evidence that host families and local organisations were often un-willing to make an additional effort to ensure that the evacuees were given sufficient help and facilities, far less a warm welcome. When 150 mothers and children arrived in Inverary from Glasgow they found that they were to be billeted in a local hall with only two lavatories, and equipped with bedding that consisted of dirty straw sacks and ancient mattresses with broad arrows painted on them, indicating that they had been used in the local gaol. When the matter was raised in the House of Commons by Campbell Stephen, Labour MP for Glasgow Camlachie, it was also pointed out that the nearby castle owned by the Duke of Argyll was largely empty and had sufficient bedrooms which could have been used, but no steps were taken to requisition the accommodation. Later, things did get better, if only modestly.

> Ultimately the Duke did take a few children and made provision for them in the basement of the castle. That is very discreditable in the circumstances in which we find ourselves. On the other hand, many of the local people were worried and anxious about what had occurred and were ready to help. There were some condemned houses that had been shut up for possibly a year. They got the keys of those houses and opened them, and many of the mothers who had been sent to this place with their children set about washing the dirty floors and cleaning up the condemned houses which had been uninhabited so long.[13]

When Stephen complained that the billets ought to have been inspected prior to the arrival of the evacuees Sir James Henderson Stewart, Conservative MP for Fife Eastern unhelpfully but pertinently interjected, 'and the children'. It was also reported that in other parts of Scotland there was equal outrage when the evacuees arrived and were lined up to allow locals to have their pick of them, one observer describing it as being like 'a slave market in the old days'.[14]

The debate echoed subsequent findings about the evacuation of women and children in the early months of the war. In his analysis of the plans and their subsequent execution the official war historian was clear that they had not worked as smoothly as had been anticipated, and that the scheme had quickly encountered problems simply because evacuation on that scale had never been attempted in the past: 'as an integral part of the plans for the protection of the civilian population, [evacuation] had largely failed to achieve its object of removing for the duration of the war most of the mothers and children in the target areas.'[15] There were many reasons for the failure. Although Anderson's commission had laid down strict guidelines for the smooth running of the evacuation scheme, it could not factor in all the human aspects. For most of those involved, like the Kennaway family and their unwilling 'guests' from Dundee it had been a case of social collision: as far as previous contact would have been concerned, the evacuees and their hosts could have been living on different planets. But for every incident of bed-wetting there were also stories of increased criminality involving evacuees – in Glasgow, for example, the number of children under the age of fourteen convicted or found guilty of theft or housebreaking was more than twice as high in 1940 as it had been before the war, and this resulted in increased delinquency in many of the reception areas. (Smashing light bulbs to hear them 'pop' was a particular problem.)[16]

There were other kinds of dislocation. People from the cities also wanted to escape the tedium of the countryside, children missed their families and loneliness made lives miserable. Religion too remained an issue. The Secretary of State for Scotland reported to the Cabinet in December 1939 that that the Archbishop of Edinburgh had issued an encyclical urging that evacuated Catholic children should be sent back home if no facilities for religious instruction existed in the reception areas.[17] In other parts of the country some Catholic priests took the view that children from their churches should run the risk of being bombed rather than receive education at non-Catholic schools in the reception areas. The argument was given added weight by the fact that the threat of bombing seemed to be waning. During the first winter of the war, with the exception of isolated raids against naval and military targets on the east coast of Scotland, the expected mass air raids had failed to materialise, and many evacuees believed that the danger had passed.

When German aircraft did make their presence felt it was a newsworthy event, and no incident was more keenly discussed than the curious crash of a Messerschmitt 110 in a field near Eaglesham in

Renfrewshire late at night on 10 May 1941. Following an erratic flight across southern central Scotland, the pilot of the aircraft baled out over Bonnyton Moor shortly after 11 p.m. and the twin-engine fighter-bomber fell to the ground and exploded. Shortly afterwards the pilot was taken into custody by a local farmer, David McLean, who then handed him over to the Home Guard. The pilot said that his name was Hauptmann (Captain) Alfred Horn and that he had 'a secret and vital message for the Duke of Hamilton', a remark that was met with some hilarity by his captors before they realised that he must be serious as he had a map showing the whereabouts of the duke's residence at nearby Dungavel. Things then moved quickly. Hamilton was summoned from RAF Turnhouse where he was wing commander, while the prisoner was transported to Maryhill Barracks where one of his guards was Corporal William Ross, later to be a post-war Labour Secretary of State for Scotland.

Only later, when the prisoner was being interrogated the following day, did it become clear that his real identity was Rudolf Hess, Hitler's deputy, who had flown to Scotland from Augsburg in the hope of meeting Hamilton; through him he hoped to 'show his sincerity and Germany's willingness for peace', the inference being that he was on an official mission to make contact with influential British personalities to discuss possible peace terms. This was one of the strangest episodes of the war, and it has given rise to a huge number of conspiracy theories about Hess's motives and the exact nature of his flight and subsequent crash. At different times it has been alleged that the pilot of the Messerschmitt was an impostor or that Hess was operating with the consent of British intelligence or that the RAF was under orders not to shoot down the aircraft when it reached British air space or, most recently (2010), that Hess came to Scotland as part of a plot hatched by MI6. All are incredible, but all gained credence at one time or another largely due to the withholding of most of the official papers concerning the incident.

When the records were released in 1992 a more banal account emerged – from a factual point of view – but none the less the story is still intriguing, not least because Hess was a high-ranking Nazi who enjoyed a close relationship with Hitler and clearly believed that he might be able to broker a peace deal between Churchill and Hitler. However, during the initial interrogation it became clear that

Hess, an ideological Nazi, had little concept about how his mission could be achieved. It also became obvious that he did not know the Duke of Hamilton except by name and reputation, having believed that the two men had met during the 1936 Olympic Games in Berlin. Equally it was made clear to Hess that Churchill's government had no intention of having any dealings with him or the regime he represented. In Germany Hitler was furious about his deputy's treachery but this was explained to the public as the onset of mental illness, as indeed it probably was. Hess was held in captivity for the rest of the war as a potential war criminal, and during that time he did develop amnesia, real or feigned, as well as other psychological disorders. As one of this interrogators, the diplomat Sir Ivone Kirkpatrick, admitted, 'the Hess episode was one of the oddest in history, and the oddest thing about it was that it was not in character.' In that sense the real impulse behind his decision might never be known.[18]

In the wake of the bombing attacks of 1941 it took time for some of the harsher realities of life on the home front to sink in. Evacuation of children had proved a mixed blessing, the blackout was unpopular and was not always strictly observed, some of the innovations such as the National Identity Card scheme were thought to be restrictive, and there had been an outbreak of 'panic buying' when rationing was first introduced in January 1940 to restrict the sale of bacon, butter and sugar. This was followed by the rationing of meat in March and tea in July, and slowly but surely the sale of just about every item of consumer interest was restricted under the Limitation of Supplies Order of 1940.

As time went on there had to be adjustments to the scheme, mainly to ensure that workers had the correct calorific intake. Coalminers received extra cheese for mealtime sandwiches but there were also regional differences. In 1942, for example, the Ministry of Food discreetly altered rationing scales to allow Scots to have additional oatmeal because of the 'difference between bread-eating England and scone-and cake-eating Scotland.'[19] Also, in the interests of fairness and good sense, pregnant women and nursing mothers were given extra allowances for food and milk. It was only when merchant ship losses started mounting that people began to see the sense of taking precautions and making sacrifices for the greater good.

Inevitably the food shortages began to make an impact on people's lives. While there is evidence to suggest that the restricted wartime diet was healthier and led to a fall in obesity, rationing was unpopular mainly because it led to monotony, and as a result attempts were made to alleviate the situation by finding other sources of food. In the country areas of Scotland there were rarely any shortages of milk or butter, and unofficial black markets flourished in which foodstuffs were bartered in return for clothes or fuel.

However these were only palliatives. By far the most successful scheme introduced by the government was the 'Dig for Victory' campaign which was the brainchild of Professor John Raeburn, who had been born in Kirkcaldy in 1912 (but brought up in Aberdeen), and had worked as a nutritionist in China and at Oxford before the war. Employed by the Ministry of Food in the agricultural planning branch in north Wales, he and his team of statisticians came up with the campaign which was led by Lord Woolton, the wartime Minister for Food. Its premise was startlingly simple, and that may explain why it was one of the most successful government initiatives on the home front. Before the war the UK imported 55 million tons of foodstuffs each year, a huge amount which meant that the country was not self-sufficient and could never be in time of war. The situation was made worse after August 1940 when the German Navy pursued a policy of unrestricted submarine warfare and British merchant ship losses began to escalate. By the following spring imports had shrunk to 28.5 million tons, less than the figure for 1917, the last time when the country had almost been brought to its knees by submarine blockade.

As the fear grew that the Germans could destroy the UK war effort by starving the country into submission, alternative methods of food production had to be found; hence the importance of Raeburn's Dig for Victory campaign. In essence it was simplicity itself. All potential cultivated land would be turned over to agricultural usage, and as a result parks, sports fields, public and private gardens were dug up and transformed into places of cultivation for all manner of crops. Even people living in tenements were encouraged to do their bit by turning over flower boxes to growing vegetables, the aim being to show that everyone was involved in the enterprise. In addition families were given permission to keep their own chickens, rabbits and goats, and at the same time 900 'pig clubs' were set up in Scotland with an estimated 6,000 pigs being raised and nurtured in private gardens and eating up scrap food.

Above all, it was a truly inspirational campaign which was backed by some of the most memorable advertising posters of the Second World War, some of them featuring cartoon characters such as Dr Carrot and Potato Pete. The aim was to encourage people to cultivate and then eat their own produce – one of the best-remembered (if not always fondly) dishes was Woolton Pie, a vegetarian concoction – but behind the propaganda pictures and the light-hearted ditties lay a serious message:

> Because of the pail, the scraps were saved,
> Because of the scraps, the pigs were saved,
> Because of the pigs, the rations were saved,
> Because of the rations, the ships were saved,
> Because of the ships, the island was saved,
> Because of the island, the Empire was saved,
> And all because of the housewife's pail.[20]

Another successful campaign was 'Make Do and Mend' featuring 'Mrs Sew-and-Sew' which encouraged people to recycle old clothes and household goods, all of which were rationed and were in short supply throughout the war. Knitting 'comforts' for service personnel was another well-supported activity, with clubs being set up in most civic centres throughout the country; one of the first to be established was the Camerons' Comfort Fund in Inverness which provided the local TA battalion – 4th Cameron Highlanders – with 950 knitted articles, together with 2,000 cigarettes and 150 packets of sweets and chocolates.[21]

Boosting morale was another important factor, and several schemes existed to help convince the population that the war was being won and that everyone had a part to play by making sure that they were involved in the process. Some schemes performed only that role and fulfilled little other useful purpose, notably the collections of scrap metal initiated by Lord Beaverbrook, Minister of Aircraft Production. At his prompting the public was asked to participate in scrap-metal drives by handing over old pots, pans and kettles, and even allowing iron railings to be cut down from outside their houses. Newspapers ran advertisements asking that people hand in anything made of metal so that the recycled scrap could be used 'to build the planes that will fly against Hitler'. Again, the scheme received massive public support and gave the impression that everyone was 'doing their bit' for their country even though, in reality, very little of the metal was ever used in aircraft construction. However, not everyone agreed with Beaverbrook's proposals, and in Blairgowrie in Perthshire the provost stubbornly refused to allow the removal of the town's elegant Victorian iron boundary railings, with the result that many original examples remained in place and did so for many years after the war, to the advantage of the local townscape.[22]

Other morale-boosting initiatives were 'Salute the Soldier' and 'Wings for Victory' weeks which took place in major towns and cities in order to boost national savings and to recognise the roles played by the armed forces. In one such event in April 1943 a damaged Messerschmitt 109 fighter aircraft was put on display in Dundee's Caird Square as part of a drive to raise funds for aircraft production. It was a great success, with the people of Dundee contributing just over £3 million. This proved to be a British record, although the result was later marred by an undignified incident in which Aberdeen council accused Dundee of gaining the record by adding in sums raised in other Angus towns.

Perhaps the greatest change that affected the entire population was the conscription of women. On 18 December 1941 the UK became the only combatant country to harness the female workforce when a National Service Act made it compulsory for unmarried women in the twenty-to-thirty age group to undertake some form of war work. In fact there already existed a possibility for women to serve in the armed forces by joining the reformed Women's Royal Naval Service (universally known as Wrens), the Auxiliary Territorial Service (the women's branch of the Territorial Army, formed in 1938) or the Women's Auxiliary Air Force (formed in June 1939), all of which allowed men to be released for frontline duties. The passing of the National Service Acts turned these voluntary services into an obligation, although conscripted women also had the opportunity of joining the Women's Transport Service, the Women's Volunteer Service, the Women's Land Army (Land Girls), the Women's Timber Corps

(Lumber Jills), the Local Defence Volunteers (Home Guard), or of working in munitions factories. The legislation was later extended to married women, although pregnant women and mothers with young children were granted exemption.

From the outset women were not allowed to undertake frontline service or carry weapons, although fifteen female pilots of the women's section of the Air Transport Auxiliary lost their lives while ferrying warplanes on active service. Instead the point about female conscription was to allow women to take the place of men in administrative jobs who might otherwise have been unable to undertake operational duties in the armed forces. This policy was made explicit in all recruiting literature, with the Women's Land Army (WLA) encouraging potential recruits with the exhortation that 'every women who joins the regular force in the Women's Land Army will take a soldier's place in wartime.'[23]

Conscription for women was a national UK undertaking, but in Scotland one of its most familiar expressions was found in the estimated 8,500 female conscripts who served as Land Girls in the Scottish Women's Land Army (SWLA). Originally created in 1917, at another time of national need, the Women's Land Army and the associated Women's Timber Corps had been reformed in the summer of 1939 and were quickly expanded to include 80,000 recruits. Although it had a military-sounding title and the Land Girls wore civilianised uniforms (corduroy breeches, shirt and tie, green pullover, hat and felt armband), the SWLA was not part of the armed forces and its members were non-combatants.

Potential recruits made application to the Department of Agriculture in Edinburgh where they were eventually interviewed and their suitability was assessed. Physical fitness for the work was considered to be most important, as was the ability to drive a motor vehicle, but all successful applicants were given full training either on a farm or at an agricultural college such as the West of Scotland Agricultural College at Auchencruive in Ayrshire (later part of the Scottish Agricultural College). Girls from rural backgrounds were almost always selected, but as with all forms of National Service throughout the war, there was a hit-or-miss element to the process, and some candidates at Auchencruive found that their fellow recruits 'hadn't a clue' when they were thrown into the training course which lasted four weeks and embraced general agricultural work, market gardening, dairy work and poultry husbandry.[24]

Following basic training – unless it had been done on a farm – recruits were sent to their first posting, and it was usually a matter of luck if the accommodation was on the farm itself or in a communal hostel. It worked both ways. Although some farm accommodation could be basic, the land girl was at least involved in the life of the farm and its rhythms of work – a few went on to marry farmers' sons or fellow employees – while hostels offered companionship and the opportunity to experience a wider variety of farm work. The SWLA hostel at Roswell in East Lothian housed eighty girls and provided labour for different farms in the surrounding area where in the main the land girls got a warm welcome.[25]

Even allowing for the passing of the years to put a gloss on what happened in the past, the experience of most Scottish land girls seems to have been positive.[26] While there were farmers who displayed initial scepticism and claimed that they preferred using German or Italian prisoners of war, they were soon turned round by the general enthusiasm and willingness to work hard which were the hallmarks of the land girls. Pay was another matter. Land girls were paid twenty-eight shillings a week, which was ten shillings less than a male farm worker, and well below the amount paid to an unskilled labourer in other occupations. While there was scope for overtime, especially during harvest, and some farmers paid an additional premium if the land girl had a driving licence, it was still a hard grind. Against that, the accommodation was subsidised, rations were generally good, and while the uniform was not really suited to agricultural work, it was smart and purposeful, and land girls made a brave show when they paraded in nearby towns. The companionship was also important, but more than anything else it was the life on the land that appealed and gave the SWLA land girls an experience which none ever forgot, especially those who came from non-farming backgrounds.

Allied to the SWLA were the 4,900 'Lumber Jills' who worked for the Women's Timber Corps which had been inaugurated in April 1942 under the auspices of the Ministry of Supply, and which grew out of the Women's Timber Service of the First World War. Scotland formed its own corps a month later as part of SWLA but with a separate identity and uniform which included smart riding breeches. As with the Land Girls, the recruits came from varied backgrounds, and all were given four weeks of basic training at centres such as Shandford Lodge near Brechin in Angus and Park House near Banchory where they received instruction in felling, cross-cutting, loading wagons and, in some cases, working with horses. Once they were sent to work on the forests, most Lumber Jills found the living accommodation fairly primitive, although some centres such as Inverchoalin Lodge, a remote shooting lodge by Loch Striven in Argyllshire, were fairly luxurious, with hot running water and comfortable rooms. Pay was modest – forty-eight shillings for those over nineteen – but against that there were deductions for food and accommodation and National Health contributions – with the result that most Lumber Jills were only left with a little pocket money. As with the Land Girls the privations were balanced by the camaraderie and the belief that the corps was making a beneficial contribution to the war effort by producing timber and freeing men for active service in the armed forces. In 2007 the Forestry Commission Scotland erected a memorial to the work of the Lumber Jills at the Queen Elizabeth Forest Park near Aberfoyle.

The conscription of women was followed by the National Service (No. 2) Act 1941, which imposed on all persons of either sex a general obligation to service in the armed forces, civil defence or industry, and extended the upper age limit of liability to service in the armed forces to fifty-one years. As a result of this ruling, the poet Hugh MacDiarmid, then aged forty-nine, was conscripted in January 1942 to work as a lathe-turner involved in the manufacture of shell bands at Mechan's Engineering Company in Scotstoun in Glasgow. This meant leaving Whalsay in Shetland where he had been living since 1933, and it also entailed temporary separation from his wife Valda and son Michael. It was back-breaking labour, especially for a man who was not in the first flush of youth: working days were nine-and-a-half hours long and overtime was compulsory on a Sunday. His problems were exacerbated that August when he was badly injured in an industrial accident involving the collapse of a pile of copper plate, and was forced to take several weeks off work. The hard grinding nature of the work took its toll on MacDiarmid, and his situation was not helped by living in a strange city, for much of the time separated from his family. It also led to a rupture with his brother Andrew Grieve, and the quarrel was never settled.

The case of Hugh MacDiarmid was not the only example of industrial conscription. From December 1943 onwards provision was also made for volunteers or randomly selected men aged eighteen to twenty-five to assist the war effort by working as coalminers, many of whose number had already been conscripted into the armed forces, thereby causing a labour shortage in the industry. They were known as 'Bevin Boys' after the creator of the scheme, Ernest Bevin, wartime Minister of Labour and National Service, and some 48,000 young men served in this way. After six weeks of training they were deployed to a coal mine to work, almost out of sight but not yet out of mind. Many of the chosen conscripts felt emasculated by not serving in the armed forces, and because they did not wear a uniform of even a distinctive badge in public, they were often given a hostile reception due to a widespread and wrong-headed belief that they were conscientious objectors. (This historical anomaly was not rectified until 2008 when the government agreed to issue a veterans' badge to recognise their role following a spirited campaign by Gordon Banks, Labour MP for Ochil and South Perthshire.[27]) Once called up, the new workforce was housed in specially constructed barrack-type hutted accommodation close to the pits, and training was carried out at thirteen pits throughout the UK, the Scottish centre being Government Training Centre Colliery at Muircockhall near Dunfermline in Fife, with accommodation at the nearby Miners Hostel at Townhill.

Some idea of the problem facing the coal industry can be seen from the contemporary productivity figures. In 1940 the industry employed a workforce of 749,000 miners who produced 224 million tons of coal, but by October 1942 this had fallen to 704,000 miners who produced 709,000 tons of coal.[28] Conscription was therefore essential to the war effort and was considered a successful innovation, but as George Ralston, a Bevin Boy at the Lady Victoria Colliery at Newtongrange in Midlothian, discovered, it was not for the fainthearted. 'The men came from all walks of life. Many of them had lived in the cities and some were from the Scottish Highlands. Some had never seen a coal mine in their lives before. It must have been a terrible shock to them. Many of us were prepared and ready to do our

National Service in one of the armed services and had some idea of what to expect. We were not prepared for the type of work we had been sent to do in the coal mines.'[29] On the credit side, Ralston also discovered that the conscript miners were well fed and that his fellow miners were generally helpful, friendly and welcoming.

Due to the exigencies of post-war shortages, the last Bevin Boys were not released until 1948, and unlike other service personnel, they were neither given demob suits nor accorded the right to return to their pre-war jobs – rights which were given by law to conscripts who had served in the armed forces.

Elsewhere life went on as best it could under the circumstances of a global war with its attendant shortages, hardships and the ever-present fear of bad news from the battle front. The social mix was also altered, albeit in most cases temporarily. There is ample oral evidence to suggest that people often found themselves caught up in situations and in the company of those they might never have encountered previously in peacetime. For the first time they saw how others lived, especially in the rough democracy imposed by conscription in the armed forces or in the civil defence services where a female graduate might find herself sharing an ARP post with 'lawyers or doctors, factory workers, strippers or dustmen'.[30] There was also a natural tendency to live for the moment, and this was reflected in popular songs and other entertainments in which it was possible to contrast the constraints of war with the glamour of escapism. It was also reflected in the ways in which relationships between the sexes were conducted, with much contemporary evidence pointing to an increase in sexual activity between younger partners, especially between men and women whose lives were constantly in danger. Again, statistical evidence is flimsy but there seems, too, to have been a modest rise in reported sexually transmitted diseases, especially in the larger cities and ports where there was an increase in the numbers of service personnel in transit.[31] There was another side effect: pregnancy. Although illegitimacy rates are an inexact indicator of sexual morality, the fact remains that across Scotland a significant proportion of illegitimate children were born to married, widowed or divorced women: in post-war Aberdeen, of the 282 women registered as having had second or more illegitimate births, 158 were married, widowed or divorced. These women accounted for almost half of the total of 359 illegitimate maternities in Aberdeen in the four years following the war.[32] Equally, there is also ample contemporary evidence to suggest that, on the contrary, wartime did not completely break down existing social shibboleths and that natural sexual reticence or fear of pregnancy meant that abstinence continued to be the order of the day.[33]

One of the best fictional portrayals of the highly charged romantic atmosphere of the home front in Scotland is Ronald Duncan's erotic ghost story 'Consanguinity', which explores a sister's incestuous love for her soldier brother when he comes home on leave in Edinburgh in the middle of the war. The plot is relatively straightforward. Two Scottish officers, one a Seaforth Highlander (Alex Maclean), the other Black Watch (Peter Buckle), find themselves on the overnight train to Edinburgh. Both have recently been in action, respectively in the Far East and North Africa. Finding that Buckle has nowhere to stay, Maclean invites him to spend his leave with himself and his sister Angela. The inevitable happens – Buckle falls for the sister and they decide to marry immediately because as Duncan explains, war has changed all the rules.

> War alone releases our personal relationships. It is not a necessary evil but a necessary pleasure. If we were honest, we would admit that all the slaughter, cruelty and suffering which war entails remain for us merely a matter of regrettable statistics. What means something to us is that war provides us with that sense of insecurity which is life, when peace has seemed as respectable and as dull as death . . . In war, we can release ourselves without guilt; indeed, our excuses become duties and any behaviour is condoned under the blanket of the great sacrifice that we curse privately but enjoy privately.[34]

Duncan was born in Southern Rhodesia, and his literary career was closely bound up with Ezra Pound and the composer Benjamin Britten, for whom he wrote the libretto *The Rape of Lucretia* (1946). Even though he was not a native-born Scot, Duncan showed a sure sense of touch in describing Edinburgh's literary scene and the Rose Street pubs with their 'coterie of affable but garrulous cadgers' whom the two soldiers meet, and one of whom is introduced as a nationalist – it has already been explained that Maclean has literary ambitions. Then something inexplicable happens. Following the marriage ceremony and the first night Buckle disappears completely, leaving no trace of his presence, and when his new wife investigates at the War Office it transpires that he had been killed at Tobruk six months earlier. The reader is left with the supposition that Buckle was either a ghost or a figment of Angela's imagination, or that she and her brother are in fact lovers enjoying a physical relationship. Lying in her bath in the honeymoon hotel in Brighton where Alex has also been staying, Angela, a self-confessed virgin, revels in the feeling that 'her limbs had drunk from her own desire' and that it was the first time that she 'had been aware of her own body as an instrument of pleasure'.

Duncan's story is matched by Bruce Marshall's novel *The Black Oxen* which was published long after the war had ended. However, its author was no stranger to conflict having served on the Western Front during the First World War when he was taken prisoner and lost a leg. After living in France he returned to the UK in June 1940 and volunteered for further military service. Latterly he served with SOE, and one his most notable works is *The White Rabbit* (1952), which told the harrowing story of the capture and torture by the Gestapo of Wing Commander F. F. E. Yeo-Thomas who was parachuted into France in 1943. His *nom de guerre* was the book's title. However, it was as a novelist that Marshall was best known. Born in Edinburgh in 1899, he was educated there and at Glenalmond before progressing to St Andrews University where his studies were interrupted by the outbreak of war in 1914. A convert to Catholicism, some his best fiction was inspired by his religious faith, and one novel, *Father Malachi's Miracle* (1931), became an international bestseller.

Marshall regarded *The Black Oxen* as his 'Scottish epic', and it is fair to say that many of the concerns and interests of his family background came together in the novel. It is set in middle-class Edinburgh in an instantly recognisable social milieu – professional, privately educated and closely interlinked – and follows the main protagonists and their ever-changing gallery of lovers from the end of the war in 1919 through to the 1970s. The period dealing with the Second World War is also astutely drawn, from the desire of the main characters to get back into uniform at the outset (particularly poignant for the old soldiers), through the ambiguities of the phoney war period to the sudden cosmopolitanism which suffused Edinburgh in the latter half of the conflict. Interspersed with a weak sub-plot involving a Soviet military mission and the security of the Russian convoys, some of the scenes involving senior officers of every nationality are particularly revealing, and demonstrate Marshall's ability to recreate the essence of that period. His central character, and presumably Marshall's alter ego, Neil Duncan, acts as a detached observer of the action and casts an acerbic eye over his fellow citizens as they refuse to let the war get in the way of their lives and their myriad love affairs: 'Was it any more absurd to fight for Utopia which would never come about than for a new misery which certainly could? A Canadian private at the far end of the [tram]car moaned that he was dreaming of a White Christmas and an Air Force plonk vomited over a corporal's puttees.'[35] Marshall died in 1987, and novels like *The Black Oxen* have been unjustly neglected, but he remains one of the few literary observers of Edinburgh middle-class life in the twentieth century.

As has been noted in the passages dealing with the war in North Africa, most of the notable Scottish war literature was written by poets who served in the Mediterranean theatre (see Chapter 10), but there was still a substantial body of work by writers who were primarily novelists.[36] In that respect perhaps the greatest novel of wartime life written by a Scottish author is Eric Linklater's *Private Angelo* (1946), a superbly fashioned picaresque satire set in the Italian campaign which he dedicated to the Eighth Army. Linklater had left Orkney in 1941 to take up an appointment in the War Office's directorate of public relations and was then sent to the Italian front in 1944 as the British official historian. Out of this experience came a love affair with the country which Linklater described as 'a state of idealistic adultery'[37] and a novel which can be compared to Jaroslev Hasek's *The Good Soldier Schweik* (1923). By any standards, the novel's central character is one of the great creations in the literature of the Second World War. An Italian soldier who ends up serving in three armies, Angelo believes that he lacks the gift of courage, and with his desertions and his pusillanimity shows that he might be right in his assertion. But as the novel proceeds and the campaign reveals seemingly unending horrors – Angelo and his fiancée are both raped, and civilians are killed indiscriminately – Linklater leads the reader towards a belief that there is more to courage than simple bravery; nobility, too, is part of the equation. Angelo might be a holy fool, but he is also astutely aware of the ultimate folly of war, saying on one occasion before an Allied bombardment of an Italian town, 'I hope you will not liberate us out of existence', an utterance that could also have found its way into other anti-war novels such as Joseph Heller's *Catch-22* (1961).

Also worthy of note is Robin Jenkins's *The Cone-Gatherers* (1955) which traces the bitter enmity amongst a group of workers on an Argyllshire estate set against the wider mayhem of modern war. Although it is not strictly a work about the Second World War, Jenkins explores the dynamics of violence as the gamekeeper Duror vents his disgust on the hunchbacked Calum whose job is to collect pine seeds so that the woods on the estate can be renewed after the war. Protected by his brother Neil, young Calum arouses equal amounts of pity and revulsion in the small community which is overseen by the unfeeling patrician Lady Runcie-Campbell. Everywhere the war intrudes – warships sail down the nearby sea loch – and with its presence humanity is tarnished. When the cone-gathering brothers refuse to rescue Lady Runcie-Campbell's son – trapped at the top of a high tree – because they are 'not her servants', their overseer reasons to himself, 'in a world that's at war we can't expect sanity from every man we meet in a wood'. Inevitably perhaps, the novel ends in tragedy with the murder of Calum by Duror and the keeper's subsequent suicide. Jenkins also wrote a number of other novels connected with the war, including *Guests of War* which deals with the evacuation of children and *A Would-Be Saint* (1978) which presents the issue of conscientious objectors through its main character Gavin Hamilton.

Before leaving the Scottish literary scene on the home front it is worth noting the final days of the poet William Soutar who had served in the Royal Navy during the First World War, and who later succumbed to ankylosing spondylitis, a form of chronic inflammatory arthritis which mainly affects the spine and the sacroiliac joint in the pelvis and can cause eventual fusion of the spine. By 1930, and for the duration of the war, he was bedridden at the family home in Perth. Fortunately his parents were in a position to look after him, and his room was transformed so that he could read and write with some ease. He received the best available medical treatment for his condition (for which there is no cure) and he entertained a steady stream of visitors, including fellow poets Maurice Lindsay, Douglas Young and Hugh MacDiarmid who edited the first collection of his poems. Best of all, he was able to concentrate on his own writing, not just poetry in Scots and English, but also the poems for children or 'bairn rhymes', for which he was perhaps best known, and a remarkable diary in which he recounted the facts of his everyday bed-bound life. As his condition worsened he became more of a pacifist, and was horrified by incidents such as the bombing of Guernica during the Spanish Civil War. By the time that war broke out he had also moved towards a new self-sufficiency and acceptance of his lot, writing in his diary on 6 October 1943, a few days before his death: 'So much can wither away from the human spirit, and yet the great gift of the ordinary day remains; the stability of the small things of life, which yet in their constancy are the greatest.'[38] He died nine days later, on 15 October 1943, having been increasingly weakened by an earlier attack of tuberculosis.

The other great poet of the period of the war was Edwin Muir who had lived in St Andrews since returning to Scotland in 1935 after his decisive visit to his native Orkney. With his wife Willa he had earned his living writing book reviews and translations of European fiction. He had also produced his major study *Scott and Scotland: The Predicament of the Scottish Writer* (1936) and in so doing had quarrelled bitterly with Hugh MacDiarmid over the viability of the Scots language as a vehicle for serious thought.

In 1942 Muir was rescued from his intellectual exile by being appointed to the staff of the British Council in Edinburgh where he joined its director Henry Harvey Wood in organising a brilliant succession of exhibitions, poetry readings and lectures, taking advantage of the fact that Scotland's capital had become home to thousands of exiled service personnel from all over Europe. Out of this came International House in Princes Street which became an intimate gathering place for all manner of events, and quickly established itself as the centre of Edinburgh's cultural life in wartime. One of the British Council's first initiatives was an exhibition in the National Gallery of Scotland entitled *The Art of Our Allies* which was mounted in May 1941. A large section was contributed by Poles, whose higher command had released known artists from military duties to contribute to an exhibition which the *Scotsman* was moved to describe as 'undoubtedly . . . one of the most interesting ever held in Scotland.'[39]

Following its success the British Council promoted further exhibitions of Polish, Czech, French, Chinese, Greek, Dutch, and Norwegian art, for which British collectors also made generous loans, thereby enabling displays of an exceptional standard to be put on public display. At the same time, and throughout the war, lunchtime concerts were held in the National Gallery, and these were considered to be the equal of Dame Myra Hess's concerts initiated at the National Gallery in London in October 1939.

Another manifestation of the collision between war and culture occurred at Port Glasgow where the Lithgow shipyards were home to the artist Stanley Spencer, who had been selected by the War Artists Advisory Committee to record the work of the Clyde shipbuilders. A product of the Slade School of Fine Art, Spencer had served on the Salonika front during the First World War and had used the experience as inspiration for much of his output in the 1920s, notably the cycle of nineteen paintings for the Sandham Memorial Chapel in Hampshire. However by the end of the 1930s his life was in chaos, dogged by an unhappy love life, financial problems and humiliating rejections. In that respect the commission from the War Artists Advisory Committee came as a lifeline, and Spencer threw himself into the work at Port Glasgow, becoming a familiar figure to the Lithgow workforce, with whom he quickly built up an easy rapport.

The results were impressive. Between May 1940 and March 1946 he spent a number of extended periods in the yards where merchant ships were built; in that period he produced *Shipbuilding on the Clyde*, a sequence of eight massive paintings, each almost six metres wide and half a metre high. Massive in scale and lofty in ambition, they resemble Renaissance frescoes, but instead of narrating religious stories they commemorate the gangs of Clydebank workers as they work in harmony to create a ship. As one reviewer described the enterprise when the frescoes were put on display at Chatham dockyard in 2010, Spencer's effort had created a thing of beauty and a celebration of an essential contribution to the nation's war effort. 'The overall effect is of the drama, busyness, grandeur and importance of the enterprise. We witness numerous welders, plumbers, riveters, riggers, burners, labourers, furnace men, rope makers, machinists and apprentices earnestly contributing their skills to a single overall purpose.'[40] So large is the work that it is held by the Imperial War Museum and is only rarely put on public display. After the war Spencer returned to his native Cookham in Berkshire where he died in 1959.

One of the problems facing those who wanted to provide entertainment during the war was the government ban on the assembly of crowds which came into force at the outbreak of hostilities. As the conflict progressed the conditions were eased, but the regulations effectively put paid to the playing of organised sport in wartime Scotland. Following the declaration of war the Scottish Rugby Union cancelled all trial and international matches, and the stadium at Murrayfield in Edinburgh was turned over to the army and used as a supply depot by the Royal Army Ordnance Corps. Clubs continued to play friendly fixtures wherever possible, and there were several matches with sides representing the armed forces, but to all intents and purposes the game went into hibernation for the duration of hostilities. The main exception was the staging of two Services' international matches against England, played each year on a home-and-away basis, with the Scottish home matches staged at Inverleith in Edinburgh. Just as had happened in the previous conflict, Scottish international rugby players joined up or were conscripted into the armed forces and fifteen of their number were killed or died on active service. Amongst them was Eric Liddell (seven caps), an Olympic gold-medal-winning sprinter who died in China on 21 February 1945 while working as a missionary.

Football was in a similar position. The season was only four games old when war was declared, with Rangers leading the First Division while Dundee were at the top of the Second Division. All player contracts were rescinded and the leagues were abandoned for the duration of the hostilities, although the Scottish Football Association initiated moves to find an alternative structure which would suit the new wartime conditions. The result was the creation of two regional (western and eastern) divisions of sixteen clubs each, but this was immediately unpopular in the east of Scotland because it cut off larger teams such as Hibernian and Heart of Midlothian from fixtures with the wealthier Glasgow sides. Other regional leagues were formed and there were also Southern League Cup and North-East League Cup competitions as well as a Summer Cup which was first won by Hibernian in the 1940–41 season. However the dearth of football spelled doom for some of the smaller clubs. Two clubs failed to survive the war – King's Park which was reborn as Stirling Albion and St Bernard's which disappeared altogether after its ground in Edinburgh was taken over for military purposes. As happened with the game of rugby, professional footballers were also called up, and this often led to many of them making guest appearances with other clubs in other parts of the country. For example, Bobby Flavell, a promising young player with Airdrieonians played for both Arsenal and Tottenham Hotspur while he was stationed near London during the war.

Football retained its ability to attract large crowds, and on a casual basis it remained very much part of the social scene in Scotland throughout the war. Cinemas were also deservedly popular as in a world before the advent of television they provided not just entertainment but also glamour and escapism. In Dundee the Caird Hall started showing films – *Gone with the Wind* played to full houses for four weeks in 1941 – and Glasgow could boast 104 screens, one of which was the iconic Cosmo in Rose Street (later the Glasgow Film Theatre) which showed movies from all over the world.

Along with the cinema, going to 'the dancing' is one of the abiding memories of Scots who lived through that period. It also managed to survive the government's temporary measure to close down dancehalls immediately after war was declared, and it continued to thrive. Glasgow alone had 159 registered dancehalls, from small local affairs to the huge and massively popular venue at the Barrowlands where the resident band of Billy McGregor and the Gaybirds played to enthusiastic crowds of dancers throughout the war. The only change was that the landmark neon sign of a man pushing a barrow was removed as part of the air-raid precautions. In Dundee Andy Lothian's band kept the music going at the Empress Ballroom, and there were other similar facilities at the Locarno on Lochee Road and the Palais in Tay Street. The only discordant note was struck at the Progress Hall in Dundee's Hilltown which quickly gained a seedy reputation for alcohol-fuelled fights involving service personnel.[41] Apart from incidents of that kind, which seemed to occur when drink and men in uniform mixed, dancing was not only popular but it also offered temporary escape from the drudgery and tensions of wartime, and scarcely a town or village did not have some kind of hall which could be used at the weekend. As Land Girl Ina Seaton found when she served with the SWLA near Gifford in East Lothian, the countryside offered all sorts of entertainments, with the possibility of the cinema twice a week and dances on a Friday night. 'You were never short of partners, you know,' she remembered. 'They were away with a Land Girl – oh, they're coming from the toon, they're toonies. Seems daft now. It was good fun, it really was.'[42]

9 Sikorski's (and other) Tourists

In the spring of 1944 the poet Hugh MacDiarmid finally managed to escape from the increasingly difficult and enervating war work to which he had been conscripted in Mechan's Engineering Company in Scotstoun in Glasgow. In circumstances which are still unclear, the poet was able to transfer to a job as Postal Officer to the Allied fleets in Greenock which entailed working in the small boat pool servicing the huge numbers of Allied vessels in the Clyde estuary. At the Tail of the Bank – the stretch of water between Greenock and Gourock – were found the assembly points for incoming and outgoing Atlantic convoys as well as safe anchorages for Allied warships. From 1940 onwards it was an exceptionally busy stretch of water, with swarms of small boats sailing to and fro between the ranks of Allied warships and merchantmen.

In his autobiography *Lucky Poet* MacDiarmid states that after making application for a transfer he was simply employed on board a Norwegian vessel, the MFV *Gurli*, which was under charter to the Admiralty. Later, in the 1980s, when MacDiarmid's biography was being written his close friend and colleague Robert Blair Wilkie claimed that political influence was brought to bear on the appointment through the intervention of Dr Robert McIntyre, general secretary of the SNP. Wilkie, a leading member of the party's General Council, had already railed against the 'insanity' of employing a middle-aged man in such unsuitable manual work and it is entirely probable that he attempted to intervene on the poet's behalf.[1] Throughout this period Wilkie and his wife Helen provided a home-from-home for MacDiarmid, and their relationship continued to be strong after the war – in 1949 both were expelled from the SNP for 'extremist behaviour'.[2]

Whatever the cause of the transfer it came as a lifeline to Mac-

Diarmid by removing him from the daily grind of hard physical work and introducing him to more suitable employment, first as a deckhand and then as an engineering officer. It also gave him first-hand experience of the way in which Scotland had been exposed to the global influences of the conflict. Not only was the Tail of the Bank home to some of the warships of the Free French Navy, together with 1,500 of their sailors at Fort Matilda, but as the assembly point for Atlantic convoys it meant that the waters 'held the biggest small boat pool in Great Britain with French, Belgian, Dutch, Scandinavian and other vessels. Greenock was as a consequence highly internationalised then and each of its public houses a veritable Babel.'[3]

The port was also home of the North Command of the Free Polish Navy which had begun arriving in Scottish waters before the outbreak of hostilities and whose ships came under the control of the Admiralty while remaining sovereign Polish territory. Of all the babel of foreign voices heard by MacDiarmid and others in the Clyde estuary, the Poles were the most insistent because as it turned out they were to leave the longest-lasting and deepest impression on the country by becoming the largest and most influential immigrant group in Scotland both during the war and in the years that followed.

With the entry of the United States into the war in late 1941 the whole complexion of the conflict began to change. Between the summer of 1940 and the Japanese attack on Pearl Harbor eighteen months later, Britain and her Commonwealth allies had been fighting alone against Nazi Germany, and the strains on their military and industrial capacities were beginning to tell. Britain was virtually under siege from constant aerial bombardment, and unrestricted German submarine warfare threatened essential supplies and the seaborne lines of communication across the world. There were huge demands on the national exchequer, and the military setbacks in North Africa and the Mediterranean had inevitably sapped morale. By then, too, the original reasons for the outbreak of the war had blurred with the passing of time and Nazi Germany's relentless subjugation of Europe.

When Poland had been invaded there were high hopes that its armed forces would be able to resist for anything up to six months – British military planners believed that the Nazi army would use the tactics of the First World War by bombarding Polish positions for several weeks before launching its attack – but the speed and aggression of the invasion had produced a relatively easy German victory. As it turned out, it was not the end of the war for the Poles but this first battleground of the conflict gave the Germans much-needed confidence about their own military abilities and seemed to prove that their tactics were unbeatable. This was confirmed eight months later when France and the Low Countries were subjected to *blitzkrieg*, leaving Hitler master of Europe from the Atlantic to the Carpathian mountains.

For the Poles it had been a shocking and bewildering experience which justifies one writer's later comment about the country's history in the twentieth century that 'Poland today is not cursed by destiny but by a brutal share of bad luck.'[4] However, it was not as if Poland was an undeveloped country or that its forces were unsuited to modern combat. In an important historical sense Poles had always known that any assault on Poland would threaten its very existence. The country's history stretched back over ten centuries but in more recent times it had been subjected to cynical carve-ups by Austria-Hungary, Prussia and Russia, and the modern state had only come into being at the end of the First World War. Even so, the Polish government was well aware of the threat posed by its acquisitive neighbours, Germany and the Soviet Union, and had taken steps to defend its territorial integrity. In the summer of 1939 the Polish Army numbered one million soldiers, and even though only half of them had been mobilised by the time of the German invasion, there were solid measures in place to fight a defensive war. In 1936 a National Defence Fund had also been instituted to raise money for modern weapons and equipment so that the people themselves felt that they had a share in their country's security.

That being said, the modernisation programme had not been completed and there were shortages of armour and modern aircraft. The tank force consisted of two armoured brigades equipped with the 7TP light tank and four independent armoured battalions, and the bulk of the cavalry was still mounted and used in the reconnaissance or mounted infantry role. (This did not make them less efficient – the Germans also relied on horses – but it gave rise to the later myth that Polish cavalry regiments attacked German armour armed only with lances and sabres.) The Polish air force was also at a disadvantage, being equipped with aircraft such as the lumbering PZL P11 fighter which was no match for its speedier German counterparts. On the other hand it possessed reliable light and medium bombers, but these failed to make much impact largely due to the dispersal of Polish aircraft in advance of the German assault. As for the navy, it escaped relatively unscathed: following a secret pre-war agreement, Operation Peking, most of the fleet of destroyers and support vessels escaped to British ports on 20 August while Polish submarines mounted a short campaign in the Baltic before making good their escape to the west.

The German plan to deal with Poland called for an attack on four fronts, the main one led by General Gerd von Rundstedt's Army Group South which would attack from the borders of Silesia, Moravia and Slovakia towards Lodz, Krakow and Warsaw. In the north there would be an attack from East Prussia, while Germany's Slovakian allies would join the attack in the south. The fourth front would be provided by uprisings of specially prepared *Selbstschutz* guerrillas of the country's German minority. Poland's terrain suited the mobile high-speed tactics used by the Germans but it did little favours to the Poles who were quickly over-stretched and their lines of communication were over-exposed and frequently under-defended. The Germans also quickly gained air superiority at an early stage in the invasion, and the terrifying bombing campaign encouraged civilians to flee from their homes, blocking roads and demoralising the Polish forces. Within three days von Rundstedt's forces had reached the River Vistula, and by 8 September they were within striking distance of Warsaw having advanced 140 miles in little over a week. As the German forces advanced they managed to split up the Polish defenders, and although the Poles inflicted heavy losses on the Germans during the fighting on the Bzura River, they were unable to counter-attack in any meaningful way. By 13 September the bulk of the Polish forces were in full retreat towards the border with Romania. With them they took President Ignacy Moscicki's government which had abandoned Warsaw soon after the invasion began.

From this point onwards Poland's fate was sealed. There were plans to defend the so-called Romanian Bridgehead behind the Vistula and San rivers but the Red Army's invasion changed the strategic balance and made further resistance impossible. The Soviets had around 800,000 soldiers under their command while the whole Polish defensive plan was geared towards halting the German onslaught from the west by rolling with the punch and then falling back. For young Polish soldiers like Władysław Fila, at the time an officer cadet, this bewildering turn of events changed everything and made further resistance impossible, not least because, as he noted later in life, 'we never expected Poland being attacked by our [eastern] neighbours.'[5]

With grim inevitability key points began falling: the city of Lwow on 22 September, symbolic Warsaw on 28 September and the huge Modlin Fortress north of the capital a day later. The Soviet intervention also changed the nature of the fighting, with large numbers of Polish officers being executed after being taken prisoners, one of the worst incidents being a mass execution at the conclusion of the Battle of Szack. On 6 October the last engagement was fought at Kock near Lublin where forces led by General Franciszek Kleeburg surrendered to the Germans. Not that the Poles gave up easily: during the fighting the Germans lost 16,343 soldiers killed in action and 30,300 wounded, a higher rate of attrition than they were to suffer in the following year's invasion of France.[6]

Despite the heaviness of the defeat and the reality that their country had been over-run by enemy armies, the Poles did not surrender, and thus began one of the most extraordinary retreats of the Second World War. As the Polish government and high command crossed over the border into Romania they did so in the certain knowledge that while the first battle had been lost the war would continue from the territory of their oldest ally, France. It was a bold declaration. Huge numbers of Poles had to get from neutral Romania and Hungary and make their way westwards across Europe, using whatever means they could. Others passed through Yugoslavia, travelling long hours by train, usually on false passports provided by the Romanians and Hungarians. Some units even managed to stay together during the long exodus, with the result that when they arrived in France a new government and Free Polish Army quickly came into being under the command of General Władysław Sikorski, an experienced soldier who combined his post with that of prime minister. By the early summer of 1940 it consisted of four infantry divisions and an armoured brigade which was earmarked to serve under the French chain of command in the south of the country. (Also formed at this time was an independent infantry brigade which served in Syria and the *Podhalanska* (Highland)

Brigade which formed in Brittany and which took part in the ill-fated operations in Norway later in the year.)

The rapid fall of French resistance in May and June 1940 was a disaster for the Poles. Not only were they badly mauled in the fighting as the Germans swung south, but the dismaying collapse of French resistance meant that the recently arrived Polish forces had to retreat once more, this time into neutral Switzerland. From there they moved to Britain where they pledged to continue the struggle with the one ally which was still capable of resisting the Germans. They arrived in a motley collection of hastily requisitioned liners and ferries, landing mainly at Southampton and Liverpool. By the middle of July there were 17,000 Polish troops on British soil – eventually the numbers would swell to 120,000 as the stragglers came in. On the whole the Poles received warm welcomes by organisations such as the Women's Voluntary Services, but the arrival of this substantial force, most of whom did not speak English, was a drain on national resources at a time when a German invasion seemed to be imminent and there was considerable perplexity within the War Office about what should be done with them.

After consideration it was decided to send them to Scotland where they would re-form and be used in defensive duties on the east coast to fill the gap left by the loss of so many of Scotland's Territorial battalions. They also needed to be re-equipped and retrained, and with an invasion expected at any moment it was essential get them to a part of the country which had a workable infrastructure and good communications.[7] For many Poles this must have been anti-climactic, but those who came to Scotland were the lucky ones. Comrades who had chosen the northern route into Lithuania were apprehended by the Red Army; others, including Władysław Fila, were captured in eastern Poland and spent the next eighteen months in Siberia, while still more who were taken prisoner in the Polish Corridor found themselves conscripted into the Nazi army and sent to Vichy France. Later still, in the summer of 1941 when Hitler ordered the Soviet Union to be attacked, surviving Polish prisoners of war were released to form a new Free Polish Army, and many of these eventually made their way to Scotland having fought in the Middle East and Italy.

For the bulk of the Free Poles of 1940 their first destination was to be Glasgow where they were housed in tented accommodation in the

city's football stadiums and other open spaces including Bellahouston
Park. From that moment they quickly emerged as the largest and most
easily identifiable of the many exiled groups which arrived in the
country following the fall of France. With their smart uniforms and
the romance of their recent fighting experiences they also became firm
favourites with many Scottish families, one historian claiming that
'many Scots, especially the ladies, were astounded by Polish good
looks and by Polish courtesy'.[8]

Most of the contemporary evidence supports the idea that the
Poles were well received when they arrived in Scotland and that the
people warmed to them 'with a combination of intense curiosity
and admiration'.[9] In Glasgow, under the direction of Lord Provost
Patrick Dollan (soon to be nicknamed 'Dollanski'), the city corporation set up canteens, and local people invited Poles into their homes.
As Władysław ('Walter') Maronski, a signaller in 8th Polish Motorised
Infantry Battalion, discovered when he arrived in St Andrews, the
Poles, too, were determined to make their presence felt amongst their
hosts: 'The first night at St Andrews began at nine o'clock when we
had the evening prayer. Before the evening prayer we sang our
national anthem [Dąbrowski's 'Mazurka' or 'Poland is not yet lost']
and this was the sound going through the whole town because before
the prayer we had to go outside, there were so many of us. And in
those days we prayed earnestly. When we made our prayer, "give us
our daily bread", that's what we meant.'[10]

The glimmer of the exotic also reached back into history. Scotland
enjoyed age-old trading links with Poland through the Baltic, and
somewhere within the national consciousness there were distant
memories of Scots fighting as mercenaries in Poland's cause in the
eighteenth century.

It was only to be expected that the enemy would learn about this
new military presence in Scotland, and the Nazi propaganda machine
responded by calling them 'General Sikorski's Tourists', a description
which the Poles adopted with self-conscious pride. However, there
was much more to the arrival of the Poles than clicking heels, kissing
hands and cutting a dash. The exiles had a job to do, and quickly set
about creating an impressive command structure to reform their army
and to begin training for the battle that lay ahead. More than anything
else it is the concentration of enthusiasm, determination and endea-

vour that marks the arrival of the Poles in Scotland. It is right to emphasise the historical romance and glamour that attended the moment, but more impressive by far is the speed and efficiency with which the Poles organised themselves so that they quickly became a familiar military presence across central and eastern Scotland.

On 3 August the Anglo-Polish Agreement for the Polish Armed Forces was signed, and this paved the way for the future structure for the Polish forces. Inevitably, the order of battle reflected Scotland's pre-eminent role as the main base for the Polish forces, but as the Free Poles were allies they had to have a separate command to allow Polish forces to operate within the area which came under the jurisdiction of Scottish Command, the headquarters of the army in Scotland at Edinburgh Castle. Polish General Headquarters (GHQ) was situated at the Rubens Hotel in London, as was the exiled Ministry of National Defence, but at the same time separate headquarters were formed in Scotland as the Poles started regrouping in their new training areas in Lanarkshire in the autumn of 1940. Two infantry brigades were formed at Biggar and Douglas with a smaller all-arms group at Crawford. Apart from the vile late summer weather and the leak-prone bell tents, two things discomfited the new arrivals: they disliked the basic British Army rations and found their replacement heavy serge battle-dress uniforms uncomfortable and unfashionable, but these drawbacks were quickly addressed by employing their own cooks and tailors to remedy the situation.

As tents were in short supply, soldiers were billeted on the local population and that helped to harmonise relations and create a feeling of fighting in common cause. Amongst those on the receiving end of Scottish hospitality in Biggar was Wiktor Tomaszewski, a young doctor, who had been returning to Poland from the US and had immediately joined the forces being formed in France: 'We had the warmest reception there. I remember very well because it was so unusual after the stay in France and suddenly coming to Great Britain here in Scotland where everyone was so friendly everywhere, wherever one was going, either in the streets or in the shops, so there was only fresh friendly faces and friendly attitudes . . . I remember very well these times.'[11]

Other Poles were less lucky because with the best will in the world the arrival of the Poles was not met with universal acclaim in every part of Scotland. Quite apart from a natural Scottish wariness of strangers, immigrant groups in Scotland in the 1930s were a distinct minority in a country whose population was in sharp decline for the first time since records began. The 1931 census shows that the population consisted of 4,842,554 people (2,325,867 males and 2,516,687 females) and that this was 39,947 lower than the previous census ten years earlier. The total number of Polish residents born in Scotland was also the lowest since 1881: 549 males and 409 females, the majority of whom lived in Lanarkshire.[12] For the first time, too, the balance of outward over inward migration had changed. 'From Returns furnished by the Board of Trade showing emigrants from Scotland and immigrants into Scotland to and from countries out of Europe, the balance of outward over inward migration overseas for the intercensal period is ascertained to be 328,764. The total loss by migration being as above stated 392,329, the difference amounting to 63,565 is apparently to be accounted for by the migration of Scottish population to countries not embraced in the Board of Trade returns referred to, i.e. to other countries of the United Kingdom and of Europe.'[13]

Politics and religion also intruded. The majority of the Poles were Roman Catholics, and this caused some animus in traditional Protestant areas, especially when soldiers extended their fraternisation to the local female population. This was to be a source of tension throughout the war, particularly in the later stages when large numbers of British conscripts were fighting in faraway overseas theatres and the presence of available single men caused obvious difficulties. Another drawback was that any Scottish girl intending to marry a Pole had to surrender her British citizenship and become, in effect, an alien, a prospect that was hardly likely to encourage her father to smile kindly on the idea of accepting a Polish son-in-law. The legal anomaly did not change until 1946 but despite that, relationships did prosper and liaisons became engagements and turned into marriages. All told, between 1941 and 1946 an estimated 10,000 marriages took place between Scots women and members of the Polish forces.[14]

In all probability suspicions about the religious divide were resolved in the same way that they were in any part of Scotland at that time. More serious and more bitter were the political differences, and this came into sharp focus when the Poles began to move into Fife in October when they were presented with their first operational orders to take over responsibility for the eastern coastal defences from Burntisland in Fife to Montrose in Angus. The 1st Rifle Brigade moved its headquarters from Biggar to Cupar in Fife with battalion headquarters in St Andrews and at Tentsmuir, while the 2nd Brigade, soon to be renamed and re-assigned as the 10th (Polish) Mechanised Cavalry Brigade set up its headquarters in Forfar. Soon Polish soldiers were to be seen in most towns along the eastern seaboard and inland as they set up military establishments in Cupar, Leven, Milnathort, Auchtermuchty, Crawford, Biggar, Douglas, Duns, Kelso, Forres, Perth, Tayport, Lossiemouth, Arbroath, Forfar and Carnoustie.[15] Much of their early work consisted of building beach defences against the threatened German invasion.

However, in Fife, where the concrete anti-tank blocks can still be seen in the sand dunes of the coastal beaches, the situation was complicated by a clear political divide. In the wealthy farmlands of the Howe of Fife and in the fishing villages of the East Neuk, north-east Fife was solidly conservative and unionist, but in the coalmining and industrialised areas of West Fife the exact opposite prevailed. Not only was this socialist territory and a coalmining centre, but the sitting Member of Parliament for West Fife was Willie Gallacher, an active trade unionist and member of the Communist Party who had been imprisoned during the First World War while serving as president of the Clyde Workers' Committee.

Despite the signing of the Molotov–Ribbentrop Pact, there was still a lively interest in left-wing circles to promote Soviet interests, and the arrival in the area of largely nationalist and anti-Communist Poles caused considerable bad feeling in the main coalfield towns of Cowdenbeath, Kelty and Lochgelly. Those hostile feelings intensified during the summer of 1941 after Hitler's forces invaded the Soviet Union which then became an important ally of the west. It did not take long for existing indifference to be transmuted into outright hostility towards the Free Poles who came to be regarded in west Fife not as gallant allies but as potential enemies of the Soviet Union.

It was an endlessly complicated situation. Following the Polish defeat in 1939 the country had been divided into areas of German and Soviet influence. Of the former, existing Germanic areas were absorbed into the Reich while a 'General Government' under Hans Frank administered an area which included most of the main cities and twelve million Poles. To all intents and purposes it became a German labour colony, where there was a brutal and systematic attempt to eradicate all traces of Polish culture and society. The first steps were also taken to eradicate the Jewish population, with half a million of their number being concentrated in the Warsaw ghetto. Conditions in the Soviet occupation zone in the east were also harsh, and there was an equally determined attempt to eradicate anything which related to Polish culture, language and history. Tens of thousands of Poles, including members of the armed forces, were forcibly transported to prison camps and state farms in Kazakhstan and beyond the Urals where they worked under terrible conditions as slave labourers. Only with Hitler's invasion of the Soviet Union in the summer of 1941 was there a change of attitude. Stalin now needed the Poles as allies, and the resulting Polish–Soviet Treaty signed on 30 July 1941 permitted the creation of a new Polish Army consisting of former prisoners of war under the command of General Władysław Anders. When these moved into Persia, a British dependency and today Iran, many Polish soldiers eventually found their way to Scotland where their presence was regarded as a double betrayal by those on the left.

There was another price to be paid by the Poles. The Soviets made territorial demands on the occupied eastern provinces, and in return supported the Union of Polish Patriots (ZPP) under the leadership of Wanda Wasilewska, a leading Polish Communist and member of the Supreme Council of the USSR, who conceded that post-war Poland would become Moscow's ally. A novelist who had fled to the Soviet Union in 1939, Wasilewska inspired mixed emotions: Communists found her inspirational but one Polish historian described the Polish Communist leader as 'the most servile exponent of Soviet ideology.'[16]

By 1943 there were virtually two Polands-in-exile, one based in London, the other in Moscow. The rivalries between them were exacerbated that same year by Sikorski's mysterious death in an aircraft accident at Gibraltar, and by the discovery of a Russian massacre of 4,000 Polish officers in the Katyn Forest near Smolensk. That helps to explain some of the enmity in west Fife, where sympathies were strong both for the Communist cause and for the idea of creating a Second Front in Western Europe to support Stalin. Put simply, many of the people working in the Fife coalfields supported the Red Army and its allies in the ZPP, and regarded General Sikorski's Tourists as traitors to that cause. For Josef Mirczynski, who had come to Scotland in 1940, that bad blood was a foretaste of the more tragic territorial issues that emerged from the Yalta Agreement which carved up Eastern Europe at the end of the war (see Chapter 12).

> Places in [west] Fife were Communist and they were not very pleased about the Polish people. Maybe the younger people were all right but the older people had a different point of view and after the war was over they all told us to go back to Poland because you have your own country and jobs. Only in these places, Fife. The rest, they were very friendly – except Dundee. If you go into the streets or into the shops or so many times into the pubs because we're not always allowed to go into the pubs they always just ignore you.[17]

In spite of difficulties such as those experienced by Mirczynski and others the Poles quickly established themselves as a formidable presence in Scotland, and in so doing set up their own institutions, a process that helped to reinforce their presence throughout the country. Apart from the headquarters of I Polish Corps at Moncrieff House near Perth and the creation of the Polish Military Staff College at Eddleston near Peebles, the Polish government-in-exile moved to create training centres for rebuilding the country once the war had ended. Various courses in law, education, medicine and veterinary science were established in the four Scottish universities, but the most notable and longest-lasting of the institutions was the creation of the Polish School of Medicine at the University of Edinburgh.

Following the arrival of the first Polish exiles, many medical students had attempted to continue their studies, but when their lack of English became a problem it was decided to address it by forming a new school where Poles would be taught by Poles in their own language and according to standards established by their government. Amongst their number was Wiktor Tomaszewsky, who joined the establishment on 22 March 1941 under the direction of Professor Antoni Jurasz and with the full support of Professor Sydney Smith, Edinburgh's distinguished Dean of Medicine. In the depths of a war which the Germans seemed to be winning the creation of the Polish Medical School was very much seen as a beacon of hope, and it was fitting that during the inauguration service in the university's McEwan Hall the organist took his music from the works of Elgar and Purcell as well as Chopin and Paderewski.[18]

Although the Polish army contingents made the deepest impression on the people of Scotland, the Free Polish Navy and Free Polish Air Force also had visible presences across Scotland. Shortly after the outbreak of hostilities the destroyers *Błyskawica* (Lightning), *Grom* (Thunder) and *Burza* (Tempest) sailed into the Firth of Forth. They were escorted into Leith where they formed the Polish Destroyer Squadron, and later redeployed to the Clyde. They were subsequently joined by the submarines *Wilk* (Wolf) and *Orzel* (Eagle), and during the following year the Free Polish Navy was strengthened by the addition of British warships and by French warships which had surrendered after the fall of France. Some thirty-eight Polish merchant vessels also managed to escape from the Baltic and joined the Allied Merchant Navy Pool, many of them operating out of the Greenock assembly point.

The Free Polish Air Force also had a presence in Scotland. Following the defeat of the homeland some 7,000 air force personnel and 90 operational aircraft had made their way to France by the summer of 1940. Following the collapse in June most managed to make good their escape, and under an agreement with the British government were incorporated into the Allied order of battle under RAF control. Two Polish squadrons, 302 (City of Posnan) and 303 (Koscluszko) served with great distinction during the Battle of Britain, the latter destroying more German aircraft than any other Hurricane squadron. Altogether 145 Polish pilots saw service in the battle and thirty lost their lives, including Josef Frontisek, a Czech pilot who flew with 303 Squadron and who was credited as being the highest-scoring pilot in the Battle of Britain with a total of twenty-eight kills. By the end of 1943, fourteen Polish squadrons were in existence and the Free Polish Air Force numbered 11,368 personnel, making it the fourth largest Allied air force.

The majority of the aircrew received their training in Scotland, and throughout the war there was a significant Polish presence in the country with various fighter squadrons flying out of Turnhouse and

Wick. Two squadrons were more or less permanent residents through-out the war. In 1940 and 1941, 309 (Land of Czerwień) Army Co-operation Squadron operated Lysander aircraft from Dunino and Crail in Fife where I Polish Corps was responsible for coastal defences. In the summer of 1941 it transferred to Longman field near Inverness where it took part in army co-operation exercises with 51st (Highland) Division, and in the following year it started receiving Mustang I fighters to enable it to serve in the fighter-reconnaissance role. One of its pilots, a trained mechanic, believed that the new aircraft had a longer range than had been imagined and gave a practical demonstration by flying a Mustang from Crail to attack targets in Norway. For using his initiative he was first reprimanded and then thanked by his commanding officer.[19] Later still the squadron transferred to Longside near Peterhead on coastal and convoy-protection duties.

The other resident Polish squadron, 304 (Land of Silesia) had an equally strenuous war serving with RAF Coastal Command. Formed originally as a bomber squadron, it transferred to Tiree in May 1942 before ending up in Benbecula in the winter of 1944–5 when it flew exhausting long-range patrols over the Atlantic using specially adapted Vickers Wellington XIV bombers to hunt for German submarines. Successful operations were few and far between, but on the night of 5 May 1944 a Wellington commanded by Squadron Leader Leslaw Miedzybrodzki came across two U-boats recharging their batteries on the surface in the Bay of Biscay and went into the attack. Despite heavy anti-aircraft from both boats, which badly damaged the aircraft leaving its fuselage with 'a hole big enough for a man to pass through', Miedzybrodzki pressed home his attack and succeeded in sinking one of the enemy submarines.[20]

Given the effort put into those long-distance patrols over the wastes of the Atlantic, Miedzybrodzki's successful attack raised spirits within the squadron, and as he remembered later it was a much-needed boost to their morale during a posting which was not one of the most attractive available to any Allied aircrew. 'The nights were long and we had problems with the wind, sheep on the runway and the mice eating our woollen uniforms which we had to hang from string, attached to the ceiling. We did not have very much contact with the local people, but when we went to get our washing done by the locals there was great difficulty because they were Gaelic speakers.'[21]

Equally debilitating, and far more dangerous, were the operations undertaken by the other three Polish bomber squadrons – 300 (Land of Masovia), 301 (Land of Pomerania) and 305 (Greater Poland). Although these operated out of bases in Lincolnshire, many of the aircrew trained in Scotland at Operational Training Units at Grange-mouth (58 OTU) and East Fortune (60 OTU). Amongst them was Władsyław Fila, who was awarded the Distinguished Flying Cross (DFC) and flew a total of forty-two missions over Germany as a bomb-aimer in a Lancaster bomber. After the war he stayed on in Scotland, and he always regarded those operations as a way of hitting back at a hated enemy: 'When I was flying deeper into German territory – some flying was nine hours or more – the deeper we went the more time I had to say several times over, that's for Warsaw which you bombarded in 1939, and that's for Posnan, and that's for Lwow, and that's for this town and that town. So we had full satisfaction of hammering them as hard as possible. And possibly the DFC I got was reward for that accuracy.'[22]

The other main Polish air force formation in Scotland was a Polish barrage balloon unit which formed part of 945 Squadron and served in north-west Glasgow before moving to the Fife coast of the Firth of Forth in the summer of 1942. By then the Polish 1st Armoured Division had come into being under the command of General Stanisław Maczek and the 1st Independent Parachute Brigade had formed at Leven in Fife out of the 4th Cadre Rifle Brigade. Many of the first Poles to arrive in Scotland were officers who formed cadres, and the preponderance of commissioned soldiers gave rise to allega-tions that they had deserted their men in France. (This was unfair: many of them had been in training at the time of the German invasion.) The original role of the paratroopers was to support an expected uprising by forces within the Polish homeland, and by September 1943 the 1st Independent Parachute Brigade numbered 2,500 officers and men under the command of Colonel Stanislaw Sosabowski, an experienced soldier who had fought earlier in Poland and France against German forces. Both formations took part in the fighting in France and north-west Europe following the D-Day invasion in June 1944 (see Chapter 11).

The Poles supplied the largest and most colourful of the European Allied forces in Scotland but they were not alone. Scotland's closest neighbours, the Norwegians, also had a visible presence in Scotland, notably at Dundee which became the main centre for their naval and air operations. The arrival of the Norwegians was especially poignant. Not only did Scotland enjoy an historic link with the country – King Eric II of Norway married Princess Margaret, daughter of King Alexander III in 1281, and there were other links over the possession of Orkney and Shetland – but the country had attracted huge credit through its efforts to hold out against Hitler's invasion plans in the spring of 1940.

In spite of attempts to retain its policy of neutrality, Norway was strategically important to both sides. The Germans relied on the country's ports, especially Narvik, for the supply of Swedish iron ore, and possession of Norway was vital for providing naval and air bases for the prosecution of the war in the Atlantic and North Sea. After some prevarication an invasion was launched on 9 April, and following a campaign which lasted two months the Nazis succeeded in occupying the country, landing their forces at Oslo, Kristiansand, Stavanger, Bergen, Trondheim and Narvik. Britain's response was to lay mines off the Norwegian coast using minelayers from Rosyth and to despatch forces, including a Polish infantry brigade, to Narvik in an attempt to support loyal Norwegian forces in stemming the invasion, but it was all too little and too late. Although the operation enjoyed some initial success the subsequent attack on France in May forced the Allies to abandon the campaign in Norway. The British alone lost 4,500 casualties, mostly from the sinking of the aircraft carrier HMS *Glorious*, and amongst other vessels lost was the Dundee-based Polish submarine *Orzel*. Amongst the Scottish regiments which took part in this ill-advised and hastily organised operation was 1st Scots Guards which lost over a hundred men as battlefield casualties or prisoners of war.

As a result of the Allied failure King Haakon VII and his government went into exile on 7 June to continue the war against Germany. The first landfall for the escaping Norwegian naval vessels was Lerwick in Shetland, a restricted area which soon became a home-from-home for the Norwegian sailors. Following the capitulation a small naval force of 13 ships and around 500 sailors left the country and inevitably, given Norway's proximity, Scotland became the main locus for its forces in exile. A Norwegian Scottish Brigade consisting of four rifle companies and a machine-gun company was formed at Dumfries. Initially it acted as a recruiting centre for exiled Norwegians, or Norwegians living in Britain, and by the end of the war 1,500 had passed through the Norwegian Reception Camp at Dumfries, many of them bound for the navy and merchant marine.

It was not until May 1941 that the Norwegians were recognised a national military unit and their relationship within the British command structure was agreed. Under the terms of the Armed Forces Agreement it was specified that the forces would be employed for 'the defence of the United Kingdom or for the purpose of regaining Norway', and that the force should be 'commanded by Norwegian officers, using Norwegian regimental colours, distinctions and badges of the Norwegian Army'.[23] Although the bulk of the Norwegian navy's future operations were to be in the English Channel, the relatively modern destroyer KNM *Sleipner* was incorporated into the Rosyth Escort Forces, whose mission was to protect the coastal convoys in an operational area which stretched from Greenock to the Thames around the north coast of Scotland. This was *Sleipner*'s main task until 1944, by which time she had been joined by a minesweeping flotilla mainly operating out of Dundee. Amongst the vessels were four Norwegian minesweepers, one of which, KNM *Thorodd*, was home to one of the most unusual crew members on any side during the conflict – Bamse, a 14-stone St Bernard dog. While *Thorodd* was based in Dundee and later in Montrose the huge creature gained considerable local fame both for his friendliness and for his uncanny ability to shepherd drunk sailors back to their billets.[24]

Dundee was also home to HMS *Ambrose*, the shore-based headquarters of the Royal Navy's 9th Submarine Flotilla which consisted of submarines representing the navies of Norway, the Netherlands, Free France and Poland. It was a unique example of naval co-operation,[25] and the flotilla enjoyed a number of successes including attacks on the German convoys and on the capital ships *Gneisenau*, *Prinz Eugen* and *Tirpitz*. Norwegian boats were also involved in landing commandos and members of SOE, and it was during one of these operations that the submarine *Uredd* was lost with all hands in February 1943. Dundee, or at least RAF Woodhaven on the Newport shore, was home to a flight of Catalina flying boats operated by 333 (Norwegian) Squadron which also flew a flight of Mosquito reconnaissance aircraft out of nearby RAF Leuchars. On the west coast 330 (Norwegian) Squadron performed similar duties, flying Sunderland flying boats out of Oban on anti-submarine patrols over the Atlantic. It has the distinction of being the first Norwegian naval air squadron to become operational during the war, flying elderly Northrop N-3PB torpedo bomber sea planes from Reykjavik in Iceland before moving south to Scotland.

For most of the people of the United Kingdom the most highly visible Allies were the personnel of the United States forces who began arriving in the country between 1942 and 1945. During that period over three million Americans, mainly men, arrived in the country or passed through it to join the invasion forces in France in north-west Europe following the D-Day landing in June 1944. Famously described as being 'over-paid, over-sexed, over-fed and over here', their arrival caused a major collision between two very different English-speaking cultures, and in some cases this led to serious social difficulties. The 'Yanks' were often homesick and bewildered by what they found in Britain, and, for their part, large swathes of the population were either bemused or unsettled by the encounter with their transatlantic cousins. Most of the Americans were based in England, firstly in East Anglia where the 8th US Army Air Force operated heavy bomber aircraft in the air war against German targets, and then across the southern counties where a huge expeditionary force started assembling for the promised cross-Channel invasion. By the end of 1942 the total stood at 241,839 but it was only a beginning: within a year the figure had risen to 918,347.[26]

Given Scotland's geographical position and the nature of the Allied tactics during this period the complement of Americans was considerably smaller. For most US service personnel their only experience of Scotland was limited to the Clyde estuary and glimpsing the far-off hills after crossing the Atlantic in cramped troopships before heading south by train. Between May 1942 and December 1944, 339 troopships arrived in the Clyde from the US, bringing with them 1,319,089 US service personnel. Some of the luckier ones had their journeys broken at US transit camps at Gourock or Househillwood in Glasgow, and could venture out into the city where they were objects of extreme curiosity. Not only were their uniforms smarter than the generally drab British Army-issue battledress but they had access to unrationed cigarettes and chocolate. Several oral history archives contain references to sightings of US soldiers in Glasgow, and these include brief encounters at the Locarno dancehall in Sauchiehall Street but even so, their numbers were never large.[27] For the most part permanent personnel were confined to parts of the central belt where numbers of US administrative staff and various specialists were based, especially in the period leading up to D-Day. Lanarkshire had the largest concentration with 1,976, while Ayrshire was home to 1,819, many of them based at Prestwick whose airport was used for the delivery of US warplanes under the lend-lease scheme. Other smaller centres included Renfrewshire (341), Midlothian (114) and Fife (206).[28]

Even at the highest levels they were confronted by misunderstandings when they met the local population. In September 1943 Lieutenant-General Omar N. Bradley and his staff flew into Prestwick at the end of the successful campaign in Sicily to prepare for the invasion of Europe. Their eventual destination was London but before travelling south they ate breakfast at Glasgow's Grand Hotel at Charing Cross. Bradley's aide and future ghostwriter Chet Hansen recorded the scene which left both sides thoroughly bewildered. Failing to understand the waitress's accent when she offered a choice of hot dishes, they plumped for the second option only to find that they had refused sausages in favour of boiled fish and tomatoes. Worse followed when they requested 'a pitcher of water' but were then presented with a pot of hot water. Eventually their request was met with the bewildered response: 'Oh, you want to drink it do you?' At the end of the meal, when they paid their bill, Hansen recalled further confusion as they struggled with the local currency: 'The Scottish girl at the cashier's desk looked on the General amusedly as she picked from his hands the proper price of the breakfast. We then asked her delicately what the proper coin was for a tip. She pointed it out and we carried our tips back to the table feeling somewhat strange in this country that was already stranger in many respects than either Africa or Sicily.'[29]

Amongst the most sensitive issues in this friendly transatlantic invasion was the sudden and largely unexpected appearance of black service personnel. At the outbreak of the war the black community in the United Kingdom never numbered more than 8,000, and they were concentrated mainly in the port areas of Cardiff, Liverpool, London and Newcastle. In most respects the United Kingdom was overwhelmingly white, and this was especially true in Scotland where numbers of Afro-Caribbeans, Africans and Asians were always low. During the eighteenth century it had been fashionable for wealthy Glasgow families to employ black servants from slave plantations in the Caribbean, and in 1881 Arthur Watson of Queen's Park Football Club became the first black footballer to play at international level for Scotland. However for the most part in the streets of Scotland coloured skins were mainly noticeable by their absence. (They remained so for many years: at the 2001 census there were only 8,025 blacks of African or Caribbean origin, a mere 0.16 per cent of Scotland's population. At the same time the UK total was 1,148,738, or roughly 2 per cent of the country's population.[30]) Bearing in mind that demographic pattern it is not surprising that both the British and the American governments gave serious thought to the possibility that the arrival of black service personnel in the United Kingdom might heighten racial tensions, and by the summer of 1942 there were only 811 black US soldiers in the country. Partly this was as a result of Washington's concern not to upset an important ally, but it was also due to the fact that throughout the inter-war years racial segregation was a fact of life in the US forces. In June 1940 the US Army had only five black officers, while the Air Corps excluded them entirely and the navy only employed blacks as mess waiters.[31]

All that changed when the US entered the war and rapidly expanded the size of its armed forces to meet the need to fight a global conflict. Figures drawn up by the Pentagon estimated that of the one million conscripts at least 10 per cent of these would be black, and that the majority would end up being posted to the United Kingdom. Officially, the US view was that the 'American negro was now integrated on a basis of complete equality in the economic and political life of the country' but there is ample evidence to suggest that there was a colour bar and that the British authorities frequently colluded in maintaining it. Asked by the US authorities for his view, Foreign Secretary Anthony Eden suggested to the American ambassador in London that the British 'climate was unsuited to negroes'.[32] Confrontations between whites and blacks were familiar occurrences throughout the war, although there is also documentation to suggest that British people generally welcomed black US service personnel and felt that the worst violence was perpetrated by white officers and non-commissioned officers in the US forces.[33]

Although the presence of black service personnel was largely peripheral to Scotland's experience during the Second World War, it did not mean that they were completely invisible. The numbers from North America were certainly small but in contrast there was a sizable concentration of black foresters from British Honduras (later Belize) in Central America who arrived in Scotland in the summer of 1941. Serving in the British Honduras Forestry Unit, these skilled foresters were based initially at three camps: Kirkpatrick in the south-west, Duns in Berwickshire and Traprain Law near Haddington; in the following year others arrived to take up work at Achnashellach, Kinlochewe and Golspie in the Western Highlands. From the outset they were engaged in essential war work in Scotland's forests, dealing with home-grown timber and mainly producing pit props, under the direction of the Ministry of Supply. This lessened the demands on merchant shipping at a time when the German submarine offensives were taking their toll on the Atlantic convoys, and the unit was also supposed to free Scottish-based forestry workers for other kinds of war work. It was also felt that the employment of the British Hondurans would have a positive effect by allowing them to send back much-needed pay to their dependants at home.

However, from the outset their treatment by the British authorities ranged from callous indifference to off-hand cruelty. Although most of the men were highly capable and used to dealing with heavy timber, they were treated as unskilled workers and paid minimum wages. Their camps contained basic facilities and their clothing was unsuited to the kind of conditions they faced in the harsh winter weather. Complaints were often ignored even when the facts were reported by visiting officials from the Ministry of Supply: 'In general, the men are living in a deplorable condition almost completely cut off from the rest of the world. They are deprived of all form of entertainment and the harsh treatment of most of them by the authorities does nothing to alleviate their sufferings . . . A great portion of [them] are miserable and desperate.'[34]

All this was in contrast to the superior facilities offered to white foresters from Australia, New Zealand and Newfoundland, and the records suggest that there was a degree of casual racism in the response to the plight of the British Honduran foresters. The same report noted that the foresters' ultimate overseeing officer, Lieutenant-General Sir Harold Carrington, was not 'very knowledgeable or indeed very interested in welfare matters or . . . in the men as individuals' and that as a result little was being done to alleviate the conditions in the Scottish logging camps.[35] Supervision was minimal, and all too often the men were left to their own devices, with the result that morale slumped and sickness was prevalent amongst the workforce.

However, instead of addressing these issues the Ministry of Supply tended to relate the men's negative response to their predicament, and by the beginning of 1943 officials discussed repatriation as the only solution, citing as reasons poor health, general inefficiency and 'associations' with white women in the camps or in the nearby communities. As was the case with the appearance of black servicemen in the rest of the UK, this latter point was considered to be a real threat, and the idea of the British Hondurans entering into relationships with local women was taken very seriously indeed. In the autumn of 1942 the Duke of Buccleuch, a leading Scottish aristocrat and landowner in the Borders, complained to the Colonial Office that 'the people in the neighbourhood [Kirkpatrick Fleming] were encouraged to be friendly to them and the girls have interpreted this rather widely . . . personally, I dislike this mixture of colour and regret that it should be allowed with no discouragement'.[36] A response was promised, but if it ever emerged it was not recorded in the archives.

Inevitably, given human nature and a willingness to make the best of a bad issue, some of the foresters looked back on their service with some gratitude. In East Lothian a jazz band was formed and played regularly in towns such as Haddington and Tranent, where the foresters' dancing abilities were admired by the local women, and, following a frosty beginning, there was an element of togetherness. Initial suspicions also blighted the arrival of the foresters in the West Highlands where one of the members of the unit, Sam Martinez, found that he really was entering a foreign country:

We went to the village of Ullapool, just three miles, a group of us, for the first time, I think it was when we went into the village, the children were all running about the street when they see us coming, they said the coal men are coming and they all disappeared and even the woman in the shop, the lasses in the shops went behind there and leave the men to serve us and I think the men were even nervous because it was the first time they seen black people.'[37]

However, the discrimination was short-lived, and not only did Martinez eventually discover that he 'couldn't find better people to deal, they organised parties, dances, entertainments, service and help us with eggs and milk and food' but he eventually fell in love and married a local girl.[38] After the war Sam Martinez stayed on in Scotland, but for most of the British Hondurans it was not a positive experience, and it was not until much later that their services were brought to public notice as accounts of their ill-treatment began to be published.[39]

The final group of tourists also came to Scotland through the exigencies of total war were German and Italian prisoners of war (POWs). The first arrivals were downed aircrew, but they were only a prelude to a growing number of enemy sailors and soldiers as Britain took the war to the Axis powers in the Atlantic and the Mediterranean, North Africa and Italy and, later, France and north-west Europe. Under the terms of the Geneva Convention of 1929, to which Britain, Germany and Italy were signatories, captured service personnel had to be treated according to strict rules, and generally these were obeyed.

All told, by the end of the war, some 400,000 Axis POWs were held in around 600 camps across the UK, all of which offered basic living facilities. Some were purpose-built camps with Nissen-hut accommodation, but most were disused buildings which could be made secure. Ration scales were the same as those used for British service personnel, and all camps offered educational and recreational facilities. International law dictated that no POW was obliged to work, but many undertook agricultural labour or bomb damage repair because it gave them the opportunity to meet locals and broke up the generally dull routine in the camps. Although fraternisation was not allowed, many POWs struck up friendships, and, in some cases, romances blossomed: at the conclusion of hostilities over 15,000 remained in the United Kingdom

In Scotland there were forty-five main camps, most of which were working establishments, and these were situated across the country in rural areas. Many were in the central belt and the east coast counties of Fife, Angus and Aberdeenshire, but there were also camps in more remote areas in Argyllshire, Caithness, Orkney, Ross-shire and Wigtownshire.[40] One of the most inaccessible camps was at Watten near Wick, which was opened in 1943 to hold high-security prisoners including Gunter D'Alquen, the editor of *Das Schwarze Korps*, the official newspaper of the *Schutzstaffel* (SS), and Otto Kretschmer, a U-boat captain known as the 'Wolf of the Atlantic' who was responsible for sinking forty-seven Allied merchant ships between 1939 and his capture in 1941. In common with others in Scottish camps they were encouraged to undertake agricultural work and, all told, by 1945 20,000 Axis POWs were working on the land in Scotland.[41] Following the invasion of France in June 1944 this figure had been swollen by the arrival of 3,435 wounded German prisoners who were brought north from the English Channel ports for emergency treatment in Scottish hospitals, part of an extraordinary operation which saw 16,576 Axis service personnel being treated in this way.[42]

For the most part the experiences of the German and Italian POWs were unremarkable. While conditions were generally good, and attempts were made to keep POWs employed either on work schemes or through educational and recreational activities, boredom was a problem, as was the stress of isolation from Germany and Italy. Even after the war had ended prisoners were denied access to information about their families, and the post-war Labour government ignored the Geneva Convention by delaying immediate repatriation. The last German POWs were not returned until November 1948, and as fraternisation had been disallowed until Christmas 1946, this caused additional strains.

Nevertheless, many POWs working on the land struck up relationships with the farming communities in which they laboured – this was more or less unavoidable – and in some cases love blossomed. In Hawick Sergeant Rudi Drabner was a POW in the local Wilton Camp, having been taken prisoner in Normandy, and following the Christmas 1946 amnesty he fell in love with Anna Scott, a local dancing champion and bus conductress. Both admitted that their relationship was fraught with difficulties from family and friends who believed that she was wrong to become involved with a German, but they persisted, and were eventually married at the end of 1947 once Rudi had been demobilised. However, years later Anna admitted that it had not been an easy decision, and many local people were affronted by their relationship: 'They said I was wasting my life. "Aren't our boys good enough for you?" That sort of thing. I never had any hostility to my face, but I knew people were talking. Men were the worst. And older people.'[43]

The collision between the different cultures also spawned one of the best novels (also made into an equally memorable film and radio play) about the POW experience in Scotland – Jessie Kesson's *Another Time, Another Place* (1983) which tells the story of a doomed love affair between Janie, the recently married young wife of an older farmer on the Black Isle, and Luigi, an Italian POW working on their farm. Any kind of liaison would shock the close-knit community, but Kesson subtly introduces the notion that while Janie is a prisoner in a loveless marriage she uses Luigi as much as he uses her. In that sense the arrival of the Italians has changed everything for her: 'The young woman felt a small surge of anticipation rising up within her at the prospect of the widening of her narrow insular world as a farm worker's wife, almost untouched by the world war that raged around her. She always felt she was missing out on some tremendous event, never more so than when she caught a glimpse of girls of her own age, resplendent in uniform, setting out for places she would never set eyes on.'[44] The affair eventually becomes public after Luigi is falsely accused of raping another girl and Janie provides him with an alibi, but that is not the end of the story. In a bleak finale it becomes clear that there is no absolution for anyone. Luigi is still arrested, and Janie and her husband are forced to remain on their farm in the closely knit rural community which now despises both of them. She is still as much a prisoner as she ever was.

During the war Kesson was a cottar's wife living at Udale Cottages, Poyntzfield, near Jemimaville on the Black Isle, where three Italian POWs were employed on the land, but she always remained coy about any autobiographical context in her novel, telling her biographer that while she was fond of the Italians and was attracted to one of them, 'she ruled herself out from the first day. 'No posseeble!'[45]

Perhaps the most significant memorials to the presence of Axis

POWs in Scotland can be found on Orkney, where Italian prisoners constructed an ornate and hauntingly beautiful chapel on Lamb Holm island, and at Cultybraggan Camp at Comrie in Perthshire which was home to hard-line Nazi officers. It would also be difficult to find a starker contrast. The Orkney chapel was built by 550 Italian soldiers who had been taken prisoner in North Africa and transported to Orkney to construct the Churchill Barrier defences. Built to block the east side of Scapa Flow, the barriers linked the Orkney Mainland in the north to the island of South Ronaldsay and the two smaller islands of Lamb Holm and Glimps Holm. The chapel was constructed out of two Nissen huts, with a façade added to replicate a chapel entrance, but it was the interior decoration which gave the building its religious intensity. Most of the work was done by Domenico Chiocchetti, a POW from Moena who painted the sanctuary end of the chapel while fellow prisoners decorated the entire interior.

On the other hand, and in deep contrast, Cultybraggan was built as Camp 21 in 1940 and eventually housed 4,000 German POWs who had been classified as 'black' or irredeemable Nazis, many of them members of the SS. Inevitably the atmosphere within the camp was tense, not least because some of the guards were Polish, and things came to a head shortly before Christmas 1944 when two German POWs were found hanged and badly beaten. Following investigations it was discovered that they had been sentenced to death as traitors by a drumhead court-martial, and eight POWs were eventually arrested. The British investigating officer was Captain John Wheatley, a lawyer whose uncle of the same name had been imprisoned as a pacifist during the First World War and had also served as Health Minister in the first Labour government of 1924. On arriving at Cultybraggan camp, Wheatley described the atmosphere inside the camp as 'extremely violent and threatening', and his work was made more difficult by the code of silence imposed by the Nazi prisoners.[46] Eventually the arrested men were sent for trial in London where five were sentenced to death and hanged at Pentonville Prison on 6 October 1945.

Many of the Nissen huts remained intact after the war when Cultybraggan was used as a training facility for the Territorial Army. In 2007 the camp was bought by the local community for use as a heritage centre and a reminder of its past use as a military camp. In the

post-war world the camp compound also housed a fully equipped
secret bunker which would have been used by the regional government in Scotland in the event of a nuclear war. Through the quirks of
time both Cultybraggan and the Lamb Holm Italian Chapel are
popular tourist attractions.

10 Striking Back

At the beginning of the summer of 1942 it suddenly seemed that the balance of the war had shifted imperceptibly in favour of the Allies. There was no decisive moment, and dangers still lay ahead, but for the first time the Allied war effort had been stabilised, and with the US in the war there were grounds for cautious optimism.

While there had been a massive setback in North Africa in May when Rommel had captured Tobruk and forced British and Dominion troops to fall back on the border with Egypt, losing 235 tanks in the process, the arrival of General Claude Auchinleck as GOC Middle East had stopped the rot. In July Rommel's forces were halted at the First Battle of El Alamein, and as a result it became clear that the Germans would not reach Alexandria that summer. In the Pacific Ocean the Japanese had also reached the limit of their advance in the Coral Sea where their naval forces were badly mauled by naval aircraft flying from the US Navy's carrier fleet. This was followed (4–7 June) by Admiral Chester Nimitz's stunning victory at Midway where, once again, the issue was settled by superior US air power.

In Europe the Germans were also facing problems in the Soviet Union which had been invaded in the previous summer. At first everything had gone the way of the advancing panzer divisions but by the onset of winter Moscow had not fallen and the German advance had stalled along a wide front with terrifyingly long lines of communication. By the spring of 1942 the campaign was still unstable, with German successes on the Caucasus front, but already the Red Army was beginning to hold ground and in some places showed that they could drive back the invaders. Ahead lay setbacks, blunders and further disappointments, and it would take time for the transatlantic alliance to gel into a working relationship, but as summer turned into autumn the Allies were no longer oppressed by the spectre of defeat.

Two great victories, at El Alamein in October and at Stalingrad during the autumn and winter months of 1942–3, gave some much-needed foundation to that optimism by proving that the Germans could be beaten and that the tide could be turned.

For the Royal Navy, though, the year had begun badly when the German battleships *Gneisenau* and *Scharnhorst* had escaped back to Germany from the French port of Brest, together with the heavy cruiser *Prinz Eugen*. Despite the valiant attempts made by Fleet Air Arm torpedo bombers to halt the ships, the 'Channel dash' was successful and reawakened fears about the threat of German capital ships acting as surface raiders from their ports in the Baltic and Norway. Earlier in the year the battleship *Tirpitz*, sister ship to *Bismarck*, arrived at Altafjord in Norway and was used almost immediately to attack the convoy PQ12. Only the arrival of a superior naval force, including the carrier HMS *Victorious*, prevented the Germans from making a successful interception. Even so, the presence of such a powerful ship as the *Tirpitz* continued to be a major concern for the Admiralty. Although she fired her guns in anger on only one occasion (covering German land forces landing at Spitsbergen), and operated only three offensive operations, the fact that she lurked in the Norwegian fjords made a her a virtual 'fleet in being'.

The potency of her threat was exposed in June 1942 when she left her base in Trondheim to meet other German forces assembling to attack convoy PQ17. Composed of thirty-five merchant ships this was one of the most heavily protected convoys of the war but its fate was sealed by a misreading of available intelligence. On hearing that the *Tirpitz* was at sea the Admiralty ordered the convoy to scatter and in the confusion twenty-two isolated and unprotected merchant ships were sunk by U-boats and aircraft in one of the worst Allied naval setbacks of the war. *Tirpitz* went into maintenance at Trondheim and then Narvik, and only just survived an order from Hitler to be decommissioned as a result of her lack of success as a surface raider.

On the ship's return in September 1943 the Admiralty attempted to neutralise the threat by attacking *Tirpitz* with a new generation of small submarine-type vessels. In April 1942 the Experimental Submarine Flotilla was formed in Portsmouth but within two months moved to a new base codenamed 'Port D' on Loch Erisort south of Stornoway on the island on Lewis. In that remote setting a small group of volunteers tested a new weapon known as the Mark I Chariot which was based on a 21-inch torpedo specially adapted to carry a two-man crew wearing bulky divers' suits. The idea was to make covert attacks on enemy warships by cutting through boom defences and placing limpet mines on the target. Training was hard: the crews had to work long hours underwater using oxygen sets while steering and manoeuvring the heavy craft, and many suffered oxygen poisoning during the process. Later in the summer the flotilla moved to a new base, Port HHZ, at Loch Cairnbawn not far from Ullapool in the north-west of Scotland, where they defied sceptics by making successful dummy attacks on the heavily defended battleship HMS *Howe*.[1]

Encouraged by this progress, and aided by intelligence from Norwegian resistance groups, an attack was planned on the *Tirpitz* which was now based at Asenfjord near Trondheim where she threatened to break out into the north Atlantic. The operation was led by Leif Larsen, the Norwegian naval officer who ran the 'Shetland Bus', and it included two Chariots and seven crew members from the Cairnbawn flotilla. The weapons were stored below the hull of the fishing boat *Arthur* and the party left for Norway from Lunna Voe on Shetland on 26 October. Two days later they reached the Norwegian coast, but a sudden storm caused the Chariots to break free and the attack had to be abandoned with the fishing boat being scuttled. All but one of the original party of ten managed to escape to Sweden, where they were eventually flown back to RAF Leuchars on board one of the regular civilian flights between Scotland and Stockholm which were operated throughout the war by Hudson and Mosquito aircraft flying under the aegis of the British Overseas Airways Corporation (BOAC).

The failure of the Chariots paved the way for another attack on the *Tirpitz*, this time by midget X-class submarines whose crews were trained at Loch Cairnbawn and Loch Striven on the Firth of Clyde. Just over 50 feet in length, the X-class submarines were designed for stealthy penetration of enemy harbours to attack individual targets, and with a pressurised hull only five and a half feet in diameter they provided desperately cramped conditions for the four-man crew. Specially equipped side-cargoes carried high explosive charges which would be dropped beneath the hull of the target. For limited running on the surface they had a diesel motor but their small size and light endurance meant that they had to be towed towards their targets by S- or T-class submarines, with the passage crews exchanging places with the attack crews at the last minute. As with the Chariots, all crew members were volunteers from the submarine service. The first prototypes came into service in March 1942, and training began immediately in the remote lochs on Scotland's west coast.[2] By September 1943 six X-craft and their crews were considered ready to make their attacks on *Tirpitz* and *Scharnhorst* in Kaafjord at the head of Altenfjord and *Lützow* in nearby Langefjord.

While the crews had accurate information from aerial reconnaissance about the ships' whereabouts, they also know that they faced formidable obstacles in the shape of submarine and anti-torpedo nets. For the attacking force there were also the perils of the actual crossing. The operational crews sailed in the relative comfort of the six 'mother' submarines but for the passage crews it was rather different as they had to endure the cramped conditions of the midgets which were towed 40 feet below the waves and needed constant trimming. Nevertheless morale was high as Rear-Admiral C. B. Fry, the senior submarine commander discovered when he visited Loch Cairnbawn on the eve of their departure on 11 and 12 September 1943: 'It was in this spirit that they went out into the night in their tiny craft to face a thousand miles of rough seas before they reached their objective, which itself to their knowledge, was protected by every conceivable device which could ensure their destruction.'[3]

Problems began even before the Norwegian coast was sighted. Two of the craft broke their tows and one of them, *X9*, was lost. Then the weather worsened as the boats entered the Arctic Circle, and it was not until 20 September that the four remaining craft, *X5* (Henty-Creer), *X6* (Cameron), *X7* (Place) and *X10* (Hudspeth) were ready to begin their attack on Altenfjord. All passed through the mine belt guarding the approaches but *X10* experienced technical problems and had to withdraw. Superb seamanship plus a little luck allowed *X6* and *X7* to get through the protective boom and position themselves beneath *Tirpitz* in the early hours of 22 September. Although both craft had to be abandoned, the resulting explosions did substantial damage to the battleship, which was out of commission for six months. Both crews escaped and were captured but Henty-Creer's *X5* was sighted, attacked by gunfire and was presumed sunk as nothing was heard of her crew again. Cameron and Place were deservedly awarded the Victoria Cross. As for Hudspeth, he called off his attack and made his way back to the mother submarine but *X10* had to be scuttled on the return voyage to Loch Cairnbawn.[4]

Further attempts to disable the German capital ships were made by the RAF using specially adapted Lancaster bombers equipped with 12,000-pound Tallboy 'earthquake' bombs. On 11 September 1944 Lancasters of 9 and 617 Squadrons left RAF Lossiemouth to attack *Tirpitz* and, after refuelling in Russia, pressed home their attack, disabling the battleship with a direct hit. A second raid followed on 29 October, and the *coup-de-grâce* was delivered on 12 November when *Tirpitz* was hit, and capsized in shallow waters near Tromsø. The day after the raid the Secretary of State for Air, Sir Archibald Sinclair, visited the squadrons at Lossiemouth and congratulated them on sinking 'one of the toughest ships in the world'. At long last the threat had been neutralised and the Royal Navy was free to move its capital ships from Scapa for service in the Far East.

Norway and the North Sea also provided the focus for the RAF's presence in Scotland in the latter stages of the war. In addition to the main fighter airfields, the war was carried on from the north-east of the country through the Banff Strike Wing from its bases at Banff and Dallachy. Originally built for training purposes, the fields came into their own in the autumn of 1944 when RAF Coastal Command moved the bulk of its squadrons from the west of England to counter the threat posed by U-boats operating from Germany and Scandinavia. By then the Battle of the Atlantic had been won, and following the fall of France the German Navy had withdrawn most of its boats from its ports on the Bay of Biscay; this redeployment gave added impetus for the creation of a force to deal with all enemy shipping in the North Sea. The result was the Banff Strike Wing which originally consisted of 144 and 404 Squadrons flying Beaufighters, and 248 and 333 (Norwegian) Squadrons flying Mosquitoes. In October 143 Squadron arrived and converted from Beaufighters to Mosquitoes, a change which necessitated a redeployment of resources, with the Beaufighters transferring to nearby Dallachy while the Mosquitoes took up residence at Banff, also known as Boyndie. Command of the wing was in the hands of Group Captain Max Aitken, son of Lord Beaverbrook, the newspaper tycoon and wartime Minister of Aircraft

Production, and amongst the crews were pilots and navigators from Australia, Canada, France, New Zealand and Norway.[5] Fighter escorts were provided by North American P-51 Mustangs of 19 Squadron based at RAF Peterhead.

Air Ministry photographic records show the extent and variety of the operations undertaken by the Banff Strike Wing in the short interval between its inception in September 1944 and the end of the war eight months later.[6] This was one of the least heralded RAF units of the war, yet its impact was enormous at a time when the Luftwaffe had all but stopped offensive operations against Scotland. Equipped with Mosquito Mark VI and Beaufighter Mark XI strike aircraft, the primary targets for the Banff Strike Wing were German surface ships and submarines operating in the North Sea, especially in Scandinavian waters. Their armament included RP-3 rockets which were devastating against shipping. Between 14 September 1944 and 4 May 1945 the Banff Strike Wing carried out regular sorties or 'Rover Patrols' against enemy shipping, and in so doing encountered difficult and heavily defended targets. Most German merchant ships travelled in convoys, and were heavily defended both by their own anti-aircraft guns and by flakships, heavily armed former whalers. Both types of aircraft also used cannon and machine-guns for aerial combat. On 21 April 1945, during one of the last sorties of the war, Mosquitoes from the strike wing encountered a force of eighteen enemy aircraft from Stavanger while flying over the North Sea. In the subsequent engagement at least ten raiders were shot down with no losses to the Mosquito force.[7]

In few other parts of the armed forces was the process of renewal more keenly felt than in the regiments which made up the reconstituted 51st (Highland) Division. Following its forced surrender at St Valéry-en-Caux the survivors made their way back to Britain as best they could, and almost immediately steps were taken to reform the division on the duplicate 9th (Scottish) Division whose forbears had fought so gallantly on the Western Front during the First World War. For Brigadier Douglas Wimberley, who had taken 1st Cameron Highlanders across to France in 1940, this was best possible outcome: 'After Dunkirk came the tragedy of St Valéry and naturally that surrender affected me much the most (like I'm sure all Highlanders). In my nightly prayers I petitioned, whatever else happened to me, the

Almighty would save me from that particular fate. Some of the remnants of the 51st were sent to an Artillery depot near Devizes. I went over with two or three Highland regiment officers, telling them the Division would come into its own again.'[8]

The process turned out to be remarkably smooth. All three regular battalions in the division were re-raised by their regiments – 1st Black Watch, 1st Gordons, 2nd Seaforth – and steps were taken to re-form the Territorial battalions and make good the losses from within the regimental system. In The Gordon Highlanders the 5th Battalion was renewed from the 7th Battalion, and joined the new division as 5/7th Gordons, while in The Argyll and Sutherland Highlanders the 7th Battalion amalgamated with the 10th Battalion. Within a short time the 9th (Scottish) Division was renumbered as the 51st (Highland) Division, with a new and instantly recognisable HD divisional badge, and quickly started building up its own sense of morale. Its head-quarters was at Rothes, Banffshire, and it was commanded by Major-General Neil Ritchie who had been adjutant of 2nd Black Watch in Mesopotamia in 1915. Other battalions started arriving to bring the new formation up to strength; these included 5th Black Watch from Angus and 7th Black Watch from Fife, both of which had spent the first part of the war training up and carrying out coastal defence duties. All the battalions were spread across the north and the north-east where they were in the home defence role, but from the outset the emphasis within the division was centred on rebuilding and then maintaining *esprit de corps*. As John McGregor put it in the war history of 5th Black Watch: 'To the Highland soldier, the 51st was *the* Division and next only to the Regiment, it commanded the same pride and loyalty.'[9]

In May 1941 Ritchie was moved to the Middle East where he eventually commanded the British Eighth Army, and his place was taken by Wimberley who immediately put his stamp on the division. Nicknamed 'Tartan Tam', he insisted that as far as was possible the soldiers within the division should be Highlanders, failing that Low-landers, and that men should always try to return to the division if they ever got separated from it. In due course he was not above poaching Scottish soldiers from other divisions, and insisted on the creation and maintenance of a fiercely Scottish (especially Highland) sense of patriotism. The battalion pipes and drums were expected to practice hard to reach high standards of perfection, and all junior officers were ordered to assemble after reveille so that they could dance reels under the direction of the pipe-major. Wimberley also insisted on high standards of discipline and keenness during training, and encouraged a competitive spirit amongst the battalions and their brigades. Only one of the units within 51ˢᵗ (Highland) Division escaped Wimberley's nationality strictures – 1/7ᵗʰ Middlesex Regiment, which served as the machine-gun battalion – but as their historian recorded, 'soon the cockneys made themselves appreciated and became friends for life with the Highlanders, civilian and military alike.'[10]

As the training continued the division was joined by a reconnaissance regiment operating armoured cars which was part of the newly formed Reconnaissance Corps; it was numbered 51ˢᵗ and wore the tam-o'-shanter, a Hunting Stewart flash on the right shoulder and the HD badge on the right. Three Royal Artillery field regiments were added (126, 127 and 128), and the intensity of training reached a new tempo during the winter of 1941–2. In March 1942 the division moved to Aldershot where it came under the South-East Command whose GOC was General Bernard Law Montgomery, a commander with whom the Highlanders were to be associated for the rest of the war.

The next step for the division was embarkation on board a large convoy of twenty-two ships, many of them well-known liners such as *Empress of Australia*, *Strathmore* and *Arundel Castle*, which was bound for an unknown destination, sailing from Glasgow, Liverpool and Southampton. The issue of pith helmets suggested that the destination was India, but for everyone it involved a long and tiring voyage round the Cape of Good Hope which lasted fifty-nine days and for most of the men felt even longer. Had it not been for a stop at Cape Town it could have been a depressing experience, but as the historian of 5ᵗʰ Black Watch remembered, the experience of a day's leave came as a time out of life after almost three years of war: 'As they came down the gangways they were greeted by lines of cars waiting to take the Jocks out for the rest of the day and night. No-one was overlooked, parties were given, wine flowed, dances had been organised with pretty partners in plenty, and all given free and with the sincere desire to ensure that the visit to Cape Town would be memorable.'[11]

During the stay in Cape Town the division's final destination became clearer when Wimberley left the convoy on 20 July to travel by flying boat to Cairo. Three weeks later the 51st (Highland) Division began arriving in Egypt where it joined the British Eighth Army as much-needed reinforcements for the fighting against the Axis forces. Immediately after arrival the division started training for desert warfare, getting used to the heat and dust, and hardening themselves for the shock of battle.

This was a difficult period for the British forces in the country. As we have seen, in June the British Eighth Army had retreated from Tobruk, which had fallen into enemy hands following a German and Italian offensive led by the charismatic Rommel; Cairo was under threat, and it seemed inevitable that another enemy assault would lead to the collapse of British power in North Africa. Morale was low, and defeat seemed inevitable. At that point Churchill decided to change the command structure by appointing Montgomery to take over the Eighth Army on 12 August. It proved to be an inspired choice, and Montgomery got to work straight away. Not only was he desperate to impose his personality and his ideology on a demoralised army, but he also wanted to get rid of the idea that there would be any withdrawal. Orders for retreat were torn up, and he immediately set about planning to take the offensive back to Rommel. His first order was brief and to the point: 'Here we will stand and fight; there will be no further withdrawal. I have ordered that all plans and instructions dealing with a further withdrawal are to be burnt, and at once. We will stand and fight here. If we can't stay here alive, then let us stay here dead.'[12]

In the time that was left to him, little more than two weeks, Montgomery had to work hard to raise morale and to restore the confidence that had been lost during the earlier reverses. He also had to produce a plan which would counter Rommel's expected offensive, and the result was a stunning defensive battle at Alam Halfa which produced a much-needed victory for the Eighth Army. It also prepared the way for a fresh offensive in the third week of October during the full moon, by which time his army would have been reinforced by 8th (Armoured) Division and 50th (Northumbrian) and 51st (Highland) Divisions. In the run-up to the attack Montgomery took time and trouble to make sure that the men of the Eighth Army, especially the newly arrived reinforcements, knew exactly what was happening and what was expected of them. He also continued his policy of inspecting units right down to battalion level and talking to the men. Mostly such visits were a fillip to morale, but there were occasional glitches: while spending time with 154 Brigade in the 51st (Highland) Division he acknowledged the presence of the regular 1st Black Watch but he appeared to be dumbfounded when told that the 7th Black Watch was a Territorial battalion from the county of Fife. According to the brigade commander, Brigadier H. W. Houldsworth, Black Watch officers 'stood gaping with their mouths open' when Montgomery admitted that he did not know where Fife was as he had 'never been to Scotland'.[13]

Fortunately Montgomery showed a surer touch in directing his next battle – the Battle of El Alamein, which began on 23 October, and which turned out to be the first decisive British land victory of the war. To the operation Montgomery brought scrupulous planning, and instilled a belief in the Eighth Army that they had the training and the equipment to defeat an enemy which was not unbeatable. It was also a set-piece battle similar to the kind that had been fought in the latter stages of the First World War, with soldiers advancing under a heavy barrage and battalions leap-frogging forward to take their objectives. As Private Roy Green, 1st Black Watch, put it, 'Alamein was First World War tactics with Second World War weapons, creeping barrages, walking through minefields ahead of armour, each man five yards apart to save casualties.'[14]

For the attack of the 51st (Highland) Division the intention was to secure 7,000 yards of desert fighting across minefields and barbed wire, with the division advancing in six channels towards their objectives. Thus 1st Gordons and 5th Black Watch advanced on the right towards Montrose, Arbroath and Forfar (Green Line) before pushing on to Turiff (red line), then on to Kintore, Dufftown and Braemar (Black Line) with Aberdeen (Blue Line) being the final objective. For 5/7th Gordons in the next channel the objectives were Elgin and Cruden (Green Line), Inch (Red Line), Strichen and Stanley (Black Line) and Ballater (Blue Line) At 9.40 p.m. a huge artillery barrage opened up as hundreds of guns fired towards the German lines. As remembered by Lieutenant Felix Barker in his war history of 5/7th Gordons it was a moment that none would forget.

Each man could see the white St Andrew's Cross on the back of the man in front of him. And as they moved forward they could not help feeling that the whole thing was rather fantastic. It was like no battle they had ever heard of, or could have imagined, in the wildest flight of imagination. Magazines were filled because it seemed out of the question to go into a major attack without rounds in the rifles, but many a man never fired a shot all that terrible night. Bayonets gleamed in the moonlight, but they were fixed as a token gesture, not so much to be used as to give confidence.[15]

The attacking force moved off shortly after 10 p.m., each battalion being guided by a navigation officer watching his compass and counting his paces to ensure accuracy. All the first objectives were quickly taken, with the follow-up forces passing through the first wave, although there were problems for 1st Black Watch when it pushed on too quickly and had to halt to wait for the artillery bombardment to pass over the enemy. By dawn the following day the second objectives had been taken and the battle moved into its next phase which Montgomery promised would be a 'dog-fight'.

All the time shelling continued on either side, and tank battles raged as British Shermans engaged the enemy lines. In some parts of the line the fighting was fiercer than others, but as Alastair Borthwick, 5th Seaforth, recorded in his autobiography, the experience of battle almost defied description.

The noise is unbelievable. If one shell be fired from one 25-pounder gun at night, the Infantryman first sees a flash far behind him and a few seconds later hears the sound of the gun. Again there is a slight pause; and far overhead a shrill sound, somewhere between a whine and a sigh and small wind blowing across the strings of a harp, grows in volume and deepens in tone until the shell roars into the ground ahead of him. There is a red flash, and an explosion which has a distinct metallic clang in it.[16]

This was the common lot of every soldier who fought at Alamein – of being under constant mortar and shell fire, and of being pinned down by artillery as the forward formations attempted to make the final breakthrough.

However, it could not last, as the speed and aggression of the Allied assault had broken the enemy's will to resist. In some parts of the line the fighting was fiercer than others, and there were a few surprises. When 5th Black Watch prepared to attack its final objective it appeared to be a tough nut to crack, as the German defenders had successfully repelled an armoured assault on their position. However, when the battalion went into the attack the following night, they found that the Germans had withdrawn, leaving behind a number of vehicles and artillery pieces. There were similar experiences for all the battalions, although 7th Black Watch found itself pinned down with New Zealand troops by heavy fire on a feature known as 'The Ben' on the Miteiriya Ridge. During the fighting the battalion lost six officers and eighty soldiers killed, and almost twice that number wounded.

However, the speed and aggression of the Allied assault had broken the enemy's will to resist, and on 3 November came the joyous conformation from the BBC that there had been 'a great victory in North Africa'. That same day Operation Supercharge was put into effect as British, Indian and New Zealand forces fought their way out of the German lines of barbed wire and minefields to allow the armoured forces to begin the chase after the now retreating German and Italian forces. Amongst them, supporting the New Zealand infantry, was The Royal Scots Greys which reverted to cavalry tactics by charging an Italian artillery battery head-on instead of attacking from the flanks. Hidden minefields were the main problem, and the Eighth Army lost heavy casualties during the pursuit phase, but the fighting in North Africa was nearing its triumphant conclusion. Soon Montgomery's advancing men were passing names which had become familiar to the Allies during the years of attack and retreat – Benghazi, Sidi Barrani, El Agheila, El Adem, Mersa Brega – as they raced towards the strategically important goal of the port of Tripoli, which fell at the end of January 1943. It was a key moment, but the war diarist of 5/7th Gordons was not overly impressed by what the battalion found when it arrived: 'Tripoli is not much: a few fly-blown shops selling razor blades and soap, and a moderately filthy Arab quarter.'[17]

Throughout his career Montgomery revealed a talent for showmanship, and in no other incident was that better displayed that in the advance on the iconic port of Tripoli. Its capture was the crowning glory of the triumph at Alamein, and Montgomery used it to reinforce the scale of Rommel's defeat and also to underline the growing strength of the Allied cause. At dawn on 23 January 1943, the first British tanks entered the port carrying infantrymen of 1st Gordon Highlanders with their pipers playing the regimental quick march 'Cock of the North', and the moment was captured by accompanying war correspondents. Two weeks later Montgomery capitalised on the feat when Churchill visited Tripoli with Alexander and Brooke and was treated to the first British victory parade of the war. It was a full-blown ceremonial affair: following a triumphal drive into the main square of Tripoli, the prime minister's party was treated to a march-past led by the pipes and drums of 51st (Highland) Division. It was a scene which greatly moved those watching, including Brooke, who recorded it in his diary.

> As I stood alongside of Winston watching the [Highland] Division march past, with the wild music of the pipes in my ears. I felt a large lump rise in my throat and a tear run down my face. I looked at Winston and saw several tears on his face, from which I knew he was being stirred inwardly by the same feelings that were causing such upheaval in me. It was partly due to the fact that the transformation of these men from their raw pink and white appearance in Ismailia to their bronzed war-hewn countenances provided a tangible and visible sign of the turn of the tide of war. The meaning of this momentous change was brought home to me more forcibly than it had been up to the present. For the first time I was beginning to live through the thrill of those first successes that were now rendering ultimate victory possible.[18]

The next stage was the advance to Tunis to link up with the First Army which was approaching to rendezvous with the Eighth Army. (A joint British and US army had landed in Morocco and Algiers at the beginning of November 1942, as part of Operation Torch. One of its more successful commanders was Lieutenant-General George S. Patton, whose name would be heard of again.) Amongst those serving in the 1st British Division was 6th Gordons, which had landed in Algiers on 9 March 1943 as part of the reinforcements after sailing from the Clyde. During the journey the ship carrying the battalion's vehicles and stores had been attacked and sunk, which meant that essential weapons such as mortars were missing during the opening rounds of the operation. (These turned up in April when the battalion also received its first supplies of the new PIAT (Projector, Infantry, Anti-Tank) weapons to replace the obsolescent Boys heavy rifle.) Minefields were also a problem, as was enemy artillery fire – in one attack eight men of D Company were killed as 6th Gordons was preparing for the first combined attack with Eighth Army.

During the night of 22 March 1943, the final assault on Tunis began in the face of sustained German artillery fire. In the opening phases 6th Gordons held the division's right flank before being relieved a week later by 6th East Surrey Regiment; the Gordons' losses were twenty killed and fifty-one wounded. In the next phase of the fighting 6th Gordons came under the command of 24th Guards Brigade, which needed to be reinforced for the attack on Djebel Bou Aoukaz on 29 April. A and D companies, under the command of Major A. G. I. Fleming, fought alongside 1st Irish Guards and succeeded in taking their objectives, despite coming under sustained counter-attack – at one point a force of twenty German tanks attacked from the rear of the battalion's position in the Gab Gab Gap. During the action thirty casualties were sustained; amongst them was Major Fleming, who was the senior of the battalion's pre-war officers.

But by then the end was in sight. On 6 April Montgomery's forces had broken through at Wadi Akarit, having breached the Mareth Line a month earlier, and the coastal route to Tunis was open. Not that it was easy going for any of the other Highland regiments. In his war memoirs Lieutenant Neil McCallum, 5/7th Gordons, left a vivid account of the sweltering conditions as the British Eighth Army continued its pursuit of the retreating Germans, adding that whereas they had the benefit of transport, the British soldiers travelled on foot: 'There was more marching, on feet soft with weeks of trench life. A hard rocky country. We marched past a large isolated house, glaringly white in the sun and from within its rough walls you could feel the invisible eyes watching. A robed Arab stood at a metal gate. The files of men marched past, boots grating on the rock, or lifting up white dust in chalky parts.'[19] With the two armies converging on Tunis, Axis resistance began to crumble – Rommel had already left the battle front, leaving General Hans-Jürgen von Arnim in command – and amidst chaotic conditions the Germans capitulated on 12 May. The fighting in North Africa had finally come to an end.

One other factor illuminates the campaign in North Africa. It produced some of the most coherent and vibrant literature of the war, so much so that comparisons were made between Cairo and Fitzrovia, an imagined literary area in London based on the Fitzroy Tavern on the corner of Charlotte Street in London, and the centre of literary gatherings in the 1930s.[20] Literary magazines such as *Orientations*, *Parade* and *Oasis* flourished, and the poet G. S. Fraser claimed that the Middle East theatre of operations 'produced far more – and at times even finer – poetry than all the years of attrition on the Western Front'.[21] Originally from Glasgow, George Sutherland Fraser had graduated in 1937 and served as a sergeant-major in the Ministry of Information, gaining from the eccentric English poet John Gawsworth (the pen name of T. I. F. Anderson) the poetic description: 'Behind his Scottish rims: | It is frightfully effectual | To look intellectual.'[22] He sat in the centre of much of what was happening in the literary publishing scene in Cairo, and he used journalistic skills learned while working on the *Press and Journal* in Aberdeen before the war. Together with the poet Keith Douglas and Lawrence Durrell, author of the *Alexandria Quartet*, Fraser epitomised everything that was lively and life-enhancing about the literary exiles living in wartime Cairo.

Douglas became one of the best poets of the Second World War, as did Hamish Henderson, who eventually served as an intelligence officer with the 51st (Highland) Division. Indeed, there is a strong case for arguing that Henderson was a soldier's poet in much the same way that Wilfred Owen was regarded in the previous conflict. By any standards, though, Henderson was an extraordinary individual, a renaissance man who felt at home in several European cultures and languages, not least those of the German and Italian soldiers facing the Eighth Army. Yet he found the truest articulation of his cultural and political beliefs in his native Scotland. Born in Blairgowrie in Perthshire in 1919, he was educated at Dulwich College and Downing College, Cambridge, and had been a regular visitor to Hitler's Germany where he worked with the Society of Friends in helping refugees to escape. On the outbreak of war he attempted to join the Cameron Highlanders but was turned down due to poor eyesight, and had to wait to be conscripted in 1940 when he joined the Pioneer Corps to work on beach defences in southern England. The following year he was commissioned into the Intelligence Corps, and by March 1943, after much cajoling, was attached to the 51st (Highland) Division, having spent time with the 1st South African Division at the time of El Alamein.

For a man who was a pacifist by instinct and inclination, Henderson's time in uniform could have caused problems, but he relished the experience because he believed that the war was a crusade against fascism, and one that had to be won. Like others who served under Wimberley, he was also passionate about the Highland regiments, becoming, as one obituarist put it, 'a Jock amongst Jocks' in a division whose 'officers flaunted proud Highland genealogies while its squaddies sang traditional lyrics in Scots and Gaelic, and its pipers represented a summation of an instrumental tradition peculiar to Scotland.'[23]

Later in life Henderson would become a renowned folklorist, but during his war service in North Africa he emerged as a powerful and sensitive poet whose wartime work was published in 1948 by John Lehmann under the title *Elegies for the Dead in Cyrenaica*. The eight elegies and the final 'Heroic Song for the Runners of Cyrene' form a body of poetry which is written from the point of a view of soldiers on both sides of the divide and underscored by Henderson's warning that 'we should not disfigure ourselves with villainy of hatred'. This led him to consider the lot of the enemy as well as his own side, and during his interrogation of a captured officer he was much taken with his observation that 'Africa changes everything. In reality we are allies, and the desert is our common enemy.' That conceit runs through all the elegies, and finds a moving expression in the 'Seventh Elegy' which mourns 'seven good Germans' killed at El Eleba:

> Seven poor bastards
> Dead in African deadland
> (tawny tousled hair under the issue blanket)
> *Wie einst Lili*
> dead in African deadland
> *einst Lile Marlene*[24]

In his introductory note to the second section of the *Elegies*, Henderson quoted from another desert war poet Sorley MacLean, whose poem '*Glac a' Bhais*' ('Death Valley') is prefaced by the observation: 'Some Nazi or other has said that the Fuehrer had restored to German manhood the "right and joy of dying in battle".' Coming across one corpse with 'face slate-grey' below the Ruweisat Ridge, MacLean saw only the pity of death, with flies swarming over grey bodies killed during the 'delirium of war':

> Whatever his desire or mishap,
> His innocence or malignity,
> He showed no pleasure in his death
> Below the Ruweisat Ridge.[25]

MacLean was another poet whose natural pacifism was balanced by the need to defeat fascism. Born in Raasay in 1911, he had been educated at the University of Edinburgh and had worked as a teacher before being conscripted into the Royal Signals. A native Gaelic speaker, he had begun writing poetry before the war, and was in correspondence with other poets such as Robert Garioch, Hugh MacDiarmid and Douglas Young. During this period, between his conscription in September 1940 and his service in North Africa, his own poetry had been fired by four relationships of varying intensity during the 1930s which resulted in the love lyrics of '*Dain do Eimhir*' ('Poems to Eimhir') in 1943. To those expressions of love and regret he grafted equally passionate political sentiments as he explored his sense of anger at the triumph of fascism after the Spanish Civil War. In '*Gaoir na h-Eorpa*' ('The Cry of Europe') the poet's sense of loss is allied to his despair for the 'poverty, anguish and grief' of the people of Spain, and typifies MacLean's attempts to forge a link between the opposing claims of love and commitment. '*Dain do Eimhir*' is widely regarded as his major achievement, and was published after he was badly wounded during the Battle of El Alamein.[26]

While living in Edinburgh and teaching at Boroughmuir High School, MacLean had collaborated with another poet and teacher Robert Garioch (Robert Garioch Sutherland, 1909–81), who produced on his own hand press *Seventeen Poems for 6d*. In common with fellow poets J. K. Annand and Norman MacCaig, Garioch (or 'Geerie' as he was always known) was Edinburgh-born, and after leaving university became a teacher. Called up into the Royal Signals, he saw action in North Africa with 201 Guards Motor Brigade during Operation Torch when a joint British-American army invaded Morocco and Tunisia prior to joining up with the Eighth Army. However, Garioch did not get the chance to finish the campaign. On 20 June, while operating a battery charger on a Ford V8 truck, he 'walked the regulation distance into the Blue, taking a shovel, after the manner prescribed for the Children of Israel in Deuteronomy, XXIII, 12–13' and quickly discovered that the Germans were in the process of over-running the Allied positions.[27] For him the war was over, and he spent the rest of his time in Italian and German prisoner-of-war camps. Later, he wrote movingly about his experiences in *Two Men and a Blanket* (1974); through a pleasing coincidence it was published by Robin Lorimer, a man in the great Scottish tradition of scholar-publishers, who had fought at the first battle of El Alamein with 11 Field Regiment Royal Artillery, serving in an anti-tank battery which knocked out eleven German tanks.[28]

The other notable Scottish poet of the Desert War was George Campbell Hay, who had tried to avoid conscription but ended up serving in the Royal Army Ordnance Corps in Tunisia as part of Operation Torch at the end of 1942. Given menial jobs – several applications to transfer to the Intelligence Corps were rejected – Hay used his time to learn Arabic and to speak to Italian prisoners of war (he was a superb linguist). At the same time he was wrestling with the problem of getting his first collection of poems through the press under the title *Wind on Loch Fyne*. Containing work in English, Scots and Gaelic, it was eventually published in 1948, and was well received. As to Hay's own position, it is perhaps best summarised in a verse from '*Teistead Mhic Iain Deorsa*' ('Mac Iain Deorsa Testifies'):

> Am I to crouch in the mud
> As if I were their slave?
> My father begat me free
> And I have not learnt to be a coward.[29]

One other thing bound together the war poets in North Africa. They were fighting over a landscape which had little in common with the other theatres of the Second World War, and the war poets seem to have been affected by its wild beauty. At first acquaintance the North African terrain was harsh, barren and inhospitable, but it was also strangely compelling, a landscape which imprinted itself on the minds of the men who fought there. Henderson described it in his first elegy 'End of a Campaign' as the 'brutish desert . . . this landscape for half-wit stunted ill-will', while the English soldier poet Jocelyn Brooke declared in his poem 'Landscape near Tobruk' that 'this land was made for war'.[30] In fact, few of the men who served there, writers or not, failed to be affected by the sheer size of the desert arena over which the two opposing armies fought, its absence of definition and the seemingly limitless horizons with few roads or tracks to break up the bare expanse of sand and scrub. Responding to its similarities to a classical sporting arena, war correspondents on both sides tended to report the conflict in an imagery which spoke of a courtly tournament involving valiant rivals. In this respect it is noteworthy that three of the Highland battalions in the 51st (Highland) Division had their Desert War histories written by young officers who went on to enjoy successful careers in broadcasting and journalism – Felix Barker, Alastair Borthwick and Andrew Todd.

The British victory in North Africa was a turning point in the war. Not only were the church bells rung throughout Britain to celebrate the Eighth Army's victory at El Alamein, but Montgomery had proved that the British soldier had nothing to fear in action against his German counterpart. Even so, it was only an interlude, if a welcome one. Giving a bloody nose to Rommel's Afrika Korps had provided a marvellous fillip for morale, but it was not the end of the war. Ahead lay two and a half years of hard fighting, and there was still much to do – in addition to dealing with the Japanese, the Allies faced a determined and ruthless enemy in Europe, where the brunt of the fighting was being borne by the Red Army in the heartlands of the Soviet Union. For the British and US forces the next stage of the war involved the capture of Sicily as a precursor to the invasion of Italy, a move which would lead to the final securing of the Mediterranean, with its vital maritime routes to India and the Far East.

The Sicilian operation called for a British seaborne assault by Montgomery's Eighth Army between Syracuse and the Pachino peninsula on the island's south-eastern coast on 10 July, while the

US I and II Armored Corps under Patton's command would land on a forty-mile front along the southern coast between Gela and Scoglitti, and Licata on the left flank. There would also be an airborne assault carried out by the US 82nd Airborne Division and the British 1st Airborne Division to attack targets in the inland area, and to secure the landing grounds. Once ashore, Montgomery planned to create a bridgehead, and to secure the ports of Syracuse and Licata before moving rapidly north to take Messina, while Patton's forces covered the left flank.

In addition to the 51st (Highland) Division, a number of other Scottish regiments were involved in the Sicilian campaign, including The Royal Scots Greys, 2nd Royal Scots Fusiliers, 2nd Cameronians and 2nd Highland Light Infantry. All the Allied forces went into the operation with the high morale that had been instilled by the successful outcome of the fighting in North Africa, but the capture of the island was not the foregone conclusion that the Allies hoped it would be. As part of XXX Corps, 51st (Highland) Division landed on the south-east corner of the island, with the 1st Canadian Division on the left, and then pushed north towards Pachino. To 1st Gordons fell the task of maintaining the bridgehead, and within a week the division had pushed 75 miles inland in what the battalion's War Diary described as 'a long and tiresome hike'.[31] The first choke point was at the town of Sferro, which covered the road and railway to Catania, and was guarded by the German Hermann Goering Division who proved to be formidable opponents.

The fighting began in extremely hot weather on 19 July, and it soon became apparent that the capture of Sferro would be no easy matter. Under heavy German shell-fire, 5th Black Watch was pinned down, and it took a great deal of effort to clear the town. During the fighting both 1st and 5/7th Gordons lost the use of their radio sets and were forced to use runners. According to Felix Barker, 5/7th Gordons, Sferro was 'nothing more than a handful of houses at a T-junction' but it proved to be an awkward position to attack.

The name of the place was in such small type that you had to peer close to the map to read it. Sferro. Yes according to the reports that was where the opposition was coming from. Sferro. Just a handful of houses. It was a little village of negligible importance, for years a lazy insignificant place housing a few poor peasants. Yet here destiny had decided that an important and bitter battle should be fought out. A little too fanciful perhaps to attribute it all to destiny! After all, as you could see from the map it was really because the enemy had seen that the land rose quite steeply behind, provided excellent cover and concealment for its 17 millimetre guns.[32]

On 10 July the first elements of 5th Division had come ashore south-west of Syracuse, the plan being for two brigades to secure the beach-head and to allow 13 Brigade to pass through it and to push inland. This was achieved successfully, and a number of Italian prisoners were taken, but before the brigade concentration area could be secured 2nd Cameronians had to take the small town of Floridia, which dominated the high ground on the north–south road. This was duly accomplished, with the battalion losing thirteen casualties killed and wounded. From there the division made its way north to Augusta where the road was littered with the detritus of war – crashed aircraft, burning vehicles and dead bodies. From there the battalion moved with the rest of the division into the Plain of Catania, which was described in the war history in the following terms:

> . . . a flat, naked depression, stretching for some twelve miles to the north, bounded on the right, or eastern side by the sea, with the port of Catania in the North-East corner. From Catania westwards ran the foothills of Etna to the high ground above Gerbini and Sferro, some fifteen miles inland to the West. The plain was principally divided by the river Simeto and its Southern tributary, the Dittaino, which both ran in the plain from West to East. From South to North the main coastal road went to Catania as did the railway, running almost parallel, but a mile or so further inland. Several secondary lines and roads served the few houses, farm buildings and signal boxes that were infrequent dots in this vast expanse.[33]

It was unpromising territory, but it had to be secured if the advance was to maintain its timetable. Unfortunately, it was also a countryside which was made for defence. Towering over the plain was the smoking bulk of Mount Etna, which the enemy used to good effect to observe the Allied movements. The Germans also enjoyed air superiority, and although some airfields had been captured by the Allies, it took time for aircraft to arrive and to mount sorties against the enemy. Topographical considerations prevented Montgomery from utilising his superiority in armour and artillery, and the lack of a decent road system meant that the infantry had to return to foot-slogging. The presence of civilians in the battlefield areas was also a hindrance. In short, after the freedom of movement enjoyed in North Africa, the Eighth Army found itself hemmed in, and the Plain of Catania proved to be a difficult hurdle. On the night of 13/14 July an airborne operation by 1 Parachute Brigade failed to take the vital bridges at Primasole, and as a result Catania remained in enemy hands.

During this phase of the advance 2nd Cameronians was able to act with armoured support from the County of London Yeomanry, although use was also made of aggressive infantry patrols. In one action on 2 August, a fighting patrol led by Lieutenant J. M. Porter destroyed two German machine-gun positions and took ten German prisoners, including an officer. Porter was awarded the Military Cross, and Corporal R. Smith the Military Medal. The next objective was the River Simieto which had to be crossed to allow the battalion to attack the town of Paterno, which fell on 6 August. Although the Germans began withdrawing a week later, it was not the end of the fighting as they took up strong defensive positions at Gerbini, six miles to the south-east, which contained an airfield as well as a railhead. The delays stymied Montgomery's plan to push rapidly up the eastern side of Sicily – Patton had made better progress on the left – and it took another week before the Allies were in a position to move jointly on Messina. By then the German and Italian high command had decided that the island was indefensible, and had laid plans to begin the evacuation on 11 August.

While the operation had taken longer to complete than the Allies had planned, Sicily fell on 16 August. Some of the gloss was taken off the victory when over 100,000 German and Italian soldiers were evacuated across the Straits of Messina to fight again in Italy, but the battle for the island showed that British and US forces could work in tandem against a determined enemy.

Before the culmination of the campaign, 6th Seaforth was taken out of the line to refit and to begin training with 5th Division for the next stage of the campaign in Italy, while the Seaforth and Cameron battalions in 51st (Highland) Division returned to Britain to start training for the long-awaited invasion of France. There was also a change of job for its experienced commander, Major-General Douglas Wimberley, who had led it so well in North Africa and Sicily: he was sent back to Britain to become commandant of the army staff college at Camberley. Before he left he issued an Order of the Day to All Ranks of the 51st (Highland) Division thanking them for their 'spirit, discipline and behaviour', and reminding them that the member regiments could not rest on their laurels. He also included a verse which he felt summed up the spirit of the Highland soldier, be he a Scot from the Highlands or Lowlands, or one of the many Englishmen who had served in the division.

> Ye canna mak' a sojer wi' braid an' trappins braw,
> Nor gie him fightin' spirit when his backs ag'in the wa'.
> It's the breedin' in the callants [young men] that winna let
>   them whine,
> The bluid o' generations frae lang, lang syne.[34]

Similar sentiments could have been addressed to the soldiers fighting in Burma. During this same period, the spring and summer of 1943, the first concrete steps had been taken to retrieve the position in Burma by adopting a more offensive attitude to the Japanese forces. For the first time, specially trained British and Indian soldiers had shown that they were capable of taking on and beating Japanese soldiers in the fastnesses of the Burmese jungle.

The author of the turnaround was Major-General Orde Wingate, a remarkable gunner officer of Scottish descent, and possessed of unorthodox opinions. Before the war he had served in Palestine, where he had emerged as a Zionist supporter, and after being recruited by SOE he had helped the Emperor Haile Selassie to return to his throne in Ethiopia in 1941. He believed that the Japanese could be beaten by inserting long-range penetration forces which would fight behind their lines and destroy vital objectives. From the outset there was a Black Watch connection. Crucially, Wingate was able to win the support of Wavell who had started his army career in The Black

Watch; in the previous year he had been transferred from the Middle East to become commander-in-chief in India, and he quickly became interested in Wingate's ideas. Amongst others attracted to the new concept was Major Bernard Fergusson, a Scot from an Ayrshire background, who had served with 2nd Black Watch in the Middle East.

Basically, Wingate rethought the traditional brigade structure and refashioned it to fight in the jungle. Fighting in eight columns supplied from the air, one of which was commanded by Fergusson, the new force was called the Chindits, after the Burmese word '*chinthe*', the mythical winged beasts which guarded Buddhist temples, and it went into action in February 1943. Operation Longcloth (as it was known) was a mixed success. The Mandalay–Myitkyina railway line was cut, but the cost was appalling. Of the 3,000 men who carried out the operation, only 2,182 came back; around 450 had been killed in action, and the remainder were either lost or had been taken prisoner. Only 600 of the force were able to return to soldiering. However, on the credit side, it sowed confusion in the minds of the Japanese high command who feared it was a precursor to a larger attack, and as result large numbers of enemy troops were used to hunt down the Chindits. Above all, Wingate had shown that the Japanese could be fought on their own terms, and on that level the Chindits were a huge propaganda success, so much so that a second operation was planned for the spring of 1944.

This time it would consist of a much larger force made up of battalions in the 70th Division which was under the command of Major-General George Symes, an experienced soldier who showed great dignity by agreeing to serve as Wingate's second-in-command, even though he was senior to him. Partly this was his soldier's duty but partly, too, Symes had been influenced by Auchinleck, the new commander-in-chief in succession to Wavell who became Viceroy of India in 1943. When it became clear that Wingate intended to break up the division's brigade and battalion structure to create new columns, Symes had been asked to stay on to reconcile his men to the Chindit concept.

In essence, a Chindit column was a reinforced rifle company of 250 men consisting of four infantry platoons; a heavy weapons platoon equipped with a Vickers .303 medium machine-gun and three-inch mortar; a commando platoon; a reconnaissance platoon; and a section of guides provided by the Burma Rifles. The changeover could have caused difficulties because the 70th Division was made up of regiments which were a roll-call of the British Army, and as Symes pointed out, many of them, including The Black Watch, had histories which stretched back over two centuries. Wingate remained oblivious to the upset he was causing by breaking up the cherished regimental system, and in the planning papers Symes fought what he called 'a battle royal' to retain individual identities 'by allotting column numbers where possible to conform with the old regimental numbers of the regular battalions'.[35] Thus it was that when 2nd Black Watch was broken up to provide two columns to the new Chindit force, they were numbered 42 and 73 (the regimental numbers of The Black Watch). The senior column, 73, was commanded by the new commanding officer Lieutenant-Colonel George Green, while the 42 column came under the command of Major David Rose.

The other Scottish regiment represented in the Chindit force was 1st Cameronians, but with them Wingate showed a less certain touch. The battalion formed 111 Brigade with 2nd King's Own Royal Regiment and 3/4th and 4/9th Gurkha Rifles, all under the command of Brigadier W. D. A. 'Joe' Lentaigne. Each battalion was divided into two columns in the Cameronians' numbered 26 and 90 to reflect the numbers of the regiment's predecessors. Training began in earnest in August 1943 with the intention that two brigades (77 and 111) would be flown in by air to create 'strongholds' at positions known as Broadway and Piccadilly, while 16 Brigade under Fergusson would march into the Indaw area from Ledo in the north. When Lieutenant-Colonel John Masters, a Gurkha officer who was later to replace Lentaigne, came to write his memoirs, he produced a telling description of the Cameronian soldiers who had been chosen to do battle against the Japanese in the fastness of the Burmese jungle.

They recruited most of their men from the streets of Glasgow, and had the reputation of being one of the toughest regiments in the British Army, in peacetime. They waged street fights with secreted bayonets and broken bottles, and, on at least one occasion in Calcutta, with rifles and ball ammunition. They carried razor blades in the peaks of their caps, with which to wipe the grin off opposing faces by a careless back swipe from the bonnet; and potatoes in their pockets, in which razor blades were stuck. No one but their own officers could handle them, and their touchy discipline vanished altogether for a week around the great Scottish fiesta of Hogmanay, New Year's Eve.[36]

Masters was also astute enough to notice that Wingate caused considerable offence to the battalion while it was training in Gwalior. Wingate was steeped in the language of the Old Testament – he counted Plymouth Brethren and the Free Church of Scotland amongst the influences on his background – and with his beard and Wolseley helmet he cut an eccentric, almost prophet-like figure. It was his habit to visit units in training and to give talks which were peppered with biblical allusions. However, when he addressed 1st Cameronians, Wingate made the mistake of telling them that many would perish in the attempt to retake Burma. As related by Masters, this was badly received by the men: 'I could sense an almost visible rising of the regimental *esprit de corps* against the general. The regiment decided he was trying to frighten them into bravery, and the real worth of Wingate's remarks – a message about sacrifice – was lost.'[37]

On 25 March 1944, the Chindit force began flying into Burma, where they landed at an airstrip codenamed 'Aberdeen' to be greeted by Wingate with the observation that they were the first Scottish troops to land at a Scottish airport in Burma. (Wingate's wife Lorna came from Aberdeenshire.) They were amongst his last official words: that same day his B-25 Mitchell aircraft crashed in an electric storm while it was transporting him to Imphal. Wingate's unexpected death changed the complexion of the operation and coloured what happened next to the Cameronian and Black Watch columns. Instead of employing the long-range penetration tactics for which they had been trained, the Chindit columns rapidly reverted to regular infantry tactics, with the exception that they were fighting in small groups in a hostile environment. Nevertheless the Black Watch columns were still able to conduct operations according to the guidelines laid down by Wingate. Both combined to conduct a well-planned ambush on the Banmauk–Indaw road on 4 April, and a week later Rose's 42 column carried out an attack on a Japanese arms dump at Singgan. Having reconnoitred the position they called up air support by radio and attacked the position on 10 April in tandem with US Air Force Mitchell and Mustang strike aircraft. It was the first time that the regiment had used such revolutionary tactics. Air support was also used to re-supply and for taking out wounded, although much depended on the skills of the columns' medical officers who often had to treat wounds and carry out operations under trying conditions. One man suffering from appendicitis was operated upon using the bent handles of mess tins for clamps and an officer's sponge for a swab.

Because Wingate died at a crucial juncture in the operation, and was unable to influence future events, it is difficult to give a complete estimate of the achievements of 1st Cameronians and 2nd Black Watch, and the other battalions which served as Chindits. The force lost 1,034 casualties killed and 2,752 wounded (Cameronian losses were 10 officers killed or wounded and 237 other ranks killed or wounded), but against that they accounted for over 10,000 casualties in the Japanese army, 5,764 of whom were killed. In his planning notes for the operation, Wingate had laid it down that no column was to fight in Burma for longer than three months at the maximum, but the exigencies of the campaign meant that both Black Watch columns were in the jungle almost twice as long. During that time they were forced to endure conditions which tested men's patience and strength. Over seventy soldiers succumbed to typhus, food was usually in short supply and the going on the ground was always hard.

During the operation the Chindits suffered dreadful privations from illness and lack of food, and came out of Burma a much-weakened and emaciated force, but the battlefield accountancy should not just be confined to figures. After landing in Burma they had operated freely against the enemy's lines of communication and sowed confusion in the minds of Japanese commanders who were never entirely certain of the force's whereabouts or intentions. As a result, a large number of troops were used in countering the threat, including one reserve division and two battalions which would otherwise have been used in the army attacking Imphal and Kohima. In that respect the suffering endured by 1st Cameronians and 2nd Black Watch made a substantial contribution to the success of the Allied war effort in Burma.

11 Victory in Europe and the Far East

No sooner had the US joined the Allied war effort than their military planners had made a strong case for an early attack on the European mainland. In fact the decision to press ahead with the invasion of north-west Europe had been taken as early as May 1943 at an Allied conference (codenamed Trident) in Washington, and planning for it began under joint US–British direction immediately after the summit had ended.

The main desiderata for the cross-Channel amphibious attack were quickly established: a landing area with shallow beaches and without obstacles which was within range of Allied air power; the neutralisation of local defences to allow a build-up which would equal the strength of the German defenders; and the presence of a large port for reinforcement and re-supply. Deception also formed part of the plan: the idea was to persuade the Germans that the assault would be made across the narrowest part of the English Channel at Pas de Calais where the beaches were shallow and led into the hinterland without the obstacles of cliffs and high ground. It also offered the opportunity to make a quick strike into the Low Countries, and from there into Germany. All those reasons made Pas de Calais the ideal place for invasion, but because it was the obvious location it was quickly discounted as the Allied planners realised that their German counterparts would deploy the bulk of their defensive forces there. By the end of the summer the plan was shown to the Allied leadership at the Quadrant conference in Quebec, which amongst other matters discussed the tactics to be used in the invasion of Europe. The chosen landing ground was the Baie de la Seine in Normandy, between Le Havre and the Cotentin peninsula, an area which met all the criteria, including a deepwater port at Cherbourg.

The initial planning called for an invasion force of three assault divisions plus airborne forces which would create a bridgehead through which reinforcements could be landed quickly to break out into Normandy and Brittany. Success would depend on the ability of the Allies to build up forces more rapidly than the Germans, and with that in mind it would be essential to deny the enemy the chance to reinforce the landing grounds by destroying road and rail communications in northern France. Although Montgomery, by then the Allied ground-forces commander, agreed with the main principles of the plan, he put forward an alternative proposal to attack in greater weight and along a broader front, and with a larger airborne contribution. This was backed by the supreme Allied commander, General Dwight D. Eisenhower, who activated his headquarters – Supreme Headquarters Allied Expeditionary Force (SHAEF) – in February 1944. It was agreed that the initial assault should be made by five divisions – two US, two British and one Canadian – with one British and two US airborne divisions operating on the flanks.

The D-Day invasion began on 6 June, with the airborne forces securing the flanks overnight while the main assault went in at dawn, preceded by a mighty bombardment from 2,000 warships in the Channel. By the end of the day the assault divisions were ashore and the five landing areas – Utah, Omaha, Gold, Sword and Juno – had been secured with the loss of less than 10,000 casualties (killed, wounded or missing), fewer than expected. The only Scottish infantry battalion in the first phase of the invasion was 1st KOSB as part of 3rd Infantry Division, which landed with 50th (Northumbrian) Division and 3rd Canadian Division. Despite fears that 3rd Division would suffer heavy casualties as the spearhead at Sword beach, the landing was relatively trouble-free, and by nightfall 1st KOSB was ashore and had assembled between Beauville and Benouville.

The next phase of the operation required the capture of the city of Caen. In Montgomery's appreciation of the post-invasion operations the battle would require three phases lasting up to eighty days in total. The first would run for twenty days, and would see the US First Army capture its objectives in the Cotentin peninsula, while the British Second Army (commanded by Lieutenant-General Sir Miles Dempsey) assaulted west of the River Orne, pivoting on Caen, to shield the US offensive. The second phase would be the beginning of the breakout, with the British forces pushing south through Falaise towards Argentan while the Americans moved towards the Loire and Quiberon Bay. Phase Three would take the Allies to the Seine, with the US First Army heading towards Paris while the British and Canadians would operate to the north between Rouen and the Channel. At the same time Patton's US Third Army would move through the US First Army's front to clear Brittany, and would then operate on the southern flank.

Following the creation of a bridgehead on the Normandy beaches, the follow-up forces began arriving in France almost immediately. Amongst them was 51st (Highland) Division, which started its deployment on the evening of 6 June, and 15th (Scottish) Division which followed a week later. During this phase it fell to 5/7th Gordons to be the first Highland battalion to come ashore, its task being to secure the bridgehead on the River Orne which had been captured by airborne forces and which the Germans desperately wanted to retake.

Almost immediately casualties began to mount, as the Germans fought desperately to prevent the Allies from moving inland. To begin with, the numbers killed in action were not particularly high, but they occurred on a daily basis − on 16 June the losses in 5/7th Gordons were 7 killed and 24 wounded − and it soon became clear that it would be no easy matter to push inland. When 5th Black Watch moved into the attack at Douvre la Deliverande they too soon discovered that the German defenders were determined to hold their ground in an attempt to push the invading Allied forces back towards the coast. By the end of the first week the battalion had lost 6 officers and 92 soldiers killed and 11 officers and 198 soldiers wounded. The relatively high figures were put into perspective by Captain John McGregor of A Company: 'When compared to the 529 casualties for the whole of the North African campaign and the 11 casualties for the Sicilian campaign it gave a clear picture of the heavy price paid.'[1] At the same time 7th Black Watch fared little better while moving up to Ranville, losing 42 casualties, mainly to heavy enemy machine-gun fire.

A divisional attack on the suburb of Colombelles to the north-east of Caen on 11 July also ran into difficulties, as the defences were stronger than had been anticipated. As casualties increased there was no option for the battalions in 153 Brigade but withdrawal. This was a particularly nasty battle as the Germans had placed observation posts on the chimneys of the factory at Colombelles, and were able to direct heavy and accurate fire onto the infantrymen as they went into the attack. The plan was for 1st Gordons to attack on the right with 5th Black Watch on the left, but despite some encouraging initial reports the assault faltered and soon became unsustainable. During the fighting 5th Black Watch suffered a further 128 casualties, including 71 killed or missing.

After the failure of this attack it became clear that 51st (Highland) Division had lost much of its fighting spirit due to exhaustion and the strain of being constantly in action and under heavy fire. Before the advance on Colombelles Major Alexander Brodie, commanding A Company, 5th Black Watch, made his feelings clear when he told his men that he 'would not hesitate to shoot anyone who ran away', and that he 'expected them to shoot me or any officer or NCO who ordered them to pack in'.[2] There were also a number of desertions, including two from 1st Black Watch which ended in tragedy – the men were apprehended and handcuffed but during the night a tank reversed into the platoon position and both men were crushed to death. 'A kind of claustrophobia affected the troops,' noted the divisional historian, 'and the continual shelling and mortaring from an unseen enemy in relatively great strength were certainly very trying.'[3]

So serious was the fall in morale that on 15 July Montgomery reported in secret to the Chief of the Imperial General Staff that the 51st (Highland) Division was no longer 'battleworthy' and 'does not fight with determination'.[4] Some idea of the collapse of fighting spirit and the widespread unrest can be found in the recollections of Captain Ian Cameron, 7th Argylls: 'Not a day passed without the battalion area being subjected to heavy shelling and mortaring and although our casualties were not heavy, there was a continual drain on personnel. In former campaigns the 51st Division had always been used aggressively and wherever there was an attack Highland Division always took part in it. This was the first time that the battalion had to sit for lengthy periods in a defensive position without launching an attack and this became very monotonous.'[5]

Another officer in the same battalion admitted that 'any orders that involved life-threatening activity were ignored or watered down, especially if given by young officers without battle training'. When

Lieutenant-Colonel (later Lieutenant-General Sir) Derek Lang took over command of 5th Camerons at the end of July, he was their fifth commanding officer in seven weeks, and Captain Fraser Burrows, an officer in the same battalion, could see morale seeping away from the men as they faced a constant diet of enemy fire: 'Nothing was easier in a night attack, but to stop, tie a bootlace and disappear. In Normandy this became more and more prevalent. We dealt with this in a number of ways; no breakfast for a start; no NAAFI [Navy, Army, Air Force Institute] rations [i.e. no cigarettes] for a week; a threat to inform their next of kin of their behaviour. The scorn of their peers was also a very effective deterrent. I had one Jock in Normandy who was marched into battle with a bayonet up his backside.'[6]

As a result of this disastrous slump in morale and fighting spirit, on 26 July, Montgomery was forced to sack the divisional commander Major-General Charles Bullen-Smith on the grounds that 'the men won't fight for you'. It was a drastic move to make in the middle of a battle that had not yet been won, but although Montgomery was loath to make it he had no option. Bullen-Smith was replaced by Major-General T. G. Rennie, a former commanding officer of 5th Black Watch who had previously been in command of 3rd Infantry Division.

At the end of July the 51st (Highland) Division was taken out of the line for a short period of rest and recuperation at Cazelle, north-west of Caen, and some of the under-strength battalions were reinforced with fresh soldiers, many of them from English regiments. For example 5/7th Gordons received forty-six reinforcements from The Duke of Wellington's Regiment, but they were quickly assimilated and soon became proud of the fact that they were 'Jocks' fighting with a distinguished Highland regiment. Ample rest and recreation and a new commander quickly helped the division to regain its old self-confidence, leaving Major Martin Lindsay, an experienced soldier temporarily in command of 1st Gordons, to comment that 'the confidence we all feel in the future is wonderful'.[7]

By then another Scottish infantry division had also been in action. Within days of arriving, the 15th (Scottish) Division made its first contact with the enemy when it was involved in the opening phase of Operation Epsom, which was intended to outflank Caen by attacking towards the River Odon with the first objectives being the villages of

Saint Manvieu and Cheux. The initial attack was in the hands of the 15th (Scottish) Division, and the ground that they fought over came to be known as the 'Scottish Corridor'. It was aptly named because it was very much a Scottish battlefield which was fought over by regiments whose histories stretched back to the seventeenth and eighteenth centuries. In his study of the Normandy campaign John Keegan makes the point that although this was the division's first experience of war 'in actuality', the Territorial battalions all had great traditions which 'encapsulated the whole of Scottish military history'. For example, 8th Royal Scots belonged 'by association to Hepburn's Regiment which had tramped the campaigning fields of Germany in the service of France during the Thirty Years War', while the men of the two HLI battalions took pride in the example provided by their antecedent regiments, the 71st and 74th Highlanders.

On the day of the attack, 26 June, the division's pipers played as the leading battalions moved up to the start line, and the men were in good spirits as they waited to go into battle. However, the day had dawned with heavy rain which meant that there could only be limited air cover. Attacking with 9th Cameronians, the men of 2nd Glasgow Highlanders (HLI) took their objectives, but the follow-up, which included 10th HLI, resulted in heavy casualties as the division advanced under 'rain and a lowering sky'. An officer in the latter battalion later recalled the ferocity of the fighting as the division forced its way forward towards Cheux: 'Machine-guns opened up at the leading companies which, shocked by the suddenness of it, went to ground. Our supporting tanks replied, the tracer ricocheting in all directions, a source of fear to all. Each time the leading companies tried to advance, they were met by heavy fire, and the advance petered out.'[8]

Armoured support was provided by 11th Armoured Division and 31st Tank Brigade, but the presence of the tanks was often a mixed blessing as they attracted heavy German defensive fire and added to the confusion. One watching staff officer noted that 'what little space was left in the lanes seemed to be filled by our own tanks, closed down and deaf to all appeals. None who was in Cheux that morning is likely to forget the confusion.'[9] In the next few days 2nd Glasgow Highlanders and 10th HLI were both involved in the fighting to the south of the River Odon where they continued to meet determined

German resistance. During the operation the 15th (Scottish) Division sustained 2,331 casualties while the losses in the 11th Armoured Division were 1,236, but Epsom was not all disaster. Although the fighting in the Scottish Corridor had not been a signal success, the Scottish battalions had lost none of their enthusiasm for the fight. As John Keegan put it, the battling performance of 2nd Argylls at Gavrus exemplified the tenacity of the resistance offered by the men and 'stood fit to rank with those other small epics of Argyll and Scottish stubbornness, the destruction of the 93rd at the battle of New Orleans and the stand of the "thin red line" at Balaclava.'[10]

This was followed on 30 July by Operation Bluecoat, which saw some of the fiercest fighting of the Normandy campaign. Its success allowed the Allies to complete the breakout from Normandy and to begin the advance on the River Seine, which was crossed on 28 August. Ahead lay the Belgian frontier and such well-known names as Amiens, Abbeville, La Bassée, Béthune and Lille, all of which were known to the Scottish Territorial battalions from the First World War. For The Royal Scots Greys there was some light relief as they crossed the Belgian border near Basly where an elderly lady emerged from her house clutching the regiment's distinctive eagle cap badge emblazoned 'Waterloo'. It had been given to her by her boyfriend in the last war, she explained, but then she looked at the men and their Sherman tanks and said sadly, 'of course, you had horses then.'[11]

Hard fighting returned in the middle of September when 8th Royal Scots was involved in the operations to secure bridgeheads over the Escaut Canal near the village of Aart. This meant advancing towards the objective during the night of 13 September and beginning the attack at dawn. The Germans put up fierce resistance, and the fighting continued for three days leaving the battalion with 163 casualties: the action was referred to later as the Battle of the Gheel Bridgehead. Despite the losses and their own exhaustion, the advance had to continue, and by 22 September 8th Royal Scots reached Eindhoven in Holland. At Fratershoef the fighting was stopped for an hour on 28 September when the Royals' commanding officer Lieutenant-Colonel P. R. Lane-Joynt agreed to a local truce with his German opposite number to allow the wounded to be brought in under a white flag. The fighting began again the next day but an officer in the battalion never forgot such a rare occurrence in warfare: 'It was a blessed relief to have an hour of peace after some most unpleasant shelling. At the end of the hour punctually to the second, one shell was fired from the German side. Clearly it was not meant to hit anything and not another shot was fired by either side for the remainder of that Thursday night. The whole episode impressed me as an odd little bit of chivalry, and we appreciated it.'[12]

The next problem for the Allies was overstretch – as the attacking forces moved away from the beachheads their supply lines became longer, and that had an impact on the speed of their advance into north-west Europe. It also meant that the war would not end in 1944 but, even so, there were some compensations for the soldiers in the Highland regiments. In September the 51st (Highland) Division took part in the operations to capture the ports of Le Havre and Dunkirk, and this was preceded by a highly emotional moment when St Valéry-en-Caux was retaken amidst scenes of great local jubilation. Each brigade in the division was placed in roughly the same positions that had been occupied by their predecessors in 1940, and that evening (3 September) the massed pipes and drums played Retreat outside the divisional headquarters at Cailleville.

From there the advance took the division into Flanders and on into Holland where the flat 'polder' low lands had been flooded, causing inevitable problems. This included a period of intensive fighting as both the 15th (Scottish) Division and the 51st (Highland) Division fought their way over a succession of formidable water obstacles towards the River Maas. During the crossing of the Schelde-Maas Canal west of Donck on 15 September, C Company of 2nd Gordons made the initial assault, with the men wearing empty sandbags over their boots and carrying the minimum of equipment in order to maintain silence and create maximum surprise.

The one port capable of giving the Allies everything they needed was Antwerp, with its huge docks, but it was still in German control and its seaward approaches were heavily mined. With winter approaching, the need to capture Antwerp and to open up the Scheldt estuary was imperative, and so it was that the men of the 52nd (Lowland) Division, which had been trained for mountain warfare and then for airborne operations, found themselves crossing the English Channel in the middle of October to support Canadian forces in a part of Europe which was below sea level. First ashore was 4/5th Royal Scots Fusiliers which landed at Ostend and regrouped in the nearby town of Deinze, near Ghent. Together with 6th Cameronians they were equipped with amphibious vehicles known as 'buffaloes', and the two-battalion force went into action on 26 October, landing in South Beveland where they soon found themselves caught up in the difficult and dangerous business of fighting in a built-up area. Faced by the onslaught, the Germans put up determined resistance and defended stubbornly to protect their positions.

To 5th KOSB fell the task of clearing the eastern part of the town as far as the Middleburg canal, and during the operation the men were under continuous German mortar fire. At the same time 4th KOSB supported 7/9th Royal Scots during the battle to capture the German headquarters in the Hotel Britannia. All the while, as the Royals' regimental war historian made clear, both battalions had to contend with atrocious conditions:

> Battle situations are frequently described as 'fluid'. Flushing literally was a fluid battle; it was aquatic in more senses than one. It began with an amphibious assault and, as it developed, the infantry often had to go into action waist deep in icy water. The waters of the Scheldt, pouring through the gaps in the sea wall, converted some of the roads into fast flowing rivers with treacherous currents at high tide and the men of the rifle companies had to hold on to each other in a human chain at some of the whirlpool spots.[13]

In spite of the difficult conditions, Flushing was in Allied hands by 3 November, allowing the Scheldt estuary to re-open to Allied shipping, and the first transport ships were able to enter Antwerp by the end of November. During the operation 4th KOSB sustained seventy-five casualties, including three killed and seven died of wounds, while 5th KOSB's losses were sixty-two, nine of whom were killed. Walcheren fell on 8 November, and 52nd (Lowland) Division's next operation was the advance towards the Rhine which took them through Holland and into Germany under the operational command of the Second British Army.

It was at this stage of the battle, when the Allies were still confident that the end of the war was in sight and when conditions were at their worst, that the Germans decided to counter-attack in the Ardennes.

The plan was the brainchild of Adolf Hitler, who reasoned as early as September that the winter weather – 'night, fog and snow' – would give the Germans the opportunity to hit back at the Allies through the dense Ardennes forest, with its narrow steep-sided valleys, and then turn rapidly north to recapture Brussels and Antwerp. The attack would split the Allies, leaving the US armies unable to come to the aid of Montgomery's 21st Army Group which would be encircled and destroyed before it could attack the Ruhr.

It did not turn out that way, but the Battle of the Bulge, as it came to be known, almost allowed the Germans to achieve their aims by creating a huge salient or 'bulge' in the Allied lines. During the battle 51st (Highland) Division in XXX Corps supported the US Ninth Army in the Ourthe Valley. Although the winter conditions were severe, one officer of the Gordons offered the opinion that it was preferable to fight over 'snow-covered hills of great beauty' which provided 'a pleasant change from the mud of Holland'.[14]

Ahead lay the equally ferocious fighting in the Reichswald which housed part of the Siegfried Line, the heavily fortified German defensive position. The 51st (Highland) Division's objective on 8 February 1945 was the town and road and rail centre of Goch, which had to be taken to secure the southern sector of the Reichswald in preparation for the crossing of the Rhine. It was a hard-fought battle which involved close-quarter fighting and, according to those who were involved in both battles, it was preceded by the heaviest enemy bombardment since El Alamein. In his memoirs, Martin Lindsay provided an honest account of the feelings which course through a soldier's mind on the eve of battle: 'I am very strung up tonight, wondering what the morrow will bring forth. I have often wondered what exactly influences the state of one's nerves. Sometimes before riding in a "chase" or making a parachute drop or a speech, I have been very much on edge, without actually feeling precisely frightened; at other times, for no apparent reason, I just haven't cared a damn. Perhaps it is something to do with one's liver!'[15]

When the attack began, matters did not go smoothly for 1st Gordons, whose A Company was over-run due to lack of armoured support, and the battalion lost three officers and twenty-one soldiers killed, and seven officers and fifty-nine soldiers wounded. The battle to take Goch lasted two days, and it is rightly counted as a Gordons' battlefield. One of several junior officers to win Military Crosses during the fighting in the Reichswald was 2nd Lieutenant Alexander Scott, 5/7th Gordons, who was a platoon commander in C Company. A wartime conscript from Aberdeen, he returned to academic life after the war and went on to become a leading poet and critic whose work in Scots was much praised. Later, he put his feelings about the battle into his poem 'Coronach (for the dead of the 5/7th Battalion, The Gordon Highlanders)':

> Waement the deid
> I never did,
> But nou I am safe awa
> I hear their wae
> Greetan greetan dark and daw,
> Their death the-streen my darg the-day.[16]

The eventual capture of Goch, followed by the fall of another strongpoint at Hekkens, opened the way for the Rhine crossing, which was begun on 23 March 1945. According to Martin Lindsay, 'Montgomery was supposed to have said that Scottish troops were the best for assaulting,' and the task was given to 15th (Scottish) and 51st (Highland) Divisions using Buffalo amphibious vehicles. During the operation 5/7th Gordons landed to the east of Rees on the opposite bank, but 1st Gordons followed 5th Black Watch in an operation which was delayed by the inability of the returning Buffaloes to climb out of the river. A description of the crossing was later written up for The Gordon Highlanders' regimental records.

> The buffaloes slowly crawled over the fields, then dipped into the water, became water-borne, and then one had the feeling of floating down out of control, yet each buffalo churned without difficulty out of Germany's greatest barrier and at the right place by the flickering green light. Once aground the buffaloes with vehicles took one 200 yards inland, those with troops deposited their load on the green fields, now baked hard by the recent fine weather, at the water's edge; two bunds [dykes] each about ten feet high stood against the skyline, otherwise the flatness was unbroken.[17]

All the Scottish battalions got safely across the river, but during the operation the 51st (Highland) Division suffered a heavy loss when General Rennie was killed during a heavy German mortar attack near the town of Rees. It was a shattering blow, as Rennie had been a popular and inspiring commander. He was succeeded by Major-General Gordon MacMillan, an experienced and well-liked Argyll and Sutherland Highlander.

To the south, 2nd Gordons crossed the Rhine opposite the village of Wolffskath and took part in the advance towards Celle, with the ultimate objective being the crossing of the River Elbe and the capture of Lübeck. Once across the river the Scottish battalions found that the German defenders were in no mood to surrender, and some units seemed to fight with a greater fanaticism as they fell back on the 'Fatherland'. Hitler Youth battalions proved to be particularly troublesome. When 2nd Gordons came across an uncompromising young woman who claimed that the Nazis would never surrender until every man was killed she received the dusty response 'that we were killing off Nazi soldiers with that purpose in view'.[18]

Nevertheless the Rhine crossing was the beginning of the end, and for the next month the 51st (Highland) Division was constantly on the move as it fought its way north towards Bremen and Bremerhaven, which was reached on 8 May. At the same time 15th (Scottish) Division reached Gros Hansdorf to the north-east of Hamburg. By 29 April, 9th Cameronians was across the River Elbe and heading for the town of Basedow where 240 German prisoners of war were taken into custody. Two days later the battalion cleared the Sachsenwald Forest where news of the impending Armistice was received. By then both 6th and 7th Cameronians had been part of the force that had broken into Bremen at the end of April. Although it had been a satisfying moment, the edge was taken off the celebrations when 6th Cameronians entered a camp at Sanbostel, halfway between Bremen and Bremerhaven. As the war history recorded, nothing could have prepared the men for their first experience of liberating a concentration camp.

> All around was a flat and desolate plain, and, in the centre, a vast cage, wherein seemed to be confined all the bestialities that even the most fertile imagination could conjure up. Everywhere there

was filth and stench and disease and hordes of dehumanised creatures with shrunken faces, cloaking their emaciated bodies in the dirty rags of their striped prison uniform. No one who did not see and smell and feel the horror of this nightmare could ever believe it. And no one who did see it and smell it and feel it could ever forget it.[19]

For all the soldiers in both divisions, and for the rest of the Allied armies, the war in Europe was over, and ahead lay the task of restoring order to the shattered country. In Lübeck the men of 2nd Gordons found that the biggest problem was the huge number of displaced persons who needed food and shelter. For 5/7th Gordons which had fought from El Alamein to the north German plain, it was the end of the road. Ahead lay demobilisation and a return to Scotland before going into suspended animation and an uncertain future. The battalion's last flourish was a splendid parade in Munich which was arranged by the US Army in the first week of June to return a drum which had been retrieved by the US 10th Armored Division during the drive into Germany. It was the only survivor of the 5th Gordons' drums which had been stored at Metz before the retreat to St Valéry in May 1940.

Because the Normandy campaign had been the precursor to the defeat of Germany it tended to overshadow the invasion of Italy in September 1943. This proved to be a lengthy and arduous task, not least because from the outset the plans were hampered by disagreements amongst the Allies, and as a result the operations were frequently bedevilled by a lack of cohesion and a shortage of resources. As we have seen, the Americans wanted to concentrate on a cross-Channel invasion followed by a rapid thrust into the enemy heartlands, while Churchill remained obsessed with attacking the 'soft underbelly of Europe', both as a means of engaging the Germans and knocking Italy out of the war. As described by his biographer Martin Gilbert, Churchill's aim was 'to persuade the Americans to follow up the imminent conquest of Sicily by the invasion of Italy at least as far as Rome, and then to assist the Yugoslav, Greek and Albanian partisans in the liberation of the Balkans, by air support, arms and coastal landings by small Commando units.'[20]

Many of the command and control problems that had bedevilled the Sicilian campaign were carried over to the Allied invasion of Italy. Alexander remained in command of Fifteenth Army Group, and Montgomery commanded the British Eighth Army, which included 51st (Highland) Division and the other Scottish regiments which had fought in Sicily, while Lieutenant-General Mark Clark commanded US Fifth Army, which included British X Corps. The plan was for the British to land at Reggio Calabria on the Italian side of the Strait of Messina (Operation Slapstick), while Clark's army landed south of Naples at Salerno (Operation Avalanche). Both invasions enjoyed mixed fortunes: the British landed unopposed and made good progress, but Clark's army encountered stubborn resistance from German land and air forces, and only the intervention of the firepower of the Royal Navy allowed the landings to proceed by the middle of the month. Although both armies then made progress in their advance northwards, lack of firm operational planning meant the campaign quickly degenerated into a remorseless slogging match. Bad weather also played havoc, with the advance to the Garigliano and Sangro rivers leaving Montgomery to complain to Brooke that there could be no hope of 'any spectacular results' in the near future.[21] Largely due to an absence of realisable aims, and the use of inchoate tactics, the Italian campaign foundered.

As a result it was also largely overlooked, especially in the wake of the D–Day landings in France. There was a tendency for the attacking divisions to be stripped of assets as the armies moved north, and this increased the feeling that the soldiers on the Italian front were being forgotten. (It was a feeling that was also familiar to the Fourteenth Army in Burma.) The mood was eventually given expression by an incident involving Lady Nancy Astor, Conservative MP for Plymouth, who had been pro-appeasement and anti-Communist before the war. In an unguarded moment she referred to soldiers of the Eighth Army in Italy as 'D-Day Dodgers'. Although there might have been an innocent reason – one of her constituents serving in Italy had signed a letter to her using that nomenclature, and she failed to recognise his sarcasm – the story gained considerable notoriety. It also gave rise to one of the most popular soldier's ballads of the war, the 'D-Day Dodgers' which was sung to the tune of the equally popular Afrika Korps song 'Lili Marlene', sung by Lale Andersen. It exists in several versions, and although the credit for the composition is often given to Lance-Sergeant Harry Pynn of the Tank Rescue Section, 19 Army Fire Brigade, the best-known version belongs to Hamish Henderson of the 51st (Highland) Division, which took part in the initial invasion of Italy.

> We're the D-Day Dodgers out in Italy –
> Always on the vino, always on the spree.
> Eighth Army scroungers and their tanks
> We live in Rome – among the Yanks.
> We are the D-Day Dodgers, way out in Italy.[22]

Throughout the campaign the song was very much a rallying call for all Allied soldiers, and it enjoyed a huge popularity, which added to Henderson's post-war reputation as one of the great poets of the Second World War.

Some idea of the hardships facing the 'D-Day Dodgers' can be found in the experiences of 2nd Royal Scots Fusiliers, who had crossed over as part of the main invasion force with XIII Corps (5th Division, 1st Canadian Division), landing to the north of Reggio at Gallico Marina. Meeting little resistance, they pushed up through Calabria towards Potenza to link up with the US Fifth Army and British X Corps which had landed at Salerno, and had immediately encountered determined German resistance. At the end of the first week the 5th Division had moved 100 miles, and by 16 September had reached the Gulf of Policastro, where XIII Corps was tasked with guarding the US Fifth Army's right flank. During the next phase of the operation, 2nd Royal Scots Fusiliers moved north from Foggia across the Trigno River into the highlands around Vinchiaturo where, as Eric Linklater makes clear in his history of the Italian campaign, things became much tougher for the advancing Allies.

> The topographical pattern of Italy, fascinating the tourist with romantic heights and stern declivities, to the soldier invading from the south is a monotonous repetition of traps and barriers, of mountain-rampart and river-ditch. From the Apennines great ribs go down to either coast, and between the ribs run meandering streams that the autumn solstice and the winter snow may enlarge with disastrous speed to roaring torrents. Every rib had to be

climbed and crossed, and every river bridged under fire from the slopes beyond. The liberation of Italy was going to be a bitter process.[23]

In those difficult conditions the battalion had its first encounter with the enemy when a fighting patrol engaged German positions on the heights north of Macchiagodena on 29 October. During advances the rifle companies of Scots Fusiliers were forced to march in single file, with the seconds-in-command leading, often in foul weather, and frequently at night. There were other local difficulties: a typical entry in the War Diary shows that problems with the mule train meant that rations failed to arrive until well into the evening. With weather worsening, the battalion took part in the assault on the German line of defences known as the Gustav Line which ran from the River Sangro on the Adriatic to the estuary of the River Garigliano on the Tyrrhenian Sea. For the Scots Fusiliers this meant acting as 17 Brigade's spearhead during the attack on German positions at Castel di Sangro and Alfadena at the end of November. Some of the peaks were higher than Ben Nevis, and the initial stages of the attack were made in pitch dark and heavy rain.

The next stage of the advance took 2nd Royal Scots Fusiliers across the River Moro to reach Lanciano, where it spent Christmas and the New Year, before pushing north again over the Garigliano. On this occasion the battalion made the crossing at the estuary, putting out to sea in amphibious boat-shaped vehicles known as DUKWs (the acronym refers to the manufacturing factories' serial letters) but as the battalion's War Diary records, the operation did not go according to plan. 'The plan for landing the Battalion on the assault beaches completely miscarried and the unit was badly disorganised at the very outset. Several things contributed to this. The principal reason was the total absence of expert navigators in the crews of the amphibious craft. Many of the drivers went too far from the coast and were consequently unable to make use of the guiding lights set out at intervals along the shore or even to see the river mouth, which should have been the surest guide.'[24] To make matters worse, the men landed close to minefields, and the rising moon provided illumination for the German machine-gunners, a position which led one officer to remark: 'we didn't much care for it . . . there seemed to be no more promising course of action than to crouch in our holes and pray for the arrival of the Sappers [military engineers].'[25] Fortunately, the next target, the town of Argento, had been evacuated by the Germans before the battalion was ordered to take it 'at all costs', but during the next action on Mount Natale, the commanding officer Lieutenant-Colonel I. D. MacInnes was killed.

By early 1944 the Allied advance had been held up in the Liri Valley south of Rome where the enemy resistance centred on the monastery at Monte Cassino, the mother-house of the Benedictine Order. It stood on high ground outside the town of the same name which had been razed to the ground, and, being partially occupied by German forces, became the scene of fierce fighting in built-up areas. At the beginning of March 1944, 6th Black Watch was committed to the campaign in Italy when it landed at Naples, having previously fought in the campaign in Tunisia. For the men under the command of Lieutenant-Colonel Brian Madden it was a baptism of fire. Although the battalion had been in continuous action in Tunis and was battle-hardened, the fighting at Monte Cassino was quite different, being dominated by constant enemy shell-fire and hard skirmishing. In the hills above the River Garigliano the men of 6th Black Watch led what was described as a 'hole and corner life' with a good deal of aggressive patrolling.[26]

There was some respite when they were taken out of the line towards the end of the month, but within a few weeks they were soon back in action again, holding another bridgehead to the north-east of Cassino. Getting there involved a lengthy route-march which was compared to passing the Lairig Ghru in the Cairngorms in the depths of winter. This was followed by a move into the sector of the town of Cassino where 6th Black Watch relieved a battalion of Coldstream Guards. Due to the closeness of the enemy there was no movement during the day, and survival for the battalion meant placing a high premium on taking cover in the sangars, fortified positions which had been built in the ruins of the houses. Supplies had to be carried in, and there was the constant danger of falling victim to enemy fire during these operations. One indication of the problems faced by the battalion comes from the statistic that British gunners fired up to 5,000 rounds of smoke shells to cover the carrying parties as they made their final approach to the British positions, and inevitably there were casualties.

Following another short period out of the line, the battalion was ordered to attack enemy positions on the River Rapido, downstream of Cassino, and to make a bridgehead. In support of the attack a squadron of tanks from the Lothians and Border Horse was put under Madden's command, and they set off in thick mist in the early morning of 13 May. By mid-morning they had reached their objective, but thick mist the following day hindered their progress and the companies began losing touch with one another, a fatal mistake given they were advancing into unknown territory. To prevent any mishaps, Madden ordered his men to form hollow squares – company by company, with the tanks in the middle – and to move off again. Hidden woods and German positions suddenly appeared in the mist-covered terrain, and there was a succession of confused fire-fights before the battalion halted on a crest where the ground suddenly started falling away. The ensuing engagement was typical of the operations around Cassino – chaotic, relentless and intense, leaving the battalion with 240 casualties killed or wounded before Polish forces finally fought their way into Monte Cassino and flew their national flag above the ruins of the monastery.

During the Cassino operations 1st Argylls had been given the task of securing a position known as the San Angelo 'Horseshoe', with 17 and 19 Brigades, while 8th Argylls was held in reserve with 78th Division to exploit the situation as the battle developed. The Scots Guards were also part of the fighting. Both the 1st and 2nd Battalions had been part of the invasion of Italy – the former had landed at Anzio in January 1944 as part of an ill-fated outflanking operation to take Rome – and played distinguished roles in the fighting at Monte Camino and Monte San Michele, but neither played any direct role in the capture of Cassino. Instead, the regiment was represented by S Company, which had been formed from new drafts, and was attached to 2nd Coldstream Guards. It was involved in some of the fiercest fighting for the position, and one of the company's officers, Captain H. F. G. Charteris, MC, left a vivid account of what it was like to fight beneath the imposing heights of the hill and its monastery.

None who saw that massive ruin, day after day, sometimes swathed in palls of dust, sometimes pink and clear in the dawn or towering blacker than night among the stars, can ever forget it. Like a face, it overhung the desiccated arena where thousands of men lay cramped and invisible as insects at the foot of a colossal bird. Lower, the outlines of Hangman's Hill and the Castle Rock on which it was difficult to believe that there was life of any kind least of all human, completed the terrible trinity of shapes.[27]

The fall of Monte Cassino opened up access to the valley of the River Liri and the coastal littoral, thus allowing the Allied infantry and armoured divisions to push north-east towards Rome. Two Scottish battalions were involved in the operations to take Rome: 2nd Cameronians and 6th Gordon Highlanders, which had been part of the invasion force at Anzio. In fact 2nd Cameronians was the first British battalion to reach the River Tiber, but political considerations obliged the US forces to enter Rome first on 5 June. A week later the battalion was in the city, and during its stay Roman Catholic soldiers were invited to a special mass in St Peter's Church.

The fall of Rome did not end the war in Italy, but sent it into a new and equally bitter phase. Before the Allies arrived in the city the Germans withdrew north to the Apennines to complete a new defensive position, known as the Gothic Line. It was at this stage of the war that 2nd Royal Scots joined 66 Infantry Brigade as part of the 1st Infantry Division in the Arno sector. Time had been set aside for training – following the surrender at Hong Kong, the new 2nd Battalion had been formed from 12th Royal Scots – but the need for troops meant that the Royals were in action north of Florence by the middle of August.

This phase of the operations kept the battalion in constant contact with the enemy, as the men patrolled aggressively on the high ground on the northern side of the Arno following the fall of Florence and the withdrawal of German forces. Not only were the Royals facing a determined enemy, but as one of their number recalled, they also had to confront difficult conditions on the ground.

In the almost complete absence of tracks, all supplies had to be carried up by mules from a mule point which was continually moving up the Arrow Route [the road from Florence to Faenza] as the advance progressed, though even then the mule parties often had to cover twelve miles or more of appalling going in the dark, in trackless country, to catch up with the ever advancing troops. As at all times four rifle companies had to be supplied, a large number of employed men of the Support and Headquarter Companies were needed to run the mule trains, and in fairness to them there were few occasions when the rations did not get through somehow.[28]

As the Germans retreated, they booby-trapped the roads with mines, and in the upper reaches of the mountains formidable defences had been constructed. It was not until the middle of September that the Royals were able to take part in a brigade attack on the enemy's positions on Monte Prefetto, and the action came as a welcome diversion following the difficult weeks of patrolling and isolated skirmishing. After two days of heavy fighting Monte Prefetto was finally taken, and the way was open to attack a neighbouring German stronghold on Monte Paganino whose approaches proved to be 'both precipitous and slippery'. Added to their problems underfoot the weather worsened with the autumn rains; the Royals had to fight over tracks 'knee-deep in mud', and the position was not taken until 20 September. This took them over the Apennines, where they were involved in further contact with the enemy at Presiola, Monte Gamberaldi, Monte Grande and Monte Castellaro. The latter position was the only one which 66 Brigade failed to take.

As September gave way to October and November, the battalion found itself fighting over some of the worst terrain experienced by British soldiers during the war in Europe.

The area [south of Bologna] was a tangle of precipitous ridges and gullies, bare and inhospitable, with very few houses to add to the comfort. It rained incessantly and occasionally snowed; it was always cold and often misty. Mule tracks were quagmires and always the plains beckoned to us tantalisingly only ten miles away. Action was confined to constant patrolling into the valley which separated us from the enemy-held ridge a mile away: artillery, mortar and *nebelwerfer* [literally 'smoke-thrower'; short-range 5.9 inch rockets] fire were incessant and often very heavy, but as we gradually improved our defences the number of casualties de-creased.[29]

In January 1945 the 1st Infantry Division handed over the Monte Grande sector to the US 85th Division and started moving south to Taranto to embark on a new deployment in Palestine. On 26 January 2nd Royal Scots sailed for Haifa which was reached five days later. During the operations in Italy the battalion's casualties had been two officers and 40 soldiers killed, 12 officers and 114 soldiers wounded, and three officers and 54 soldiers missing. The plan was to give the 1st Infantry Division a period of intensive training in river crossing and the use of armour before returning it to Italy in June, but the end of the war in Europe on 8 May put paid to that idea. By an odd coincidence, having left Italy the previous November when 4th Indian Division was deployed in Greece, 2nd Camerons ended the war in the Struma Valley on the Salonika Front, the place that the same battalion had been stationed at the time of the Armistice in 1918.

The war was also coming to an end in the Far East, where the reconquest of Burma in 1944 and 1945 proved to be one of the great sagas in the histories of the British and Indian armies. The longest sustained campaign of the Second World War, it was fought over a harsh terrain which included deep jungle as well as desert and mountain. It was often war to the knife, with opposing soldiers caught in bitter close-quarter combat, and those who surrendered were rarely granted much mercy. It began with a painful retreat and ended with a famous victory which relied as much on the endurance and fortitude of the Allied troops as it did on the skill of their commanders. It involved soldiers from Britain, India, Burma, China, Nepal, the United States and West Africa, and because the campaign was almost as long as the war itself, it saw the introduction of innovations such as the use of air power in support of ground troops, and modern radios to guide the strike and supply aircraft to reach their targets.

As a result of the Chindits' morale-boosting initiatives in 1943, British soldiers began to realise that they could fight in the jungle on equal terms with the Japanese and that they could take the war back to an enemy previously thought to be 'super-human'. Amongst the battalions involved in the new offensive was 1st Royal Scots, which had been given intensive jungle training at Belgaum on the dry Deccan plateau where they formed part of 4 Brigade in 2nd Infantry Division. This proved to be a crucial period in the development of the battalion's fighting capabilities, and according to the regimental war historian they were taught that 'the jungle is your best friend . . . you can live in the jungle, and you can live on the jungle – in the jungle you will find all you need to keep alive. There will of course be many dangers, but they need not get you down . . . As for the Japs in the jungle, you can beat them at their own game'.[30]

The opportunity to put this new thinking into practice came in the spring of 1944 when the Japanese, under General Renya Mutaguchi, opened a major offensive across the River Chindwin to attack Imphal and Kohima in Assam. This would give the Japanese the springboard to invade India, and for that reason it was imperative for the British and Indian forces not just to hold those two key points but also the railhead at Dimapur, which was the end of the supply line from India.

In the middle of April, 1st Royal Scots was flown into the area and landed at Dimapur and Jorhat where they went straight into the fighting; first contact with the enemy was made on 19 April. It was a desperate situation. At the time Kohima was garrisoned by a single battalion (4th Royal West Kent Regiment) together with some details of the Assam Rifles, and the initiative was firmly with the Japanese as the British took up their positions close to the town. For the Royals this involved sending out fighting patrols against the enemy, and they soon found that it was going to be a long and wearisome experience. Writing after the war, the adjutant Captain F. C. Currie recalled that although the jungle training came into its own, it was still difficult to pin down and kill the enemy.

> The Japs were well dug in on a steep cliff. We could not see them, but they could see us. We probed all round them, lost about a dozen men and then the Company withdrew. Our losses had not been heavy, but we had the unsatisfactory feeling that we had lost some very good men, and we could not swear to having killed a single Jap. It was our first attempt to turn the little yellow rats out of their holes without supporting fire, and our last. Just another jungle warfare lesson learnt and, all things considered, it was cheap at the price. It had no effect on our morale, but it made us very cross indeed.[31]

Following several more equally tough encounters the Royals moved westwards and began the slow slog of clearing the Japanese from their positions around Kohima. Some of the fiercest fighting took place at positions known as Pavilion Hill, GPT Ridge, Aradura Spur and the Pimple. Throughout this phase the battalion was given tremendous help by the local Naga hill-men who acted as porters and provided nothing but loyal and unstinting service. Kohima was a hard and unyielding battle which tested the Royals to the full, but the tenacity and courage of the British and Indian forces paid off on 31 May when the Japanese began to withdraw. The decision was taken – against orders – by the Japanese commander Lieutenant General Kotuku Sato to save his forces from 'futile annihilation', and it brought to an end 64 days of fighting which left the Japanese with 6,000 casualties and the British and Indian forces with 4,000 casualties. During that period the Royals lost one officer and 37 soldiers killed, and 7 officers and 115 soldiers wounded. The last action was fought on 6 June at Viswema, which allowed 2nd Division to move towards Imphal and complete the Allied offensive to drive back the attacking Japanese forces.

Three other Scottish infantry battalions were involved at Kohima – 2nd King's Own Scottish Borderers, 1st Seaforth and 1st Camerons, which had arrived in India in the summer of 1942. After a period of intensive training the latter battalion moved up to the Assam border as part of 2nd Division in April 1944. The orders were terse and to the point: open the road to Kohima and then re-capture it. On 14 April, 1st Camerons took part in the first set-piece action to retake a position called Bunker Hill under the direction of Brigadier V. P. S. Hawkins, 5 Brigade, who left a vivid picture in his diary of the Camerons as they went into action.

I spotted David Graham, one of the Company Commanders, walking about as if there were no Japs there and controlling his chaps magnificently. We actually saw him take a bullet through his shoulder and fall over as he was in the act of throwing a bomb. The actual attack went exactly as we hoped. There were no Japs on the back of the hill, and the Camerons were in full possession one half-hour after they first appeared. We afterwards counted seventy-five dead Japs on the position, and the total Cameron casualties were under twenty.[32]

After the battle, Bunker Hill was christened Cameron Hill. From there the brigade fought its way towards Garrison Hill which was the only part of Kohima garrisoned by Allied troops. This involved hard fighting against a determined enemy during which, according to one officer's account, the Camerons came to admire the enemy's capacity to withstand air strikes by RAF fighter-bombers and 'to learn of the tenacity of the little Nip [Japanese soldier] and his amazing ability to do wonders in underground defence'.[33] Kohima was eventually re-taken on 25 June but at a cost: the casualties in 1st Camerons were 6 officers and 86 soldiers killed or missing, and 5 officers and 186 soldiers wounded. The names of the dead are remembered on a memorial stone designed by Alan M'Killop, a Camerons' officer who had trained at Edinburgh College of Art.

At the time of the fighting at Imphal and Kohima, 1st Seaforth took part in operations which were designed to confuse the Japanese during the Chindits' airborne assault, and which involved an attack on the headquarters of the Japanese 15th Division at Kasom. Fresh impetus was provided by the rumour that the senior enemy commander was accompanied by his favourite Geisha girls, and although this turned out not to be the case, the position was taken on the night of 14/15 April, forcing the enemy to withdraw. By then the monsoon had begun and the Allies found themselves operating in conditions which tested their morale and their ingenuity. In the heavy rain tracks disappeared altogether leaving impassable quagmires, food was often in short supply, malaria was an ever-present danger and the remaining pockets of Japanese resistance had to be cleared. An entry from the diary of Major R. D. Maclagan, 1st Seaforth gives a good idea of the conditions soldiers had to endure during the monsoon: 'Rain, which had started at dawn, continued heavily and relentlessly all day. Conditions were extremely unpleasant. It was bitterly cold, particularly on Nippon Hill, which, covered with craters and shell holes, was completely devoid of any cover. Communication by wireless was hopeless, all transmitting sets having long before gone out of commission due to the intense rain.'[34]

It could have been a difficult phase, but with the Japanese back on the other side of the Chindwin there was the satisfaction of knowing that the enemy had been defeated. The war in Burma was now entering its final phase and the Allies decided on a twin assault which saw General Sir William Slim's Fourteenth Army attack the enemy on the line between Mandalay and Pakkoku (Operation Capital), while a second amphibious and airborne assault on Rangoon was planned at the beginning of 1945 (Operation Dracula). Slim's intention was to break out from the Kohima area and to make a four-pronged advance towards Indaw, Schwebo, Myinmu and Pakkoku. At the same time Lieutenant General Sir Philip Christison's XV Corps would move into the Arakan and re-capture the airfields, which would extend Allied air cover to Rangoon and the border with Thailand. The offensive opened on 3 December when the 11th East African Division and the 20th Indian Division crossed the Chindwin and began advancing, with little sign of Japanese resistance. Faced by less opposition than he had expected, Slim decided to feint towards Mandalay while driving towards Meiktila, a key communications centre. Once the upper reaches of the River Irrawaddy had been seized, the way would be open to race south to Rangoon.

For the Camerons this meant taking part in 2nd Division's move towards Schwebo, which had to be cleared before moving on to Ywathitgyi on the River Irrawaddy. During the river crossing on 24 February, 1st Camerons and 7th Worcesters formed the bridgehead, with 1st Royal Welch Fusiliers on the left flank, and, as recounted by Major I. J. Swanson in the regimental records, this called for a good deal of ingenuity: 'Rowing on a fast river wasn't the same as a stagnant pond; and some of our boats had already started going around in crazy circles. Somehow or other we settled down and paddling became a routine. The current was far stronger than had been calculated, but we seemed reasonably controlled, while overhead a Boston aircraft flew backwards and forwards to drown the noise of our oars.'[35]

It could have been a difficult phase, but with the Japanese back on the other side of the Chindwin there was the satisfaction of knowing that the enemy was in the process of being defeated. As the Japanese historian of the Burma campaign, Kojimo Noboru, put it, they were 'no longer a body of soldiers, but a herd of exhausted men' stricken by dysentery, typhus and malaria.[36]

For those on the winning side, though, it was rather different. Padre Crichton Robertson of 1st Royal Scots remembered that the conditions brought out the best in the men, who refused to be down-hearted and always rallied even when 'hungry, tired, soaked to the skin with a foul night ahead of us'. And then there was a memorable moment on the return march at Kamjong where dreams of food became reality when a mule train brought in much-needed rations after days of want. 'How we cheered! Food, and again food. Delicious bully, tasty Army biscuits; we ate everything. We had to rest at Kamjong for twenty-four hours to get our strength back and to digest the huge meals we had.'[37]

The road to Rangoon lay ahead. Mandalay fell to the 19th Indian Division on 13 March, while the 2nd Division, attacking from the west, captured Fort Ava. During this final phase of the operations the Royals were in constant contact with the enemy, although one action almost ended in farce. After capturing the railway station at Paleik an elaborate attack was planned on the nearby railway works at Myitnge, but no assault was needed and no shots were fired as the Japanese had already withdrawn. On 2 May the remaining Japanese were cut off in the Arakan, and the next day the first units entered Rangoon following amphibious landings by the 26th Indian Division. For the Japanese in Burma the war was over, and fighting came to an end on 14 August, after the dropping of atomic bombs on the cities of Hiroshima and Nagasaki.

Two other Scottish battalions were involved in the Burma campaign – 8th and 9th Gordon Highlanders, Territorial battalions which served as anti-tank gunners and as an armoured regiment operating Sherman tanks. The 9th Battalion had arrived in Bombay towards the end of July 1942, and on their arrival at Sialkot the officers and men received the tidings that the battalion would be converted into an armoured regiment, serving in the Royal Armoured Corps as 116th Regiment (Gordon Highlanders). Although the pipe band continued in being, and flashes of Gordon tartan were worn, 9th Gordons had become an armoured regiment and the men became 'troopers'. Slowly but surely the first tanks began to appear – elderly and under-gunned US Lee and Grant models – and it was not until the end of 1943 that the first modern Shermans arrived. The new regiment was assigned to 255 Tank Brigade in the 44th Indian Armoured Division. For the 8th Gordons there was also a lengthy voyage to India by way of South Africa, and as 100th (Gordon Highlanders) Anti-Tank Regiment, Royal Artillery, the renamed battalion joined 2nd Division at Ahmednagar equipped with 6-pounder anti-tank guns. Later the new formation was re-equipped with 3-inch mortars so that it could also be used in the infantry role.

Throughout the battle for Kohima the guns and mortars of the Gordons supported 2nd Division positions including those of The Royal Scots and Royal Scots Fusiliers. With batteries scattered over a large area it was impossible for the commanding officer Lieutenant-Colonel D. B. Anderson to maintain any central control, so that individual commanders had to reply on their own judgement. One troop of mortars fired 600 rounds in a ten-hour period, fighting in a battle which broke the back of the attempted Japanese invasion. The operations in the 'Railway Corridor' also brought the battalion into frequent contact with the enemy, fighting major actions at Nansan-kyin, Pinbaw and at the railway town of Mawlu on 27 October.

At this stage the Gordons armoured regiment entered the fray when it joined 7th Indian Division in its drive towards Meiktila in December 1944. The regiment was in continuous action for a month, and quickly discovered that operating a tank in extreme temperatures was a hazardous and exhausting business. At the beginning of April Meiktila with its railhead and two airfields fell into the hands of the advancing Fourteenth Army, and at long last the road to Rangoon was open. During this phase the Gordons acted as a spearhead force for 5th Indian Division, together with 7th and 16th Cavalry and 3/9th Jat Regiment, all of the Indian Army. There was a close call at Pyinmana where the bridge had been mined, but the Japanese sapper charged with the task fell asleep and woke to find the British and Indian tanks making the crossing. By the time the war came to an end with the capitulation of Japan on 14 August, 116th Gordons were still in action, and to their men falls the honour of being the last armoured regiment to come out of action in the war against the Japanese in Burma.

12 Brave New World

For everyone who lived through those tumultuous days of spring 1945 the approaching end of the war came as a great relief. It had been a long and bruising six years, and because no one in the country had been left unaffected by the conflict with its casualties, hardships and deprivations, the fact that the conclusion was in sight brought added hope and a sense of optimism.

Ever since the invasion of France in June 1944 and the advance towards Nazi Germany in the latter half of the year, there had been huge expectation that victory was around the corner, but it had taken another winter of hard fighting before it became clear that the enemy was on the point of collapse. The first harbinger had been the Rhine crossings which had been spearheaded by 15th (Scottish) Division and 51st (Highland) Division, and this was followed by the advance to the Elbe, while the Red Army pushed on inexorably from the east. On 30 April Hitler committed suicide, and this was followed a week later by the unconditional surrender of the German forces in Europe. Long awaited, Victory in Europe (VE) Day was announced on 8 May (a day later for the Soviet Union), and although the war against Japan had not ended and continued to involve Scottish service personnel, it was still possible for hundreds of thousands of people to take time off and celebrate the defeat of Nazi Germany.

In expectation of the public need to mark the end of the war, the Home Secretary had established an Interdepartmental Committee as early as 11 September 1944 'to consider the arrangements which should be made for celebrating the cessation of hostilities with Germany'. While it was concerned primarily with events in London, which would be the fulcrum of the nation's celebrations, the committee also took advice from the Scottish Office so that due recognition could be given to the needs of the people of Scotland. From the outset it was agreed that the main focus of the celebrations should be 'light and illumination' – a good choice after the years of blackout – but it was also acknowledged that sobriety should be the order of the day, that 'the present war differs from the last in that it has directly involved the Home Front and it may be assumed that the mood of the country when hostilities cease will not be one of universal noisy rejoicing.'[1]

Even so, the committee recognised that a degree of licence would be in order, and while the main recommendations were not pre-scriptive they reflected the need to celebrate the end of a conflict which had brought great misery and hardship to the nation. The main desiderata were the inclusion of the following: the cease-fire to be signalled by the 'all clear'; street lighting to be increased; searchlights to be switched on, but no guns or maroons to be fired; licensed premises to be opened for an extra hour, with additional supplies of beer but not spirits; theatres and dancehalls to be opened; bonfires to be lit; and church bells to be rung.

Before the Scottish Office responded to the proposals a meeting was held on 22 September with the Chief Constables of Glasgow and Edinburgh, and it was agreed to offer the following comments to the committee. The two officers were opposed to any extension of the licence for alcohol as well as for the extended opening of billiard saloons, 'as few people would spend armistice night in such places' but they agreed that dancehalls could be kept open to 1 a.m. in Edinburgh because 'most patrons could walk home'. However, the same dis-pensation would not apply in Glasgow due to transport difficulties. Above all they wanted 'to avoid the hooliganism which may develop amongst an excited crowd with nothing to do.'[2]

It was also agreed that services of thanksgiving should be held on the first Sunday after VE Day, one at St Paul's in London which would be attended by the king, and the other at St Giles in Edinburgh which would be attended by the Lord High Commissioner, the Marquis of Linlithgow. There was a slight hiatus when the Scottish Office reported on 11 April 1945 that the latter commemoration would form part of a regular Sunday service, and as St Giles was a parish church its congregation would have first call on seats, but this was solved by reassurances that the scale of the Edinburgh service would be restricted compared to the service in St Paul's.

There was more consternation when it came to the decision to broadcast messages of loyalty to the king from all the armed forces and those representing civilians and the civil defence services. The draft for the latter included the phrase 'our battle honours are British names' but an official in the Scottish Home Department pointed out that the majority were English, and that only Clydeside and Belfast had been included amongst the names of the main cities which had been bombed by the Luftwaffe. Further dissatisfaction was caused by the prevalence of English accents in the BBC broadcasts, 'with the consequent spate of complaints from North of the Border'; this attracted a proposal from the Scottish Office that the message of loyalty from the Metropolitan Police need not be 'a pure [English] accent'. Instead, they proffered the suggestion that 'it is, of course, possible that one of the numerous Scottish members of the Metropolitan Police might be chosen; if a native of Inverness, of which I know there is at least one, were selected, he might, of course, be taken for an Englishman!'[3] Another suggestion was that the readers of the messages from the fishing or agricultural sectors should be Scots.

As it turned out, the celebrations for VE Day were generally muted, although there were large crowds in the streets in the main Scottish centres, and in many of them it was not unknown for alcoholic drink to have been taken. The following day most sectors of the press noted the orderly spirit that had generally prevailed, and that there had been none of the drunken revelry that had accompanied the Armistice of 1918. Not everyone was happy: to the obvious displeasure of the Edinburgh press, the castle had not been illuminated in order to save money – fuel was still in short supply and it had been thought frivolous to waste it on extravagant public displays.[4]

If anything, though, the celebrations for the end of the fighting against Japan – known as VJ Day – were the exact opposite of what had happened on VE Day. Perhaps it was because this really was the end of the war, and perhaps it helped that it was summertime and that two days' holiday with pay had been granted. It might also have helped that by coincidence the day was also marked by the State Opening of Parliament.[5] Throughout Scotland there was an outbreak of joy and relief with large gatherings in the streets in all the main cities – the Ross Bandstand in Edinburgh's Princes Street was packed with dancers, mainly women, due to the shortage of men on war service –

and there was a feeling of release that had been missing three months earlier. Only a few voices were heard criticising the use of the atom bomb, 'this awful weapon' (Churchill's words) which had brought the war to a precipitate end when two bombs were exploded over the cities of Hiroshima and Nagasaki.

Those killed in Japan during the last days of the war were part of the estimated 57 million people who died during the conflict – the exact figure will probably never be known. Of the estimated 260,000 British war deaths, some 10 per cent would have been Scots although, once again, it is difficult to compute a precise figure as conscription was carried out on a UK basis.[6] All told some 60,000 civilians were killed in the whole of the United Kingdom, mainly as a result of bombing, and of those 2,520 were killed in Scotland with a further 5,725 injured or detained in hospital.[7] The territorial connections of the Scottish regiments had also been loosened during the conflict, and this brought about a reduction in casualties. As the war progressed reinforcements and battlefield casualty replacements came from all over the UK, with the result that most Scottish infantry regiments contained large numbers of soldiers from outside Scotland and their traditional recruiting territories.

For those who had survived the experience of war, though, demobilisation was not always the happy event servicemen and servicewomen had long anticipated. Although there were improvements on the same situation in 1919, there were unacceptable delays which led to strikes in army and RAF bases in the Far East where there were cases of near mutiny by men no longer prepared to accept wartime conditions of discomfort. The most serious of these involved 13th Parachute Regiment which mutinied at Muar camp near Kuala Lumpur in Malaya (later Malaysia) in May 1946. It was not the only trouble. Many reunions were blighted by evidence of marital infidelity or a failure by returning combatants to re-adapt to civilian life. In July 1945, a soldier from 1st Royal Scots Fusiliers stabbed his wife when he returned from India on compassionate leave to find that she had been made pregnant by an Italian prisoner of war. Instead of facing a possible death sentence, the jealous husband was sentenced to five years in prison for manslaughter; he was the first of several similar soldier offenders to be treated in this way.[8]

By then the war was over; now the Allies had to deal with the future of the world they had fought for. In Scotland the service personnel of the Allied forces began to go home, and the country said farewell to temporary residents who had trained and served amongst them for so long or who had been enemy prisoners of war. Due to the need to retain essential personnel to work on the land, the last German and Italian prisoners of war were not released until 1948, but for most of the Allies there was a rapid transformation in their fortunes. Free French Navy ships left the Clyde to return home to a country which had created a new republican constitution and had elected General Charles de Gaulle as head of the provisional government.

The Norwegians were also on their way home. Following the German capitulation some 40,000 members of the Norwegian resistance occupied key points and began arresting Quisling members of the collaborationist administration. At the same time the German army commander General Franz Friedrich Böhme was ordered to surrender to representatives of Scottish Command who had flown immediately to Oslo on the cessation of hostilities. This was followed by the dispatch of the first occupation forces – 1st Airborne Division, a Special Air Services Brigade and the Norwegian Brigade. On 11 May General Andrew Thorne, as Commander Allied Liberation Force Norway, and Crown Prince Olav, together with senior British officers and Norwegian ministers, left Rosyth on board the fast minelayer HMS *Ariadne*. Other Rosyth-based ships taking part in Operation Kingdom were the cruiser HMS *Devonshire*, the destroyers HMS *Iroquois*, HMS *Savage* and HMS *Scourge*, the fast minelayer HMS *Apollo* and the Norwegian destroyer *Arendal*. They arrived in Oslo to receive a rapturous welcome; as Thorne later told his wife: 'Everyone who had a boat or could get into someone else's did so and came out to cheer him [Crown Prince Olav] and the squadron. The only one who didn't appreciate it was the German officer naval pilot who came on board off Lista lighthouse. It must have been very humiliating for his feelings to see the real joy and gladness in the faces of the people.'[9]

Months of planning by Scottish Command had finally paid off. Although Thorne did not have to lead an invasion force to recapture Norway the administration for the Allied Mission to Norway was in place, and there was a smooth transition from German occupation to rule by a caretaker government, all overseen by Scottish Command. It was no easy task. German forces had to be disarmed and rounded up prior to being returned to Germany; food supplies and fuel had to be imported; aggressive interest from the Soviet military command had to be countered; and steps had to be taken to stabilise the local political situation. On 7 June, exactly five years after the capitulation of Norway, King Haakon returned to Oslo and was greeted by Thorne with the simple welcome: 'Sir, I return to you your kingdom.'

Others were less lucky. Most of the Poles who had come to Scotland in 1940 had continued the fight against Nazi Germany because they believed that in no small measure their sacrifices would enable them to return to their homeland. It was not to be. Following the invasion of France the 1st Polish Armoured Division had been heavily involved in the fighting, and together with 1st Polish Parachute Brigade had fought their way into northern Germany under British command. In Italy Lieutenant-General Władysław Anders's 2nd Polish Corps had played a key part in the operations, and Polish soldiers had distinguished themselves in the fierce fighting to take the German position at Monte Cassino during the advance towards Rome.

However, as the war came to an end it was already clear that the Poles were to become pawns in the carve-up of Eastern Europe which had been agreed by the Allies at their planning conferences in Tehran in November 1943 and Yalta in February 1945. At the first summit the western Allies conceded to Stalin's demands for the extension of Poland's borders westwards to the rivers Oder and Neisse to include German territory, while much of eastern Poland was ceded to the Soviet Union. At the second summit this secret accord was agreed and the Soviet Union was given virtual hegemony over most of eastern Europe, with Poland becoming a satellite of the Kremlin. By then, of course, the Red Army had occupied most of the territory in question, but the agreement, under Article VII of the protocol was still regarded as acquiescence and a betrayal of the Poles fighting in the west.

A new situation has been created in Poland as a result of her complete liberation by the Red Army. This calls for the establishment of a Polish Provisional Government which can be more broadly based than was possible before the recent liberation of the western part of Poland. The Provisional Government which is now functioning in Poland should therefore be reorganized on a broader democratic basis with the inclusion of democratic leaders from Poland itself and from Poles abroad. This new Government should then be called the Polish Provisional Government of National Unity.[10]

This decision effectively sidelined the Polish government-in-exile in London, and gave the advantage to the Soviet-backed home government in Warsaw. For the Poles fighting in the west it was both a betrayal and a death knell. For the British government which had encouraged the Polish government-in-exile in London, and which had relied on Polish forces for the prosecution of the war against Germany, it also proved to be a very sensitive situation and one that caused no little shame. Small wonder that when the news about Yalta became common knowledge the Poles felt that all their efforts had been in vain. At the time Władysław Fila's Lancaster squadron was preparing to fly a mission deep into eastern Germany in support of the advancing Red Army, and the reaction of the Polish bomber crews was perhaps predictable.

The feeling was very, very highly strung. Quite a number of aircrew took off their flying gear including parachute. They threw it into the corner in the briefing room and they said from today onwards our war is over and we are not flying any more because we have no reason and no purpose to fight any more. Well, commanding officer informed Bomber Command about the feeling of the squadron. Air Marshal came to our squadron, he addressed us and then he was asking the commanding officer to ask individual crew whether we are prepared to fly that night to give support to advancing Russians. Strangely enough our Lancaster had the letter O for Oboe and we were first on the list. We were asked, O for Oboe are you prepared to fly tonight or not? Members of my crew ask me to reply, I said yes we are flying. Next crew are you flying? Yes, no and so on. So on that night instead of 14 or 15 aircrew flying I think that about half of them went actually to give that support in agreement with Bomber Command. But the rest of them gave up flying altogether, some of them were crying that Poland was betrayed so badly by the friend Britain for whom we gave everything to win the war.[11]

There was another fallout. For the Poles who came from eastern Poland, many of whom had been released in 1941 and joined the western allies in the Middle East, the prospect of returning was not appealing as their homeland was now in Soviet territory. Others, too, decided that there was little future in going home, and of the 240,000 Poles under British command only 105,000 were repatriated.[12] With the help of the Polish Resettlement Corps, which offered help in finding work, the rest stayed on, many of them because they had married local women and were already raising families. Large numbers remained and settled in Scotland, especially in the Border counties and in the counties of Angus, Fife and Perthshire where they had done their training. In the early days some suffered hostility from a small section of Scots on the left who supported the Soviet Union or were anti-Catholic, but by and large the assimilation of former Polish soldiers into Scottish life was one of the success stories of the post-war world.

Although the government-in-exile suffered many vicissitudes and much internal squabbling, it remained in being in London until it was dissolved following the collapse of the Communist government in Warsaw in 1989. And by one of history's quirks there was a second friendly Polish 'invasion' in the first decade of the twenty-first century when some 50,000 young Poles took advantage of their country's entry into the European Union to come to work in Scotland. They too were greeted as welcome visitors.[13]

Scotland, too, had been affected by political decisions made during the course of the Second World War. Even before the fighting stopped, and peace of a kind returned to a shattered globe, the first steps had been taken to try to ensure that it would be a world fit for heroes. In fact the theme was much more intense than a simple appeal to the optimism that had accompanied the end of the previous conflict. For the beleaguered British people who had withstood almost six years of continuous warfare when for much of the time they themselves had been on the front line, the predominant emotion was 'never again'. They had seen what could be achieved when people combined in common cause, and the experience of coalition government with united war aims had provided them with the foundations for a new beginning. Now it was their time and they were determined to make the most of it.

Many of their hopes were based on the principles embodied in William Beveridge's Social Insurance and Allied Services report which had provided the blueprint for a comprehensive post-war 'cradle to the grave' welfare state. Published in December 1942, its timing was doubly fortuitous. Not only did it bring the promise of change but it provided hope at the very moment when it seemed that the war could be won following the victories at El Alamein and Stalingrad. Not surprisingly, perhaps, because it caught the mood of the moment it became an instant bestseller, with a print run of over 600,000 copies plus many thousands more in a truncated version which was distributed to members of the armed forces. Within a few weeks of publication it was estimated that nineteen out of twenty people had heard of the report and mainly understood the gist of its findings.[14] From that point onwards support for the Labour Party began to grow, and although the wartime electoral truce held firm and support for Churchill never wavered, there was a distinct shift leftwards in the second half of the war as people dared to dream of a New Jerusalem.

Such attitudes were not altogether surprising. During the war people had become used to a collectivist approach to government. They could see what might be achieved by state interventionism on a grand scale, and did not want to return to the *laissez-faire* attitudes of the 1930s which had failed to deliver economic recovery. The coalition government had demonstrated what could be done when the will of the country was bent towards defeating the enemy, and with over five million men and women conscripted into national service they wanted that mood to continue into the peacetime years. Nothing else would do. If the evil of fascism could be extirpated by united national resolve then surely a similar effort could be made to defeat poverty, unemployment and social exclusion.

There was, too, the added incentive that thousands of men and women had fought and risked their lives on the front line and were not prepared to see their sacrifices dissipated by political inaction. As a returning Black Watch soldier put it when he went back to the Braes of Angus and an uncertain future in hill farming: 'These were men who had been fighting in North Africa and Europe and they weren't prepared to go back to damp, tied farm cottages and the minimum agricultural wage.'[15]

The real problem, though, had little to do with implementing those hopes; it was finding the money in a world in which Britain was economically exhausted and saddled with a debt of over £3 billion. Hopes were all very well, but the stark reality was that money was in desperately short supply. The situation in Scotland was both similar and dissimilar to what was happening elsewhere in the United Kingdom, and there was a tentative reaction from the Scottish Office when Churchill requested initial ideas for reconstruction during what was described as 'the period of Transition which would lie between the two stages of War and settled Peace'. When asked to respond on 3 November 1943 the specifically Scottish subjects identified by Scottish Home Department were solidly utilitarian: demobilisation as it related to the fire and police service and ARP; release of buildings and land used for war purposes; the creation of a revised electoral register; the repair and re-conversion of requisitioned fishing boats; clearance of mines; recruitment of police; and liquidation of the evacuation scheme.[16]

At that early stage very little was said about deeper issues such as poverty, low pay, poor health and, above all, inadequate housing which had always offered challenges for social reform and which was still a desperate problem, especially in the western end of the central belt. Bomb damage had been severe in Glasgow and the Clyde estuary following the blitz of 1941, but the sorry truth was that the existing housing stock could not cope with the massive overcrowding that afflicted the area. In 1943 Glasgow's Town Clerk revealed that 700,000 people were crammed into an area of barely 1,800 acres, with the bulk of them living in the three square miles of the city centre.[17] Other large conurbations in the west of Scotland were just as badly affected with high population densities. Even before the war had broken out the Scottish Office had estimated that 250,000 new houses were required in Scotland, and following the 1941 blitz officials recognised that bomb damage would have increased that number.

Clearly this problem had to be solved before other associated health care and economic issues could be successfully addressed, and after the initial summarising of the main issues, re-housing quickly became one of the major planks in Scotland's post-war recovery programme. On 13 March 1941, at a time when Clydebank was being bombed in the first of the heavy raids on Scotland, a Joint Memorandum on

Reconstruction was produced by Mr J. Westwood and Mr J. S. Wedderburn and presented to the Secretary of State.

> If we are to tackle these problems [town and country planning] effectively there must be planning before the end of the war so that on the cessation of hostilities we can start on this work at once. Scotland ought to be Town and Country planned as speedily as possible and legislation ought to be fully examined with a view to removing all delaying obstacles . . .
>
> This raises the question of whether or not the provision of these services should be left in the hands of existing Local Authorities. Whilst Local Authorities have done much to help in this problem, the problem is so big and calls for such speedy action that it would seem that the best way to deal with the building programme is by means of a National organisation and National direction and aim at the building of 30,000 houses per annum.[18]

In fact their estimates were not misplaced, and they were astute enough to point out that it was not just housing but the business of construction itself that would be beneficial to society, as house building would absorb the maximum labour and provide outlets for a wide variety of jobs. At its simplest, civil servants in the Scottish Home Department quickly realised that the nation's housing stock would be inadequate for post-war needs, and that the deficit would have to be made good by a massive rebuilding programme. With the problem being most acute in Glasgow and the Clyde valley, the efforts for the post-war period centred on a phased development plan which would ease higher densities of occupancy while attempting to keep people within existing residential areas. By the end of June 1945 sites had been approved across the area for the construction of 128,000 houses, and the Scottish Special Housing Association in association with local authorities had invited tenders for the immediate construction of 5,000 new homes.[19] However, from the outset it was conceded that in Glasgow at least it would be impossible to resettle everyone within the city boundaries, and that there would be overspill owing to an acute shortage of available buildings and existing space on which to construct low- and high-density housing.

It would take time and effort to redress the country's long-standing ills and to make a reality of the hopes expressed in the Beveridge report, but in other respects Scotland emerged in reasonably good shape to meet the expectations of the brave new world. That this was the case was due in no small measure to the system of good governance which had been instituted by Tom Johnston. Throughout his reign as Scottish Secretary he had been given a free hand and had used it mainly to good effect. While his Council of State had not emerged as a realistic working model for devolution, it had overseen a number of worthwhile innovations, and under Johnston's direction positive steps had been taken to plan for the kind of country which he hoped would emerge from the mayhem of war. In 1945, as the war drew to a close, Johnston was entitled to claim that 'we were no longer representatives of an old nation in decay, but of a young virile people lit up with the assurance that whatever men dare in unison they can do.'[20]

It was a bold claim, and typical of the optimism that Johnston brought to everything that he had done during the war, but what did it mean in practice? For a start, the Council of State had authorised the establishment of thirty-two sub-committees which looked at various aspects of post-war planning, the first of which had met as early as 1941, and which produced voluminous files dealing with subjects as various as juvenile delinquency and sheep farming. Even today it is impossible not to be moved by the sense of hope that permeated the first tentative steps taken by politicians and civil servants as they met in wartime Edinburgh to discuss a far-from-certain future.[21]

As we have seen, the pioneering work of the Emergency Hospitals Scheme and the Clyde Basin Scheme had already shown what could be done by producing the groundwork for a prototype National Health Service in Scotland, and Johnston himself had used his position in the Cabinet to work closely with like-minded English colleagues such as the Minister of Health Henry Willink. There was also a blueprint already in place in the Cathcart Report of 1936 which recommended, amongst other proposals, the establishment of health centres run by general practitioners and the need to institute a sound system of health education as a preventative measure – no bad thing, considering the low state of personal health in the country as a whole. Together with the need to reform education and to provide financial benefits for sickness, unemployment and old age, the idea of state intervention had gathered pace during the war, and as the end of the fighting loomed a growing majority of the population was desperate to embrace the social reforms promised by Beveridge.

However, it was never going to be easy for the political establishment to understand that a sea change was taking place in people's thinking. By 1944 the wartime electoral truce was already under pressure as the need for reform became ever more pressing. That same year Churchill acknowledged that a general election would be fought after Germany had been defeated, and it was agreed that arrangements would be made to allow members of the armed forces to participate in the poll. By the beginning of the following year the gloves had been removed, albeit carefully, as the main political parties began to plan for the forthcoming contest. In January 1945 Attlee told Labour supporters that he sensed a swing to the left, with people telling him that they had seen the country come first in war and now they wanted to see it come first in peace. This was answered by Churchill at the Conservative Party's conference on 15 March when he accused Labour of pandering to Communism by seeking to introduce 'sweeping proposals which imply not only the destruction of the life of our whole existing system of society and life and labour, but the creation and enforcement of another system, a system borrowed from foreign lands and alien minds'. Although the parties maintained the solidarity of the wartime coalition to the end of its life, the first cracks had appeared by the spring of 1945, and it took three by-election defeats in April to show which way the wind was blowing. Two of them were in Scotland, and while they did not break the mould of British politics, they were indicative of a dissatisfaction with the kind of Conservative politics which had prevailed before the war.

The first of the by-elections took place in the Motherwell and Wishaw constituency on 12 April, following the death in a motoring accident of the sitting incumbent James Walker, Labour MP since 1935. There were only two candidates: Alexander Anderson, representing Labour, and Dr Robert McIntyre, the secretary of the SNP who fought his campaign on the grounds of 'national freedom based on self-government for Scotland and the restoration of national sovereignty by the establishment of a democratic Scottish government, whose authority will be limited only by such agreements as will be freely entered into with other nations, in order to further international co-operation and world peace'. Acting on the principle agreed in 1942, that the SNP should contest elections in its own right and not just as a means of promoting home rule, McIntyre fought a good campaign in which he called on the people of Scotland to take responsibility for their own future. Backed by strong local support, McIntyre won the by-election, beating Anderson by 617 votes and thereby becoming the SNP's first member of parliament. While the turnout was low, at 58 per cent, it vindicated the SNP's wartime decision that the party could contest elections with hope of success. McIntyre then caused minor controversy when he failed to follow parliamentary procedure by refusing to accept the traditional sponsorship of a fellow MP before taking his seat at Westminster.

As it turned out, it was something of a flash in the pan as McIntyre failed to hold the seat at the general election three months later, and hopes of an SNP breakthrough were stillborn. However, it did serve notice that in a post-war election nothing could be taken for granted – tellingly, for what happened next, during McIntyre's campaign the local press published messages of support from Scottish soldiers serving overseas.

The second Scottish by-election held in the same month was equally momentous: standing as an Independent, the distinguished biologist and Rector of Glasgow University Sir John Boyd Orr won the Combined Scottish Universities seat by 20,197 votes to 8,177, beating his Liberal rival R. M. Munro with a 70 per cent swing. Once again there was a negative outcome for the Coalition government, as Munro's candidacy had been endorsed by Churchill. A week later there was a further shock when the safe Conservative seat of Chelmsford in Essex was lost to Wing Commander Ernest Millington, a wartime bomber pilot representing the short-lived Common Wealth Party which backed a co-operative socialist policy. After winning the seat Millington claimed that 'the people are tired of the old order and want a new plan'; once again, as happened in Scotland, he was supported by service personnel with homes in the constituency.

If the April 1945 by-elections could be taken as portents, they demonstrated that Common Wealth's leader Sir Richard Acland was probably correct when he insisted that 'Socialists had nothing to fear from the myth of the Churchill prestige'. On the face of it, it must have seemed inconceivable that Britain's wartime leader would have difficulty winning votes in the forthcoming general election which had been fixed to take place on 5 July, and which would take up to three weeks to conclude. He was the architect of victory and his standing in the country was immense, so much so that when Churchill made a triumphal trip around Britain in the last week of June he was given an ecstatic reception. In no other place was the enthusiasm greater than in Scotland. In Glasgow the *Daily Express* reported 'a tempest of cheering and shouting compared with which even some of the exciting scenes which the Prime Minister had seen this week were a mild vapour'.[22] Thousands leaned from tenement windows to cheer him as his cavalcade made its way along Paisley Road, and a tickertape welcome awaited him in Sauchiehall Street, while 50,000 gathered to listen to him speak in Princes Street Gardens in Edinburgh.

Churchill was both surprised and delighted by the response, and he would not have been human had he not believed that he was heading for a substantial victory. But behind the personal enthusiasm for the wartime prime minister lay a huge groundswell of antipathy towards the Conservative Party, which was generally held to be responsible for all the ills of the previous decade – the Depression and its accompanying high levels of unemployment, the scandal of poverty and lack of investment, and the policy of appeasement which had failed to prevent war with Nazi Germany. People might have admired Churchill as a war leader, but they did not like the Conservatives who seemed to lack the necessary policies to address post-war problems and had been lukewarm about the idea of social change. Because this would be a 'khaki election', with all servicemen and servicewomen being included in the vote – either by proxy or by post – their presence was another imponderable.

Shortly before polling day a Gallup poll conducted in 195 of the UK's 640 constituencies gave Labour a narrow lead, but the election was followed by the anti-climax of having to wait another three weeks for the result to be known. The outcome was astonishing. Labour had won 393 seats to the Conservatives' 213, while the Liberals all but disappeared with only 12 seats. There were 22 independents, but none of these were SNP, which had lost its only seat, Motherwell. Otherwise the political landscape in Scotland reflected the scale of the Labour victory: Labour had won 47.9 per cent of the vote, the

Conservatives had won 40.3 per cent, the Liberals had won 5.6 per cent, while the SNP share was 1.3 per cent.[23] With over one million people having voted for Labour in Scotland, it was by far the dominant party, although the Conservatives had continued to make a good showing outside the central belt and in most rural areas. Inevitably the new order changed Scotland's political landscape, especially as the incoming Labour government was intent on creating a 'New Britain' which would make unemployment a thing of the past and introduce a new system of benefits, the 'Welfare State', which would address poverty, health care and education, and in so doing produce 'cradle to the grave' security for the people of the UK.

The reforms had a distinctly British feel in that most of them were settled on a UK basis, but there were regional or national differences, the most notable occurring in the National Health Service. When the NHS in Scotland came into being on 5 July 1948 it already had solid foundations, and to all intents and purposes was built on what already existed. Through pre-war innovations such as the Highlands and Islands Medical Services and the wartime Emergency Hospital Service, Scotland already possessed a system of treatment which was very different (and superior) to what was on offer elsewhere in the UK, and this offered a secure foundation for the new service. There was also an existing infrastructure which allowed for the creation of separate legislation for the fledgling health service in Scotland. The country's teaching hospitals enjoyed a working relationship with regional hospital boards, and the existence of the Scottish Home and Health Department had created an administrative system for medical staff and civil servants alike. Finally, when Health Minister Aneurin Bevan canvassed his ideas the British Medical Association in Scotland largely supported them, while they were rejected initially by doctors in England. From the very outset the NHS in Scotland would be a very different organisation, even though it was fully integrated into the UK system. The only distinctly Scottish concept that failed to materialise was the creation of the all-inclusive health centres offering a variety of services including dentistry, as promised in chapter six of the booklet which was sent to every potential patient in Scotland at the time of the foundation of the Scottish Health Service.[24]

Health was not the first nationalised service to be vested and brought into the public domain. In the previous year, on Monday

6 January 1947, plain blue flags bearing the initials NCB (National Coal Board) had been unfurled on staffs at all of Scotland's 187 coal mines to mark the moment when the industry came under public ownership. (Officially, vesting day was 1 January, but in Scotland the new year holiday and the weekend had delayed the ceremonies to the beginning of the first working week.) At the Bowhill Colliery near Cardenden in Fife the ceremony was conducted by the pit's oldest working miner, John Herd, and by its youngest entrant, Adam Drummond, and as the *Dunfermline Press* reported 'many informal "smokers" were held throughout the district as part of the general celebrations'.[25] Similar celebratory events were held across Scotland to mark a moment which most Scottish miners had demanded throughout their working lives, and although it came at a time of recession within the industry the common reaction was one of passionate satisfaction. In Scotland the new industry was managed by its Scottish Division, one of eight geographical divisions, each under a divisional board which reported to the NCB.

Also nationalised at this time were the railways: the pre-war 'Big Four' companies were amalgamated under the auspices of the British Transport Commission (BTC) which had wider responsibilities including docks and inland waterways, hotels, London Transport and road transport. BTC's Railway Executive traded as British Railways with six different regions, the Scottish Region being responsible for all operations within Scotland. The former companies were London Midland and Scottish; London and North-Eastern; and Southern and Great Western. The priority in the immediate aftermath of nationalisation was to repair wartime damage and clear the backlog of maintenance work, and, in Scotland's case, to return locomotives and rolling stock which had been moved south to replace war-damaged stock. Plans were also laid to begin replacing steam with electric and diesel-powered locomotives and multiple units, and in the 1955 modernisation proposals Glasgow benefited from its 190 miles of suburban lines being replaced with electric power at a cost of £18 million.[26]

The new industrial and social welfare order had repercussions for nationalism. Although home rule did not disappear immediately from Labour's agenda, it was seen increasingly as being irrelevant at a time when the national UK government was engaged in pushing through the welfare state, a move which enjoyed widespread public support. It also has to be said that by then the concept of political nationalism had suffered during the war against Nazi Germany, and the SNP had become marginalised as an irrelevance. Increasingly Labour in Scotland began to adopt a passive unionist line, and support for any kind of devolution began to wane. As interpreters of this period have put it, to most outsiders the SNP looked 'more of a sect than a party'.[27] Nationalism did not disappear altogether. Although the party spent the next twenty years in a limbo (largely of its own making), nationalism in its widest sense continued to exist within the interstices of the country's political and cultural life.

Some of its promptings were predictably romantic, and brought some excitement to the post-war world. On Christmas Day 1950, a group of four students (Ian Hamilton, Gavin Vernon, Kay Matheson and Alan Stuart) broke into Westminster Abbey and removed the Stone of Destiny (or Stone of Scone) from beneath the Coronation Chair and returned it to Scotland. The incident received a huge amount of publicity, and while much of the comment was of the outraged variety, it also gave satisfaction to idealists and closet nationalists everywhere. Such was the stone's historical significance – as the coronation stone for Scottish kings it had been taken to London in 1296 by King Edward I – it was the best-known symbol of Scottish nationhood, and down the years frequent demands had been made for its return. On those grounds alone its removal seemed to make good a historical grievance and reawakened interest, albeit fitfully and tangentially, in nationalist politics. It also spawned doubts about the stone's authenticity (it was found to be broken), and when it was placed secretly in Arbroath Abbey a few months later rumours abounded that it was a fake (these were almost certainly untrue).

Three years later, at the time of the coronation of Queen Elizabeth II, there was a further protest against regal symbolism when activists blew up a number of post boxes in protest against the new queen's title and its incorrect relationship to Scotland, but these activities did little more than generate publicity and the issue was soon forgotten. However it was not the end of the matter as far as the Stone of Destiny was concerned. Towards the end of the century, to most people's surprise, Prime Minister John Major announced that the stone would be returned to Scotland on St Andrew's Day 1996, and it was subsequently put on display with other regalia in the Crown Room at Edinburgh Castle. The decision was announced at a time when the fortunes of the Conservative government were at a low ebb, especially in Scotland, but Major's decision provides a good inkling of the stone's symbolic importance in Scottish life.

Nationalism, or at least a sense of national cultural identity, also infused the post-war literary scene. On the conclusion of hostilities the poet Hugh MacDiarmid was made redundant from his wartime work, and at Douglas Young's suggestion he joined the SNP to stand as a candidate for the Kelvingrove constituency in the post-war election. This was won by Labour (J. L. Williams, 12,273) with MacDiarmid (C. M. Grieve) in third place (1,314). Finding himself unemployed, MacDiarmid took employment as a journalist with the *Carlisle Journal* while his wife and son remained in Glasgow. As ever, he retained a deep interest in literature, producing his second *Selected Poems* in 1946 and involving himself in a literary row which erupted that same year in the correspondence columns of the *Glasgow Herald* over the use of Scots. It had been sparked by a lecture which had been broadcast on the BBC by the archivist and historian James Fergusson of Kilkerran who coined the phrase 'plastic Scots' to describe the literary language used by MacDiarmid and his followers. Fergusson was the scion of a noted Ayrshire family – his brother was Brigadier Bernard Fergusson – and later became a noted holder of the post of Keeper of the Records, but his broadcast, in which he denigrated poetry in Scots as a 'bastard language' caused uproar, with other writers joining in an increasingly outraged correspondence.

Seen from the perspective of a later age, the row has all the ingredients of the kind of writers' spat or 'flyting' which typified Scottish letters in the age of MacDiarmid, but at the time it was solidly based on a realistic attempt to bring some stylistic and lexicographical coherence to the use of Scots in contemporary poetry and prose. Also known as 'Lallans', a word used by both Robert Burns and Robert Louis Stevenson, Scots as a poetic language had always been in wide general use, and since the 1920s it had been associated with Mac-Diarmid's post-war Scottish renaissance movement. Fergusson disputed the use of this kind of language and reserved much of his bile for Young, whom he regarded as a fake because he 'and his companions will hardly believe that the language in which they are claiming that they naturally express themselves in poetry bears other than the remotest relation to any form of Scots current today.'[28]

The argument was taken a stage further when Fergusson claimed that the poets, or self-styled 'makars', were motivated by political reasons and were attempting to disassociate contemporary Scottish literature from English literary traditions. To this charge Young took grave exception, and in an address given at the Masonic Hall in Glasgow on 22 December 1946, he offered a stern rebuttal and laid out his stall for the position that he believed should be taken by post-war poets in Scotland. His speech was later issued as a pamphlet by the literary publisher William MacLellan: 'Now this allegation contains but a partial truth, for the Makars – I believe I can say all of them – share a desire to re-establish the cultural contacts of Lallans as a national language fit for all purposes of verse, and indeed of literature generally. If in the pursuit of this aim some of them are more or less militantly Anglophobe, that is a necessary result of the imperialist tendency of the English language in Scotland, claiming and by Act of Parliament securing a monopoly in schools and so forth.'[29]

To drive home the point, Young mischievously claimed that only a few years previously the *Glasgow Herald* had criticised the Nazi policy of Germanification in its occupied territories, notably Poland, yet it was not inclined to support a similar status for the Scots language. The correspondence was concluded at the end of December, but Young and his fellow makars took the issue of 'plastic Scots' further the following year at a meeting of poets known as the Makars' Club in the Abbotsford bar in Edinburgh's Rose Street on 11 April 1947. Chaired by the poet A. D. Mackie, it produced the *Scots Style Sheet*, a regularised orthography of the correct use of Scots, and amongst those who created it were Young and a host of younger poets who had served in the Second World War including J. K. Annand, Robert Garioch, Maurice Lindsay and Alexander Scott. While the political involvement was subsidiary to the literary intention, the *Scots Style Sheet* helped to regularise the use of Lallans, and many of those involved regarded it as a political statement of intent.[30]

Other moves were more practical, and were aimed at giving some renewed substance to the structure of political nationalism following the wartime splits within the movement. Following McIntyre's failure to hold Motherwell and the generally insipid performance at the 1945 election, the SNP adopted a manifesto which went hell-for-leather for independence, while MacCormick, having stood unsuccessfully as a Liberal, continued to put his faith in consensus politics.

The result was the creation of the Scottish Convention which aimed to swing the people of Scotland behind an irresistible tide of support for the creation of a single-chamber assembly which would have responsibility for Scottish affairs within the UK government. It held its first Scottish National Assembly in Glasgow in March 1947, and culminated its business with a third assembly which was held in the General Assembly Hall of the Church of Scotland in Edinburgh on 29 October 1949. It proved to be a sonorous occasion, and one that positively reeked of history, for in allying the movement to a covenant, MacCormick had self-consciously related it to the Solemn League and Covenant of 1643 which bound Scottish and English Presbyterians in common cause to support the ideals of the reformed church. Delegates signed up for change and put their names to the call for the creation of 'a parliament with adequate legislative authority in Scottish affairs'. It was a fine thing to attempt, and MacCormick had not been far wrong when he insisted that if Scotland wanted to change direction he and his fellow Covenanters had to seize the historical moment: 'We can use the Scottish Convention to that end. It is open to us all. It will become what the Scottish people make of it. Will it be another of the high dreams and sudden cold awakening with which our history has so often been familiar? Or will it be the promise kept at last and the giving of what is ours to the world?'[31]

MacCormick's questions were soon answered, although not in the manner he might have wished. Around two million people put their names to the document, but no number of signatures could have changed the status quo, and home rule remained a romantic dream. The National Covenant gave voice to a widespread nationalist sentiment and satisfied the longings of those who craved change, but nothing came of the initiative. It gathered signatures, but that was all: as a result political nationalism, and along with it the SNP, went into a long decline, so much so that Arthur Donaldson was able to remark that 'all the activists of the SNP could have been the complement of a small passenger aircraft, and had they flown together and crashed without survivors, the cause of independence would have been lost to view for many years.'[32]

Yet by an odd quirk the encroachment of nationalism into Scotland's cultural and political life did not bring with it a narrow parochialism. Far from it: during the war the country had grown used to the sight of overseas service personnel, most of them from European countries, and while most had returned within months of the war ending, some echoes of their presence remained.

As we have seen, the British Council had responded to the foreign invasion by arranging a series of cultural events and establishing International House in Edinburgh's Princes Street as a gathering place for poetry readings, discussions and opportunities to learn and study English. The mastermind behind this initiative was Henry Harvey Wood, an able administrator and cultural ambassador who had been born and brought up in Edinburgh and who had been recruited by the British Council after failing his medical for military service. At any time Wood would have been a valuable addition to a nation's cultural life, and his contribution in Scotland proved to be decisive. Towards the end of the war Rudolf Bing, the distinguished manager of the Glyndebourne Festival, had been investigating the possibility of setting up a festival which 'might establish in Britain a centre of world resort for lovers of music, drama, opera, ballet and the graphic arts'. During one fateful meeting at the end of 1944 with British Council officials in a restaurant in London's Hanover Square, Bing was persuaded by Wood's argument that Edinburgh would be the right location, provided that it attracted sufficient local and civic support.

Despite the enthusiasm which had been generated at the meeting, Wood had to work hard to convince potential supporters in Edinburgh, notably Lord Provost Sir John Falconer and Murray Watson, editor of the *Scotsman*, but eventually a decision was taken to mount the festival in August 1947. Problems still abounded, and would continue to dog the project – one of Wood's biographers claimed that 'the festival plan almost foundered on the rocks of apathy, civic obstruction, and local government politics' – but the first ever Edinburgh International Festival was a triumph.[33] As the recently demobbed poet Maurice Lindsay put it, 'it is impossible to exaggerate the impact the Festival made upon us in that long-ago sunny summer, when Europe was still in the process of dragging itself out of the shadows of war.'[34] Even the sun shone throughout the event, and the closing concert by the Vienna Philharmonic was hailed as a manifestation of 'the unconquerable spirit of European civilisation'. No one who heard Kathleen Ferrier singing Mahler's *Das Lied von der Erde* to Bruno Walter's conducting, ever forgot the experience.

There was another side-effect. From the outset the festival was firmly international in its approach. It was also solidly British in its execution but Scottish in its location, and therein lay a problem. Early complaints about the lack of a Scottish cultural input (not all of them received from within Scotland) were quickly addressed by the decision to revive the Scottish morality play *Ane Plesant Satyre of the Thrie Estaitis* by Scotland's first known dramatist, Sir David Lyndsay of the Mount, which was the highlight of the second Edinburgh International Festival in 1948. This was an inspired decision because from the very outset the portents were not promising. While the play had undoubted literary integrity, it had only been performed twice since its first staging at the Royal Court in Linlithgow on Twelfth Night, 1540. It was also seven hours long, prolix and written in Scots, and there existed no modern version capable of being staged in contemporary terms. Against that, and strongly in its favour, Lyndsay's play was richly humorous, with a strong satirical bent, and it mixed comedy with moral seriousness. Above all, in its central character John the Common-Weill, who represents the welfare of the nation, it possessed one of the great levelling democrats in Scottish literature, a figure who would be instantly recognisable anywhere in the post-war world.

If Lyndsay's play could be cut down and the language revised for a modern audience it would make an ideal vehicle for the fledgling festival. Fortunately the project was put in the hands of the noted producer and impresario Tyrone Guthrie, who engaged the playwright Robert Kemp to adapt it for a modern audience. Then the bold step was taken to mount the production in the General Assembly Hall of the Church of Scotland on the Mound in Edinburgh. All were inspired decisions, and the production of the *Satyre* was an instant success. Largely this was due to the sense of innovation and Guthrie's bold staging, but the play's main theme of a satirical attack on the Thrie Estaitis was represented by the characters Spiritualitie (the first estate, or clergy), Temporalitie (the second estate, or secular lords) and Merchand (the third estate, or burgesses). Other characters include Rex Humanitas, Divyne Correctioune, Gude Counsall plus a host of richly comic figures, and the play concludes with the cleansing of the nation and the reform of the estates. There is little doubt that audiences responded to the play's main theme, and its message that countries can be corrupted by false leaders who are beguiled by pride and hypocrisy – in a moment of high symbolism the second act opens with the estates entering backwards to signify their moral and political recidivism.

Despite occasional financial and organisational vicissitudes and local carping, the festival never looked back, becoming in time one of the world's great civilising celebrations and one of the brightest ornaments in Scottish cultural life. And yet, despite this brief revival of national values the overwhelming spirit of the age was governed not by a sense of being Scottish but of being British. This came about mainly a result of the government's promotion of the war effort, which historians later summed up as embracing 'an idealised British national identity'.[35] Because the direction of the war had been in the hands of the Westminster government, and because the Ministry of Information promoted the concept of the British island race in much of its wartime propaganda output, the idea of everyone being in it together grew, and quickly became established as a national (UK) ideal. This is borne out by many local intelligence reports conducted in the aftermath of the first bombing raids against British cities in 1940. When it became clear that London was on the receiving end of the worst of the attacks, people in Dundee were reported to have said: 'if only they [German bombers] would give us a turn, they might give London a night's rest.'[36]

Conscription also introduced an equality of effort, as well as taking young men and women out of Scotland to serve or work elsewhere in the United Kingdom and further afield in the British Empire where Britain, or England, was the central binding factor. When Maurice Lindsay returned to live and work in 'shabby down-at-heel' Glasgow as a journalist and broadcaster he decided quite early on to stop writing in Scots – his first collection *Hurlygush* appeared in 1948 – and returned to writing in English, having taken 'a conscious decision to write only in the language I spoke daily'.[37] Although he had been an avid pro-Scots advocate during the *Glasgow Herald*'s debate in 1946, and although he decided that his future working life should be spent in Scotland where he emerged as a gifted writer and energetic cultural activist, the rest of Lindsay's substantial poetic output was to be principally in English. There is an uneasy metaphor here for Scotland's condition in the aftermath of the Second World War: it was possible to be British, or unionist, while retaining Scottish or nationalist sensibilities.

Within five years of the first demobilisations and the introduction of the Welfare State, Scotland began to change out of all recognition. Two elections in quick succession, in February 1950 and October 1951, cut Labour's majority and in Scotland left the once great Liberal Party with only one seat, Orkney and Shetland (Jo Grimond). The Conservatives returned to power, as they did again in 1955 when they won 36 of Scotland's 71 seats, a feat they were not to repeat again. In 1959 Labour won 38 seats to the Conservative's 32, although the latter remained in power at Westminster. However, with the economic situation declining in Scotland, the writing was on the wall, and in the 1964 election the Conservatives lost heavily, winning only 24 seats, while Labour took 43 seats to help them secure a small overall majority in London. For the first time in several decades there was a resurgence of interest in the SNP which took second place to Labour in West Lothian.

Against a background of further decline a new economic plan was announced for Scotland at the beginning of 1966, but despite the estimated investment of £2,000 million the heavy industries were already in trouble. The NCB estimated that only 48 pits would still be open by 1970, and demand for shipbuilding had fallen to such an extent that the UK's global share had fallen to 13 per cent by 1965, with the Clyde's share of that total only 34 per cent.[38]

It was perhaps not surprising that the SNP re-emerged in the 1966 election, doubling its vote and coming second in three hotly contested constituencies, a feat that prepared the ground for the party winning the Hamilton by-election in November 1967. In the decade that followed that surprising breakthrough, nationalism returned to the political agenda, and as a result Labour once more came to embrace the concept of home rule; at a meeting held in Glasgow in August 1974 it ended the strict unionist stance which it had adopted after the

Second World War, thereby paving the way for the first devolution referendum in 1979.

Sixty years earlier when Scotland had gone into the war to defend the rights of small nations a Liberal-sponsored home rule bill had been on the verge of becoming law, only to be swept away in the storm that engulfed the rest of Europe. During the inter-war years devolution remained in the national consciousness, albeit fitfully in the dire economic climate, only to disappear once more in the crusade to defeat Nazi Germany and imperialist Japan. During that time the Liberals all but vanished and the Conservatives went into the long decline which saw them become a marginal party in Scotland by the end of the twentieth century. For good or for ill – in the west of Scotland, perhaps the latter – in the second half of the twentieth century Labour remained the dominant party with its own command culture. At the same time the country had to accept the decline and eventual death of its heavy industries as reliance on public sector employment and, later, the financial sector, became paramount. From that point of view it was an odd outcome for those who had served their country during the Second World War and wanted the world they inherited to be a better place.

However, on the credit side, the conflict had helped to end *laissez-faire* politics, and paved the way for an inclusive and interventionist approach to government which would benefit everyone. Hopes were high in Scotland that this would lead to a prosperous future of full employment and decent housing with development areas, inward investment and the creation of new towns at Cumbernauld, East Kilbride, Glenrothes, Irvine and Livingstone. Central to Labour's post-war philosophy was a belief that never again should Scotland be forced to return to the bad old days of unemployment, lack of investment, endemic poverty and social malaise that had followed the First World War. If that earlier conflict had been the war which had been fought to end war, then the Second World War would be the war which ushered in a brave new world of social justice and economic parity. Or, as Tom Johnston put it so eloquently in his memoirs, in the unity of the war years lay the strength which should accompany the peace: 'if only we could lift great social crusades like better housing and health from the arena of partisan strife, what magnificent achievements could be ours.'[39]

It did not quite turn out that way, but the experience of the war had proved many things to the people of Scotland. After the false hopes of the 1920s and the doldrums of the 1930s, a sense of common cause had been created, and in the election of the post-war Labour government with its reforming instincts Scots had been shown that they had nothing to fear but fear itself, if only they could rise above all their trepidations and learn to master them. As 1945 drew to a close it was very far from being a sombre prospect, and most importantly of all it was one which thousands of Scots yearned to embrace as their rightful inheritance.

Epilogue
The Beginning of a New Song

On a warm and pleasant summer's morning on the first day of July 1999, the Crown of Scotland was paraded before the people of Scotland in a ceremony presided over by the Duke of Hamilton, Scotland's premier peer, before it was placed in front of the Queen in the General Assembly Hall of the Church of Scotland, the temporary chamber of Scotland's new parliament. It was the centrepiece of a day of festivities to mark the reopening of Scotland's parliament in which public celebration was mixed with ceremonial to mark a new beginning in the country's history. Crowds lined the Royal Mile, soldiers were on parade, bands played and later Concorde swooped across the Edinburgh skyline accompanied by the Red Arrows, the RAF's spectacular display team. As the Queen finished her speech, a specially commissioned mace was unveiled in public for the first time, a gift from Her Majesty marking the new parliament's authority.

But for all the pageantry there was a distinct lack of the kind of high pomp and ceremony that usually marks national occasions of this kind. It was certainly an historic moment, but as the new First Minister Donald Dewar reminded everyone in his opening speech, it was a turning point not just in the history of Scotland, but also in the history of democracy within the United Kingdom.

This is about more than our politics and our laws. This is about who we are, how we carry ourselves. And in the quiet moments of today – if there are any – we might hear some echoes from the past: the shout of the welder in the din of the great Clyde shipyards, the speak of the Mearns rooted in the land, the discourse of the Enlightenment when Edinburgh and Glasgow were indeed a light held to the intellectual life of Europe, the wild cry of the great pipes and back to the distant noise of battles in the days of Bruce and Wallace.

Dewar had every reason to wax eloquent, as he was one of the architects of that historic moment and, quite rightly, had emerged as Scotland's founding First Minister. For one day at least, many of the squabbles which had proceeded the event were forgotten – notably the row over the cost and the design of the new parliament building which was still taking shape, slowly, laboriously and expensively, at the foot of the Royal Mile opposite the Palace of Holyroodhouse. Instead of looking back and complaining, those who celebrated the occasion hoped that a bright dawn was breaking, that 'new politics' would be at the heart of a fresh way of doing things, and that Scotland had at last gained home rule in reasonable measure. After an absence of just under three hundred years it seemed that once again Scotland's parliament had come back into its own. All told, it was very much a Scottish day in which the actual ceremonial was short and well-judged, while as far as was possible a human face was put on the public celebrations. Few present at the opening ceremony will forget Sheena Wellington's luminous rendition of Robert Burns's great song 'A Man's a Man' or the reading of eleven-year-old Amy Linekar's poem 'How to Create a Great Country'.

It also represented the general desire of the Scottish people to take their fate back into their own hands. Two years earlier on 11 September 1997, Scotland had gone to the polls in a referendum on devolution, and the result was overwhelmingly positive, with 74 per cent voting in favour of a Scottish parliament and 63 per cent voting for the parliament to have powers to vary the basic rate of income tax. From that point onwards things proceeded quickly and tolerably smoothly, and the following year saw the emergence of the Scotland Act which paved the way for the creation of the new Scottish parliament.

Although its powers were limited in that the body could only pass legislation on devolved matters, which included education, health, agriculture and justice, devolution helped to settle the issue of home rule which had existed since 1914 and which had aggravated the body politic in the years that followed. Before the new parliament came into being, between the revitalisation of the SNP in the late 1960s and the change in Scotland's economic and political fortunes which followed, the devolution movement (as it became) was subject to many false dawns, frequently bewildering changes of fortune, underhand horse-trading and (this being Scotland) considerable blood-letting and character assassination.

Scotland's political history in the second half of the twentieth century is not the purpose of this narrative, and so it can be briefly told. As we have seen, in the immediate aftermath of the Second World War nationalism had ceased to be a burning issue and the SNP had gone into a sharp decline, but according to the writer John Herdman, by the late 1960s it had 'moved almost stealthily to a position from which it would be able to launch a significant raid on mainstream politics and deliver a strike at the heart of the unionist establishment'.[1] One result of this improvement was the party's success at Hamilton in 1967 and its continuing popular support in the following decade. The pinnacle was reached in the general election of October 1974 when the SNP polled almost a third of all votes in Scotland and returned eleven MPs to the Westminster parliament.

At the same time there was a renewal of cultural nationalism which, while not related in any direct way to party politics, was centred on the status and well-being of the country's artistic life, especially its literature. In 1967 the magazine *Scottish International* was founded under the editorship of Robert Tait with a policy of embracing political as well as cultural matters and providing a platform for debate. That same year also saw the arrival of the nationalist magazine *Catalyst* which aimed to 'stimulate discussion in the question of an independent Scotland'.[2] Then, four years later, the literary magazine *Lines Review* gave over its summer issue to the publication of a polemical essay by the poet Alan Jackson entitled 'The Knitted Claymore: An Essay on Culture and Nationalism' which became the subject of heated argument and prompted a long-running and equally impassioned correspondence in the pages of the *Scotsman*. Other manifestations included the 1974 production of the play *The Cheviot, the Stag and the Black, Black Oil* by the radical 7:84 Theatre Company which cast a leery eye at Highland history, from the Clearances to the recent exploitation of oil in the North Sea. It too provoked a huge amount of questioning of Scotland's role and the need for change.

The discovery of oil also played a role in stimulating that national conversation. The SNP adopted the slogan 'It's Scotland's Oil', and a debate was sparked about the revenues and their ownership, the implication being that these should be purely for the benefit of the Scots. At a time of mounting unemployment, particularly in the declining heavy industries, arguments of that kind carried popular resonance. The decade was also marked by some spectacular political jousting with 'Nat-bashing' being a feature on both the left and the right. At one stage the SNP were anathematised as 'Tartan Tories' but there were also those within the Labour, Liberal and Conservative parties who understood the potency of the demands for devolution or home rule. Those tensions formed the backdrop to the introduction of a Scotland Bill formulating the creation of a Scottish Assembly, which received the Royal assent on 31 July 1978 and which would become law if it survived a referendum the following year.

Thanks to a complicated system of scoring the results (a 40 per cent majority was required), a modest turnout and some last-minute political chicanery, the 1979 referendum failed to win the necessary support and for the time being devolution was out for the count. But it was not yet dead. The following decade saw a renewal of mainly positive action to revive the debate and keep the issue alive, and by the end of the 1980s devolution was still a potent political issue. It also crossed the party-political divide and gained widespread support through the creation of the Campaign for a Scottish Assembly, which was followed in 1989 by the Scottish Constitutional Convention under the joint chairmanship of Lord Ewing of Kirkford and Sir David Steel MP. This represented the latest attempt to harness public opinion by encouraging pro-devolution groups and individuals within Scottish politics and civic life and its final report *Scotland's Parliament, Scotland's Right*, published on 30 November 1995 provided a blueprint for devolution which had a profound influence on the creation of future policy.

Following the return of the deeply unpopular (in Scotland at least) Conservative government under John Major in 1992, a final push was provided by other pro-devolution groups such as Scotland United, Democracy for Scotland and, above all, Common Cause, and a real head of steam was created. With an election looming in 1997, the Labour Party promised in its manifesto to create a Scottish parliament, and when it came to power under Prime Minister Tony Blair – as it did in May with a huge majority – the detailed proposals were unveiled in the White Paper *Scotland's Parliament* (Cmd. 3658) on 24 July 1997.[3]

Suddenly the future had arrived, and with it the great matter of home rule had finally been resolved; this was indeed the 'settled will of the Scottish people', as had been promised by devolution's supporters. It was not perfect. There was considerable dissatisfaction with the Additional Member System form of proportional representation, which used closed party lists to elect members in addition to constituency members, who are elected using the standard first-past-the-post system, and in the early stages at least there was much carping about the standards of debate and parliamentary behaviour, but the new parliament quickly settled in, and by its tenth anniversary the institution had become just that, part and parcel of the fabric of Scottish life. So low-key was the occasion that many MSPs did not attend when parliament was once more addressed by the Queen on 1 July 2010. By then an SNP administration had been in power for three years, albeit as a minority administration; by then the parliament was in its new home; and by then, too, the fledgling institution had learned how to fly.

Within four years of that breakthrough, the SNP scored an impressive electoral success, winning the General Election in May 2011 by taking 69 of 129 seats and emerging as the country's first majority government. After his party's breakthrough, First Minister Alex Salmond announced that he would proceed with plans to hold a referendum on Scottish independence.

All this had come about during the course of the so-called 'short' twentieth century, which began in 1914 when the world went to war, and ended with the breakdown of communism and the equally sudden collapse of Cold War confrontation in the century's last decade. Concern about Scottish home rule bookended that period, but its middle portion was dominated by what has been called the 'high point of modern British unionism' when Scotland at war embraced a sense of British nationhood as at no other period in the country's history.[4]

On one level that assessment is not far off the mark. There were many types of glue which kept the British fabric intact during the Second World War – from Churchill's soaring rhetoric which preached the concept of patriotic independence, to the overwhelming and well-understood need to defeat a vicious fascist enemy – but within the interstices of political life in Scotland the feelings of nationhood were never far away. It was never expressed in a vainglorious or pretentious way, but from the concept of being British and being part of a successful team was born a belief that in the post-war years anything might be possible when people united to do the best for themselves and their country. That was the real legacy of the Second World War for a people who had learned that it was possible to keep the faith.

There were, of course, setbacks in the years that followed. The New Jerusalem promised by Labour failed to materialise even though the National Health Service remained its greatest monument. All over the UK, but especially in Scotland, the bulk of the heavy industries sank to rise no more, and many of the loftier hopes for a better and more caring society remained the stuff of dreams. But out of the wreckage of 1945 came the spoor of something new and different. Although no one could possibly have foreseen it during that first summer of victory, when all seemed to be for the best in the best of all possible worlds, the first steps were being taken to create a world in which it would be possible to assert a sense of Scottish nationhood while remaining inside the curtilage of the British nation-state. Like a late spring it reached fruition before the twentieth century proper came to an end, and in so doing the devolution settlement gave proof to the people of Scotland that the new system of governance could work – and, what is more, work well.

Notes

Prologue

1. http://www.empireexhibition1938.co.uk.
2. *Glasgow Herald*, 6 October 1936.
3. *Glasgow Herald*, 11 September 1930.
4. Harvie, *No Gods and Precious Few Heroes*, p. 40.
5. Peebles, *Warship Building on the Clyde*, p. 139.
6. *Glasgow Herald*, 6 October 1936.
7. Crampsey, *Empire Exhibition*, p. 43.
8. Lindsay, *Portrait of Glasgow*, p. 192.
9. *Evening Citizen*, 5 May 1938.
10. *Glasgow Herald*, 31 October 1938.

1 Here We Go Again

1. David Newlands, 'Structural Change and the Scottish Regions 1914–45', Devine, Lee and Peden, *Transformation of Scotland*, pp. 165–8.
2. *Report of the Scottish Liberal Land Inquiry Committee 1927–1928* Glasgow: Scottish Liberal Federation 1928, p. 311.
3. Muir, *Scottish Journey*, pp. 18–19.
4. Ibid., p. 60.
5. Ibid., pp. 87–94.
6. Ibid., p. 140.
7. NA CAB 24/272 Report of the Commissioner for the Special Areas in Scotland, Papers Nos 255(37)–275(37), 12 November 1937.
8. Muir, *Scottish Journey*, p. 234.
9. Bold, *MacDiarmid*, pp. 101–02.
10. Hugh MacDiarmid, 'Causerie', *Scottish Chapbook*, vol. I, no. 3, October 1922.
11. Compton Mackenzie, *Pictish Review*, November 1927.
12. Kellas, *Modern Scotland*, p. 138; Harvie, *Scotland and Nationalism*, pp. 51–2; Finlay, *Modern Scotland*, p. 167.

13. C. H. Douglas, 'The Delusion of Super-Production', *English Review*, December 1918.

14. Linklater, *Magnus Merriman*, p. 102.

15. Muir, *Scottish Journey*, p. 234.

16. *Die Letzten Wochen vor Kriegenausbruch, 9 August bis 3 September 1939*, Akten zur Deutschen Auswartigen Politik, Gottingen: Vandenhoek & Ruprecht, 1956, vol. 7, p. 171.

17. Brian Bond ed., *Chief of Staff. The Diaries of Lieutenant General Sir Henry Pownall*, London: Leo Cooper, 1972, p. 221.

18. NA WO 167/755 War Office: British Expeditionary Force, France: War Diaries, Second World War, War Diary, 5th HLI, 26 August 1939.

19. Hansard, House of Commons Debate, 31 October 1939 vol. 352 cc 1829–902.

20. NAS HH 48/66, Police War Duties, Circular No. 4796: Objects Dropped From The Air Etc.

21. Lindsay, *Thank You for Having Me*, p. 46.

22. Recent historians have questioned the use of the term *blitzkrieg* and argue that von Rundstedt was using enhanced encirclement tactics.

23. Bill King, MacDougall, *Voices from War*, p. 190; Constance A.C. Ross, *The Herald*, 2 September 2009.

24. *Edinburgh Evening News*, 3 September 1939.

25. NAS HH 50/6, Sinking of ss *Athenia*, Donald Maclean to Scottish Office, 7 September 1939.

26. Ibid., Department of Health, 24 November 1939.

27. NA ADM 178/194 Loss of HM Submarine Oxley: Board of Inquiry, 1939.

28. NA DO 131 Records of the Children's Overseas Reception Board.

29. NLS Acc 5540, Box 23, James Kennaway, treatment for 'Flowers', pp. 38.

30. NA CAB 66/9/33 Northern Barrage and other Mining Requirements at Home, Memorandum by the First Lord of the Admiralty, 7 July 1940.

31. Martin Gilbert, *Churchill: A Life*, London: Heinemann, pp. 626–7.

32. NA ADM 199/158 Loss of HMS *Royal Oak*: Board of Inquiry, 1940.

33. NA ADM 115/5790 Main Fleet Base, Scapa Flow: Inception, Development and History 1937–1945.

34. The first German aircraft to be shot down was a Messerschmitt 109 fighter which was hit while attacking three Fairey Battle strike aircraft over Aachen in Belgium on 20 September. Six days later a Blackburn Sea Skua of 803 Squadron flying from HMS *Ark Royal* shot down a Dornier Do 18 flying boat 250 miles north-west of Heligoland.

35. NA AIR 27/1384 Air Ministry and successors: Operations Record Books, Squadrons, 224 Squadron, September–December 1939.

36. 224 Squadron's kill has been disputed but it is listed in the archives of the Royal Air Force Museum at Hendon.
37. *Scotsman*, 17 October 1939.
38. NA AIR 25/232 Air Ministry and Ministry of Defence: Operations Record Books, Groups, No. 13 (Fighter) Group, Operations Record Book, July 1939–December 1940.

2 Phoney War

1. Leo Amery, *My Political Life*, vol. III, London, 1955, p. 330.
2. NA CAB 65/2/37, War Cabinet and Cabinet: Minutes (WM and CM Series), The Naval Situation – HMS Nelson.
3. Jeffrey, *This Present Emergency*, p. 60.
4. *Dundee Courier*, 3 August, 1940.
5. NA CAB 15/37, Government War Book, Chapter X.
6. Urquhart, *Forgotten Highlander*, pp. 14–20.
7. Bill King, MacDougall, *Voices from War*, p. 194.
8. Trevor Royle, *Flowers of the Forest: Scotland and the First World War*, Edinburgh: Birlinn, 2506, pp. 284–5.
9. Eddie Mathieson, MacDougall, *Voices from War*, p. 218.
10. Paterson, *Pontius Pilate's Bodyguard*, vol. I, p. 387.
11. Barnett, *Britain and Her Army*, p. 410.
12. Trevor Royle, *The Argyll and Sutherland Highlanders: A Concise History*, Edinburgh and London: Mainstream, 2008, p. 154.
13. Sir Frederick Pile, *Ack-Ack*, London: Harrap, 1949, p. 115.
14. Order of Battle, 51st (Highland) Division, May 1940, Salmond, *51st Highland Division*, pp. 7–8.
15. Salmond, *51st Highland Division*, p. 4.
16. Fergusson, *Black Watch and the King's Enemies*, p. 19.
17. NLS Acc 7380 Wimberley Papers, Box 13 (i).
18. David, *Churchill's Sacrifice of the Highland Division*, pp. 6–7.
19. NA WO 167/710 War Office: British Expeditionary Force, France: War Diaries, Second World War, 1st Black Watch, March 1940.
20. Delaforce, *Monty's Highlanders*, p. 13.
21. Order of Battle 15th (Scottish) Division, Martin, *Fifteenth Scottish Division*, p. 3.
22. Martin, *Fifteenth Scottish Division*, pp. 355–9.
23. Order of Battle, 52nd (Lowland) Division, September 1939, Blake, *Mountain and Flood*, p. 228.
24. Sebag-Montefiore, *Dunkirk*, p. 482.
25. Alanbrooke, *War Diaries*, p. 80.
26. NA WO 167/815 War Office: British Expeditionary Force, War Diaries, Second World War, 7th/9th Royal Scots, May 1940.

27. Lancastria Association Scotland website, http://www.lancastria.org.uk/home.html.
28. *Scotsman*, 26 July 1940.
29. Ibid.
30. *Glasgow Herald*, 4 July 1940.
31. NA ADM 199/2133 Admiralty Casualty Report, *Arandora Star*.
32. NAS AD 57/23 Correspondence of Lord Advocate's Department concerning case of Antonio Mancini, a naturalised British subject, drowned on the *Arandora Star* after she was torpedoed and sunk by a German U-Boat on 2 July 1940.
33. NA HO45/25755 Detainees in Scotland: appearance before the Scottish Advisory Committee; list of Detainees held in Barlinnie Prison 1940.
34. Wendy Ugolini, 'The Internal Enemy "Other": Recovering the World War Two Narratives of Italian Scottish Women', *Journal of Scottish Historical Studies*, vol. 24, no. 1, July 2005, p. 149.
35. *Edinburgh Evening News*, 11 June 1940; *Glasgow Herald*, 11 June 1940; *Greenock Telegraph*, 11 June 1940.
36. Joseph Pia, MacDougall, *Voices from War*, p. 308.
37. NAS HH 55/57, Scottish Home Department, Special Branch Report, December 1943.
38. *Scotsman*, 18 February 1940.

3 Defeat, Retreat and Making Do

1. NA WO 167/747 War Office: British Expeditionary Force, France: War Diaries, Second World War, 6th Gordon Highlanders, May 1940.
2. *Historical Records of the Cameron Highlanders*, vol. V, p. 123.
3. Muir, *First of Foot*, p. 55.
4. Ibid., p. 79.
5. Kemp, *Royal Scots Fusiliers*, p. 40.
6. Ibid.
7. Sir John Smyth, *The Only Enemy*, London: Hutchinson, 1959, pp. 146–7.
8. Gunning, *Borderers in Battle*, p. 41.
9. Fergusson, *Black Watch and the King's Enemies*, pp. 32–3.
10. David, *Churchill's Sacrifice of the Highland Division*, p. 233.
11. Ibid., pp. 230–1.
12. NA WO 167/704 War Office: British Expeditionary Force, France: War Diaries, Second World War, 7th Argyll and Sutherland Highlanders, June 1940.
13. David, *Churchill's Sacrifice of the Highland Division*, pp. 238–41.

14. Angus Hay of Seaton, The 51st (Highland) Division and St Valéry-en-Caux, France 1940, unpublished lecture Stirling Smith Art Gallery and Museum, 4 November 2008.
15. Urquhart, *Forgotten Highlander*, p. 66.
16. Miles, *Life of a Regiment*, vol. V, p. 89.
17. Rose, *Who Dies Fighting*, p. 9.
18. Stewart, *Thin Red Line*, p. 23.
19. NA WO 106/2574A, Wavell, Report on Malaya Campaign.
20. Miles, *Life of a Regiment*, vol. V, p. 111.
21. Urquhart, *Forgotten Highlander*, pp. 96–7.
22. NA CAB 120/570, Cabinet Office: Minister of Defence Secretariat: Records, Churchill to Ismay, 7 January 1940.
23. McBain, *A Regiment at War*, p. 93.
24. Muir, *First of Foot*, p. 81.
25. Ibid., p. 91.
26. David Pinkerton, *The Thistle*, October 1946.
27. Paterson, *Pontius Pilate's Bodyguard*, vol. II, p. 117.
28. Muir, *First of Foot*, pp. 120–21.
29. Ibid., p. 110.
30. McBain, *A Regiment at War*, p. 156.
31. Richard Hillary, *The Last Enemy*, London: Macmillan, 1942, p. 100.
32. NA AIR 27/2074–2078, 602 Squadron Operations Record Books, January 1940–July 1945; NA AIR 27/2079–2081 603 Squadron Operations Record Books, September 1925–July 1945.

4 Frontline Scotland

1. NA CAB 21/596 Scottish Administration: Reorganisation of Offices (Scotland) Bill, 1938, and Act, 1939.
2. Johnston, *Memories*, p. 135.
3. NAS HH 31/5/2 *Forward* socialist newspaper: copies forwarded to Lord Advocate with expression of concern as to anti-war sentiment contained in some articles.
4. Tom Johnston, leader in *Forward*, 24 September 1938.
5. Hansard, House of Commons Debate 18 April 1939 vol. 346 cc 170–3 170, Civil Defence Regional Commissioners.
6. Christopher Durston, *Cromwell's Major-Generals: Godly Government during the English Revolution*, Manchester: Manchester University Press, 2001, pp. 5–12.
7. NA CAB 23/97, Cabinet 4 (39), War Cabinet and Cabinet: Minutes, 1 February 1939.
8. NA CAB 23/96, Cabinet 53 (38), War Cabinet and Cabinet: Minutes, 7 November 1938.

9. Ibid.
10. Glasgow City Archives & Special Collections, Minutes of Glasgow Corporation, Special Committee on Air Raid Precautions, 28 May 1936.
11. Glasgow City Archives & Special Collections, DCD 2/2, Records of the Civil Defence Department, 'Provision of Shelter Accommodation', Glasgow, 1942, p. 15.
12. *Edinburgh Evening News*, 5 September 1939.
13. Memories of Skene Street (now Gilcomstoun) School, Aberdeen 1939–1945, James G. Pittendrigh (late of 19 Chapel Street, Aberdeen), http://www.gilcomstoun.aberdeen.sch.uk/memories.htm.
14. Osborne, *Home Guard*, pp. 23–6.
15. NA WO 32/10016 Home Guard: Dress and Badges (Code66(B)): Scottish Home Guard; headgear.
16. Osborne, *Home Guard*, p. 43.
17. Alanbrooke, *War Diaries*, p. 89.
18. Osborne, *Home Guard*, pp. 66–7.
19. Linklater, *Compton Mackenzie*, pp. 289–90.
20. Ibid., p. 291.
21. NA WO 199/3251 Letters to and from the War Office concerning Auxiliary Units, January 1941–June 1942.
22. William Paul and Trevor Royle, 'Scotland's Secret Army', *Scotland on Sunday, Spectrum*, 24 June 1990, pp. 27–8; Lindsay, *Forgotten General*, p. 151.
23. Ibid., William Paul and Trevor Royle, 'Diary of a Scots Guerrilla', p. 27.
24. 'Auxiliary Units Operational State 1941', Appendix C, Lampe, *Last Ditch*, p. 159.
25. NAS ED3/362 Dispersal of National Treasures in an Emergency.
26. Ibid., Notes of meeting at St Andrew's House on Wednesday 27 July 1949 on plans for safeguarding national art treasures in time of war.
27. NA CAB 66/9/35 Estimated Scale of Air Attack upon the United Kingdom. Memorandum by the Prime Minister, 9 July 1940.
28. IWM 11929 EDS Collection, Operation Sealion.
29. Ibid., *Informationsheft GB*.
30. Trevor Royle, 'Operation Sealion: Hitler's Blueprint for Invasion', *Scotland on Sunday Magazine*, 17 June 1990, p. 24.
31. IWM 11929, EDS Collection, *Sonderfahndungsliste GB*.
32. Noël Coward, *Future Indefinite*, London: Heinemann, 1954, p. 113.
33. William Paul, interview with Naomi Mitchison, *Scotland on Sunday Magazine*, 17 June 1990, p. 23.
34. Douglas Macleod, 'The Thistle, the Shamrock and the Swastika', BBC Radio Scotland, 1993.

35. NA KV 5/3 The Security Service: Organisation (OF series) Files, Anglo-German Fellowship, 1 January 1935–31 December 1940.

36. NLS Acc. 3721 Muirhead papers, Box 89/27 Correspondence with Douglas Young, Young to Muirhead, 1 August 1940.

37. NA KV 4/188 Liddell Diaries. Volume 4 of the diary kept by Guy Liddell, the head of the Security Service's B Division, during the Second World War, 2 February 1941–30 November 1941.

38. Susan R. Wilson (ed.), *The Correspondence between Hugh MacDiarmid and Sorley MacLean*, Edinburgh: Edinburgh University Press, 2010, p. 188.

39. Hay, *Poems and Songs*, pp. 464–5.

5 Scotland's Conscience, Moral and Political

1. *Scotsman*, 23 December 1901.

2. Hansard House of Commons Debate 14 May 1912 vol. 38 cc 958–9.

3. *The Scotland Bill: Some Constitutional and Representational Aspects*, House of Commons Research Paper 98/3, 7 January 1998.

4. Harvie, *Scotland and Nationalism*, p. 51.

5. Young, *Chasing an Ancient Greek*, p. 58.

6. Young, *Auntran Blads*, p. 24.

7. Compton Mackenzie, *On Moral Courage*, London: Collins, 1954, pp. 150–51.

8. William Douglas-Home's oldest brother was Lord Dunglass, who had served as parliamentary private secretary to Chamberlain, and who later became a Conservative prime minister as Sir Alec Douglas-Home. Later in the war, in October 1944, William Douglas-Home was court-martialled and imprisoned for refusing to take part in an attack on Le Havre because he knew that the Allied assault would cause civilian casualties.

9. Open letter to John MacCormick, by Arthur Donaldson, *Scottish News and Comment*, August 1942.

10. John Couzin, *Radical Glasgow: A Skeletal Sketch of Glasgow's Radical Tradition*, Glasgow: Volone Press, 2003, p. 70.

11. NA CAB 24/285, Military Training Bill, 30 April 1939.

12. NAS HH 50/63 Emergency: Membership of Conscientious Objectors' Tribunals.

13. Morgan, 'Stanza 99 The New Divan', *The New Divan*, p. 56.

14. J. K. Annand, MacDougall, ed., *Voices from War*, p. 181.

15. Annand, 'Atlantic 1941', *Selected Poems*, p. 22.

16. Norman MacCaig, MacDougall, ed., *Voices from War*, pp. 282–3.

17. Ibid., p. 286.

18. Ibid.

19. NAS HH 50/63 Emergency: Membership of Conscientious Objectors' Tribunals.
20. *Scotsman*, 23 January 1944.
21. NAS HH 16/253/1–2 Criminal case file: Douglas Cuthbert Colquhoun Young.
22. Marr, *Battle for Scotland*, p. 93.
23. Sir John Martin, *Downing Street: The War Years*, London: Bloomsbury, 1991, p. 42.
24. Johnston, *Memories*, p. 146.
25. Ibid., p. 148.
26. NAS HH 50/166, Scottish Council on Post-War Problems, Minutes of the first meeting of the Scottish Council on Post-War Problems, 29 September 1941.
27. Ibid.
28. Johnston, *Memories*, p. 150.
29. *Report of the Committee on Hydro-electric Development in Scotland*, London: HMSO, 1942.
30. Johnston, *Memories*, p. 150.
31. Robert Rhodes James, *Bob Boothby: A Portrait*, London: Hodder & Stoughton, 1991, p. 311.
32. NA CAB 124/680 Discussions on the future of economic controls, August–September 1944.
33. NAS HH50/170, Fifth Meeting of the Scottish Council on Post-War Problems, 1942.
34. David Newlands, 'The Regional Economies of Scotland', Devine, Lee and Peden (eds), *The Transformation of Scotland*, pp. 165–9.
35. NAS HH 50/168, Third meeting of the Scottish Council on Post-war Problems, 8 December 1941.
36. Slaven, *Development of the West of Scotland*, p. 210.
37. Murray, *Agriculture,* pp. 170–71.
38. Ibid., Appendix Table XIII, Changes in Net Income Per Farm by Type of Farming Groups in England and Wales and in Scotland 1940–1 to 1944–5, p. 383.
39. *Report of the Royal Commission on the Housing of the Industrial Population of Scotland, Rural and Urban*, Edinburgh: HMSO, 1917, para 1052.
40. Johnston, *Memories*, p. 152.
41. *Summary Report of the Department of Health for Scotland for 1945*, Cmd. 6661, London: HMSO, 1945, p. 15.
42. Titmuss, *Problems of Social Policy*, p. 496.
43. NAS HH 50/ Report of the Committee on Scottish Health Services.
44. Ibid., p. 472.
45. NA CAB 65/41 War Cabinet and Cabinet: Minutes (WM and CM Series), 15 February 1944.
46. Johnston, *Memories*, p. 164.

47. Harvie, *No Gods and Precious Few Heroes*, p. 103.
48. NA CAB 87/72 War Cabinet and Cabinet: Committees on Reconstruction, Supply and other matters: Minutes and Papers (RP, SLAO and other Series).

6 Total War

1. 'The Great Destruction' by a Clydesider, *Clydebank Press*, 25 April 1941.
2. There are detailed accounts of the raids in Macleod, *River of Fire* and Jeffrey, *This Time of Crisis*, pp. 49–81.
3. Taylor, *Luftwaffe over Scotland*, pp. 68–9.
4. NAS HH 50/1 Department of Health for Scotland, The Clydebank Air Raids of March 13–15 1941, A note on the department's activities, April 1941.
5. NAS HH 50/2 Office of the Regional Commissioner – Scotland Region, Raids on Clydeside 13th/14th and 14th/15th March 1941.
6. Ibid., Office of the Regional Commissioner – Scotland Region, Raids on Clydeside 13th/14th and 14th/15th March 1941.
7. NAS HH 50/3 Raids on Clydeside Area, Dept of Health, Further reports bringing situation to date, 18 March 1941.
8. NAS HH 50/2 Department of Health for Scotland, Blitz of Clydeside – appreciation from a medical point of view by Chief Medical Officer, 29 April 1941.
9. NAS HH 50/2 Office of the Regional Commissioner – Scotland Region, Raids on Clydeside 13th/14th and 14th/15th March 1941.
10. Ibid.
11. NAS HH 50/2 Scottish Office, Home Intelligence, Clydebank Raid, 9 April 1941.
12. NAS HH 50/3 Air raids on Scotland, Preliminary situation report as at 08.00 hours, 8th April.
13. Blitz map of Greenock, McLean Museum and Galleries, Inverclyde Council.
14. Ibid., Blitz map.
15. NAS HH 50/103, Office of the Regional Commissioner – Scotland Region, Raids on Clydeside 5th/6th and 6th/7th May 1941.
16. NAS HH 50/165 Narrative of raid on Aberdeen and District 21/22 April 1943.
17. NAS HH 50/160–65 Heavy explosive and incendiary missiles dropped in Scotland 1939–45.
18. NA CAB 102/419 Battle of the United Kingdom Ports, C. B. A. Behrens.
19. NA INF 1/292, Home Intelligence Weekly Reports, 26 March–2 April 1941.

20. *United States Strategic Bombing Survey. Over-All Report (European War)*, Washington: Government Printing Office, 1945.
21. NA WO 166/16335 2 H.Q. Military Port Cairnryan, January–December 1944.
22. NA ADM 234/369, Naval Staff History – Second World War, No. 22 Arctic Convoys 1941–5.
23. J. K. Annand, McDougall, *Voices from War*, p. 186.
24. Annand, 'Atlantic Convoy', *Selected Poems*, p. 9.
25. Fergusson, *Black Watch and the King's Enemies*, p. 69.
26. NA WO 169/348 War Office: British Forces, Middle East: War Diaries, Second World War, 2nd Queen's Own Cameron Highlanders.
27. Stockman, *Seaforth Highlanders*, pp. 93–4.
28. Lieutenant-Colonel R. W. Jackson and Captain J. S. Purvis, 'Memories of the Arakan, 1943', *The Thistle*, April 1946.
29. Allen, *Longest War*, pp. 114–16.
30. Gunning, *Borderers in Battle*, p. 63.
31. Ibid., pp. 220–21.
32. Trevor Royle, *The King's Own Scottish Borderers: A Concise History*, Edinburgh: Mainstream, 2009, p. 189.

7   The Arsenal of War

1. NA ADM 1/9549 Preparation for War (Military) (46): Naval Command in the North Sea, English Channel and Western Approaches: organisation in event of war.
2. Lavery, *Shield of Empire*, p. 386.
3. NA WO 166/17949, War Office: Home Forces: War Diaries, Second World War, Scottish Command.
4. P. J. G. Ransom, *Iron Road: The Railway in Scotland*, Edinburgh: Birlinn, 2007, p. 171.
5. Gordon Donaldson, *Northwards by Sea*, Edinburgh: Paul Harris Publishing, 1978, pp. 46–7.
6. Palmer, Roy (ed.), *What a Lovely War: British Soldiers' Songs from the Boer War to the Present Day*, London: Michael Joseph, 1990, pp. 147–50.
7. Fortress Orkney Project: *The Orkney Blast*, Orkney Museums and Heritage, Scapa Flow Visitor Centre & Museum, 2009.
8. Lavery, *Shield of Empire*, pp. 318–320.
9. Ibid., pp. 311–14.
10. Mackenzie, *Secret History of SOE*, p. 69.
11. In 2005 the National War Museum of Scotland mounted the groundbreaking exhibition *Commando Country*, and this was followed by Stuart Allan's important history with the same title.

12. The full story is told in David Howarth, *The Shetland Bus*, London: Thomas Nelson, 1951. Howarth, a British naval officer, was second-in-command at the headquarters at Lunna House.

13. Mackenzie, *Secret History of SOE*, p. 651.

14. Ibid., pp. 654–7.

15. Allan, *Commando Country*, p. 168.

16. NA WO 188/2783 Gruinard Island following contamination by anthrax: annual inspections; correspondence.

17. McBain, *Regiment at War*, p. 229.

18. NA HS 2/221, Special Operations Executive: Group C, Scandinavia: Registered Files, Top level planning activities: Operation Apostle.

19. NA WO 219/310 Supreme Headquarters Allied Expeditionary Force: Military Headquarters Papers, Second World War , Operation Fortitude, cover plan for Overlord.

20. Wilmot, *Struggle for Europe*, p. 200.

21. NA CAB 106/1122, A Short History of the Deception or 'Cover' Plan for the Normandy Campaign in 1944, Colonel Roderick Macleod.

22. NA DEFE 28/49 Wingate Report, vol. II, Extract from Interrogation of General Jodl in 1946 on Norway.

23. Peebles, *Warshipbuilding on the Clyde*, p. 73 and p. 139.

24. Ibid., p. 140.

25. Johnston, *Ships for a Nation*, p. 219.

26. Slaven, *Development of the West of Scotland*, p. 211.

27. Ibid., p. 215.

28. J. G. Bullen, 'Aluminium: Scotland's Major Part in the Light Metal Age', C. A. Oakley (ed.), *Scottish Industry*, Glasgow: The Scottish Council (Development and Industry), 1953, pp. 163–9.

29. Table 3, *Ministry of Fuel and Power Statistical Digest*, Cmd. 6920, London: HMSO, 1945.

30. Slaven, *Development of the West of Scotland*, p. 210.

31. *The Economist*, 19 July 1941; Court, *Coal*, p. 109.

32. *Keeping the Home Fires Burning, The Bevin Boys: The Forgotten Men of the Home Front*, Newtongrange: Scottish Mining Museum, 2009, p. 6.

33. Court, *Coal*, p. 390.

34. Hansard, House of Commons Debate, 7 February 1940, vol. 357 cc 188.

35. Inman, *Labour in the Munitions Industries*, p. 44.

36. Postan, *British War Production*, Appendix 4.

37. Postan, Hay and Scott, *Design and Development of Weapons* , pp. 6–9.

38. Kohan, *Works and Buildings*, p. 377.

39. *Evening Times* (Glasgow), 3 September 2010.

40. *Report by a Court of Inquiry Concerning a Dispute at an Engineering Undertaking in Scotland*, Cmnd. 6474, 1943, Appendix V.

41. *New Propeller*, December 1943.

42. Professor Mary Davies, *The Labour Movement and the Second World War*, Centre for Trade Union Studies, London Metropolitan University, TUC Library Collections, London Metropolitan University.
43. David Newlands, 'The Regional Economies of Scotland', Devine, Lee and Peden, eds, *Transformation of Scotland*, pp. 168–74.
44. Lenman, *Economic History of Scotland*, p. 237.

8 Home Front

1. NAS HH 50/137 Celebration of the Termination of Organised Hostilities in Europe (VE Day), Arrangements.
2. NAS HH 50/104, Survey of sending and receiving areas, circulars etc.
3. NAS BR/LNE/8/370 Files of General Manager (Scottish Area) on the undernoted subjects: Evacuation of civilian population – Edinburgh, Glasgow and Dundee Areas.
4. NAS HH 50/104, Evacuation Papers, DHS Circular 34/1939, 9 October 1939.
5. NAS HH 50/114 General publicity: consideration and drafting of press articles, including extract articles in "Dundee Courier" and "Sunday Post" criticising the evacuation scheme.
6. Titmuss, *Problems of Social Policy*, p. 180.
7. Alastair Dunnett, *Among Friends: An Autobiography*, London: Century, 1984, p. 110.
8. Leader in the *Lancet*, 7 October 1939, ii, p. 794.
9. NLS Acc 5540, Box 23, James Kennaway, treatment for 'Flowers', pp. 29–31.
10. Jenkins, *Guests of War*, pp. 11–12.
11. Ibid., p. 285.
12. Titmuss, *Problems of Social Policy*, p. 172.
13. Hansard, House of Commons Debate, 14 September 1939, vol. 351 cc 802–66.
14. Ibid.
15. Titmuss, *Problems of Social Policy*, p. 172.
16. Hansard, House of Commons Debate, 27 March 1945, vol. 409, cc 1324.
17. Titmuss, *Problems of Social Policy*, p. 179.
18. NAS RH 4/202 Papers relating to Anglo-German relations and the landing of Rudolph Hess, Hitler's deputy, in Scotland on 10 May 1941.
19. Hammond, *Food*, p. 287.
20. NA MAF 45 Ministry of Agriculture and Fisheries and Ministry of Agriculture, Fisheries and Food: Information and Publicity Correspondence and Papers.
21. Letter, *Inverness Courier*, 11 January 1940.

22. *Blairgowrie Conservation Area Appraisal*, Perth and Kinross Council, 2005, p. 12.
23. NAS AF/59 Agriculture Labour, Safety and Wages Files.
24. Interview with Anna Searson (née Murray). Edwards, *Scotland's Land Girls*, pp. 117–18.
25. Interview with Laura Bauld, ibid., 112–14.
26. 'Land Girls and Lumber Jill' exhibition, National Museums of Scotland, 2010–11, http://www.nms.ac.uk/our_museums/war_museum/land_girls_and_lumber_jills.aspx.
27. Hansard, House of Commons Debate, 25 July 2006, cc 843 Bevin Boys.
28. Joe Hicks and Graeme Allen, *A Century of Change: Trends in UK Statistics since 1900*, IX, Energy Production and Mining Employment, House of Commons Research Paper 99/III, 21 December 1999, p. 19.
29. *Keeping the Home Fires Burning, The Bevin Boys: The Forgotten Men of the Home Front*, Newtongrange: Scottish Mining Museum, 2009, p. 24.
30. Gardiner, *Blitz*, p. 367.
31. NAS CO /102, Association of County Councils, Venereal Disease, Treatment, 1942.
32. Barbara Thompson, 'Social Study of Illegitimate Pregnancies', *British Journal of Social Medicine*, 1956, vol. 10, pp. 75–87.
33. For a fuller discussion see John Costello, *Love, Sex and War: Changing Values, 1939–45*. William Collins, London, 1985.
34. Duncan, 'Consanguinity', *Perfect Mistress*, pp. 12–13.
35. Marshall, *The Black Oxen*, p. 263.
36. Douglas Gifford, 'Literature and World War Two', Ian Brown and Alan Riach, eds, *The Edinburgh Companion to Twentieth Century Scottish Literature*, Edinburgh: Edinburgh University Press, 2009.
37. Eric Linklater, *Fanfare for a Tin Hat*, London, p. 316.
38. Soutar, *Diaries*, p. 205.
39. *Scotsman*, 16 May 1941.
40. Christine Lindey, 'Resonance And Renewal: Stanley Spencer', *Morning Star*, 12 November 2010.
41. Andrew Murray Scott, *Modern Dundee: Life in the City since World War Two*, Derby: Beedon Books, 2002, pp. 23–4.
42. Interview with Petrina (Ina) Lithgow (née Seaton). Edwards, *Scotland's Land Girls*, p. 142.

9 Sikorski's (and other) Tourists

1. Letter from Robert Blair Wilkie to Alan Bold, Bold, *MacDiarmid*, p. 445.
2. Michael Donnelly, obituary of Robert Blair Wilkie, the *Herald*, 8 December 1998.

3. MacDiarmid, *The Company I've Kept*, pp. 187–8.
4. Neal Ascherson, 'Phantoms that haunt the people return', *Observer*, 11 April 2010.
5. Interview with Wladyslaw Fila, Trevor Royle, 'General Sikorski's Tourists', BBC Scotland, 10 October 1988.
6. Kennedy, Robert M., *The German Campaign in Poland, 1939*, Zenger: Washington DC, 1978.
7. NA CAB 66/11/238, Organisation of Allied Naval, Army and Air Contingents. Report by the Chiefs of Staff Committee, 4 September 1940.
8. Henderson, *Lion and the Eagle*, p. 9.
9. 'The Poles in Scotland 1940–1950', Peter D. Strachura (ed.), *The Poles in Britain 1940–2000: From Betrayal to Assimilation*, London: Taylor & Francis, 2004, p. 49.
10. Interview with Wladyslaw Maronski, Royle, 'General Sikorski's Tourists'.
11. Interview with Wiktor Tomaszewski, Royle, 'General Sikorski's Tourists'.
12. Lipka, James (ed.), Section 1 Regional Distribution of Poles in Scotland, Part 1: 1871–1931, *Polish Residents in Scotland: A Statistical Sourcebook based on the Census of Scotland 1861–2001*, website http://www.angelfire.com/jazz/ntstar/scotpolesintro.htm.
13. *Census of Scotland: Preliminary Report of the Fourteenth Census of Scotland*, Part II, General Summary, (Edinburgh: HMSO, 1931), pp. v–vii.
14. 'Celebrating the Links between Scotland and Poland', *Scotland Now Archive*, http://www.friendsofscotland.gov.uk/scotlandnow.
15. D. M. Henderson, *The Poles and Scotland*, The Scots at War Trust website, http://www.scotsatwar.org.uk/AZ/poles&scotland.htm p. 4.
16. Joseph Garlinski, *Poland in the Second World War*, New York: Palgrave Macmillan, 1985, p. 156.
17. Interview with Josef Mirczynski, Royle, 'General Sikorsky's Tourists'.
18. *Polish School of Medicine at the University of Edinburgh*, Edinburgh: Oliver & Boyd, 1942, p. 149.
19. Carswell, *For Your Freedom and Ours*, p. 20.
20. M. Lisiewicz, J. Baykowski, J. Glebocki, R. Gluski, and Dr W. Czerwinski, eds, *Destiny Can Wait: The Polish Air Force in the Second World War*, London: Heinemann, 1948, pp. 203–5.
21. Interview with Leslaw Miedzybrodzki, Henderson (ed.), *Lion and the Eagle*, p. 85.
22. Interview with Wladyslaw Fila, Royle, 'General Sikorski's Tourists'.
23. *Armed Forces Agreement, Texts Composing the Arrangements between His Majesty's Government in the United Kingdom and the Royal Norwegian*

Government in Respect of the Norwegian Forces in the United Kingdom, Appendices I, II and III, 28 May 1941.

24. The dog's story is told in Whitson and Orr, *Sea Dog Bamse*.

25. Mark C. Jones, 'Experiment at Dundee: The Royal Navy's 9th Submarine Flotilla and Multinational Naval Cooperation during World War II', *The Journal of Military History*, 72 (October 2008): pp. 1179–212.

26. US Army Troop Build-Up in the United Kingdom, January 1941 to May 1944, Reynolds, *Rich Relations*, pp. 103.

27. *WW2 People's War: An Archive of World War Two Memories*, Written by the public, gathered by the BBC, http://www.bbc.co.uk/ww2peopleswar.

28. US Troop Distribution in the UK by County, 31 October 1944, Reynolds, *Rich Relations*, pp. 396–7.

29. Omar N. Bradley, with Chester Hansen, *A Soldier's Life*, New York, 1951, pp. 170–71.

30. *Population Estimates by Ethnic Group*, Census April 2001, Office for National Statistics, 2001.

31. Morris J. Macgregor Jnr, *Integration of the Armed Forces, 1940–1965* Washington DC: 1981, pp. 3–7.

32. NA FO 954/298, Private Office Papers of Sir Anthony Eden, Earl of Avon, Secretary of State for Foreign Affairs, 1 September 1942.

33. NA CO 537/1224, 'Colour Discrimination in the United Kingdom,', Proposed Legislation, May 1946.

34. NA CO 876/43, British Honduras Forestry Unit – Health and Welfare, 1942–3.

35. NA CO 876/41, British Honduras Forestry Unit – Health and Welfare, 1941–2.

36. NA CO 876/41, Duke of Buccleuch to Harold Macmillan, 30 September 1942.

37. *Serving Britain During Wartime: A Positive or Negative Experience? The Case of the British Honduran Forestry Unit*, London: Imperial War Museum, 2008, p. 5.

38. Ibid., p. 6.

39. Martin Hennessey, *Independent*, 20 February 1995.

40. Roger J. G. Thomas. *Twentieth-Century Military Recording Project: Prisoner of War Camps 1939–1945*, Project Report, Swindon: English Heritage, 2003, pp. 18–53.

41. David Marshall, 'Scottish Agriculture during the War', *Transactions of the Highland and Agricultural Society of Scotland*, 58 (1946), pp. 37–47.

42. NAS HH 50/17 Emergency Hospital Scheme Weekly Rates, 7 April 1945.

43. Couples who overcome prejudice: Rudi and Anna Drabner, *Daily Telegraph*, 15 May 2009.

44. Kesson, *Another Time, Another Place*, p. 8.
45. Isobel Murray, *Jessie Kesson: Writing her Life*, Edinburgh: Canongate, 2000, pp. 160–61.
46. John Wheatley, *One Man's Judgement: An Autobiography*, London: Butterworths, 1987, p. 45.

10   Striking Back

1. NA ADM1/13410 Naval Training: Specially constructed craft for training submarine personnel in Loch Corrie (Port HHX) and Loch Cairnbawn (Port HHZ).
2. NA ADM1/12880 Complements of Ships and Establishments (7): Small submersible craft (X-craft, Chariots and Welman craft) combination as 12th S/M Flotilla: complementing, administration and training, 1943.
3. Admiralty, *His Majesty's Submarines*, London: HMSO, 1947, p. 61.
4. The full account of the attack is told in C. E. T. Warren and James Benson, *Above us the Waves: The Story of Midget Submarines and Human Torpedoes*, London: Harrap, 1953.
5. Bruce Barrymore Halpenny, *Fight for the Sky*, London: Patrick Stephens, 1986, p. 41.
6. NA AIR 26/597 Banff Mosquito Strike Wing: photographic record of operations, September 1944–May 1945.
7. Obituary of Air Chief Marshal Sir Christopher Foxley-Norris, *Daily Telegraph*, 29 September 2003.
8. NLS Acc. 6119, Wimberley Papers, Box 2, Part 4.
9. McGregor, *Spirit of Angus*, p. 9.
10. P. K. Kemp, *The Middlesex Regiment, 1919–1952*, Aldershot: Gale & Polden, 1956, p. 129.
11. McGregor, *Spirit of Angus*, p. 26.
12. Hamilton, *Monty: The Making of the Field Marshal*, p. 198.
13. Delaforce, *Monty's Highlanders*, p. 33.
14. Ibid., p. 51.
15. Barker, *Gordon Highlanders in North Africa and Sicily*, p. 6.
16. Borthwick, *Sans Peur*, p. 34.
17. NA WO 175 War Office: Allied Forces, North Africa (British Element): War Diaries, Second World War, 1st Gordon Highlanders.
18. Alanbrooke, *War Diaries*, pp. 378–9.
19. McCallum, *Journey with a Pistol*, p. 98.
20. Sinclair, *War like a Wasp*, pp. 130–31.
21. Selwyn, Victor, ed., *Return to Oasis: War Poems and Recollections from the Middle East 1940–1946*, London: Shepheard Walwyn, 1980, p. xix.

22. Ibid.
23. Angus Calder, 'Hamish Henderson', *Independent*, 12 March 2002.
24. Henderson, *Elegies*, p. 37.
25. MacLean, *Selected Poems*, p. 122.
26. Sorley MacLean, ed. Christopher Whyte, *Poems to Eimhir*, Glasgow: Association for Scottish Literary Studies, 2002.
27. Garioch, *Two Men and a Blanket*, p. 8.
28. Obituary, Robin Lorimer, *The Times*, 24 August 1996.
29. Hay, *Collected Poems and Songs*, p. 77.
30. Jocelyn Brooke, 'Landscape near Tobruk', John Lehmann, ed., *Penguin New Writing 21*, Harmondsorth: Penguin Books, 1944.
31. NA WO 175 War Office: Allied Forces, North Africa (British Element): War Diaries, Second World War, 1st Gordon Highlanders.
32. Barker, *Gordon Highlanders in North Africa and Sicily*, p. 25.
33. Barclay, *History of The Cameronians*, p. 113.
34. NLS Acc. 6119, Wimberley Papers, Box 2, Part 4.
35. NA CAB 101/182, Correspondence on Operation 'Thursday' (second Chindit expedition), Symes to Major-General S. Woodburn Kirby, February 1958.
36. John Masters, *The Road Past Mandalay*, London: Michael Joseph, 1961, p. 136.
37. Ibid., p. 146.

11 Victory in Europe and the Far East

1. McGregor, *Spirit of Angus*, p. 123.
2. Delaforce, *Monty's Highlanders*, p. 138.
3. Salmond, *51st Highland Division*, p. 145.
4. Hamilton, *Monty: Master of the Battlefield*, pp. 701–2.
5. Delaforce, *Monty's Highlanders*, p. 143.
6. Ibid.
7. Lindsay, *So Few Got Through*, p. 38.
8. Keegan, *Six Armies in Normandy*, p. 175.
9. Ibid., p. 176.
10. Ibid., p. 181.
11. Michael Blackcock, *The Royal Scots Greys*, London: Leo Cooper, 1971, p. 102.
12. Muir, *First of Foot*, pp. 333–4.
13. Ibid., pp. 342–55.
14. Miles, *Life of a Regiment*, vol. V, pp. 320–24.
15. Lindsay, *So Few Got Through*, p. 183.
16. Scott, 'Coronach (For the dead of the 5/7th Battalion, The Gordon Highlanders)', *Selected Poems*, p. 12.

17. Miles, *Life of a Regiment*, vol. V, p. 346.
18. Ibid., pp. 351–2.
19. Barclay, *History of the Cameronians*, p. 221.
20. Martin Gilbert, *Churchill: A Life*, London: Heinemann, 1991, p. 767.
21. Hamilton, *Monty: Master of the Battlefield*, p. 227.
22. Neat, *Henderson*, pp. 153–5.
23. Linklater, *Campaign in Italy*, p. 100.
24. NA WO 170/1471 War Office: Central Mediterranean Forces, (British Element): War Diaries, Second World War, 2nd Royal Scots Fusiliers.
25. Kemp, *History of the Royal Scots Fusiliers*, p. 197.
26. Madden, *6th Black Watch*, pp. 37–47.
27. Wallace Kinloch and Ralph Couser, *350 Glorious Years, 1642–1990*, London: RHQ Scots Guards, 1993, p. 152.
28. McBain, *Regiment, at War*, p. 178.
29. Ibid., p. 180.
30. Muir, *First of Foot*, pp. 154–5.
31. F. C. Currie, 'Kohima 1944', *Thistle*, January 1946.
32. Hawkins' Diary, *Historical Records of the Queen's Own Cameron Highlanders*, vol. V, p. 156.
33. Ibid., p. 159.
34. Sym, *Seaforth Highlanders*, p. 285.
35. *Historical Records of the Queen's Own Cameron Highlanders*, vol. V, p. 179.
36. Allen, *Longest War*, pp, 514–23.
37. Muir, *First of Foot*, p. 180.

12 Brave New World

1. NAS HH 50/136 Report of the Interdepartmental Conference of Arrangements for Celebrating the Cessation of Hostilities with Germany 3 October 1944.
2. Ibid.
3. NAS HH 50/137 Scottish Home Department memorandum, 20 April 1945.
4. *Edinburgh Evening News*, 9 May 1945.
5. NAS HH 50/138 Celebration of the Termination of Organised Hostilities (VJ Day).
6. John Ellis, *World War II : A Statistical Survey*, London: Facts on File, 1993.
7. NAS HH 50/160–165 Heavy explosive and incendiary missiles dropped in Scotland 1939–45.
8. Allport, *Demobbed*, pp. 1–3.

9. Lindsay, *Forgotten General*, p. 174.

10. *A Decade of American Foreign Policy: Basic Documents, 1941–49, Article VII Poland, Prepared at the Request of the Senate Committee on Foreign Relations by the Staff of the Committee and the Department of State.* Washington, DC: Government Printing Office, 1950, pp. 23–8.

11. Interview with Wladyslaw Fila, Royle, 'General Sikorski's Tourists'.

12. Carswell, *For Your Freedom and Ours*, pp. 27–9.

13. 'Polish immigrants swell Scotland's new baby boom', *Scotsman*, 15 June 2007.

14. Clarke, *Hope and Glory*, p. 214.

15. *Glens Folk*, Kirriemuir: Community of the Glens, 2000, p. 57.

16. NAS HH 50/144 Post-War Planning Response to Memorandum by the Prime Minister and Minister of Defence, 19 October 1943.

17. Slaven, *Development of the West of Scotland*, p. 249.

18. NAS HH 50/201 Joint Memorandum on Reconstruction by Mr J. Westwood and Mr J. S. Wedderburn, to Secretary of State, 13 March 1941.

19. Kohan, *Works and Buildings*, p. 431.

20. Johnston, *Memories*, p. 169.

21. The files are contained in NAS HH 50/144–155 Post-War Planning and NAS HH 50/166–192 Scottish Council on Post-War Problems.

22. *Scottish Daily Express*, 28 June 1945.

23. *UK Election Statistics 1945–2000*, House of Commons Research Paper 01/37, 29 March 2001, p. 12.

24. *Your Health Service: How It Will Work in Scotland*, Edinburgh: HMSO, 1948, pp. 22–3.

25. *Dunfermline Press*, 7 January 1947.

26. *Modernisation and Re-equipment of British Railways*, London: British Transport Commission, 1955, p. 14.

27. Marr, *Battle for Scotland*, p. 95; Devine, *Scottish Nation*, p. 565.

28. Editorial, *Glasgow Herald*, 28 November 1946.

29. Douglas Young, *Plastic Scots and the Scottish Literary Tradition: An Authoritative Introduction to a Controversy*, Glasgow: William Mac-Lellan, 1946, pp. 19–20.

30. Alan Bold, ed., *The Letters of Hugh MacDiarmid*, London: Hamish Hamilton, 1984, p. 788.

31. John MacCormick, *Scottish Convention: An Experiment in Democracy*, Glasgow: William MacLellan for the Scottish Convention, 1943, p. 43.

32. Marr, *Battle for Scotland*, p. 116.

33. Eileen Miller, 'Henry Harvey Wood', *New Oxford Dictionary of National Biography*, Oxford: OUP, 2004.

34. Lindsay, *Thank You for Having Me*, p. 126.

35. Finlay, *Modern Scotland*, p. 184.

36. NA INF 1/292, Home Intelligence Weekly Reports, 30 September–
    9 October 1940.
37. Lindsay, *Thank You for Having Me*, p. 116.
38. *The Scottish Economy 1965 to 1970, a Plan for Expansion*, Cmnd. 2864.
39. Johnston, *Memories*, p. 170.

Epilogue

1. Herdman, *Some Renaissance Cultural Wars*, pp. 11–12.
2. Editorial, *Catalyst*, December 1967.
3. Isobel White and Jessica Yonwin, 'Devolution in Scotland', Standard
   Note: SN/PC/3000, Edinburgh: Parliament and Constitution Centre, 2004.
4. Devine, *Scottish Nation*, p. 565.

Bibliography

Official Papers and Records

Glasgow City Archives and Special Collections

Imperial War Museum: Department of Sound Records (IWM)

National Archives, Kew (NA)

ADM 116 Admiralty: Record Office: Cases

ADM 178 Admiralty: Naval Courts Martial Cases, Boards of Inquiry Reports, and Other Papers (Supplementary Series)

ADM 199 Admiralty: War History Cases and Papers, Second World War

AIR 27 Air Ministry and successors: Operations Record Books, Squadrons

AIR 28 Air Ministry and Ministry of Defence: Operations Record Books, Royal Air Force Stations

AIR 50 Air Ministry: Combat Reports, Second World War

CAB 65 War Cabinet minutes, 1939–45

CAB 66 War Cabinet memoranda (CP and WP) 1939–45

CAB 67 War Cabinet memoranda (WP[G]), 1939–45

CAB 68 War Cabinet memoranda (WP[R]), 1939–45

CAB 73 Air Raid Precautions Registered Files 1931–57

CAB 106 Historical Section Files (Archivist and Librarian Series)

DEFE 28 Ministry of Defence: Directorate of Forward Plans: Registered Files

HO 186 Air Raid Precautions Registered Files 1931–57

HO 207 Home Office and Ministry of Home Security: Civil Defence Regions, Headquarters and Regional Files, 1935–57

HS 2 Special Operations Executive: Group C, Scandinavia: Registered Files

WO 165 War Office: Directorates (Various): War Diaries, Second World War

WO 166 War Office: Home Forces: War Diaries, Second World War

WO 167 War Office: British Expeditionary Force, France: War Diaries, Second World War

WO 168 War Office: British North West Expeditionary Force, Norway: War Diaries, Second World War

WO 169 War Office: British Forces, Middle East: War Diaries, Second World War

WO 171 War Office: Allied Expeditionary Force, North West Europe (British Element): War Diaries, Second World War

WO 172 War Office: British and Allied Land Forces, South East Asia: War Diaries, Second World War

WO 175 War Office: Allied Forces, North Africa (British Element): War Diaries, Second World War

WO 197 War Office: British Expeditionary Force, France: Military Headquarters Papers, Second World War

WO 198 War Office: North West Expeditionary Force, Norway: Military Headquarters Papers, Second World War

WO 199 War Office: Home Forces: Military Headquarters Papers, Second World War

National Archives of Scotland (NAS)

AF 59 Agriculture, Labour, Safety and Wages Files
HH 50 Second World War Files

National Library of Scotland (NLS)

Acc. 10517 Papers of Christopher Murray Grieve (Hugh MacDiarmid)
Acc. 5862 Papers of Tom Johnston
Acc. 5540 Papers of James Kennaway
Acc. 3721 Papers of the Scottish Secretariat and Roland Eugene Muirhead
Acc. 6119 Papers of Major-General Douglas Wimberley
Acc. 7380 Papers of Major-General Douglas Wimberley relating to the 51st (Highland) Division
Acc. 7656 Papers of Arthur Woodburn

Scottish National War Museum

Commando Country exhibition, October 2006–February 2008
Land Girls and Lumber Jill exhibition, February 2010–February 2011

Newspapers and Journals

Blackwood's Magazine
Courier and Argus (Dundee)
Daily Telegraph
Dundee Advertiser
Dunfermline Press
The Economist
Evening Dispatch (Edinburgh)
Evening News (Edinburgh)
Evening Times (Glasgow)
Glasgow Herald (later the *Herald*)
Greenock Telegraph
Inverness Courier
Lancet
Manchester Guardian (later the *Guardian*)
Orcadian
Scotsman
Shetland Times
Stornoway Gazette
Thistle (The Royal Scots)
The Times

Service Histories, Personal Accounts, Fiction and Poetry

Annand, J. K., *Selected Poems* (Edinburgh, 1992)
Barclay, Brigadier C. N., *The History of The Cameronians (Scottish Rifles)*, vol. III 1933–46 (London, 1949)
Barker, Felix, *Gordon Highlanders in North Africa and Sicily* (Sidcup, 1944)
Blake, George, *Mountain and Flood: History of the 52nd (Lowland) Division 1939–1946* (Glasgow, 1950)
Borthwick, Alastair, *Sans Peur: 5th Battalion Seaforth Highlanders in World War II* (Stirling, 1946)
Byrne, Michael, ed., *Collected Poems and Songs of George Campbell Hay* (Edinburgh, 2003)
Carswell, Allan, *For Your Freedom and Ours: Poland, Scotland and the Second World War* (Edinburgh, 1993)
Cochrane, Peter, *Charlie Company: In Service with C Company 2nd Queen's Own Cameron Highlanders 1940–1944* (London, 1977)
David, Saul, *Churchill's Sacrifice of the Highland Division France, 1940*, London, 1994
Delaforce, Patrick, *Monty's Highlanders, 51st Highland Division in World War Two* (Brighton, 1997)
Duncan, Ronald, *The Perfect Mistress* (London, 1969)

Edwards, Elaine M., ed., *Scotland's Land Girls: Breeches, Bombers and Backaches* (Edinburgh, 2010)

Elliott, W. A., *Esprit de Corps: A Scots Guards Officer on Active Service 1943–1945* (Wilby, 1996)

Fairrie, Lieutenant-Colonel Angus, *Queen's Own Highlanders (Seaforth and Camerons)* (Golspie, 1998) 2nd revised edition of *Cuidich 'n Righ: A History of the Queen's Own Highlanders* (Golspie, 1983)

Fergusson, Bernard, *Beyond the Chindwin* (London, 1944)

—, *The Wild Green Earth* (London, 1946)

—, *The Black Watch and the King's Enemies* (London, 1950)

Ford, James Allan, *The Brave White Flag* (London, 1961)

Garioch, Robert, *Two Men and a Blanket: A Prisoner of War's Story* (Edinburgh, 1975)

Henderson, Diana M., *The Lion and the Eagle: Polish Second World War Veterans in Scotland* (Dunfermline, 2001)

Henderson, Hamish, *Elegies for the Dead in Cyrenaica* (London, 1948)

Historical Records Committee, *Historical Records of the Cameron Highlanders*, vol. V (Edinburgh, 1909–62)

Jenkins, Robin, *The Cone-Gatherers* (London, 1955)

—, *Guests of War* (London, 1956)

Johnston, Captain R. T., Steward, Captain D. N., and Dunlop, Rev. A. Ian, eds, *Campaign in Europe: The Story of the 10th Battalion the Highland Light Infantry* (Glasgow, 1945)

Johnston, Thomas, *Memories* (London, 1952)

Kemp, J. C., *The History of the Royal Scots Fusiliers, 1919–1959* (Glasgow, 1963)

Kesson, Jessie, *Another Time, Another Place* (London, 1983)

Lavery, Brian, *Shield of Empire: The Royal Navy and Scotland* (Edinburgh, 2007)

Lindsay, Donald, *Forgotten General: A Life of Andrew Thorne* (Salisbury, 1987)

Lindsay, Martin, *So Few Got Through* (London, 1946)

Lindsay, Maurice, *Portrait of Glasgow* (London, 1972)

—, *Thank You for Having Me* (London, 1983)

Linklater, Eric, *The Highland Division* (London, 1942)

—, *Private Angelo* (London, 1946)

—, *The Campaign in Italy* (London, 1951)

McBain, S. W., *A Regiment at War: The Royal Scots 1939–1945*, (Edinburgh, 1988)

McCallum, Neil, *Journey with a Pistol* (London, 1959)

MacDiarmid, Hugh, *Lucky Poet: A Self-Study in Literature and Political Ideas* (London, 1943)

—, *The Company I've Kept* (London, 1966)

MacDougall, Ian, ed., *Voices from War and Some Labour Struggles: Personal*

Recollections of War in Our Century by Scots Men and Women (Edinburgh, 1995)

McGregor, John, *The Spirit of Angus: The War History of the County's Battalion of the Black Watch* (Chichester, 1988)

MacLean, Sorley, *Spring Tide and Neap Tide: Selected Poems 1932–1972* (Edinbugh, 1977)

Macleod, John, *River of Fire: The Clydebank Blitz* (Edinburgh, 2010)

MacRoberts, Douglas, *Lions Rampant: The Story of 602 Spitfire Squadron* (London, 1985)

Madden, B. J. G., *History of the 6th Battalion The Black Watch* (Perth, 1948)

Marshall, Bruce, *The Black Oxen* (London, 1972)

Martin, H. G., *The Fifteenth Scottish Division 1939–1945* (Edinburgh and London, 1948)

Miles, Wilfrid, *The Life of a Regiment: The Gordon Highlanders*, vol. V, 1919–45 (Aberdeen, 1961)

Morgan, Edwin, *The New Divan* (Manchester, 1977)

Nancarrow, F. G., *Glasgow's Fighter Squadron* (London, 1942)

Osborne, Brian D., *The People's Army: Home Guard in Scotland 1940–1944* (Edinburgh, 2009)

Paterson, Robert H., *Pontius Pilate's Bodyguard: A History of the First or the Royal Regiment of Foot, The Royal Scots (The Royal Regiment)*, vol. 2 (Edinburgh, 2000)

Rose, Angus, *Who Dies Fighting* (London, 1944)

Salmond, J. B., *The History of the 51st Highland Division 1939–1945* (Edinburgh and London, 1953)

Scott, Alexander, *Selected Poems* (Preston, 1975)

Smith, David J., *Action Stations: Military Airfields of Scotland, the North-East and Northern Ireland* (London, 1989)

Soutar, William, *Diaries of a Dying Man* (Edinburgh, 1954)

Stewart, I. M., *The Thin Red Line: 2nd Argylls in Malaya* (London, 1947)

Stockman, Jim, *Seaforth Highlanders: A Fighting Soldier Remembers* (Somerton, 1987)

Sym, Colonel John, *Seaforth Highlanders* (Aldershot, 1962)

Todd, Andrew, *The Elephant at War: The 2nd Battalion Seaforth Highlanders* (Bishop Auckland, 1998)

Urquhart, Alistair, *The Forgotten Highlander: My incredible story of survival during the war in the Far East* (London, 2010)

White, Peter, *With the Jocks: A Soldier's Struggle for Europe 1944–45* (Stroud, 2001)

Whitson, Angus and Orr, Andrew, *Sea Dog Bamse: World War II Canine Hero* (Edinburgh, 2008)

Young, Douglas, *Auntran Blads: An Outwale o Verses* (Glasgow, 1943)

—, *Chasing an Ancient Greek* (London, 1950)

Secondary Sources (selected)

Scotland

Allan, Stuart, *Commando Country* (Edinburgh, 2007)

Bold, Alan, *MacDiarmid* (London, 1988)

Crampsey, Robert, *The Empire Exhibition of 1938: The Last Durbar* (Edinburgh, 1988)

Devine, T. M., *The Scottish Nation 1700–2000* (London, 2001)

Ferguson, William, *Scotland: 1689 to the Present* (Edinburgh, 1968)

Finlay, Richard, *Modern Scotland 1914–2000* (London, 2004)

Gordon, Eleanor and Breitenbach, Esther, eds, *Out of Bounds: Women in Scottish Society 1800–1945* (Edinburgh, 1992)

Harvie, Christopher, *Scotland and Nationalism: Scottish Society and Politics 1707–1977* (London, 1977)

—, *No Gods and Precious Few Heroes: Twentieth Century Scotland* (Edinburgh, 1998)

Herdman, John, *Some Renaissance Cultural Wars* (Blair Atholl, 2010)

Hutchison, I. G. C., *Scottish Politics in the Twentieth Century* (Basingstoke, 2001)

Jeffrey, Andrew, *This Dangerous Menace: Dundee and the River Tay at War 1939 to 1945* (Edinburgh, 1991)

—, *This Present Emergency: Edinburgh, the River Forth and South-East Scotland in the Second World War* (Edinburgh, 1992)

—, *This Time of Crisis: Glasgow, the West of Scotland and the North-Western Approaches in the Second World War* (Edinburgh, 1993)

Johnston, Ian, *Beardmore Built: The Rise and Fall of a Clyde Shipyard* (Clydebank, 1993)

—, *Ships for a Nation: John Brown & Company Clydebank* (West Dunbartonshire, 2000)

Kellas, J. G., *Modern Scotland* (London, 1968)

Knox, W. W., *Industrial Nation: Work, Culture and Society in Scotland 1800 to the Present* (Edinburgh, 1999)

Linklater, Andro, *Compton Mackenzie: A Life* (London, 1987)

McCrae, Morrice, *The National Health Service in Scotland: Origins and Ideals 1900–1950* (Edinburgh, 2003)

Marr, Andrew, *The Battle for Scotland* (London, 1992)

Mileham, P. J. R., *Scottish Regiments* (Tunbridge Wells, 1988)

Muir, Edwin, *Scottish Journey* (London, 1935)

Neat, Timothy, *Hamish Henderson: A Biography*, vol. I (Edinburgh, 2007)

Nimmo, Ian, *Scotland at War* (Runcorn, 1989)

Peebles, Hugh, *Warship Building on the Clyde: Naval Orders and the Prosperity of the Clyde Shipbuilding Industry* (Edinburgh, 1987)

Slaven, Anthony, *The Development of the West of Scotland 1750–1960* (London, 1975)

Smout, T. C., *A Century of the Scottish People 1830–1950* (London, 1984)
Taylor, Les, *Luftwaffe over Scotland* (Dunbeath, 2010)
Walker, Graham, *Thomas Johnston* (Manchester, 1988)

Secondary Sources (selected)

Second World War

Alanbrooke, Field Marshal Lord, Alex Danchev and Daniel Todman eds, *War Diaries 1939–1945* (London, 2001)
Allen, Louis, *Burma: The Longest War 1941–45* (London, 1984)
Allport, Alan, *Demobbed: Coming Home after the Second World War* (London, 2009)
Barnett, Correlli, *Britain and Her Army* (London, 1970)
Beevor, Antony, *D-Day: The Battle for Normandy* (London, 2009)
Calder, Angus, *The Myth of the Blitz* (London, 1991)
Court, W. H. B., *Coal* (History of the Second World War: United Kingdom Civil Series) (London, 1951)
Dear, I. C. B., ed., *The Oxford Companion to the Second World War* (Oxford, 1995)
Douglas-Hamilton, James, *The Truth about Rudolf Hess* (Edinburgh, 1993)
Gardiner, Juliet, *The Blitz* (London, 2010)
Gillman, Peter and Leni, *Collar the Lot! How Britain Interned and Expelled its Wartime Refugees* (London, 1980)
Hamilton, Nigel, *Monty: Master of the Battlefield* (London, 1983)
Hammond, R. J., *Food: The Growth of Policy* (History of the Second World War: United Kingdom Civil Series) (London, 1951)
Hastings, Max, *Overlord: D-Day and the Battle for Normandy* (London, 1984)
—, *Armageddon: The Battle for Germany 1944–45* (London, 2004)
—, *Finest Years: Churchill as Warlord* (London, 2009)
Inman, P., *Labour in the Munitions Industries* (History of the Second World War: United Kingdom Civil Series) (London, 1957)
Jones, Helen, *British Civilians in the Front Line: Air Raids, Productivity and Wartime Culture, 1939–1945* (Manchester, 2006)
Keegan, John, *The Second World War* (London, 1989)
—, *Six Armies in Normandy* (London, 1982)
Kohan, C. M., *Works and Buildings* (History of the Second World War: United Kingdom Civil Series) (London, 1952)
Lampe, David, *The Last Ditch* (London, 1968)
Mackenzie, William, *The Secret History of SOE* (London, 2000)
McLynn, Frank, *The Burma Campaign: Disaster into Triumph* (London, 2010)
Murray, Keith A. H. *Agriculture* (History of the Second World War: United Kingdom Civil Series) (London, 1950)

Padfield, Peter, *War Beneath the Sea: Submarine Conflict 1939–1945* (London, 1995)

Postan, M. M., Hay, D. and Scott, J. D., *Design and Development of Weapons: Studies in Government and Industrial Organisation* (History of the Second World War: United Kingdom Civil Series) (London, 1964)

Postan, M. M., *British War Production* (History of the Second World War: United Kingdom Civil Series) (London, 1952)

Reynolds, David, *Rich Relations: The American Population of Britain 1942–1945* (London, 1995)

Roberts, Andrew, *Masters and Commanders: The Military Geniuses Who Led the West to Victory in WWII* (London, 2008)

—, *The Storm of War: A New History of the Second World War* (London, 2009)

Sebag-Montefiore, Simon, *Dunkirk: Fight to the Last Man* (London, 2006)

Sinclair, Andrew, *War Like a Wasp: The Lost Decade of the 1940s* (London, 1989)

Titmuss, Richard M., *Problems of Social Policy* (History of the Second World War: United Kingdom Civil Series) (London, 1950)

Wilmot, Chester, *The Struggle for Europe* (London, 1952)

Websites

http://www.bbc.co.uk/ww2peopleswar
http://www.rememberingscotlandatwar.org.uk
http://www.scotsatwar.org.uk

Index